LIBRARY IN A BOOK

TOBACCO INDUSTRY AND SMOKING

Fred C. Pampel

Facts On File, Inc.

TOBACCO INDUSTRY AND SMOKING

Copyright © 2004 by Fred C. Pampel
Graphs copyright © 2004 Facts On File

All rights reserved. No part of this book may be reproduced or utilized in any form or by any means, electronic or mechanical, including photocopying, recording, or by any information storage or retrieval systems, without permission in writing from the publisher. For information contact:

Facts On File, Inc.
132 West 31st Street
New York NY 10001

Library of Congress Cataloging-in-Publication Data
Pampel, Fred C.
    Tobacco industry and smoking / Fred C. Pampel.
    p. cm.—(Library in a book)
Includes bibliographical references and index.
    ISBN 0-8160-5450-9
    1. Smoking—United States. 2. Tobacco industry—United States. 3. Smoking. 4. Tobacco habit. I. Title. II. Series.
    HV5760. P36 2004
    338.4'767973'0973—dc21   2003013236

Facts On File books are available at special discounts when purchased in bulk quantities for businesses, associations, institutions, or sales promotions. Please call our Special Sales Department in New York at (212) 967-8800 or (800) 322-8755.

You can find Facts On File on the World Wide Web at http://www.factsonfile.com

Text design by Ron Monteleone
Graphs by Sholto Ainslie

Printed in the United States of America

MP Hermitage 10 9 8 7 6 5 4 3 2 1

This book is printed on acid-free paper.

SHATFORD LIBRARY

APR - - 2005

PASA... ... ...LLEGE
1570 E. COLORADO BLVD
PASADENA, CA 91106

CONTENTS

WITHDRAWN

PART III
APPENDICES

PART I

OVERVIEW OF THE TOPIC

CHAPTER 1

INTRODUCTION TO THE TOBACCO INDUSTRY AND SMOKING

Cigarette smoking is the single largest preventable cause of premature death in the United States today. Estimates of the number of yearly deaths from smoking-related causes exceed 400,000 (about one-sixth of all deaths), and smokers can expect to die 13–14 years earlier than nonsmokers. The situation has improved since the famous 1964 report of the surgeon general on the harm of cigarettes, but it remains serious. Despite falling cigarette use in past decades, 23 percent of the U.S. population in the year 2000 smoked, and another 22 percent used to smoke—making nearly half the population vulnerable to the risks of early death. Worse, young people today continue to adopt the habit at about the same rate as 10 years ago. No wonder the U.S. surgeon general views smoking as the nation's number one public health problem.

Given that few incentives seem to remain for smoking cigarettes today, the persistence of the problem seems puzzling. Public warnings about the harm to health of smoking are so well known that people actually overestimate the risks; taxes and lawsuits against tobacco companies make the cost of cigarettes a substantial budget drain; prohibitions against smoking in office buildings, public facilities, and even restaurants and bars force smokers into outside streets, alleyways, and quarantined rooms; and nonsmokers feel free to criticize smokers as a public nuisance and shame them for their inability to stop a destructive habit.

Still, more than 40 million persons continue to act in ways that harm their health. Cigarette smoking is spreading across the globe and countering the decline in the United States and in European nations. China, for example, now has one of the world's highest rates of cigarette consumption.

3

Efforts to make the United States and the world smoke-free have a long way to go.

What lies behind these trends? Many suggest that the promotion and advertising efforts of the tobacco industry combined with the addictive properties of cigarette smoke explain the persistence and proliferation of the habit. Private attorneys and attorneys general of many states have, in representing addicted smokers and public health programs that pay for health problems of smokers, blamed the tobacco companies for the situation. Juries appear to agree, as they have become increasingly willing to award plaintiffs large damages in suits against tobacco companies. In a major turn of events, the tobacco industry, under pressure, has consented to make payments to state governments for the health costs inflicted on smokers.

Yet, describing the problem seems easier than dealing with it. At one extreme, antismoking advocates, who tend to view smokers as manipulated by tobacco advertising and utterly addicted once they begin, favor stringent controls and litigation. At the other extreme, defenders of smoking note that Congress has not outlawed tobacco products, and adults can reasonably decide to risk a shorter life in order to enjoy the pleasure they get from cigarettes. They worry about the threat of antismoking policies to individual rights.

Stated in less extreme but still controversial terms, the following questions have engaged the public in recent years.

- Should tobacco be regulated by the government much as other drugs are regulated?
- Is the tobacco industry, despite the mandated warnings on cigarette products, responsible for the harm of cigarettes?
- Can consumers make their own decisions about cigarette smoking, or have tobacco ads manipulated people, particularly youngsters, to adopt a harmful product?
- Does secondhand smoke from the cigarettes of others represent a serious threat to nonsmokers that requires banning smoking in all public indoor places, including restaurants and bars?
- Why do people continue a habit that so clearly harms their health? Can policies counter the attractions to smoking?

Far from obscure issues of concern only to doctors and lawyers, the debates over tobacco use and smoking policies affect most everyone in their daily lives.

THE RISE OF TOBACCO, 1870–1950

EARLY FORMS OF TOBACCO USE

A plant native to the Americas, tobacco was first cultivated in the Andes Mountains in present-day Peru and Ecuador as far back as 5000 B.C.[1] In the centuries to follow, use of the plant spread across the two continents and into the Caribbean islands. Properly prepared, tobacco could be sniffed into the nose, inserted into the mouth for chewing, or brewed like tea to make a drink. When so used, it had some medicinal properties: Tobacco's mild narcotic could ease the pain of toothache, wounds, and snakebites. And, as a powerful insecticide, it could be used for a variety of purposes. However, it had more appeal when burned and inhaled. Tobacco could be smoked after it was dried, chopped, inserted, and burned in a pipe, or after it was rolled into a leaf similar to today's cigars. When burned, tobacco seemed to have religious properties, as the smoke would rise up toward the gods in heaven.

Something more than these religious and practical purposes, however, accounts for the spread of tobacco use among diverse tribes and regions of the Americas. Inhaling the smoke into the mouth and lungs could disperse tobacco chemicals into the bloodstream and give users a mild, pleasurable experience. Smokers might find the process of inhaling to be soothing, but the chemical makeup of tobacco must have contributed to its popularity—otherwise, smoking of different plant products would have become more common. The rewards of tobacco and its main chemical stimulant, nicotine, have attracted humans for as long as the plant has been known.

Tobacco came to have social as well as physical value. Its properties made it a logical medium for youth to prove their passage into adulthood, for those relaxing and socializing to pass the time, and for competing tribes to share a common experience. Tribal shamans would blow smoke over sacred objects, warriors would smoke before battle, and the dead would be buried with their pipes. Although these activities most often involved men rather than women, they played a central part in the social life of American tribal societies.

Upon landing in the New World in 1492 and making contact with the native peoples, Christopher Columbus and his sailors received a gift of tobacco leaves, and some of the crew members later accepted the offer of the local American Indians to follow their custom by smoking the dried plant in a long pipe. Reputed to have become habitual users during their stay, the sailors were the first Europeans to try the practice.[2] Columbus returned to Spain with stories of the product but only a few seeds and leaves. Focused on obtaining gold from the New World, Columbus and other explorers did not realize at the time what influence and economic value this product would come to have.

Tobacco Industry and Smoking

Later brought back to Spain and Portugal in usable form during the 1550s, tobacco was first thought by Europeans to have special medicinal value, and physicians and others would plant it in palace gardens for this reason. Early on it was used mostly as snuff and mostly by health fanatics. Some claimed wondrous results from the product, recommending it as a cure for bad breath, kidney stones, and wounds from poison arrows. It soon spread from Spain and Portugal to France, Italy, and Germany. In France, Jean Nicot promoted the curative powers of tobacco to the queen, and history rewarded him: The plant was formally named *Nicotiana tabacum* and the crucial chemical in the plant was termed *nicotine*.

English explorers John Hawkins, Walter Raleigh, and Francis Drake brought the product to England starting in the 1560s, where it spread rapidly.[3] The English favored use of a pipe for their new habit. The handsome and elegant Walter Raleigh popularized the new behavior until it became something of a craze, and he even persuaded elderly Queen Elizabeth I to try it. Smoking turned into a habit common among patrons of William Shakespeare's Globe Theatre and surrounding forums of entertainment in London, and it was the subject of an English-language book in 1595.

While many lauded the pleasurable, even narcotic properties of smoking, others found the new habit disgusting and wicked. Most famously, King James I of Great Britain published a pamphlet in 1604, soon after his coronation, criticizing the product and rebuking smokers. In harsh words he stated, "Smoking is a custom loathsome to the eye, hateful to the nose, harmful to the brain, dangerous to the lungs, and in the black, stinking fume thereof, resembling the horrible Stygian smoke of the pit that is bottomless."[4] His critical voice along with those of the emerging Puritan movement could not, however, overcome the attraction to the product and to the profits made by growers in the New World. The king soon tried to discourage its use with new taxes, but tobacco continued its growth in the English-speaking world.

The first successful American commercial crop was cultivated in Jamestown, Virginia, in 1612 by Englishman John Rolfe (who a few years later married the Wampanoag princess Pocahontas). Within seven years, tobacco had become the colony's largest export. Reflecting its Puritan background, the northern colony of Massachusetts prohibited tobacco, but such opposition did not prevent the product from becoming a central part of the American economy. Tobacco was so popular in the South that it could be used as a form of money and as a dowry in marriage. It had such a central place in the economy and the wealth of citizens that high taxes placed on the product once led Virginia planters to rebel against the colonial governor. By the time of the American Revolution, tobacco was such an important commodity that Benjamin Franklin used it as collateral in obtaining loans from France to support the war effort.

Tobacco use took various forms in the United States. During the colonial period, the pipe remained generally popular, but aristocrats tended to use snuff and those in rural areas tended to use chew. For a brief period in history, pipe smoking was also popular among women (the wife of President Andrew Jackson, first elected to the office in 1829, smoked a pipe as the first lady). Cigars were new at the time, and cigarettes were rare. Only the destitute, who rolled discarded tobacco bits, used cigarettes; that form of smoking product accordingly gained little acceptance by more respectable parts of colonial society. One exception to the disrepute of cigarettes was during a brief period in revolutionary France (1789–94) when many viewed cigarettes as a way to show solidarity with the lower class.

During the first part of the 19th century, however, tobacco use in the United States declined. The U.S. government had begun taxing tobacco in 1794, and a few leading scientists and public figures (including Benjamin Rush, a physician and signer of the Declaration of Independence) claimed that tobacco was harmful to one's health. Snuff became unfashionable, and pipe smoking and chew remained common largely in rural areas. Other tobacco products started to appear more commonly but did not yet gain widespread popularity; for example, troops during the Civil War used hand-rolled cigarettes because they were cheap, convenient, and easy to carry, yet most did not continue with the habit afterward. In fact, men tended to view cigarettes after the Civil War as effeminate and suited for dandies and Europeans in big cities. Outside rural areas, chew was increasingly viewed as unsanitary; the presence of spittoons containing spit tobacco juice and the sight of tobacco stains on floors in cities repelled many respectable people. Cigars became popular among the growing affluent business class after the Civil War, and many leaders such as President Ulysses Grant (who later died of throat cancer) and General Robert E. Lee smoked cigars regularly. Perhaps because of their expense, however, cigars did not attract widespread adoption.

THE SPREAD OF MANUFACTURED CIGARETTES

Historians mark 1870 as the starting point for widespread cigarette smoking in the United States. Prior to this year the use of tobacco seemed a curious habit that appealed to just a few groups, hardly a habit that would become an important part of society. It brought a mild form of pleasure, but the common forms of tobacco produced harshness in the smoke that made inhalation unpleasant. Moreover the process of smoking pipes and cigars was slow and tedious—suited for leisurely paced socializing but not for daily activities. Chew was unsanitary, snuff was pretentious, and cigarettes were bohemian. With the decline of tobacco use over the last 70 years, the market for greater sales seemed limited. Several new developments, however, made for changes in attitudes toward one tobacco product—cigarettes.

What led to the changes and the widespread adoption of the product over the next century? Slowly and steadily, improvements in the product itself and its suitability for modern life combined to make cigarettes widely popular. In terms of the product, manufacturers made their cigarette tobacco less harsh and more flavorful. Consisting of mild and sweet tobacco plants that were cured to make the leaves even milder and sweeter, cigarettes became easier for persons to tolerate and inhale. As discovered in 1839, bright tobacco, grown in Virginia and North Carolina, developed an unusually sweet and pleasant taste when cured in a certain way and could be smoked in greater quantities than previous forms. Another tobacco plant, white burley, first developed in Ohio in 1866, could absorb additives better than other products. Soon, sweeteners and flavors added to the tobacco also attracted new users. In addition to having a better taste, the new products had higher nicotine levels.

By itself, however, better flavor did not lead to widespread use of cigarettes. The product needed to be presented in a way that consumers would find attractive. In the past, tobacco was sold in lots that required smokers to roll their own cigarettes, which made it hard to identify a certain tobacco with a product name and identity. The creation of manufactured cigarettes that came in small boxes not only avoided the need for smokers to roll their own cigarettes but also allowed producers to display the name of the cigarette on the box. From this packaging came the emergence of tobacco brands that would attract smoker loyalty and, with the coming of advertising and promotion, the desire to buy new products. Producers could advertise their brands by name to gain new smokers and could offer picture cards that smokers liked.

Manufacturers soon realized that increasing demand for cigarettes from advertising and promotion of particular brands would do little to help the industry if they could not supply the product at an affordable price. Hiring workers to roll each cigarette by hand was expensive and kept the production costs of cigarettes high. The tobacco industry fell behind other manufacturers in its lack of a mechanized means to turn out cigarettes. A major innovation thus came with a machine invented and patented by James Bonsack in 1881. The machine dropped a small amount of granulated tobacco onto paper, shaped the paper and tobacco into a tube, and then cut the tube into equal-sized cigarettes. By 1884 the machine could produce 200 cigarettes a minute.

Combined with a helpful decrease in excise taxes on cigarettes, the ability of machines to reduce labor costs in factories made it possible to sell cigarettes to retailers at lower prices than before. Able to make larger profits themselves, the retailers did more than in the past to promote cigarettes. Cigarette manufacturers did not get a higher rate of profit with the lower prices they charged to retailers but did increase their profit through higher sales.

Cigarettes also led to a different form of smoking that seemed well suited to changing social life at the end of the 1800s. Cigars and pipes typically did not require inhaling to enjoy; rather, the pleasure came from the drawn-out process of preparing to smoke and from the aroma of the tobacco fumes. With continued effort required to keep cigars and pipes lit, they were enjoyed during leisurely talks after dinner and during periods of inactivity. Smokeless tobacco in the form of snuff or chew could be used on the go and spit on the ground by farmers and residents of rural areas, but spitting was not a habit suited for modern life in cities. In contrast to these other products, cigarettes fit the continuous, sometimes frantic activity in cities. They could be carried conveniently, lit easily, and smoked quickly. (The invention of small paper matchbooks added to the ease of use.) Clerical workers in cities, for example, could more handily smoke cigarettes than cigars or pipes while they worked. Cigarettes, more than other tobacco products, also involved social sharing: Their inexpensive cost allowed for giving them out upon request, and lighting another's cigarette signified friendship or intimacy. Although cigars remained well liked for special occasions, the smaller cigarettes became common for everyday activities.

Perhaps more important, cigarette smoking had a different and more attractive physiological effect. Smoke from cigars and pipe tobacco had properties that made inhaling unpleasant. As with chew, cigars and pipe tobacco delivered nicotine to the body through the mouth. However, cigarettes could deliver nicotine more efficiently than the other products. Cigarette tobacco had chemical properties that made inhaling easier to learn and tolerate. Because the lungs more than the mouth cavity have enormous absorbent properties, inhaling smoke effectively delivered nicotine to the body, efficiently evoked the mild narcotic pleasure, and resulted in addiction. Smokers consequently found it harder to moderate or stop their habit when they used cigarettes.

Past fashions in tobacco use had led to preferences for snuff, pipes, chew, large cigars, and small cigars, but these new trends and developments would make cigarettes the dominant product in the late 19th century and into the early 20th century. By 1924 more than 80 percent of families spent at least part of their budget on tobacco. In a study in 1935–36, about 2.23 percent of the budget of the typical American family went to tobacco products.[5] Economic downturns might produce some modest changes in cigarette use. Purchase of cheaper brands of cigarettes rather than premium brands and even use of cheap tobacco to roll one's own cigarettes became popular during periods of high unemployment and low income (particularly during the Great Depression of the 1930s). Otherwise, cigarette use spread steadily.

Some figures can describe the rise of manufactured cigarettes in the United States. In 1870 the number of cigarettes smoked per person was 0.36—in other words, less than a single cigarette a year on average. In 1879 cigars remained the most common tobacco product, followed by tobaccos for snuff, pipe, and chewing. By 1900, however, the figures for cigarettes per person had risen to 35 and by 1938 to 1,268. In the 30 years from 1870 to 1900, consumption per person had increased by 9,700 percent, and in the following 38 years from 1900 to 1938, it increased by another 3,600 percent. In 1900 tobacco for cigarettes constituted only 2.4 percent of all manufactured tobacco, and by the early 1930s it represented more than 40 percent. Smoking tobacco for pipes, the next most popular brand, composed 30 percent; cigars, 15 percent; chew, 10 percent; and snuff, 5 percent. The popularity of cigarettes would continue to rise.

COMPETITION AND MONOPOLY IN THE TOBACCO INDUSTRY

As with most industries during the late 1800s, the tobacco industry grew initially through the entrepreneurship of thousands of small businessmen. In 1864, there were no major American cigarette manufacturers, and premade cigarettes were imported from Europe, Turkey, and Russia. In response to concerns about the use of cigarettes by soldiers and to the desire of the government for revenue, new taxes were placed on the manufactured cigarettes, most of which were paid by importers. Domestic cigarettes made with the bright tobacco leaf were largely handrolled and used by those living outside the larger cities of the eastern United States who could not afford the high prices of the imported brands.

The growth of the American tobacco industry came with efforts to sell cigarettes made of domestic tobacco. F. S. Kinney in 1868 began to sell pre-rolled cigarettes largely with American bright tobacco in a store in lower Manhattan. Experimenting with various blends and even adding sugar and licorice flavor, Kinney had much success with his brands in New York City. Keeping his prices lower than the imports, he placed the cigarettes in paper rather than cardboard packages. Businesses copied his strategy in other neighborhoods, cities, and states.

Lewis Ginter, who began in the cigarette business in 1840, used his base in Richmond, Virginia, to become the first national distributor of cigarettes. Also using bright tobacco from the Virginia and North Carolina area that smokers found so appealing, he marketed his product to all parts of the country. Although not the first to use factories to roll cigarettes, Ginter began producing cigarettes in large numbers in the 1870s and contributed to the early rise of cigarette smoking. He also exploited the advantages of white burley tobacco in absorbing sweeteners and flavors by producing and marketing new flavored brands of cigarettes.

Despite Ginter's success in selling his product across much of the nation, the tobacco industry in the 1870s still consisted of hundreds of small manufacturers. In 1877, for example, government tax authorities had registered 121 cigarette brands, and local brands left uncounted by national authorities would add even more to the total.[6] The competition between small companies resulted in overproduction of cigarettes, low prices, and small profit margins. Those in the cigar business thought that the cigarette industry would collapse, and cigars would continue their traditional dominance as the tobacco product of choice. In fact, efforts to organize and monopolize the cigarette industry would put it on a sound financial basis and would lead to some of the most successful and powerful business enterprises in the United States.

James Buchanan (Buck) Duke, the man most responsible for the shape of the modern tobacco industry—and also for the spread of cigarettes—played much the same role as did John D. Rockefeller in the oil industry and J. P. Morgan in the financial industry. In 1874, he joined his father and brother to found a tobacco firm, W. Duke Sons and Company, in Durham, North Carolina. Duke's father, Washington Duke, had established a small business that produced chewing tobacco from the bright tobacco leaf. Eventually taking over the business, Buck gave up competing against more well known brands of chewing tobacco, such as Bull Durham, and began to produce cigarettes in 1881. The competition for the product was less fierce but so was the demand from tobacco users. A wildly overwrought quote from the *New York Times* in 1883 reveals the prejudice at the time against cigarettes: "If this pernicious habit obtains among adult Americans the ruin of the Republic is close at hand."[7]

Duke showed his tremendous organizational and managerial skills in making his cigarette business successful and creating a major industrial empire. By exploiting the development of the cigarette rolling machine—he leased machines for his factories from the inventor, James Bonsack, beginning in 1884—and using his lower costs to encourage retailers to push his product, he made strong inroads on the market. With considerable expense devoted to advertising and hiring talented salespeople to further market his brand, Duke became the nation's largest cigarette manufacturer. Yet he was not satisfied. He wanted to control the industry, not just lead it.

To the dismay of his competitors, Duke intensified his advertising efforts and price-cutting strategy in the late 1880s. He bought out companies with profit margins so thin they could not invest in the machines and advertising to compete with Duke. Other, more successful companies promised to fight back, but most soon gave in and agreed to merge with Duke. In 1890 Duke, at age 33, became the first president of the American Tobacco Company. The firm produced 90 percent of domestic cigarettes and soon began trying to overtake the chewing and snuff companies in addition to cigarette companies.

Although wildly successful in creating a profitable enterprise that enriched all those involved, Duke created enemies with his strategies. No sooner had he founded the American Tobacco Company than an antitrust suit in North Carolina aimed to dissolve the company. Other suits followed, and President Theodore Roosevelt came to oppose the trust. In 1907 the circuit court found that subsidiaries of the American Tobacco Company had violated the Sherman Anti-Trust Act. With eventual support of the decision by the U.S. Supreme Court, the American Tobacco Company in 1911 had to be dissolved into four firms: Liggett and Myers, Reynolds, Lorillard, and American, all companies that would remain important forces behind cigarette production and use in years to come.

Duke's trust not only made him rich but also made cigarettes a national product with increasing acceptance and prices that a mass market of people with modest incomes could afford. Duke retired soon after the breakup of his company and devoted his wealth to expanding a small college, which was later renamed Duke University. However, his efforts to create an efficiently and rationally organized industry for growing, curing, manufacturing, marketing, and selling tobacco contributed to the spread of the product's use. Although several companies rather than one major company now existed, each one continued and even expanded the efficient generation of profits. They did so in part because of the nature of the product but also by advertising and promoting their products. Such efforts would become the key to success among these companies, and in the future several of the most famous brands—Camel, Lucky Strike, and Chesterfield—would emerge and further contribute to the growth of the industry.

ANTISMOKING MOVEMENTS

Given the enormous success of the industry, the spread of cigarettes created a backlash of resistance. During the early 1900s largely rural Protestants protested against the spreading vice of alcohol, especially among the largely immigrant Catholics and the new affluent middle classes in cities.[8] With much the same motivation the Anti-Tobacco Society was founded in 1849, publication of an antitobacco journal began in 1857, and warnings about the harm of tobacco use emerged in 1849 and 1857. The opposition to cigarettes was neither as strong nor as successful as the opposition to alcohol and did not result in national prohibition of the product, as occurred for alcohol from 1919 to 1933. While drinking became associated with debauchery, saloons, prostitution, gambling, fighting, marital discord, and drunkenness, smoking had none of these drawbacks. Cigarettes and tobacco were sold by respectable businesses, did not lead to inebriation, and were used by respectable members of society in everyday life.

Still, substantial opposition to smoking surfaced for several reasons. Because the purpose of tobacco seemed to involve little more than the search for frivolous pleasure, religious groups such as the Seventh-Day Adventists and the Women's Christian Temperance Union (WCTU) opposed its use. Although no one knew the extent of the harm smoking could cause, critics saw it as unhealthy for smokers, unpleasant for nonsmokers, and lacking social merit. Cigarettes received special criticism: Cigars and pipes seemed more dignified and less noticeable; in contrast, the tendency for people to smoke cigarettes in public and to become habituated to the daily use of cigarettes aroused the concern of crusaders. More than other tobacco products, cigarette use led to addiction and revealed weakness of character.

Antismoking groups showed particular concern about the tendency of youth to smoke, worrying that it reflected a sense of rebellion and lack of respect for authority. Young boys seemed particularly attracted to cards that were included in many packages of cigarettes. Sometimes these cards included pictures of attractive actresses in provocative poses and famous athletes whom children would want to emulate. The cards might even be used for betting games. Furthermore smoking seemed especially common among delinquent youth and soon became associated with truancy and petty crime.

Responding to these negative characteristics of cigarette use among adults and young people, a powerful antismoking movement emerged from the temperance movement. Its leader, Lucy Page Gaston, a single schoolteacher and WCTU member, came to have much influence on the public's view of smoking. Through her tireless efforts, she significantly slowed the spread of cigarette use. In 1899 she founded the Chicago Anti-Cigarette League using the model of antialcohol groups. Two years later she founded the National Anti-Cigarette League and soon became one of the country's best-known reformers. She held rallies in schools and towns in which she decried the poisons brought into the body by cigarettes and noted cases of known murderers and criminals who smoked. She recruited converts to her organization, promoted city health clinics where smokers could go to quit the habit, and urged legislatures to ban the product. In 1920 she ran unsuccessfully for the Republican Party presidential nomination.

Her antismoking movement had some success. North Dakota, Tennessee, and Iowa first prohibited cigarette smoking in the 1890s, and 11 other states followed with prohibition in the first two decades of the new century. Other laws prevented teachers and school officials from smoking, banned passengers from smoking in railway cars and in the New York City subways, and required persons buying cigarettes to be at least 16 years old. Many famous Americans supported these antismoking efforts: Henry Ford, the successful car manufacturer, wrote a pamphlet for young people entitled "The Case Against the Little White Slaver," and Thomas Edison, the inventor, claimed that cigarettes released poisons into the body and destroyed brain cells.

In the end, however, cigarette use continued its steady upward increase. Laws to ban smoking did not stop the habit, much as Prohibition did not stop the use of alcohol. In fact the efforts to deny people the chance to use cigarettes may have intensified their appeal in some quarters. States repealed their prohibitions against smoking (except among minors) by the end of the 1920s, with Indiana being the first state to do so in 1909. Gaston continued her campaign against cigarettes into the 1920s, later focusing on limiting their adoption by women. In support of this goal the Women's Christian Temperance Union also sponsored thousands of antismoking events. The efforts failed to slow the spread of cigarettes. Gaston died in 1924, ironically of throat cancer, having had only short-term success. Not until some 50 years later would antismoking crusades have real success.

SMOKING BECOMES WIDELY FASHIONABLE

Despite its steady growth, cigarette smoking in the early 20th century remained somewhat tainted. As one historian described it, "Red blooded men smoked cigars and pipes and chewed tobacco" while the cigarette had "the taint of the dude, the sissy, and the underworld."[9] Consistent with such attitudes, cigar production reached a new record in 1917. True popularity of cigarettes would come only with their adoption by men as a symbol of rugged masculinity and by women as a symbol of freedom and independence.

Changes in the attitudes of men toward smoking began with World War I. During U.S. participation in the war from 1917 to 1918, cigarettes became popular among soldiers. Entering late into the war, American soldiers picked up the habit from British troops but were also encouraged to smoke by the free or inexpensive cigarettes supplied by the government to the armed forces; tobacco firms wisely made cigarettes available to the government for such distribution at low cost. General John Pershing, the commander of the U.S. troops, revealed the importance of cigarettes to soldiers when he stated, "You ask what we need to win this war. I answer tobacco, as much as bullets. Tobacco is as indispensable as the daily ration. We must have thousands of tons of it without delay."[10] Charitable organizations responded by sending cigarettes to soldiers overseas.

Cigarettes were easy to carry in battle and convenient to light up during breaks in fighting. Sharing them created bonds among unit members and helped pass the time during periods of inactivity. Moreover some said that cigarette smoking helped calm the nerves when watching and waiting for the enemy. Smoking might even have given a soldier a sense of confidence and resolve when holding a cigarette between his lips in periods of danger. During the terrible battles of the war, providing a cigarette to an injured or dying soldier became a sign of compassion, an act of civility for someone suffering.

Cigarette manufacturers quickly took advantage of the popularity of cigarette smoking among soldiers. By associating the habit with patriotic fighters, advertisers could displace common views that smoking was a habit of delinquent youth, members of the underworld, and European dandies. The respectability of soldiers countered criticisms of antismoking organizations. Indeed the opposition of the American Legion and soldiers to smoking bans contributed to the repeal of state laws in the 1920s. Building on this new constituency, advertisers created patriotic copy. One such ad in 1918 depicted a muscular and determined-looking sailor standing next to a tall, sleek bomb and holding a cigarette; the ad states, "I'd shell out my last 18 cents for Murad (The Turkish Cigarette)."[11]

Along with targeting soldiers who had returned from the war, the tobacco industry knew it had to appeal to young people. Without having present-day knowledge about the addictiveness of cigarettes, the industry realized that continued growth of cigarette sales depended on the acceptance of the product by new generations. Advertisements that appealed too directly to young people would be seen as wrongly influencing children; however, testimonials by adult sports stars and celebrities could indirectly appeal to youth, who tend to have a strong sense of hero worship. A 27-year-old Charles Lindbergh, for example, lit a cigarette after his famous flight across the Atlantic.

A new market for cigarette use among women also emerged in the 1920s. Smoking by women was not unknown in the United States. In colonial times aristocratic women used snuff, and rural women smoked pipes, much like their spouses. However, with the decline in popularity of snuff and pipes, women dropped the use of tobacco and did not adopt the cigars and chew used by men later in the 1800s. Becoming largely a male activity, tobacco consumption seemed unfeminine and inappropriate for women. Men would, accordingly, segregate themselves from women after dinner in a special room to smoke cigars and would often wear special smoking jackets so regular jackets did not smell of tobacco. Women largely took the lead in antismoking movements.

The early use of cigarettes in the late 1800s thus began as a male fashion. Smoking by women in private was frowned on, and smoking in public was seen as outrageous. For example, in 1904 a New York City policeman arrested a woman for smoking in a car on Fifth Avenue, and a 1908 ordinance in New York City made public smoking for women illegal. An 18-year-old woman was expelled from Michigan State Normal College for smoking in 1922. Women nonetheless began to adopt the habit as it became popular among men but did so more in privacy.

Tobacco firms recognized that they could double their market if women smoked as much as men. Toward the goal of gaining more female converts, the first advertisement aimed at women occurred in 1919 for Helmar cigarettes, and by the 1920s such ads were common. The early ads were relatively tame because tobacco companies did not want to violate public taboos too severely, but they represented a new strategy in the battle to gain smokers. By 1929 women consumed about 12 percent of all cigarettes.[12]

The adoption of cigarettes by women coincided with advances toward greater freedom in other arenas of social life. Voting in elections had since the founding of the country been limited to men, but protests by women suffragists had led to ratification of the Nineteenth Amendment to the Constitution in 1920, granting women the right to vote. The right of women to smoke, in both private and public, emerged about the same time and was seen by some as, like voting, an issue of women's freedom. Other behaviors once restricted in public, such as dancing and wearing bathing suits, became acceptable for women, along with cigarette smoking. Tobacco companies aimed to exploit these new desires by challenging social conventions. Rejecting traditional views of women as protectors of moral purity, advertisers promoted images of women as stylish, autonomous, and sexually alluring.

Some figures show the rise in female smoking. In 1923, 5 percent of smokers were women, but by 1931 the figure had risen to 14 percent. Smoking levels among women lagged behind those of men but were still substantial. A 1937 survey found that 26 percent of women smoked an average of 2.4 cigarettes a day, compared to 60 percent of men who smoked an average of 7.2 cigarettes a day.[13]

With cigarettes viewed by youth as a behavior that helped establish their identity as adults, by men as a behavior that helped establish their masculine identity, and by women as a behavior that helped establish themselves as modern and independent, the negative perceptions that had been associated for decades with cigarettes largely disappeared. Movie stars, sports figures, adventurers, physicians, college students, beautiful women, and rugged men smoked—and tobacco advertisements did all they could to publicize such usage. The decades after the 1870s, and particularly the 1920s, thus revealed a major change in American social life: An innovative behavior that many had once viewed with suspicion as a worrisome vice and organized to protest, outlaw, and reform became not only tolerated but embraced. Overcoming the efforts of its one-time opponents, smoking became a norm that men and women followed without much thought to its long-term consequences.

THE INFLUENCE OF ADVERTISING

Cigarette manufacturers learned early that competition for sales had to involve something other than price or product distinctiveness. James Duke discovered that cutting prices destroyed the prestige of a cigarette brand, associating it with the poor and disadvantaged and thereby reducing its sales. If having the lowest prices offered no means to success, neither did differences in the product. The public liked certain types of tobacco, certain packaging, and certain kinds of flavor in their cigarettes. Makers developed new products that smokers liked, but other makers would imitate the new brands. In both price and product, different brands of cigarettes varied little.

As Duke demonstrated, the key to gaining sales was advertising and promotion. Even given similarities in price and flavor with others, a particular brand could through advertising and promotions develop brand loyalty among its users and increase its sales to new buyers. After spending nearly 20 percent of his company's gross income on advertising in his successful attempt during the 1880s to weaken rivals and create the American Tobacco Company, Duke had eliminated most competition and reduced the need for so much advertising. Yet he did not do away with it altogether. Advertising could help attract new smokers and help keep cigarette consumption rising. In contrast advertising never emerged as important for cigars, where product differences in prices, shapes, flavor, and tobacco leaves offered the major source of appeal to customers. The markets for pipe tobacco and chew also responded less to high expenditures on advertising than the market for cigarettes did. Advertising and cigarettes became closely associated.

Upon breakup of Duke's cigarette trust into four companies, advertising competition among tobacco firms accelerated. In 1913 an advertising campaign of Richard J. Reynolds for Camel cigarettes helped make the product the nation's most popular, capturing 40 percent of the market by 1919; the R. J. Reynolds Tobacco Company subsequently grew into one of the nation's most successful. Large two-page ads that appeared in the popular *Saturday Evening Post* magazine proclaiming "The Camels Are Coming" piqued the interest of smokers. Smokers also liked the more flavorful blend of Turkish and American tobaccos in the cigarette that resembled more expensive imports. Responding to this success, other companies promoted their own products. American Tobacco introduced Lucky Strike cigarettes, and Liggett and Myers introduced Chesterfield cigarettes about the same time as Camel cigarettes. Each brand developed advertising to identify a particular image and would dominate sales in the decades to follow.

The problem for tobacco firms that gained market share through advertising was that their brands were easily displaced by advertising campaigns from other companies. The rise and fall of the major brands showed in the replacement of the top-selling Camels in the 1920s by Lucky Strikes. George Washington Hill, the president of American Tobacco, followed the precepts of his predecessor, James Duke, by using advertising to make Lucky Strike cigarettes the top seller. Chesterfields also took the lead in sales in the 1930s. Trends in sales thus followed innovations in advertising more than innovations in product and price.

Sometimes ads highlighted factual claims that one brand had superior flavor, was less irritating, and used better tobacco. Lucky Strike cigarettes claimed that physicians favored their brand, and other companies followed suit with statements that their product soothed the nerves and protected the throat. Such assertions led editors of the *Journal of the American Medical Association (JAMA)* to criticize cigarette advertisements for promising unproven benefits. However, the real appeal of ads was emotional. Much as they do today, ads in the first part of the century associated smoking with other pleasurable activities, relied on testimonies of celebrities, and depicted cigarettes as enjoyable. Camel ads, already associated by virtue of the name with the exotic Middle East, proclaimed the strong desire for their product with the slogan "I'd Walk a Mile for a Camel." Reminding smokers of the pleasant aroma of browned bread, Lucky Strike emphasized that its tobacco was toasted. Chesterfield cigarettes claimed, "They Satisfy."

Advertising also targeted specific subgroups with their images and appeals. Advertising for women often took special forms. Lucky Strike advised women in 1928 to reach for a Lucky rather than a sweet, appealing to the growing desire for young women to maintain a thin figure. A new cigarette brand from England, Marlboro, aimed to capture the female market by proclaiming that the product was as "Mild as May." Chesterfield cigarettes hired Bette Davis and Marlene Dietrich to advertise their products. Other brands emphasized that their cigarette was lighter and prettier than those smoked by men. In 1926 one Chesterfield ad reflected a new, more provocative approach: It showed a young woman asking a handsome male smoker to "blow some my way."

Did advertising contribute to the growth of cigarette use? On the surface it would certainly appear so. Advertising of cigarettes rose at a pace similar to cigarette consumption, and advertising campaigns certainly had success in making one brand more popular than others. The tobacco companies believed in advertising and used it to increase their market share. However, it is hard to show that coinciding trends in advertising and smoking result from causal forces. The increased acceptability and fashionableness of smoking among wide segments of the U.S. population could have encouraged both more smoking and more advertising. Indeed advertising may have followed the growth of cigarettes among various groups by appealing to those already using the product.[14]

DOCUMENTING THE HARM OF TOBACCO, 1950–1990

EARLY WARNINGS ABOUT CIGARETTES

Cigarette consumption continued its upward growth rate throughout the first half of the 20th century. Given the widespread acceptability of the practice, the number of cigarettes smoked per capita rose from 1,485 in 1930 to 1,976 in 1940. Aided by the consumption of cigarettes by U.S. soldiers in World War II (1941–45) and advertising campaigns emphasizing the war efforts of the tobacco companies, smoking rose even faster during the 1940s. By 1950 smoking per capita reached a new high of 3,552—nearly twice as high as only 10 years earlier. The major controversies came not from health concerns but from conflict over profits. Tobacco farmers had during the Great Depression survived financial ruin only by receiving government price supports, while tobacco manufacturers continued to earn high profits. A price-fixing suit against the tobacco companies in 1941 led to a fine but not to low profits. A later shortage of tobacco in the United States during the war years raised the price of cigarettes and further benefited the industry. After the war the demand for American cigarettes increased sharply in Europe, where production facilities had been destroyed.

However, growth of cigarettes slowed during the 1950s. To some degree the market had simply reached saturation: Anyone who would be prone to smoke had likely already tried and continued the habit. More important, people responded to new evidence on the damage to health caused by cigarettes. Per person cigarette consumption actually fell after 1952 and did not return to its previous peak until 1958. Scientific evidence had accumulated for some time, but new articles about the risks of smoking in popular magazines during the years of the 1950s may have worried smokers. The change in smoking habits was not dramatic—the behavior remained common and acceptable—but it was the start of larger changes to follow.

In hindsight one wonders why the scientific community and the population did not come sooner to the conclusion that smoking harms health. Antismoking advocates had for decades noted the potential harm of smoking. The slang term for cigarettes—*coffin nails*—certainly implied that the product was damaging. And most anyone could wonder if the large amount of smoke being inhaled into the lungs and the body would bring injury and if smoker's coughs reflected underlying problems. Perhaps the sometimes exaggerated and unscientific claims of antismoking advocates made the general public suspicious of health warnings about cigarettes, or perhaps the advertising claims, sometimes supported by physicians, that smoking brought energy and good health soothed doubts people had about smoking. Overall, however, the main reasons for the lack of attention to the risks of smoking were that the harm of smoking took several decades to emerge at a time when most people worried about diseases such as scarlet fever, influenza, and tuberculosis that killed more quickly and that scientific evidence had not yet clearly demonstrated the harm. The general medical consensus was that, when done in moderation, smoking was not dangerous.

Those looking for such evidence could by 1950 find articles published in reputable scientific journals that warned of the risk of smoking. A 1930 study by researchers in Cologne, Germany, identified a correlation between cancer and smoking, and in 1938 Dr. Raymond Pearl of Johns Hopkins University reported that smokers did not live as long as nonsmokers. Those following the trends in lung cancer noted that the death rates for men had risen from two per 100,000 in 1910 to 22 per 100,000 in 1950—an 11-fold increase. The rise in lung cancer came a few decades later than the rise in smoking, but otherwise the upward trends matched. Despite denials from cigarette companies, such evidence led scientists to suspect cigarettes as a source of the increased incidence in lung cancer. Still, proof was harder to obtain: As noted in considering the relationship between advertising expenditures and cigarette consumption, proving cause and effect from these statistical correlations is always difficult.

Other studies in the 1940s demonstrated that tobacco extract could induce cancer in laboratory animals; that cigarette smoking was associated with coronary heart disease as well as lung cancer; and that chewing tobacco led to mouth cancer. Still, defenders of the habit could dismiss the evidence as preliminary and tout the health benefits of smoking. The pleasure gained from smoking seemed for many to outweigh possible risks. Even *JAMA* was not sufficiently convinced by the evidence of the harm of smoking in the 1940s to refuse inclusion of cigarette advertisements in the publication. The American Cancer Society, clearly concerned about cigarette use, admitted that no definitive evidence at the time linked smoking to lung cancer.

The year 1950 marked a turning point in scientific evidence and attitudes about smoking. In that year a groundbreaking study demonstrated in stark terms the association between smoking and lung cancer by examining individuals rather than statistical trends. Ernest Wynder, a medical student at Washington University in St. Louis, Missouri, persuaded his professor, Dr. Evarts A. Graham, to participate with him in a study of smoking and lung cancer. A smoker himself, Graham was not enthusiastic about the project or the ability to prove a connection between smoking and lung cancer but

Introduction to the Tobacco Industry and Smoking

agreed to collaborate. With support from the American Cancer Society, the investigators surveyed 605 patients with lung cancer and then surveyed a set of patients without lung cancer yet matched in background to the lung cancer patients. The results were striking: Of the lung cancer patients 96.5 percent smoked compared to 73.7 percent of the other patients. The 22.8 percent difference between the groups represented a huge effect in comparison to other factors known to influence lung cancer; only rarely did medical studies find differences this large.

Soon after, another study demonstrated even more strongly that cigarettes increased the risk of death. Rather than gather current lung cancer patients and ask about their past habits, a better study design would identify healthy smokers and nonsmokers and follow them into the future to see if deaths occurred more commonly among one group than the other. In 1952 Dr. E. Cuyler Hammond and Dr. Daniel Horn of the American Cancer Society—themselves both smokers—began a huge study of 187,000 men aged 50 to 69. After obtaining information on the current health, background, and smoking habits of the subjects, they merely kept track of deaths in their sample. After only 22 months, they found that smokers had a death rate 1.5 times higher than nonsmokers and that heavy smokers (a pack or more a day) had death rates 2.5 times higher than nonsmokers. With all causes combined, 150 smokers and 250 heavy smokers died for every 100 nonsmokers who died. For lung cancer, smokers had death rates seven times higher than nonsmokers; for every 100 nonsmokers who died of lung cancer, 700 smokers died.

A 1954 study of 40,000 physicians aged 35 and over in Britain replicated these results. Dr. Richard Doll and Dr. A. Bradford Hill found that after four and a half years mild smokers had death rates from lung cancer that were seven times higher than nonsmokers, moderate smokers had lung cancer death rates that were 12 times higher, and heavy smokers had death rates that were 24 times higher. These figures were shockingly high. Since these findings came from a sample of physicians—a group of highly educated and affluent individuals who, other than with the habit of some to smoke, would live healthy lives—critics could not say that unhealthy lifestyles, ignorance of healthy behaviors, and poverty could account for the high death rate among smokers. That same year Wynder and Graham reported that they produced skin cancer in 44 percent of the mice they had painted with tobacco tar condensed from cigarette smoke.

The scientific evidence entered the public consciousness through a series of articles in *Reader's Digest*, whose editors and publishers took an early stand against tobacco. (The magazine had published an article in 1924 that questioned the safety of cigarettes, but without supporting scientific evidence, it did not provoke much concern.) *Reader's Digest* articles in the 1950s on "How Harmful Are Cigarettes," "Cancer by the Carton," and "The

21

Growing Horror of Lung Cancer" alerted the public to the new evidence of the hazards of smoking. Along with similar articles in *Ladies' Home Journal*, the *New Republic*, and *Consumer Reports*, early concerns began to take shape. In 1954, for example, the American Cancer Society adopted a resolution recognizing a connection between smoking and lung cancer, and in 1958 the Consumer's Union recommended that smokers quit or cut down to avoid health risks.

THE 1964 SURGEON GENERAL'S REPORT ON SMOKING AND HEALTH

As study after study replicated the results of Wynder and Graham, Hammond and Horn, and Doll and Hill, the mounting evidence of the danger of cigarettes for health could not be ignored. Although many medical researchers criticized the studies as insufficiently rigorous in their scientific methods and defended the habit, others became increasingly vigorous in their criticism of smoking. To make a strong impression on the public, those critical of cigarettes believed that the government should make a statement on the effects of smoking, yet federal agencies worried that government support of efforts to control tobacco would harm the economy, create resistance in Congress, and make enemies of powerful tobacco companies.

With pressure from a few in Congress and organizations such as the American Cancer Society and the American Public Health Association, President John F. Kennedy referred the matter to then surgeon general Luther Terry, who agreed to supervise a comprehensive review of the evidence on smoking and health. Although part of the Public Health Service, the surgeon general was an appointed position that involved little in the way of bureaucratic administration and focused largely on informing the public and health professionals about matters relating to public health. In 1957 Surgeon General Dr. Leroy F. Burney had issued a mild statement that confirmed cigarette smoking was a cause of lung cancer and in 1959 published an article on his findings in *JAMA*. Still, his carefully qualified statements received more in the way of harsh attacks from the tobacco industry than recognition of the problem from the public.

Surgeon General Terry, on the other hand, took the approach of convening in 1962 an advisory committee of 10 biomedical experts from the nation's most prestigious universities and research institutes. The committee undertook a review of the evidence and completed a 387-page report that remained secret until its release on January 11, 1964. In the words of Terry, "The report hit the country like a bombshell. It was front page news and a lead story on every radio and television station in the United States and many abroad. The report not only carried a strong condemnation of tobacco usage, especially cigarette smoking, but conveyed its message in such clear and concise language that it could not be misunderstood."[15] More than a summary of scientific findings, the report and the recommended actions bluntly told people interested in their health and in a long life to give up or avoid smoking.

The publicity received by the report showed in the immediate reaction of the public. For the first two months after the report, cigarette consumption declined by 20 percent, and tobacco companies worried about the collapse of the industry. Although the short-term decline did not last, the overall per capita consumption in 1964 fell to 4,143 from the 1963 peak of 4,286. By itself a small decline, it nonetheless represented a major turn of events in the longtime span of the cigarette's largely uninterrupted upward climb.

Building on the reaction, the surgeon general recommended new public policies to deal with the problem. With nonsmoking the best way to reduce risks, policies would aim to have smokers give up the habit and prevent nonsmokers from starting. The recommended actions included an educational campaign on smoking and health, labels on cigarette packages to warn about the hazards, and restrictions on advertising.

After the first report on health and smoking, the surgeon general continued as an advocate against smoking, and beginning in 1967 the Office of the Surgeon General released reports nearly every year. The reports generally summarized recent research on the health consequences of smoking but eventually came to focus on specific themes. For example, a 1980 report focused on women, a 1981 report focused on changes in cigarette products, and a 1983 report focused on cardiovascular disease. A 1982 report from Everett Koop, the newly appointed surgeon general in the Reagan administration, on the relationship between smoking and cancer noted an encouraging decline in cigarette use from the time of the first report. It further noted in strong language that the consequences of smoking were still "the most important public issue of our time," and that cigarettes were "the chief, single, avoidable cause of death in our society."[16] The report presented evidence that 21 percent of all U.S. deaths were due to cancer, and 30 percent of those were attributable to smoking. More so than previous surgeons general, Koop became a fierce critic of smoking, approached his task with missionary zeal, and reported on the harm of smoking in several other influential reports during his tenure.

NICOTINE ADDICTION

Given the publicity of the 1964 Surgeon General's report and the desire of nearly all people to avoid dying early, it would seem that the evidence against smoking would lead to the disappearance of the habit. The percentage of the U.S. population that smoked did indeed decline, as did the overall consumption of cigarettes, but not as fast as public health advocates would have liked. In 1965, 52 percent of adult males and 34 percent of adult females smoked. Just over 20 years later, the percentages had fallen to 33 and 28, respectively—a significant decline but far from creating a smoke-free society. A substantial part of the U.S. population continued to smoke. Moreover per person consumption fell from its 1963 peak of 4,286 to 3,969 by 1970 but rose again to 4,112 by 1973—not an encouraging change. The number of cigarettes smoked per person fell less than the percentage of smokers because those continuing the habit consumed an increasing number of cigarettes.

The slow shift in behavior did not mean that smokers rejected the evidence about the harm of smoking and the benefits of quitting. Rather, they wanted to quit but found the process difficult. Researchers could have predicted as much. Personal experiences over the years demonstrated that cigarette smoking was at least habit forming if not addictive. The 1964 Surgeon General's committee that authored the report recognized this fact. Some members desired to label cigarettes and the nicotine they contained as addictive, but others believed more cautiously that the evidence could not yet prove this claim. Many saw smoking as a habit, but one substantially different from addictions to drugs such as heroin and cocaine. Hard drugs required increasing amounts to satisfy the craving, but smokers of cigarettes seemed to get along on the same daily allotment. Moreover, labeling millions of smokers as addicts—akin to drug and alcohol abusers—might offend enough people to blunt the major message of the Surgeon General's report about the harm of smoking.

After the 1964 report two groups continued to research the addictiveness of nicotine—scientists employed by tobacco companies and scientists in research universities or institutes. The tobacco companies had recognized the addictive qualities of tobacco early on, but to avoid obvious negative publicity that they were enslaving smokers much as drug dealers enslaved heroin addicts, they kept the information in-house. According to documents released many years later during a civil suit, the tobacco company Brown and Williamson was informed in 1962 of research done by its parent company, British American Tobacco, that showed smokers needed continued intake of the drugging element of cigarettes to maintain physiological and emotional equilibrium. One executive wrote in a memo (that would prove damning in the suit), "We are, then, in the business of selling nicotine, an addictive drug effective in the release of stress mechanisms."[17] Cautious executives did not want to make this claim public.

Independent researchers also began to accumulate evidence of the addictive properties of cigarettes and nicotine. In one 1967 study at the University of Michigan Medical School, smokers were injected with a substance that, unknown to them, consisted of either nicotine or a placebo. Those injected with nicotine cut their consumption of cigarettes, as they received little additional lift from the cigarettes.[18] Other studies systematically described the difficulties smokers faced in stopping. Although the majority (70 percent) of smokers today state they want to quit, few can do so—only about 6 percent succeed for more than a year. The quit rate for cigarettes is lower than for many hard drugs, which reveals the powerful hold of cigarettes over smokers.

In terms of feeding an addiction, cigarettes turn out to work well as a delivery system. They allow smokers to conveniently regulate their ingestion of nicotine. After lighting up and inhaling a cigarette, nicotine reaches the brain in minutes. It stimulates electrical activity in the brain, increases metabolic activity in the body, raises the heart beat, and causes skeletal muscles to relax. Serving as both a stimulant and relaxant, nicotine mildly improves the performance of everyday tasks and moderates mood swings.[19] It can stay in the body for hours, but as it leaves, the desire to smoke grows. Lighting up and inhaling on a regular basis feeds the body's need for more nicotine. In this way the use of cigarettes is self-reinforcing.

Viewing cigarette use as an addiction presents a different perspective on the pleasures of smoking. Smokers often state that they find smoking soothing, as the stimulant properties of nicotine for the brain can help one focus on the task at hand, and the relaxing properties for the muscles ease physical stress. Yet, the soothing nature of cigarettes may really come from the delivery of nicotine, which relieves addictive cravings and the physical discomfort caused by the cravings. In other words, cigarettes and nicotine may in the first place cause the negative feelings that more cigarettes and nicotine later remedy.

The difficulty in quitting and the evidence of addiction show in several withdrawal symptoms. Giving up smoking causes strong cravings for the product that, when not satisfied, produce irritability, restlessness, depression, anxiety, sleep disorder, and physical discomfort. Those with these symptoms often have trouble concentrating on daily tasks. The withdrawal symptoms largely disappear after three to four weeks, but the cravings remain for much longer periods, sometimes indefinitely; former smokers often say they miss the habit years after they have stopped. This continued attraction results not so much from the physical dependence but from the memory of the pleasurable feelings (stimulation of the mind and relaxation of the muscles) and behaviors (eating, drinking alcohol, socializing) associated with smoking.

In 1988 the Office of the Surgeon General released another report that this time focused on nicotine addiction. The report stated bluntly, "The processes that determine tobacco addiction are similar to those that determine addiction to other drugs, including illegal drugs."[20] Willing to go beyond statements in previous reports of the Surgeon General, the 1988 report clearly laid out its definition of addiction and how nicotine had properties similar to hard drugs. In general terms addiction involves behavior that is controlled by a substance that causes changes in mood from its effects on the brain. Nicotine causes changes in mood through its effect on the brain (unlike, say, food that improves mood by meeting requirements for nourishment) and compels smokers to act in ways that damage themselves and society. As with addiction to hard drugs, addiction to nicotine produces uncomfortable withdrawal symptoms that require smokers to light up again. Such addiction occurs not only from cigarettes but also from smokeless tobacco (and less so, cigars and pipes), which distributes nicotine to the body through the mouth.

That many smokers quit successfully does not, according to the report, negate the claim of nicotine addiction. Spontaneous remission or unaided quitting occurs among 30 percent of hard drug users but leaves many others who face difficulties in trying to end their dependence on the addictive substances. For both drugs and cigarettes, some people are more prone to becoming addicted than others and have a more difficult time quitting. Such variation occurs in most human behavior and simply means that susceptibility to cigarette addiction, if not universal, is common. Of course, cigarettes are legal and most hard drugs are not. Hard drugs more than cigarettes negatively affect the ability of addicts to participate in daily life, increase the criminal actions associated with the habit, and produce more disgust in conventional society. Still, the control of one's actions by an artificial substance and the difficulty in ending the reliance on the substance make the products similar.

Several important implications follow from these conclusions about addiction. First, smokers and those considering taking up the habit must be made aware of their addiction. By realizing that their habit comes not from a personal choice, they may be more motivated to reject or quit the habit. This would seem especially important to young people, who may begin the habit not realizing that it will addict them for decades to come. Second, education alone cannot get most smokers to quit. Many smokers fully understand the advantages of not smoking, but the addiction makes quitting difficult. For those unable to quit on their own, interventions must involve some sort of medical treatment of the addiction. Third, unlike earlier anti-smoking advocates, such groups today do not criticize smokers for their weakness but instead view them as victims of an addiction. More than smokers the tobacco companies that encouraged the addiction with their advertising, product marketing, and pricing strategies become the villains.

ADVERTISING TO YOUNG PEOPLE

Given the evidence of the addictiveness of smoking, public health experts turned their focus to the problem of teen smoking. Once a young person overcomes the initial unpleasant sensations and takes up smoking on a regular basis, he or she will become a long-term, perhaps even lifelong, smoker. The earlier the addiction occurs, the longer a smoker will remain a customer.

Nearly all smokers first tried cigarettes before age 20, and those who passed that age without smoking seldom ever begin. Teens might know of the harm of smoking to health but tend to think that they will have plenty of time to quit before health problems develop and underestimate the difficulty in quitting.[21] The teenage years thus prove critical in the adoption of cigarette smoking.

While recognizing the need to appeal to teenagers, the tobacco industry did not want to undermine its formally declared statement that smoking was an adult habit by appealing directly to minors. Advertising could indirectly appeal to adolescents, however, by associating traits valued by the young with smoking. Ads did not need to use teen models or students in schools but could show young adults involved in activities that youth want to enjoy. They would depict smokers as young, physically active, cool, independent, attractive to the opposite sex, and able to fully enjoy life's pleasures. Tobacco companies could, within limits, advertise in magazines and on radio and television shows that attracted the young as well as adults so they could not be accused of targeting youth alone. *Playboy*, for example, often appeals to adolescent males and includes many cigarette ads. Similarly, tobacco company sponsorship of sporting events, such as auto racing, women's tennis tournaments, and rock and jazz music concerts influence youth.

The sheer number of ads could also increase the misperception among young people that cigarettes had achieved a high level of popularity and acceptance outside their own families and schools. Until recent restriction, ads in magazines, on billboards, in sports stadiums, on racing cars, and in store displays were hard to miss. Point-of-purchase advertisements in retail outlets that sell cigarette products can easily be seen by youth. A 1992 Gallup poll found that 87 percent of surveyed adolescents could recall having seen one or more tobacco company advertisements. Even relatively young children are aware of cigarette advertising.

The most glaring and disconcerting effort of tobacco companies to attract young smokers came from the Joe Camel campaign sponsored by R. J. Reynolds for Camel cigarettes. Based on a $75 million campaign that began in 1987, the Joe Camel ads used a cartoon character along with adult models. In the ads, Joe Camel appeared as a cool party animal, with a cigarette, sporting sunglasses and a tuxedo, and with adoring young women nearby.

27

Joe Camel also appeared on T-shirts, sweatshirts, posters, mugs, and beach sandals. The images and products appeared to be geared toward young children as well as teens—few adults would be attracted to a brand by a cartoon camel and cheap products. A study published in 1991 in *JAMA* found that a shocking 90 percent of six-year-olds could identify Joe Camel and knew his connection to cigarettes.[22]

Combined with the mounting evidence of the addictiveness of cigarette smoking, the ads directed at young children and teens encouraged the Office of the Surgeon General and antismoking organizations to further emphasize the harm of cigarette advertising. Reports by the Surgeon General's office included long chapters on the manipulation of youth by smoking advertisements and the effects of the ads on the adoption of cigarettes.[23] Much controversy exists over the effectiveness of advertising, and teens can see through the appeals of ads directed at them. Still, documenting the harmful effects of tobacco had moved from medical studies of the physical harm (for both addiction and mortality) to social science studies of the social factors behind youthful adoption of cigarette smoking.

RESPONSE OF THE TOBACCO INDUSTRY

The emerging negative evidence about cigarettes in the 1950s led at least in part to a drop in sales during the middle of the decade. In an attempt to continue generating profits at past levels, tobacco companies addressed these health concerns. In 1954 they formed the Tobacco Industry Research Council (TIRC). The council aimed to counter the negative publicity about cigarettes with its own studies, press releases, and propaganda on smoking. Tobacco executives, representatives of the council, and some physicians and scientists assured the public that the harm of smoking was overstated and moderate cigarette use was safe.

The debate between critics and defenders of cigarettes often centered on the validity of the scientific evidence. The key statistical issue concerned the ability of studies to demonstrate the causal harm of cigarettes. The fact that smokers experienced premature mortality did not prove cause and effect; for example, one respected psychologist in England, Hans Eysenck, suggested that persons unable to express anger, fear, and anxiety were prone to both smoking and early death.[24] These personality traits, both inborn and learned, could account for an observed but ultimately unfounded association between smoking and lung cancer. An appropriate study would have to make sure that the personality traits of smokers and nonsmokers did not differ before concluding that smoking caused lung cancer. Scientists replied that premature death from lung cancer in societies with little cigarette smoking occurred rarely, even though the personality traits seen to cause both smoking and cancer were common in those societies. Yet, defenders of tobacco could always point to possible alternative explanations.

Other scientists with no vested interest in either the theories of the causes of cancer or the defense of tobacco companies nonetheless remained cautious about the criticisms of cigarette smoking. These scientists tended to wait for improved methodology and replication before reaching a firm conclusion about the hazards of tobacco. *JAMA* was slow, for example, to give scientific backing to claims about the perils of smoking. Ernest Wynder, one of the first researchers to identify the connection between smoking and lung cancer, faced much criticism for his work. In the 1960s the director of research at the Sloan-Kettering Institute called Wynder's claims irresponsible but also accepted annual cash gifts from Philip Morris on behalf of the institute. Antismoking campaigns point out that the tobacco industry supported many such skeptical researchers with funding.

The battle of experts would prove futile, however—the emerging evidence against smoking was too strong. As internal industry documents released in the 1990s would show, many in the tobacco industry in the 1960s and 1970s were fully aware of the hazards of their product. The documents proposed that nicotine was addictive and smoking caused cancer. Manufacturers searched for tobacco leaves and ingredients that would most effectively deliver the chemical and limit the harm of the product, all the while publicly denying both the addictiveness and perils of smoking. This dishonesty may have kept sales from falling further but would provide grounds of fraud and misrepresentation for groups to later sue tobacco companies.

Rather than trying to convince hard-line critics of its case, the tobacco industry believed it should focus on appealing to those with more moderate views about the need to make changes in the smoking habits of the population. In trying to do so, tobacco ads in the 1950s claimed that cigarettes were safe. Philip Morris offered "A Cigarette That Takes the Fear Out of Smoking"; R. J. Reynolds said that "More Doctors Smoke Camels"; Chesterfield promised the benefits of "30 Years of Tobacco Research." However, these ads may have worsened rather than soothed the worries smokers had about cigarettes.

More effective ads took another form: They indirectly associated smoking with health. The Marlboro Country ads came to prominence in television and magazines in the 1960s in a campaign developed by the famous advertising executive Leo F. Burnett. The ads featured the Marlboro Man, a ruggedly handsome cowboy who lived and worked outdoors in open mountain country and enjoyed a life of hard work, fresh air, and scenic beauty. The ads did not have to state that the Marlboro Man did not look like he would succumb to lung cancer. Other ads also showed young, healthy, and active people smoking cigarettes while enthusiastically enjoying themselves.

Tobacco Industry and Smoking

Tobacco ads touting health claims drew the ire of the federal agency in charge of regulating business practices. The Federal Trade Commission (FTC) had since the 1950s expressed concerns about the claims made on behalf of cigarettes in advertising. Later, at the time of the 1964 Surgeon General's report on health and smoking, the commission began an investigation of cigarette advertising, concluding that some ads made false health claims, and others misleadingly implied that smokers gained vigor, sexual attractiveness, and virility from cigarettes. Hoping to preempt government interference, the tobacco industry promised to self-regulate its ads. It would no longer allow industry members to make claims that did not have medical or scientific proof or that misrepresented the social benefits of cigarettes. The effort could not, however, forestall proposals by the FTC and eventual legislation from Congress to include warnings on cigarette packages and advertisements, and the policy of self-regulation was dropped.

The tobacco industry financed several other efforts to discredit claims against cigarettes in the areas of politics, the law, public relations, and the media.[25] First, recognizing the importance of the political as well as the medical battle, a consortium of the major tobacco firms hired a lobbyist to represent their interests in Washington, D.C. Their lobbyist, Earl C. Clements, a retired representative and senator from Kentucky who had close ties to his former colleagues in Congress and to the Lyndon Johnson White House, testified formally and lobbied informally. He shrewdly led the discussion toward economic issues and away from health issues. Politicians worried about the economic harm new laws to restrict cigarette sales and advertising might bring to growers, factory workers, retailers, advertising outlets, and cities, such as Richmond, Virginia, and Winston-Salem, North Carolina, that depended on the industry. Clements's lobbying could not stop movements to restrict advertising and require warning messages on cigarettes but did stall more drastic measures.

Second, the tobacco firms hired a committee in 1963 of six well-known and successful lawyers to defend the legal interests of the industry. Early suits against the tobacco companies had failed, but the evidence presented by the Office of the Surgeon General might make the manufacturers liable for future suits. Worried that even one loss would open the floodgates of suits from other smokers, the industry prepared to fight expensive legal battles until the end. Hiring the best legal talent would prove crucial in this effort.

Third, to help publicize their views about cigarettes, tobacco firms funded the Tobacco Institute (TI), which opened in Washington, D.C., in 1958. Like any trade organization, the TI emphasized the economic importance of the industry and the dependence of millions of people on its fortunes. In addition, it extended the efforts of the TIRC to dispute the evidence behind claims of the dangers of smoking, highlighted the rights of smokers to enjoy their freely chosen pleasure, and emphasized the First Amendment rights of companies to free speech in commercial advertising.

Fourth, through its financial support of research organizations, writers, magazines, and publishers, the tobacco industry promoted its own views about smoking. Articles and books arguing for the safety of cigarettes appeared regularly, and copies of these articles and books received wide distribution free of charge. The publication of one 1967 book, *It Is Safe to Smoke*, turned out to have been subsidized by the tobacco industry.[26] Ads filled with one or two pages of dense text offered a detailed defense of smoking and the rights of consumers to enjoy the habit. With ads entitled "A Frank Statement to Cigarette Smokers" or "Do Cigarette Companies Want Kids to Smoke? No," the tobacco industry could purchase space in magazines when it could not publish regular articles.

These efforts could not, however, halt the growing antismoking movement. In the years after the Surgeon General's 1964 report the industry had to respond to multiple threats to its well-being and profits. They met these threats with, from their point of view, varied degrees of success.

- In 1964 the FTC proposed requiring a warning on cigarette packages and in advertisements to counter what they viewed as deceptive advertising. After proposing self-regulation, the industry appealed to allies in Congress, many of whom represented tobacco-growing regions and states, for protection from the proposed regulations. Congress responded by preventing the FTC from taking action on the issue. In reaction to the lobbying efforts of the tobacco industry, the House and Senate in 1965 instead required a mild warning on cigarette packages but not advertisements. The warning stated, "Caution—Cigarette Smoking May Be Hazardous to Your Health."

- The Federal Communications Commission (FCC) agreed with a 1966 petition of a New York City lawyer, John F. Banzhaf III, that the fairness doctrine applied to cigarette advertising. Based on the view that the airways are a public resource, the fairness doctrine required equal time for presentation of competing views. Although typically applied to politicians and political parties, the fairness doctrine was extended by the decision of the commission to require the airing of antismoking ads to balance smoking commercials. Much to the concern of the tobacco industry, these antismoking ads proved effective.

- Continuing its efforts against tobacco advertising, the FTC proposed to ban cigarette advertisements from radio and television. The tobacco industry again appealed to Congress for protection, but antismoking legislators had grown in power. After much struggle, the tobacco industry first agreed to voluntarily remove their ads and then went along with a bill that banned the ads beginning on January 2, 1971 (after filling the airways with commercials during the New Year's Day football bowl games).

- Congress required that a stronger warning appear on cigarette packages and the same warning be included on advertisements. The warning stated, "The Surgeon General Has Determined That Cigarette Smoking Is Dangerous to Your Health."

- Joseph Califano, head of the Department of Health, Education, and Welfare under President Jimmy Carter, proposed several actions in 1978 to fight cigarette smoking. He wanted to raise taxes on cigarettes, use the government proceeds from the taxes for antismoking campaigns and programs, eliminate smoking on airplanes and in restaurants, and end government subsidies to tobacco growers. However, Califano received little support from the Carter administration. Opposition from tobacco growers, retail establishments, and cigarette makers was sufficient to block these proposals.

- On the legal front the tobacco industry lawyers had since the first filing in 1954 successfully defeated suits brought by smokers against them. In part due to the resources of tobacco firms in fighting them, few early suits even reached a jury. However, in 1988, Rose Cipollone won a $400,000 judgment against the Liggett Group for the failure of the cigarette manufacturer to warn her about the dangers of its product. Although the decision was later overturned and the family of the deceased Mrs. Cipollone dropped continued appeals to the Supreme Court after the costs rose beyond their means, the jury award represented a major defeat for the tobacco company against claims that it was liable for the harm of cigarettes. (More serious legal problems would come in the 1990s.)

Overall, the years after the 1964 Surgeon General's report were not good ones for the tobacco industry. Both the sales and the image of the industry suffered. In response to the troubles, however, the industry could follow past strategies by continuing its advertising, promotion expenditures, and product development.

CHANGES IN THE TOBACCO INDUSTRY

The cigarette industry had over the first part of the 20th century overcome opposition to its product and gained widespread respect and high profits. Cigars, the one-time major competitor of cigarettes, became associated with older rather than younger generations and had fallen on hard times. In 1950, having done its part in the efforts against Nazi Germany and imperial Japan in World War II and facing no opposition from antismoking crusaders, the industry could expect to benefit from the booming economy after the war. The three major cigarette brands, Camel, Lucky Strike, and Chesterfield, continued to dominate the market as they had for decades. Confident executives would not have predicted the threats to the financial condition of the companies that would soon come or recognize the new shape their business would take.

Economic problems for tobacco in the 1950s related to marketing as well as to health. With levels of smoking near the maximum, the market could not likely grow by attracting more smokers (except of course at the younger ages, when new smokers would first start). At the time, more than 50 percent of men ages 18 and over smoked. Those who did not smoke were unlikely to take up the habit, as they would have already had their chance to begin but for whatever reason did not like the habit. Fewer women smoked, between 20 and 30 percent. Without special efforts to create products that better appealed to women, it seemed unlikely that they would reach the high smoking levels of men. Thus, under current sales and production strategies, the market of smokers had reached saturation.

One way to increase sales came not from attracting more smokers but from encouraging each smoker to consume more cigarettes. Sales of cigarettes in cartons made a new package easily available to smokers when they finished an old one. Sales of cigarettes in ubiquitous vending machines similarly made it easy to find cigarettes outside the home. These changes made smoking even more than in the past an activity not reserved for special times and places, but something that one could indulge in throughout the day.

Perhaps more important, cigarette companies developed a new form of cigarettes—king size—that might lead to more smoking. Slightly longer than regular cigarettes, king-size cigarettes had more tobacco and cost a few pennies more per pack. Smokers could consume the same number of cigarettes each day but use more tobacco and pay more. The growing affluence of the U.S. population allowed smokers to pay the higher costs and contributed to the profits of the tobacco company. New brands of king-size cigarettes, such as Pall Mall, Winston, and Marlboro, became more popular than the older standard brands. Chesterfield cigarettes, in response, began to appear in both regular and king size.

Other efforts to distinguish one brand from another emerged. Cigarettes with filters grew in popularity, particularly among women, as did mentholated cigarettes. Filter cigarettes had been introduced in 1936 but did not become well liked until the publicity in the 1950s about health concerns. Although the attraction to these innovations involved more than health concerns, cigarettes with filters and menthol could, in their advertising, appeal to the health conscious. New filtered products such as Winston, L&M,

Kent, and Viceroy grew in sales, in part based on advertisements that emphasized the ability of filters to purify cigarette smoke and make the habit safer and cleaner. The filters would in fact only modestly reduce the risks of cigarettes, but smokers felt reassured. Health claims were also made about mentholated cigarettes: They were cleaner, fresher, and tastier than other cigarettes. Kool cigarettes, the first popular brand to add peppermint extract to tobacco to form a menthol cigarette, used a name that implied that the cigarette smoke would be less irritating and hot.

The tobacco companies also conducted research to find a safer cigarette and successfully marketed some low-tar and low-nicotine cigarettes. During the 1950s cigarette makers often made claims about the tar content—the particles contained in the residue or by-product of the burning of tobacco that are inhaled with tobacco smoke—of their cigarettes. Because tar was a major source of the harmful effects of tobacco use on health (but also a major source of tobacco flavor), cigarette makers hoped that low-tar cigarettes would attract smokers worried about their health. Competition among cigarette manufacturers over sales of low-tar cigarettes that occurred in the 1950s became known as the tar derby. The low-tar and health claims made on behalf of the cigarettes became so confusing that the FTC took over testing for cigarette tar. However, smokers either rejected low-tar cigarettes with filters that cleansed the smoke so much as to significantly lose flavor or puffed harder and longer to obtain the same chemicals from the low-tar cigarettes as from regular cigarettes. Efforts in the 1980s and 1990s to market smokeless cigarettes and nicotine-free cigarettes flopped altogether.

The new types and brands of cigarettes and the competition they generated led to more choices for smokers. In 1941 the top three brands captured 72 percent of the market, while in 1961 the top three sellers had 48 percent of the market.[27] Consumers less often adopted a brand for life than in the past but would switch quickly to another brand based on advertisements or new cigarette styles. Brands proliferated at an even faster pace in the 1960s and 1970s in the hope of finding a new winner; for example, Virginia Slims (which used the slogan "You've Come a Long Way Baby") targeted younger, more independent women. By 1978 smokers had their choice among 190 different brands and brand types.

The major tobacco companies remained dominant. Reynolds, American, and Liggett and Myers, products of the trust breakup in 1911, remained the top three companies in 1961. Three other companies, Lorillard, Brown and Williamson, and Philip Morris, rounded out the top six. Although still profitable, the companies recognized the need to diversify in the face of growing antitobacco sentiments. Philip Morris, for example, purchased the Miller Brewing Company and Seven-Up; R. J. Reynolds purchased several food businesses and eventually merged with Nabisco; Liggett and Myers purchased liquor distilling and other companies to form the Liggett Group and later the Brooke Group. Lorillard was acquired by a business conglomerate, Loews Corporation, which also owns movie theater and hotel companies. Diversification over the years represented an implicit recognition by tobacco companies that they needed to protect themselves from the likely decline of the cigarette business in the United States. They would in the future also employ another strategy for survival by turning their attention to new markets outside the United States—developing nations where there were few smokers and little organized opposition to the smoking industry.

RECENT TRENDS AND PATTERNS, 1990–PRESENT

THE SLOWING RATE OF DECLINE

Negative publicity about the harm of cigarette smoking, the addictiveness of nicotine, and the efforts of tobacco companies to promote self-destructive behavior produced a decline in cigarette smoking. Reviewing the trends since 1964, the 1989 Surgeon General's report could point to substantial progress.[28] The number of cigarettes consumed per adult fell from 4,269 in 1964 to 2,827 in 1990. From 1965 to 1990, the percentage of male smokers fell from 51.9 to 28.4, and the percentage of female smokers fell from 33.9 to 22.8. The decline among males exceeded that among females in large part because males were at higher levels in 1965. Despite a greater decline in smoking among light and moderate smokers, who were less addicted to nicotine than heavy smokers, the trends encouraged public health officials.

Smoking among youth declined much as it did for older groups during the years from 1964 to 1990. Because youth smoking would foretell future trends at older ages, progress against smoking before age 18 had special importance. For young adults 18–24, male smokers fell from 54.1 percent of the age group in 1965 to 25.1 percent in 1990, and female smokers fell from 37.3 to 22.4 percent over the same period. Yearly surveys of high school seniors, which began in 1976, revealed a similar decline in daily smoking until 1990. For boys, such smoking fell from 28 percent to 18 percent and for girls from 29 percent to 19 percent.

The downward trends in current smoking stemmed in part from fewer people ever starting the habit but also from more people quitting. An increase in the percentage of former smokers represented progress against smoking. In 1965, 19.8 percent of males said they used to smoke but currently did not, and 8 percent of females said they used to smoke but currently did not. In 1990, 30.3 percent of males and 19.5 percent of females fit the category of former smokers. In terms of those who never smoked, the percentages rose for males from 28.3 in 1965 to 41.3 in 1990. For females, however, the trend for "never smokers" was less positive: It changed little from 58.1 percent in 1965 to 57.7 in 1990. The drop in current smoking among females largely comes from the rise in former rather than never smokers.

Although some signs of decline continued, the rate of decline in cigarette smoking slowed. Among adults from 1990 to 1998, the percentages of current male smokers fell by only two percent—from 28.4 to 26.4. For females the decline was even smaller, falling from 22.8 to 22.0. Among smokers in the 1990s light and moderate consumption of cigarettes increased relative to heavy smoking, but with no smoking, the percentages appear slow to change. Overall, after some 35 years of antismoking efforts, about one-quarter of the U.S. population continued with the habit. Given the population of the United States, these percentages translate into roughly 40–50 million current smokers and about an equal number of former smokers.

Concerning trends among young people during the 1990s, rather than falling, rates of smoking in fact showed some increases. From 1990 to 1998 current smoking among young men ages 18–24 rose from 25.1 to 31.5 percent, and current smoking among young women of the same age group rose from 22.4 to 25.1 percent. Among high school seniors, daily smoking among boys and girls remained at about 18 to 19 percent in both 1990 and 2000. More specifically, the trends show a rise from a low point in 1992 of around 16 percent to about 25 percent in 1997. Since 1997, however, smoking among high school seniors has fallen each year, and most public officials hope that the trend will continue downward. In any case, the rise and then fall leave current levels of smoking about the same presently as a decade ago.

Through its Healthy People Goals for 2010, the U.S. government strives to reduce current smoking rates among high school students to below 16 percent.[29] That goal is reachable only if the trends of decline in the last few years among high school students continue. For all adults the goal is to reduce smoking to 12 percent—a goal that is also possible to reach but unlikely given the experiences over the last decade. Reaching the goal would require major efforts at getting adult smokers to quit.

Why the slowdown? Continued declines may become more difficult as the remaining smokers are those most attracted and addicted to cigarettes. Those best able to resist starting to smoke and to quit once they start will likely have already done so, and those who currently smoke may have the most trouble stopping. The slowdown in smoking also likely relates to the efforts of the tobacco industry. Lower cigarette prices in the early 1990s and the increased availability of bargain brands contributed in particular to a rise in smoking rates among young people. Conversely, rising prices in the late 1990s and early 2000s help explain the decline. Advertising and promotional expenditures by tobacco companies, which grew throughout the 1990s, also may moderate the potential for smoking to decline. For example, an issue of *People* magazine with a cover story on "Teens and Sex"—a story likely to attract young readers—contained 14 pages of cigarette ads. Antismoking advocates argue that some of the ads would appeal especially to young people: a picture of a slim young model in tight-fighting clothes with the label "Totally Kool" and a Marlboro ad promoting adventure gear and depicting youthful mountain climbers.

Cigars have for most of the last half century declined in popularity, although they enjoyed resurgent popularity in the 1990s. In 1970, 16.2 percent of men smoked cigars. The figure fell to 3.5 percent by 1991 but rose to 8.4 percent in 1998 (female cigar smoking remained negligible over the period). As shown by the popularity of *Cigar Aficionado* magazine and cigar bars, the resurgence of cigar smoking involves desires to enjoy their flavor and aroma, much as one enjoys gourmet food and quality liquor. Furthermore, the new found status associated with cigar smoking may reflect a trend of "chic" among young men. The largest increase has thus come in the consumption of premium cigars, particularly among white males ages 25–34. Although for most cigar smoking involves an occasional pleasure rather than a day-long habit, the health risks faced by occasional cigar smokers are greater than for those who abstain altogether from tobacco products.

Smokeless tobacco has also failed to decline in the 1990s, staying at 5 to 6 percent use among men (female use is negligible). Pipe smoking has declined among men after a brief period of popularity in the 1960s. Use of bidis, a tobacco product common in India but new to the United States, has increased among youth. Bidis are small brown cigarettes that are hand rolled in a leaf and tied at one end by a string. About 12 percent of high school girls and 17 percent of high school boys have tried the product, but few use it on a regular basis. About 5 percent of high school students have tried Kreteks, a kind of cigarette that mixes tobacco and clove spice.

Smoking figures have only recently began to be gathered for pregnant women but appear more favorable than the figures for smoking in general. The percent of live births in which mothers reported smoking during pregnancy fell from 19.5 in 1989 to 12.9 in 1998. The percentage of heavy smokers (more than one pack a day) among pregnant women fell from 6.6 percent to 3.8 percent. However, since many women may hide their smoking habit from physicians and researchers, the levels may be artificially low. Smoking by pregnant women harms not just the smokers themselves but also retards the growth of the fetus, increases the risk of a stillborn birth, and often results in low birth weight babies. The decline over time may result in part from the growing embarrassment among pregnant smokers and greater willingness to misreport their habits.

Tobacco Industry and Smoking

WHO SMOKES?

The decline in cigarette smoking from the 1960s to the 1990s involved some groups more than others and as a result has in recent years come to concentrate smoking among persons with certain social characteristics. The groups that now have the highest smoking rates also appear to consist of individuals whose attraction to the habit is most difficult to change. Assuming that the decline in smoking occurs among those who most strongly desire or are best able to avoid or give up the habit, those who do smoke will be the most resistant to change. Who are these people? In simplest terms they are those people whose physiology and psychology make them most prone to addiction, who find the most enjoyment from cigarettes, and who are most attracted to the image of cigarette smokers. However, these people are concentrated in some groups more than in others.

Gender and Age

Perhaps surprisingly, gender and age no longer distinguish strongly between smokers and nonsmokers. In regards to gender, men continue to smoke more than women, but the traditionally large differences have declined, particularly among the young. For high school seniors, smoking differences between the sexes are negligible and for all ages difference reach at most 5 percent. The equality between the sexes reflects the faster decline among males in recent decades. This trend may come from the strong efforts of tobacco companies to appeal to women with their products and the desire of women to act in ways that assert their independence and freedom. More simply, the slow rate of decline among females may merely reflect the fact that they adopted the habit later than males and have not yet had as much time as males to reject the habit.[30]

In regards to age the percentages of current smokers differ little among those under age 65. At ages 18–24, 26.8 percent of persons smoke; at ages 25–44, 27.0 percent of persons smoke; and at ages 45–64, 24.0 percent of persons smoke. The percentage falls to 9.7 percent at ages 65 and over, largely because older persons have had longer to quit and face more serious health conditions that require quitting. In addition, fewer smokers than non smokers survive to old age. Otherwise, smoking today appears similar across ages and generations.

Socioeconomic Status

Educational attainment, occupational prestige, and income levels reflect the major components of socioeconomic status (SES). In general, the higher the SES of a person, the less likely he or she is to smoke. This trend has strengthened over the years, which increasingly concentrates smoking among low SES groups. The most recent figures available show that 34 percent of high school dropouts smoke, while 13 percent of those with a college degree smoke.[31] Data on income and occupational differences in smoking are harder to come by but reveal much the same pattern. Those living at poverty level are more likely to smoke than those with income above the poverty level, and among those above poverty level, smoking declines as income increases. Similarly those in high prestige occupations with high education and high earnings—professionals (lawyers, doctors, professors), corporate managers, and technical specialists (computer programmers, engineers)—smoke the least. Persons in lower-level white-collar occupations, such as salespeople, administrators, store clerks, and secretaries, smoke more than persons in higher status occupations. And persons in lower status occupations such as factory workers, truck drivers, construction workers, and cleaning service people smoke the most.

Race and Ethnicity

Race and ethnic differences in smoking relate to SES differences, as minority groups tend to have lower education and income than whites. African Americans once smoked more than whites, but the difference has largely disappeared. In 1974, for example, 44.0 percent of blacks and 36.4 percent of whites smoked. In 2000, the percentages equaled 23.2 for blacks and 24.1 for whites. Among young people, smoking among blacks has declined dramatically and has contributed to the similar rates across races. Figures for high school seniors show that less than 10 percent of black youth smoke— a percentage substantially lower than for whites.

Among other race and ethnic groups, Native Americans have the highest rates of smoking, and Hispanics and Asian Americans have the lowest rates. For example, among women, 22.4 percent of non-Hispanic white females smoke, compared to 42.5 percent of Native American women, 13.3 percent of Hispanic women, and 7.6 percent of Asian and Pacific Islander women. The low rates for Hispanics and Asian Americans may stem from the relatively large portion of recent immigrants in these groups who were not exposed to the habit as much in their country of origin as those born in the United States.

Residence

Smoking across states in the United States demonstrates no strong regional pattern. In 2000, the highest rates were in Kentucky (30.5 percent), Nevada (29.1 percent), and Missouri (27.2 percent), while Utah (12.9), California (17.2), and Minnesota (19.8 percent) had the lowest rates. Within states, smoking tends to be more common in rural areas, a pattern that reverses the earlier tendency for city dwellers to be smokers. Concerns over healthy lifestyles and the higher SES in cities contribute to this new pattern.

Religion

Few differences in smoking exist across religious denominations, and to the extent that they do, they likely reflect differences in education and income among members of various religions. However, attending church regularly, regardless of denomination, relates closely to nonsmoking. For example, among those who attend church weekly, 17 percent smoke, while among those who never attend church, 44 percent smoke. Highly religious persons had for centuries rejected smoking as a worldly pleasure that, if not sinful, did little to bring one closer to God. Such beliefs do much today to distinguish smokers from nonsmokers.

Youth

The same factors affecting adult patterns of smoking also influence smoking of girls and boys, but the social characteristics of parents prove as important as the social characteristics of the youth themselves. Based again on data for high school seniors, youthful smokers have the following characteristics.[32]

- Those with less educated parents are more likely to smoke than those with highly educated parents.
- Those growing up in a rural area are more likely to smoke than those growing up in a large city or suburb.
- Those living alone or with only one parent are more likely to smoke than those living with both parents.
- Those performing poorly in school and not planning to go to college are more likely to smoke than those doing well in school and planning to go to college.
- Those saying religion is not important in their lives are more likely to smoke than those saying religion is important or very important in their lives.
- Those holding jobs and earning more income are more likely to smoke than those without jobs (and presumably devoting more time to academics).
- Those participating in delinquent and criminal activities are more likely to smoke than those not participating in such activities.

These relationships reflect only tendencies. Smoking cuts across all teen social groups, and many persons with characteristics that should make them prone to smoke nonetheless reject the habit, just as others not prone to smoke take up the habit. The same point holds in describing group differences in smoking adults. Still, group tendencies exist and offer insights into the social forces behind individual decisions to smoke or not to smoke.

REASONS FOR SMOKING

Information obtained from smokers on the reasons they started and continue seldom proves insightful. They state that they smoke because they enjoy it and because it is too hard to stop. That answer merely raises other questions. Why do some people enjoy it more and find it harder to stop than others? What factors underlie the attraction to smoking among the quarter of the U.S. population that continues the habit? If smoking brings addiction, physical pleasure, and psychological rewards, why do some give into these rewards but not others? The answers to the questions must consider physiological, psychological, economic, cultural, and social factors.[33]

Biological differences across individuals help explain why some smoke. Studies of twins have found that a genetic predisposition to smoke passes across generations. For example, those who start smoking at an early age have different chemical receptors in the brain than others and metabolize nicotine differently than others. Those physically prone to stronger addiction will find the withdrawal symptoms more painful and smoking more difficult to stop.

Psychological traits affect the tendency to adopt and continue smoking. Impulsive individuals may lack the ability to control their behavior in general and may lack the ability to resist the temptation to smoke in particular. Those with fewer coping skills to deal with their problems and those fatalistic about what happens to them may give into temptation to smoke more than others. Those prone psychologically to risk taking and sensation seeking may take up and continue smoking. Lastly, extroverted personality types, whose outgoing and engaging behavior is highly valued, are more likely to smoke than introverted personality types.

Prosmoking beliefs and attitudes increase the likelihood of smoking. Smokers often believe that their habit helps to control weight, improve mood, and realize a desirable image. Use of cigarettes can, among teens in particular, help smokers feel cool, confident, and part of a group. Similarly the desire of young women to control their weight with smoking and emulate the glamorous images of thinness found in magazines, advertising, movies, and television contributes to their smoking. However, researchers understand less about why some come to accept these beliefs and others reject them; perhaps those addicted to smoking use their beliefs to justify their addiction.

Tobacco Industry and Smoking

Obtaining a release from social stress through the mild narcotic effect of nicotine motivates smokers to continue the habit. The propensity to smoke, despite its long-term harm and immediate financial cost, may serve as a short-term coping mechanism to deal with difficult circumstances. Smokers say that cigarettes give them a boost, help them concentrate, and make them feel better. Indulging in the addictive pleasures of nicotine may help in dealing with daily problems and tasks. Youth in particular, given the difficulties they face entering into the adult world, may find smoking helps alleviate their stress. Yet smoking may reduce stress largely because it relieves the withdrawal symptoms produced by the lack of nicotine. If smoking relieves stress, it also produces more stress.

The smoking of parents and friends can lead adolescents to take up the habit themselves. Teens may directly imitate the behavior of those they feel close to or may adopt the beliefs and attitudes of parents and friends that lead indirectly to smoking. Those whose parents smoke are much more likely to smoke themselves than those whose parents do not smoke. Similarly those whose friends smoke are much more likely to smoke themselves than those whose friends do not smoke. In short, social influences affect the decision to smoke. If, for example, peers offer support for smoking and parents offer opposition to smoking, those with stronger ties to peers than parents will be more likely to smoke. In much the same way, lack of involvement in school, sports teams, and religious organizations—all groups that oppose tobacco use—will increase smoking.

Advertising serves as a major source of the attraction to smoking, particularly among young people. According to many experts, the attractive and glamorous images of smokers in magazine ads lead young people to imitate those images by smoking (cartoonlike characters such as Joe Camel influence even grade-school children). Advertising images may also appeal to rebellious youth by implying a connection between smoking and independence and to girls by implying a connection between smoking and sophistication.

Perhaps a more useful way to understand the question of why people smoke requires considering not what attracts people to cigarettes, but what prevents them from acting on this attraction. History has shown that billions throughout the world have found the stimulating and addictive effects of cigarettes hard to resist. What gives some special motivation to resist? Reasons for not smoking might include worry about the long-term health effects, impairment of athletic performance, unpleasant smell and taste, reactions of nonsmoking friends, and monetary costs.

Lastly, a small and sometimes vocal group maintains they smoke simply because they enjoy the habit and resent the accusations of antismoking groups that their decisions are illegitimate. In the words of one writer who smokes, "I believe life should be savored rather than lengthened, and I am ready to fight [those] trying to make me switch." Another writer states, "Cigarettes improve my short-term concentration, aid my digestion, make me a finer writer and a better dinner companion, and, in several other ways, prolong my life."[34] Some smokers claim they have not been manipulated by advertising images, are not addicted and irrational, were not misled by tobacco companies, and did not act out of insecurity or impulsiveness. Such explanations give smokers the responsibility for their decisions.

NEGATIVE PUBLIC OPINIONS ABOUT SMOKING

As smoking has become concentrated in a smaller part of the U.S. population, the negative attitudes toward the habit have grown—even among smokers. In terms of their views on the harm of smoking, there is virtually unanimous agreement among smokers and nonsmokers alike. A 1999 Gallup poll found that 92 percent of respondents answered "Yes" when asked, "Does smoking cause lung cancer?" Eighty-eight percent of smokers and 93 percent of nonsmokers agreed with the statement. A clear consensus on the relationship between smoking and health has emerged, and this consensus represents a substantial change from the past. In 1954, only 41 percent agreed with the statement. The largest increase came in the 1960s, when the agreement jumped from 45 percent to 71 percent, but the steady negative publicity about smoking since then has raised agreement another 21 percent since 1969.

Other evidence suggests that smokers recognize the harm they are doing to themselves with the habit. When asked in a poll, 77 percent of smokers said they would like to quit, 66 percent said they have made a serious effort to quit (but failed), and 87 percent said they wish they had never started. In one study that asked smokers and nonsmokers to estimate the harm of smoking in terms of the added risk of death, the likelihood of dying from a smoking-related cause, and the years of life lost, both groups overstated the risks identified by the scientific literature.[35] Their answers demonstrate in stark terms that smokers recognize the serious health risks they face.

Despite knowing, even exaggerating the harm of smoking, smokers and nonsmokers alike do not support banning the product altogether. According to surveys, the public views smoking as a personal choice that citizens should be free to make; only 16 percent want to make smoking illegal. Although they attribute some blame to the tobacco companies for encouraging smoking, 55 percent of survey respondents say that smokers themselves are completely or mostly to blame. Nonsmokers prefer that separate smoking areas be set aside in public places but otherwise respect the right of smokers to light up. They reason that, if smoking is a legal personal choice, it should not be banned altogether from public, and society should willingly make some accommodations for smokers. Most people also fear that outright banning of smoking may lead to banning of other products such as alcohol and to excess power of the government to regulate the behavior of citizens. This view fits with the belief held by a majority of the public that all tobacco ads should not be banned. In the end, most citizens want to balance the right of smokers to engage in their habit with the right of nonsmokers to enjoy smoke-free air.

The belief in the right to smoke does not, however, mean that the public in general and nonsmokers in particular fully respect smokers. If people believe that smoking involves a personal choice, then they also will blame individuals for that choice and sometimes even view smoking as "deviant conduct."[36] Smokers must tolerate urgings from their family, friends, doctors, neighbors, workmates, teachers, religious leaders, media, and government to stop. Nonsmokers feel free to criticize and shame smokers for their inability to stop a destructive habit. Segregation of smokers in airports, restaurants, and office buildings makes smokers feel separate from the rest of society, even sometimes as victims of discrimination. Smokers have the right to choose to use tobacco, but that choice comes with a social as well as a personal health cost.

The negative view of smoking and smokers perhaps shows most clearly in surveys of high school seniors, whose beliefs reflect the future public opinion of adults.[37] About 66 percent prefer to date people who do not smoke, 55 percent think that being a smoker reflects poor judgment, and 70 percent see smoking as a dirty habit. Less than 10 percent of high school students think that smokers look mature and sophisticated, or cool and calm—most see smokers as insecure and foolish. These negative beliefs are more typically held among nonsmokers more than smokers but overall reveal a general distaste for the habit among the general public.

A psychologist at the University of Pennsylvania has coined the term *moralization* to describe the process that translates antismoking preferences into views of cigarette use as an immoral act.[38] Moralization shows not just in the dislike of cigarette smoking but in the outrage of nonsmokers when confronted by undesired cigarette smoke, in the crusading views of antismoking advocates, and in the association of smoking with weakness. As a result of this process, smoking can produce disgust more than disagreement, criticism more than indifference, and condemnation more than understanding.

On one hand, the negative views of smoking should discourage the habit, as most people aim to follow the conventional norms of society. On the other hand, the common antismoking views may in some ways make the habit all the more attractive to some, and the sometimes zealous efforts to control individual smoking behavior can produce a backlash among those valuing independence and individualism against the forces of conformity.

Smoking has always involved a sense of daring, but with the negative views of the habit these days, it may offer this appeal even more than in the past.

The negative perceptions about cigarette use have led some concerned about the potential abuse of government power to oppose public health efforts against smoking.[39] These critics see antismoking efforts as the attempt of one group to impose its own tastes and preferences on another group and to do so through the use of government force, censorship, economic penalty, and vilification. The end result of the more zealous forms of cigarette control is a form of puritanical repression much like the one that led to alcohol prohibition.[40] In answer to these accusations the 2000 report of the Surgeon General's office states, "It would be hard to deny that moral zealotry has entered into the contemporary movement to reduce smoking," but also that "it would be equally hard to argue that zealotry is the dominant element in the movement."[41] Most policymakers and voters accept tobacco control efforts because the efforts stem largely from medical and scientific evidence and aim to promote the health of the population.

LIGHT CIGARETTES

In the 1960s public health officials concluded that if smokers could not quit using cigarettes, it would be better for their health if they smoked low-tar cigarettes.[42] A shift to these products would not eliminate tobacco-caused cancer but would reduce its prevalence. With the endorsement of low-tar cigarettes by public health authorities, tobacco companies began to engineer new products. They created and marketed low-tar and low-nicotine cigarettes that came to be called "light" or "ultra light" cigarettes. The determination of tar and nicotine in a cigarette came from a machine that smoked the cigarette and measured the tar and nicotine yield (known as the machine-measured yield).

During the last 50 years changes in cigarette design and manufacturing have produced a 60 percent decline in machine-measured tar and nicotine yields. While cigarettes in 1955 averaged 35 milligrams of tar, they now average around 10 milligrams.[43] Nicotine in cigarettes has dropped just as much. Presently, lower-yield cigarettes dominate the market. About 98 percent of cigarettes sold are filtered, and about 65 percent of cigarettes sold are classified as low-tar products (the machine-measured tar is less than 15 milligrams per cigarette). A partial list of these products includes the following brands: Marlboro Lights, Camel Lights, Kool Lights, Merit Lights, Winston Lights, Salem Lights, Newport Lights, Now, Vantage, Carlton, Virginia Slims Lights, and Parliament Lights.

To a large extent smokers choose these brands because they think that these cigarettes are the healthier choice and might make it easier in the future to quit. Surveys find that smokers most concerned about the health risks of cigarettes and most interested in quitting are also most likely to use low-tar and low-nicotine cigarettes. Tobacco companies spend heavily to promote these products, and advertisements aim to attract smokers wanting a safer product.

Along with light cigarettes, other types of cigarette products have increased in popularity. Several smaller companies market cigarettes that use tobacco without any additives or inorganic substances. As natural products, these cigarettes might be viewed by smokers as healthier. The Liggett Group sold their traditional brands such as Chesterfield and Lark to concentrate on developing and marketing a new low-nicotine cigarette to aid smokers wanting to quit. Still other companies sell clove cigarettes that contain some tobacco but not as much as regular cigarettes. None of these products has become a big seller, but as a group they meet demand from a growing segment of smokers who prefer nontraditional types of cigarettes.

The National Cancer Institute argues, however, that despite earlier claims, light cigarettes offer little health benefit.[44] They may in fact increase the risk to health by leading smokers to try the lighter brands rather than quit altogether. The new brands also fail to reduce the harm of tar, the absorption of nicotine, and the rates of lung cancer for two reasons. First, smokers either inhale light cigarettes more intensely to get more flavor and nicotine or they increase the number of cigarettes they smoke per day. Second, tobacco companies placed ventilation holes in the filters that could be easily blocked by a smoker's lips or fingers and therefore often fail to dilute the delivery of tar and nicotine. Cigarettes that yield low tar in machines do not always deliver the same benefit when smoked by people. As a result recent epidemiological studies reveal little health value from the growth of light cigarettes. Smokers of light cigarettes are no more likely to quit or live longer than smokers of regular cigarettes.

Tobacco companies have recently come to deny the safety of light or low-tar yield cigarettes. Philip Morris, for example, has circulated notices with some of their brands. The notices state that the tar and nicotine levels are not necessarily good indicators of how much of these substances smokers inhale and that smokers should not assume that low-tar cigarettes are less harmful than other cigarettes. Critics of the tobacco industry claim that this effort is merely a way to absolve them of liability for the harm caused by so-called safe cigarettes. Indeed many suits have been filed on behalf of smokers of light cigarettes. Based on the claim that cigarette companies misled smokers about the safety of light cigarettes, law firms are soliciting smokers of light or safe cigarettes who have been diagnosed with smoking-related illnesses.

TOBACCO USE IN MINORITY COMMUNITIES

Compared to white non-Hispanics, Native Americans have higher levels of smoking, African Americans have similar levels of smoking, and Hispanics and Asian Americans have lower levels of smoking. Yet as smoking has declined in the general population, tobacco companies have done more to target smokers and potential smokers in the minority communities. Besides directing appeals to these communities with advertising, the tobacco industry has done much to provide economic support.

A report of the Surgeon General's office on tobacco use among minority groups notes that several actions of the tobacco industry have strengthened its standing in the African-American community.[45] Tobacco companies were among the first in the South to hire African Americans in their factories, to provide management opportunities for African Americans, and to employ African Americans as models and spokespersons for their products. By placing advertisements in African-American publications, tobacco companies have helped to support minority businesses. Companies have also contributed funding to community agencies and civil rights organizations, sponsored cultural events, and supported African-American political candidates.

Along with providing economic support, the tobacco companies have targeted certain types of advertising to appeal to African Americans. In general, cigarette ads are more common in magazines for African Americans, such as *Ebony, Essence,* and *Jet,* than in magazines for the general population, such as *Time, People,* and *Mademoiselle.* More specifically, mentholated cigarettes, which are particularly popular among African Americans, are heavily advertised in publications with a minority readership. One new cigarette product, Uptown, was by all appearances introduced by R. J. Reynolds to appeal specifically to African Americans, but protests led the company to withdraw the product after early tests. In any case advertising targeted at minority groups may contribute to use of cigarettes in their communities.

Involvement of tobacco companies in other minority communities has not been as extensive as in the African-American community, but they do make an effort to reach all minority groups. They sponsor activities to enhance racial or ethnic pride, such as Mexican rodeos, American Indian pow-wows, Chinese New year festivities, and Cinco de Mayo festivities. They also direct advertising to Hispanic, Asian-American, and Native American communities. Outdoor advertising of cigarettes was (until banned) more commonly located in urban minority communities than in white parts of cities and suburbs. In-store displays appear more commonly in small city convenience stores in ethnic communities. And specific brands were targeted for minority groups: Rio and Dorado for Hispanics, Mild Seven (a popular cigarette in Japan) for Asian Americans, and American Spirit for Native Americans.

On the one hand, these efforts of cigarette makers reflect economic power of minority groups. When other product makers often ignore minorities in their promotions and advertising, the attention of cigarette makers provides an economic boost to often disadvantaged communities. On the other hand, with life expectancy in most minority communities already lower than average, the promotion of cigarettes threatens to maintain that disadvantage. Critics in minority communities and government agencies have worked hard to oppose special efforts by tobacco companies to appeal to vulnerable minorities.

CONTINUED SUCCESS OF THE TOBACCO INDUSTRY

It might seem that the negative publicity about smoking, the views of smokers as lacking self-control and breaking conventions, and the decline in smoking in the United States would have weakened the tobacco industry. The public increasingly views the tobacco industry and its executives as evil in their efforts to addict young people. The negative views not only have reduced sales but have led to legal judgments that have imposed billions of dollars in damages on the tobacco companies. Indeed, some companies have had to lay off workers in recent years, and it would seem that the industry must be close to bankruptcy.

But in fact the tobacco industry is thriving. It has changed form, has suffered defeats, and lost the respect and profits it once had, but it still does quite well. Across the world it enjoys $300 billion in sales annually, sells 15 billion cigarettes each day, and produces 5.5 trillion cigarettes a year—about 1,000 for each child and adult on the globe. In economic terms the sales and production costs offer a potential for profit that most industries would envy. If government and private suits raise the legal costs of tobacco firms, they can pass those costs on to consumers. If markets in the United States and other high-income countries shrink as citizens increasingly reject smoking, they can focus on new markets outside these nations. If they are portrayed as morally evil, they can justify their industry in terms of providing a legal product that adults enjoy. Morals aside, the industry has continued to enjoy economic success.

In the present-day United States 97 percent of cigarettes are produced by five companies that are collectively called Big Tobacco. The largest U.S. company is Philip Morris, originally a British firm that entered the American market with a small office in New York City in 1902. In the last 50 years, Philip Morris has earned the largest share of the American market and follows only the China National Cigarette Company in its share of the world market. Philip Morris has gained special publicity over the years in part because of its successful Marlboro brand, but also because it has most aggressively fought antismoking forces and acts most unrepentant in promoting its product. The second largest company, British American Tobacco, owns Brown and Williamson, a tobacco manufacturer much in the news in recent years after the public release of its internal documents about nicotine, addiction, and youth advertising. The third largest company, R. J. Reynolds, makes Camel, Winston, and Salem cigarettes, and at one time led in cigarette sales in the United States. However, some unwise mergers, including an expensive purchase of Nabisco, saddled the company with so much debt that it had to sell much of its business and has lost market share to other companies. The fourth and smaller company is Lorillard, maker of Newport cigarettes. The last and smallest company, Liggett Tobacco (earlier part of the Liggett Group and now part of the Brooke Group), has played a prominent role in industry legal battles.

The continued success of these firms stems from the nature of their product. Cigarettes differ from almost all other consumer items: Their addictive nature keeps customers returning, and the unique properties of inhaling cigarette smoke and ingesting nicotine mean that no other product can take its place. Combined with the low cost of producing cigarettes, these properties make for a high profit margin. In one analysis, most of the cost of a pack of cigarettes ($7.50 in late 2003 in New York City) goes to taxes and retailer markup. The production, advertising, marketing, and legal costs of the companies equal only $1.45 per pack, and profit equals 28¢.[46]

The future for tobacco companies looks strong because the world presents a huge market for expansion. As cigarette use declines in high-income, more developed countries, attention of tobacco companies has turned to middle and low-income, less developed countries. Vast populations in developing countries have had less opportunity to use the products and represent a growing market. A few figures illustrate the global patterns of change in tobacco use. From 1970 to 1990, cigarettes consumed per adult age 15 and over fell by 9 percent in more developed countries and rose by 64 percent in less developed countries—a net increase in world consumption of 18 percent. Consumption per person has, for example, risen by 160 percent in China, 66 percent in Egypt, and 36 percent in India. Projections suggest that, largely because of growth in the developing world, the approximately 1.1 billion smokers in 1995 will rise to 1.6 billion by 2025.[47]

The trends in smoking in developing nations obviously concern public health officials, who now refer to a *worldwide* smoking epidemic. They decry the adoption of a behavior that will reduce life span across the globe at the same time other forces of development, medicine, and public health serve to increase its longevity. With tobacco deaths currently numbering about 4 million per year worldwide (about one in 10 adult deaths), they may plausibly number 10 million (about one in six adult deaths) by 2030, with most occurring in developing regions.

On another level public health officials find it disturbing that the spread of tobacco use across large parts of the globe counters the increasingly successful efforts in the United States to combat cigarette use and restrict the power of the tobacco industry. Despite facing higher taxes, judicial setbacks, negative publicity, legislative restrictions, and a declining market in many high-income nations such as the United States, the tobacco industry has maintained its profitability—and its ability to promote the use of tobacco—through global sales and marketing efforts. During recent decades of globalization and trade liberalization, penetration of markets by multinational tobacco corporations has led to price cuts, widespread media advertising, escalating competition for sales, efforts to promote positive images of smokers, and greater sales and profits. Calls for public health efforts against tobacco around the world, including an international treaty that would create consistent antismoking policies worldwide, have strengthened. However, these efforts have had limited effects so far on the spread of tobacco use.

CURRENT KNOWLEDGE ABOUT SMOKING AND HEALTH

DETAILING THE RISKS

Tobacco smoke contains more than 4,000 known compounds that enter the lungs along with various gases. These compounds include nicotine, which passes into the bloodstream through the lungs, affects cells throughout the body, and produces an addictive physical and mental reaction. They also include 43 different substances identified as carcinogens (or cancer-causing substances) and carbon monoxide, a colorless, odorless, and highly toxic gas. The exact processes of how these compounds adversely affect the body are not always well understood, but studies have clearly documented the association between absorption of these tobacco smoke compounds and health problems.

Among the known adverse consequences of cigarette smoking are increases in death from heart disease (the most common cause of death in the United States), diseases of the arteries, lung and throat cancer, cancers of numerous other organs (bladder, pancreas, kidney, stomach, and cervix), and chronic obstructive pulmonary disease (chronic bronchitis and emphysema). Numerous studies have demonstrated these relationships, but the Cancer Prevention Study II from 1982 to 1986 provides data on a large number of Americans.[48] The study examined the smoking habits of more than 1.2 million volunteers and then followed them over the next four years to record information on the cause of death for those who died during the period. The key statistics came from the rate of death for current smokers, former smokers, and never smokers. With the huge sample the study was able to examine the effect of smoking on relatively rare causes of death.

According to the results the risks of lung cancer for current male and female smokers are 22.4 and 11.9 times higher, respectively, than they are for nonsmokers. Called relative risk ratios, these numbers indicate that for every nonsmoker who dies of lung cancer, 22 current male smokers and 12 current female smokers die. The risks of lung cancer for former smokers are lower than current smokers but still high. For every nonsmoker who dies of lung cancer, nine former male smokers and five former female smokers die. Quitting smoking reduces the risks of lung cancer but does not eliminate them altogether. Other cancers, although not as common as lung cancer, also appear more among smokers and former smokers. Compared to never smokers, current male smokers have relative risks of 27.5 for lip and mouth cancer, 7.6 for esophagus cancer, 2.9 for kidney cancer, and 2.9 for bladder cancer.

Cigarette smoking also increases the risks of heart disease. At ages 35–64, 2.8 current male smokers and 3.0 current female smokers die of heart disease for every nonsmoker who dies of heart disease. For former male and female smokers, the relative risks are 1.7 and 1.4. While these risks are lower than for lung cancer, they translate into more smoking-related deaths. Since more people in the United States die of heart disease each year than any other cause—about 725,000 in 1998—the added risk of premature death for smokers contributes substantially to loss of life. Smoking thus accounts for roughly 20 percent of heart disease deaths.

Two other diseases deserve special attention because of their prevalence and close association with smoking. For every nonsmoker who dies of a stroke at ages 35–64, 3.7 current male smokers, 4.8 current female smokers, 1.4 former male smokers, and 1.4 former female smokers die of a stroke. Chronic obstructive pulmonary disease (COPD), which includes emphysema, chronic bronchitis, and other diseases that block the flow of air into the lungs, also occurs more commonly among smokers. For every nonsmoker who dies of COPD, 9.6 current male smokers, 10.5 current female smokers, 8.8 former male smokers, and 7.0 former female smokers die of the disease.

Averaged across all causes of death, current male smokers are 2.3 times as likely to die prematurely as male never smokers, and current female smokers are 1.9 times as likely to die prematurely as female never smokers (the risks for former male and female smokers are, respectively, 1.6 and 1.3). Similarly, risks for heavy smokers to die prematurely of these diseases are higher than for light smokers, and risks for former smokers who used cigarettes for a long period are higher than those who used cigarettes for a short period. From the point of view of the individual, smokers can expect to live 13–14 fewer years on average than nonsmokers. Of course, some smokers will live as long as or longer than nonsmokers and some smokers will die at a very young age, so the 13–14 years represent an average; nonetheless, the average figure provides a useful summary.

Based on the higher risks of death among former and current smokers, and on the prevalence of former and current smokers in the U.S. population, the 1989 Surgeon General's report computed the number of deaths due to cigarettes. If former and current smokers had the same risks of death as never smokers, then there would be more than 400,000 fewer deaths. This number makes the harm of smoking easy to summarize and understand—400,000 deaths a year from smoking make for a national tragedy. Considering impairment from sickness and disability further adds to the costs of smoking. Compared to nonsmokers, smokers have more breathing, bone, eye, and movement problems.

Although traditionally less likely to use tobacco than men, women are seriously affected by smoking-related mortality, which led the World Health Organization to publish a short book, *Women and Tobacco*, in 1992,[49] and the Office of the Surgeon General to publish a report of more than 600 pages in 2001 on *Women and Smoking*.[50] Relative risks of death for female smokers are lower than for males, perhaps because they inhale less and use milder cigarette brands. Still, in 1997, 165,000 women died prematurely from smoking, and since 1980 about 3 million women have died prematurely from smoking. Lung cancer has even replaced breast cancer as the major form of cancer death among women. As much effort needs to go into dealing with female smoking and its health consequences as with male smoking and its health consequences.

The risks of death from other forms of tobacco use are also elevated, although not to the same degree as from cigarette smoking. The estimated mortality rate of cigar smokers was 39 percent higher than for those who smoked neither cigarettes nor cigars, and the estimated mortality rate of pipe smokers was 29 percent higher than for those who smoked neither cigarettes nor pipes. Smokeless tobacco, taken in the form of chew placed in the cheek or snuff placed between the lower gum and lip, experienced renewed popularity with the warnings against cigarettes. Because smokeless tobacco does not involve the inhalation of smoke and associated byproducts into the lungs but still gives a nicotine kick, it seemed a good alternative to cigarettes. According to one study, however, the risks of mouth cancer were four times higher for moderate users of smokeless tobacco and seven times higher for heavy users than for nonusers. Translating the statistics into something more meaningful to potential users, a story of a 19-year-old Oklahoman received much publicity.[51] He began using smokeless tobacco as a teen, became addicted, and developed tongue cancer, which spread and killed him. Although use of smokeless tobacco never reached the levels of cigarettes, and mouth cancer is rarer than lung cancer and heart disease, users of smokeless tobacco face heightened risks of death.

The cost to life from smoking also includes nonsmokers through environmental tobacco smoke, sometimes called passive, or involuntary, smoking. Although the risks are not to the same extent as they are for smokers who directly inhale cigarette smoke, the lung cancer rates among nonsmoking women whose husbands smoke are 24 percent higher than for nonsmoking women whose husbands do not smoke.[52] Other studies find heightened levels of a blood product of nicotine in the blood of nonsmokers who are exposed to smokers in the workplace or who have friends who smoke. The results imply that those nonsmokers who breathe smoke in restaurants, bars, office buildings, and public facilities may also face higher risks of sickness and death. These findings help justify segregation of smokers and nonsmokers in public places, and the banning of indoor smoking altogether in many facilities. However, a debate over the harm of environmental tobacco has ensued, as critics are not convinced that the amount of secondhand smoke inhaled in public places reaches levels high enough to cause serious harm. Despite such criticism government agencies continue to maintain that secondhand smoke represents an important health risk and to push for clean indoor air regulations.

Children, infants, and fetuses can also suffer from the smoking of their parents. Women who smoke during pregnancy are more likely to have a miscarriage or give birth to a stillborn baby than women who do not smoke while pregnant. Smoking during pregnancy also leads to higher risks of low birth-weight babies and may slow the brain development of children as they grow older. These effects come in part from the sharing of the chemically altered blood of smoking mothers with their fetuses. Later, smoking by either or both parents in the house can increase the risks of asthma and infections among older children who breathe the secondhand smoke.

PREVENTING SMOKING

Because youth typically try cigarettes for the first time between ages 11 and 15 (grades six through 10), and most who continue to smoke as adults have started by age 20, prevention programs must begin at young ages. Nonsmoking adults rarely take up the habit, so most resources for prevention go to school-based programs. It might seem logical that presenting information on the damage of cigarette use would prevent youths from smoking, but the evidence shows the contrary. According to the Surgeon General's 1994 report on youth and smoking, "Knowledge of the long-term health consequences of smoking has not been a strong predictor of adolescent onset . . . perhaps because virtually all U.S. adolescents—smokers and nonsmokers alike—are aware of the long-term health effects of smoking."[53] Similarly a study of trends in smoking initiation from 1944 to 1988 concludes, "The public health campaign . . . has had limited or no impact on younger persons.[54] Thus, as the World Bank has observed, "In general, young people appear to be less responsive to information about the health effects of tobacco than older adults."[55]

Besides presenting information on the risks of smoking, the programs need to recognize that youth are highly influenced by their peers, their reactions to advertising, and perceptions of the prevalence of smoking in the larger society. Understanding the risks of smoking brings little benefit if youth remain attracted by the images of advertisements and lack skills to resist pressures from others to smoke. Teaching youngsters about the social skills needed to resist manipulation by advertisements and the pressures of others to smoke needs to accompany teaching them about the physical costs of smoking.

To be successful, programs also must make an intensive effort at change. Early antismoking programs had little success in changing behavior because they tended to be short in duration, small in size, and isolated from the larger context of the school and community. More recent programs have, in contrast, been more effective because they have expanded the limited form of early programs. Programs with the best results last years rather than weeks (one program, for example, consists of 30 classes over three grades), and they incorporate antismoking efforts into general health education for students. In addition, these programs view antismoking efforts as part of school and community goals rather than as a single class. The more intensive the effort to change the views of the students, the more successful the program will be.

Multifaceted programs that include all these components can reduce smoking among teenagers by 20 to 40 percent. Moreover they are similarly effective across diverse regions of the country, urban and rural areas, race and ethnic groups, and teaching styles and curriculum. The SHOUT (Students Helping Others Understand Tobacco) program, for example, consists of 18 class sessions in seventh and eighth grade and then continued telephone and mail contact in ninth grade. The intensive effort has reduced current smoking by 33 percent by the end of grade nine.

However, even these multifaceted programs can have short-lived benefits. Without continued effort, the benefits of antismoking programs disappear during high school and after. Once programs end, the influence of peers and the media can overwhelm earlier antismoking messages. Delaying the start of smoking brings health benefits, but it would be best to prevent the adoption of cigarette smoking into adulthood. Longer-term programs that follow-up school-based efforts have some potential to reach this latter goal, but the continual effort of antismoking education requires a major commitment and higher expense.

Based on the knowledge of the characteristics of programs that most successfully reduce smoking among youth, the Centers for Disease Control and Prevention (CDC) in 1994 developed a set of national guidelines to prevent tobacco use and addiction. The guidelines suggest that tobacco prevention education programs should

- develop and enforce school policies that prohibit tobacco use by all students, staff, and visitors during school-related activities;
- begin in kindergarten and continue through 12th grade, with particularly intensive efforts in middle and junior high school grades;
- cover the consequences of tobacco use, social norms of tobacco use, reasons for use of tobacco by youth, and the social influences that promote tobacco use, and then teach social skills to resist these influences on smoking; and
- work to improve curriculum implementation and overall program effectiveness through the training of teachers.

State-based surveys of antismoking programs have found that the guidelines have not been widely adopted. Most schools are smoke free, but few have implemented the education programs recommended by the CDC and research. In 1994 only 4 percent of the middle, junior, and high schools in the nation had comprehensive tobacco use programs.[56] Although efforts may have improved since 1994, the demands on schools of these programs are intense. Moreover the models of smoking outside school remain regardless of the efforts within schools to prevent smoking.

SMOKING CESSATION

Although preventing youth from starting to smoke is ideal, helping those who have already begun smoking will also reduce cigarette and tobacco consumption. Specialists refer to smoking cessation as nicotine addiction management because management of the addiction that makes quitting hard can help in the process. With smoking treated as a chronic disease of addiction, those trying to stop can expect remission, relapse, and difficulty in changing. Smokers need to continue their efforts without blaming themselves or attributing their problems in stopping to character weakness.

Consistent with the addiction framework and the difficulty in stopping smoking, those smokers trying to quit have a high failure rate. In fact, only 6 percent of attempts in quitting succeed for a month, and only 3 to 5 percent succeed for a year or more. Yet the low rate of success, when accumulated over time, can do much to reduce smoking. Individuals who have failed to stop in the past may with additional attempts succeed. Thus about 44 million Americans today are former smokers—about the same number as current smokers. Since former smokers have lower rates of death than current smokers (although the rates are still higher than never smokers), quitting can improve the health of the U.S. population.

Those groups most successful in quitting once had high rates of smoking but now have relatively low rates of smoking. More men than women, more older than younger persons, and more highly educated and affluent persons than less-educated and poor persons have successfully quit. The differences in quitting do not relate to interest, as members of all groups express the desire to give up the habit (an average of 70 percent of the total U.S. population of smokers), but some groups more than others have either stronger motivation or better ability to realize their goal.

Most former smokers ended their habit on their own, usually by simply stopping and resisting the impulse to start again (a practice known as "going cold turkey"). Those able to quit most easily may have weaker physical addictions and withdrawal symptoms or greater motivation and willpower. Over the years, however, those who can most easily quit will have already done so, leaving among the population of smokers those most addicted to the product and likely to have the hardest time quitting. As a result, longtime smokers need special help in stopping. Research has identified five approaches to aiding smokers, each of which shows some effectiveness but varies from the others in cost and efficiency.[57]

First, large-scale public health programs focus on the full population of smokers. Transmitting smoking cessation messages through the media, at work, and in the community can bring crucial information to this population and help some to quit; however, such programs work best when they extend beyond the local community to become state or nationwide. Moreover smokers may need something more tangible or personal than public health messages to motivate them. Although such messages can reach large numbers of smokers at an inexpensive cost, they so far have had only limited effects.

Second, the simple process of distributing self-help manuals may help some smokers stop. Antismoking organizations and the government can cheaply produce self-help manuals and distribute them easily to large numbers of smokers. They can further tailor the style and format of the manuals to specific gender, race, ethnic, and education groups. Such efforts appear to produce a small but consistent benefit, one that favors those less addicted to cigarettes and most motivated to change. Manuals listing telephone numbers that readers can call for help sometimes do better to promote cessation, but such calls again mostly help those already strongly motivated to stop and less addicted to nicotine.

Third, minimal clinical interventions that involve the efforts of health care personnel to urge smokers to stop can have modest effects. Clinicians who not only ask patients if they smoke but also advise them to quit can help provide the motivation their patients need. With 70 percent of smokers already saying they want to quit, the urging of physicians, nurses, and other health care personnel can do much to get smokers to take the first steps to stop their habit. If clinicians also appraise the willingness of smokers to stop, assist those who want to stop, and check on the progress of the patients who attempt to stop, they can then do more to aid smoking cessation. When treated as part of regular health care checkups, these minimal clinical interventions involve little cost and can do more than self-help manuals alone.

Fourth, intensive clinical intervention requires the most cost and effort but works better than less-intensive procedures, particularly for highly addicted smokers. Such interventions would include multisession counseling over a period of at least five months to develop problem-solving or coping skills. Other procedures include hypnosis, acupuncture, behavioral reward conditioning, and simultaneous weight-control procedures. The drawbacks of intensive procedures involve the high expense and coverage of only a small part of the smoking population. Moreover, the types of intervention available change so quickly that scientists have difficulty evaluating them. This method has demonstrated some success in clinical studies, however, and may help certain groups of smokers.

Fifth, pharmacological approaches that treat the physical reactions to smoking cessation and nicotine withdrawal with medications can help smokers quit. Companies widely promote nicotine replacement therapy in the form of gum or patches (and less commonly nicotine nasal spray and inhalers). Abundant evidence demonstrates the value of these products, and clinicians highly recommended them. Combined with more socially based methods of support, use of nicotine replacement therapy appears promising. Antidepressant medications, notably bupropion and perhaps serotonin reuptake inhibitors such as Prozac and Zoloft, may also help. Many who quit smoking experience depression, and clinical studies of bupropion and nicotine replacement theory find that the combination increases the quit rate over those using nicotine replacement therapy alone. Other antidepressants may bring similar benefits but have not been thoroughly studied in regard to smoking. In terms of both cost and success, these approaches represent a compromise between the inexpensive but less successful reliance on self-help manuals and doctor's advice, and the expensive but more effective and intensive interventions.

Based on these results authorities recommend that public health agencies make counseling and treatment programs available to those who need them. This might include covering the costs of the programs with insurance or providing free or low-cost programs to low-income persons. In addition they recommend large-scale public health interventions that extend local community efforts to include whole states. Statewide tobacco control programs have had some success in changing the smoking behavior of adults (less so for youth) and result in a decline in tobacco consumption. The programs not only increase public health messages and treatment opportunities but also raise taxes as a means to regulate tobacco. Combined with intensive counseling and nicotine replacement therapy for some smokers, comprehensive efforts to change the social environment that supports smoking appear promising.

REGULATING TOBACCO

ECONOMIC STRATEGIES

Outside of making the product illegal or restricting its use in some public places, the government can do little directly to prevent adults from smoking. For minors the known harm of cigarette smoking and antitobacco educational campaigns will ideally prevent them from wanting to purchase cigarettes, but otherwise restrictions are necessary. States have laws to prohibit the sale of cigarettes to minors (under 18), but teens can get around the restrictions.

A potentially more effective approach to reducing youth smoking involves raising taxes. Economic studies have demonstrated that increases in cigarette prices significantly reduce cigarette smoking. Based on statistics that show a 10 percent increase in price will reduce overall consumption of cigarettes by 3 to 5 percent, the increase in the cost of a pack of cigarettes from a price of $3.60 by 36 cents (or 10 percent) will reduce the cigarettes smoked in the United States—currently at about 2,000 per adult per year—by 80 cigarettes. Doubling the price or increasing it by 100 percent would, at least theoretically, reduce smoking by 800 cigarettes. Of course, as cigarette prices get too high, problems of smuggling, stealing, and use of hand-rolled cigarettes grow, and raising prices will do less to reduce smoking. Still, prices have an important influence on cigarette purchases.

High prices not only reduce the average number of cigarettes consumed by smokers but lead some to give up the habit altogether. Because young people and lower-income people have less money, raising prices does more to reduce their smoking than that of older and higher-income people. And because discouraging young people from smoking helps prevent lifelong addiction, and given that the poor have high rates of smoking, raising prices will affect smoking among these groups of special concern.

Although pricing relates to the decisions of the tobacco industry, governments regulate the cost of cigarettes to consumers with taxes. Federal, state, and local excise (per unit) taxes on cigarette purchases represent a substantial cost. These taxes vary across states but generally represent a significant part of the total charge. New Jersey has the highest excise tax, equal to $2.05 per pack. New York State has an excise tax of $1.50 per pack, but New York City has an additional excise tax of $1.50. Virginia includes only a 2.5 percent excise tax to go with its 11 percent sales tax. Federal taxes had long been about 8¢ per pack until the 1980s, when they rose to 16¢ per pack. By 2002 the taxes had grown to 39¢ a pack. As a percentage of the average cigarette price, federal taxes reached a peak in 1996 of 31.6 percent and have fallen since then to 22.1 percent because companies have raised the nontax prices they charge for cigarettes (in absolute terms, the taxes increased).

The taxes on cigarettes in the United States may seem high relative to the taxes on other products, but they remain well below those in most other high-income nations. In the United Kingdom, taxes make up 82 percent of the average price of cigarettes, in Germany they are 72 percent, and in France they represent 75 percent. European nations tend in general to tax more highly than the United States, but even Canada imposes cigarette taxes equal to 66 percent of the average price. Furthermore, a 500 percent increase in taxes in Canada between 1982 and 1992 coincided with a steep decline in smoking. The U.S. tax rates of 21 to 47 percent therefore fall substantially below these other nations, perhaps explained in part because the United States is also a large tobacco producer. In any case tobacco opponents argue that much room remains to raise cigarette taxes.

The 2000 Surgeon General's report on reducing tobacco use concludes that substantial increases in the excise tax could reduce smoking considerably and moderate the adverse health effects caused by smoking.[58] Higher taxes could pay off even more in the future as young people, discouraged by high prices from starting to smoke, would live out their lives as nonsmokers. They could also increase government revenues to be used for health and education-related programs. In all, raising taxes to increase prices may be the most effective regulatory strategy available to federal, state, and local governments.

Another economic effort to regulate tobacco relates to growers. Since the Great Depression federal subsidies to tobacco growers have helped them stay in business and have helped keep the price of tobacco leaf low for purchase by tobacco companies. Congress has been unable to eliminate these subsidies, but other developments may increase the price of raw tobacco and therefore increase the price of cigarettes and reduce smoking. Tobacco growers filed a class-action suit in 2002 against tobacco companies, accusing them of price fixing; if successful the suit may force manufacturers to pay higher prices for their tobacco and pass on the higher cost to consumers. In Maryland the state has begun paying tobacco farmers for not growing tobacco, all but eliminating the state's crop; fewer tobacco farmers could also raise the price to manufacturers of purchasing U.S.-grown tobacco.

REGULATION OF INFORMATION

The government has some, but far-from-complete, power to regulate the information tobacco companies provide to consumers through advertising and packaging. Below is a list of major regulatory actions.

- In 1955 the FTC objected to claims made by cigarette ads that certain brands improved health.
- In 1957 Congress held hearings on deceptive ads about filter-tip cigarettes.
- In 1965 Congress required a mild warning statement on cigarette packages.
- In 1967 the FCC in enforcing its fairness doctrine required television and radio stations to air antismoking ads in order to counter the views presented in cigarette ads.
- In 1971 Congress banned tobacco ads from the public airways used by television and radio stations and required warnings in magazine advertisements.
- In 1984 the Smoking Education Act required that four strongly worded warnings be rotated on cigarette packages and advertisements.
- In 1986 the Comprehensive Smokeless Tobacco Health Education Act required three rotated warning labels on smokeless tobacco packages.

More recently the FTC leveled a complaint against R. J. Reynolds for using the Joe Camel or Old Joe cartoon character in its ads. The 1997 complaint argued that the ads appealed to minors who by law could not purchase cigarettes and were not old enough to fully evaluate or understand the information available on the harm of smoking. A 1994 suit in California had also accused the ads of violating California laws on unfair competition. After failing in the California supreme court to have the suit dismissed, Reynolds ended Joe Camel ads and promotions in California. As part of the 1998 nationwide settlement of lawsuits, the company stopped the Joe Camel campaign nationwide. However, advertising to minors continues as a major source of dispute between the tobacco companies and their opponents in the government, judiciary, and private-sector groups.

The government also now requires that cigarette manufacturers include information on tar levels and nicotine levels in advertisements. Manufacturers need not print this information on cigarette packages, and only those brands with low tar and low nicotine choose to do so. The hope is that smokers will use the information they have to purchase brands with low amounts of the harmful products. The government has also required cigarette makers to report to the government any additives they include in their cigarettes, and the government makes this information available to the public but again does not require the information to be printed on cigarette packages. Manufacturers of smokeless tobacco must report the nicotine content of their products, but cigars, pipe tobacco, and fine-cut cigarette tobacco for roll-your-own cigarettes face no such regulations.

Despite their ability to regulate information, government agencies have not, in the absence of congressional legislation, been able to regulate the product itself. In the 1990s the head of the Food and Drug Administration (FDA), Dr. David Kessler, attempted such regulation but ultimately the effort failed. Claiming that cigarettes are in essence a delivery system for an addictive substance, nicotine, the FDA suggested that ads with the words *satisfaction, strength,* and *impact* were describing the pharmacological effects of cigarettes. The FDA also cited evidence from tobacco industry documents that manufacturers manipulated the levels of nicotine in their cigarettes to strengthen their addictiveness. As it did for other drugs, then, the FDA proposed to regulate cigarettes. Since the FDA already regulated nicotine in the form of patches and gum, why shouldn't it regulate the nicotine in cigarettes? The agency thus proposed to use this regulatory power to restrict the sales of cigarettes without obtaining new congressional legislation. The regulations would, among other things, require that the tobacco industry spend $150 million a year to support prevention education among children and ban promotional items, free samples, color ads in magazines with more than 15 percent of the readership under age 18, and sponsorship of sporting or entertainment events using brand names.

Joined by retailers and advertisers, the tobacco industry responded to the proposed regulations by filing lawsuits that claimed the FDA did not have jurisdiction. Proposed legislation in Congress also threatened to bar the FDA from regulating tobacco. President Bill Clinton nonetheless approved the new FDA rules on August 23, 1996. The final rules changed somewhat by emphasizing more strongly the need to protect minors and by eliminating the required $150 million payment from the tobacco companies for antismoking education but maintained the goal of regulating the industry under existing law.

However, lower courts largely invalidated the regulations by concluding that existing statutes did not give the FDA the authority it claimed. After appeals, the U.S. Supreme Court on March 21, 2000, affirmed by 5-4 the lower court decision against the FDA. Although recognizing the harm of cigarette use by minors that motivated the FDA, the Supreme Court majority agreed that Congress in previous laws did not intend to give the FDA regulatory control over tobacco. The Court noted that Congress had throughout history treated tobacco differently from other drugs under the purview of the FDA.

CLEAN INDOOR AIR REGULATIONS

The most widely supported regulations of tobacco relate to protecting nonsmokers (and, to a lesser degree, smokers) from the tobacco smoke of others. Environmental tobacco smoke, or ETS, sometimes called secondhand smoke, and the breathing of such smoke (sometimes called passive or involuntary smoking) can have serious health consequences for nonsmokers. The scientific evidence of these consequences is much weaker than for actual use of cigarettes, and much debate remains about the seriousness of the problem. Yet in 1986, reports from the Office of the Surgeon General and the National Academy of Sciences concluded that ETS causes lung cancer in nonsmokers and labeled it as a known carcinogen. The harm of ETS appears greatest for those exposed to high levels inside homes and buildings, such as spouses and children of family members who smoke heavily at home and workers in businesses such as bars where there is much smoking. For those exposed only occasionally to small amounts of ETS, the health threats may be small, but the unpleasantness of breathing in fumes annoys many nonsmokers (and sometimes other smokers).

Regulating ETS has strong support. Public opinion surveys indicate that people respect the rights of smokers to enjoy their tobacco, if they are aware of the harm it does themselves, but also the rights of nonsmokers to stay free from the unwanted smoke of others and from the risks of involuntary smoking. Likewise a majority of smokers accept the need to place restrictions on where they can light up. In the private realm, stores, hotels, and restaurants have therefore done much to segregate smokers or prohibit smoking altogether. Employers also support restrictions on smoking because limiting access to cigarettes in the workplace increases the productivity of workers, reduces the risks of accidents, and limits insurance costs. They also have an obligation to protect workers from risk of injury while on the job, and protecting them from cigarette smoking fits this obligation.

Government regulations have extended and encouraged private efforts to create clean indoor air. In 1988 Congress banned smoking on domestic air flights of less than two hours and later extended the restriction to all public U.S. flights. Similar federal restrictions involving interstate commerce and travel apply to trains and buses. Federal government buildings are now also smoke-free. Numerous state and local restrictions exist as well. Most states limit smoking in public buildings such as hospitals and airports, and some even limit smoking in private buildings. Most businesses have followed suit by requiring workers to go outside or to special rooms to smoke. In 2000, for example, a survey across 19 states found that the percentage of workers whose companies had a smoke-free policy ranged from 61 (Mississippi) to 84 (Montana).

Current battles to implement further smoking restrictions generally occur at the local level and involve banning smoking altogether in restaurants and bars. Separate smoking sections in restaurants and bars are common but may not do enough to separate nonsmokers from tobacco fumes. Moreover nonsmoking employees of restaurants and bars must breathe passive smoke in the smoking sections of their places of employment. Many cities have therefore banned smoking in restaurants and bars. Berkeley, California, was the first city to do so in 1977; Los Angeles followed in 1993, San Francisco in 1994, and New York City in 2003. However, many in the food and drink industry fear a loss of business from such restrictions and have worked to prevent wider implementation of the restrictions.

Advocates of clean indoor air regulations suggest that protection from ETS will not only protect the health of smokers and nonsmokers but also discourage smokers from continuing the habit or consuming as many cigarettes as they would otherwise. The need to go to a separate room or outside to smoke limits, they argue, the number of cigarettes that can be consumed each day and may create enough trouble to encourage smokers to give up the habit altogether. Perhaps the inability to light up after a meal in restaurants further changes the motivation of smokers to continue the habit. Regardless of their effects on the consumption of cigarettes by smokers, increasing restrictions on smoking in public indoor places will no doubt continue.

LITIGATION

Litigation involves the use of private law by victims of cigarette use or their surrogates to receive compensation for the injuries they suffered. Using the tort (a word derived from Middle English meaning "injury") system, plaintiffs bring action against tobacco companies to obtain damages for wrongful behavior. The suits are extraordinarily expensive, particularly since tobacco companies use whatever resources they think necessary to win the cases. Only the plaintiffs and their lawyers receive the monetary damages and gain the benefits of winning a suit, but they also bear the cost. From the point of view of policymakers, litigation is an inefficient form of regulation since court cases take a long time, are extremely costly, and usually give the awards from a victory to only a few beneficiaries. Rather than a direct form of action of the government on behalf of its citizens, litigation on behalf of individuals can only indirectly regulate tobacco.

Still the indirect efforts can bring public health benefits. Legal victories against tobacco companies can raise prices, which discourages smoking. A few years back, Philip Morris had to raise the prices of its cigarettes by about 10 percent to cover the costs of a legal settlement, and today about 50¢ of every pack of cigarettes go to paying legal settlements and legal fees. Legal victories can also discourage tobacco companies from making misleading claims about the safety of their products, selling products to uninformed consumers, and making unsafe products. After decades of denying the harm and addictiveness of tobacco, industry executives have admitted to these problems as part of legal settlements. Legal victories can help educate the public about the ways tobacco companies aim to manipulate them with ads and promotions. The anger felt by victims about this treatment can motivate further action against tobacco companies. Legal victories can reduce the political and economic power of the tobacco companies. Although they enjoyed much political clout in the past, tobacco companies have lost much of their ability to influence legislators and government executives, in part because of the negative publicity that has emerged in litigation. And legal victories bring in new advocates on behalf of public health—trial lawyers. Although motivated in part by contingency fees, lawyers have brought new energy and strategies to the battle against the tobacco companies.

These public health benefits have come slowly. A review of the history of litigation distinguishes three waves of suits, with only the most recent having been successful. The first wave began in 1954 with early suits against the tobacco companies based on the emerging evidence of the harm of smoking. The suits claimed that tobacco companies were negligent in not warning smokers of the possible harm of the product, or that tobacco companies offered an implied warranty for the safety of the product. Few suits reached trial, as tobacco companies outspent their adversaries and delayed proceedings until the financial losses led the plaintiffs to withdraw. For those plaintiffs who did endure, courts did not favorably receive claims of either negligence or implied warranty. None of the suits resulted in victory against tobacco companies.

The second wave began in 1983 with two changes in strategy. Groups representing plaintiffs began to pool resources so that they could outlast the expensive delaying tactics of tobacco lawyers. Also, a new legal argument claimed that tobacco companies were strictly liable for a product that causes addiction and kills users. As with victims of a faulty automobile or electrical appliance, smokers claimed cigarette manufacturers were responsible for the harm of their product. The tobacco industry in turn responded that smokers were not harmed by cigarettes, and even if they were, they knew of the harm, at least since the warnings placed on cigarette packages in the mid-1960s, but freely chose to continue smoking. To counter claims of addiction, the lawyers could point to millions of smokers who had quit the habit. Lawyers for Rose Cipollone, a dying smoker, used this strategy to place liability on the cigarette maker and won an award of $400,000 in 1988, but the arguments of the tobacco lawyers ultimately won in appeal and her survivors eventually dropped the suit. After the first two waves of litigation, no plaintiff or plaintiff's attorney had yet recovered any money from the tobacco companies.

The third and only successful wave began in 1992 soon after the final decision in the Cipollone case. The new approach relied more on class-action rather than individual suits in order to further pool resources. A class-action suit enables a group of persons suffering from a common injury to bring suit. The action on behalf of a large number of people increases the total amount that can be awarded. Although the injured parties must share the benefits of the class and individually receive much less than in a regular suit, a successful class-action suit would impose daunting costs on the tobacco companies. Moreover, the contingency fees for trial lawyers would reach levels high enough to motivate legal firms to invest in suits. Plaintiffs in many suits of this third wave of litigation enjoyed greater financial resources than in the past.

The legal strategy of this third wave also took a new form. Rather than merely claiming harm from cigarettes, plaintiffs accused the tobacco companies of intentional misrepresentation, concealment, and failure to disclose information about the addictiveness and harm of smoking. Supporting these accusations required evidence that tobacco companies indeed knew of the harm of their products, and this evidence came from the unlikely and unexpected public release of internal industry documents. Merrill Williams, an employee of a Louisville law firm with access to the files of Brown and Williamson Tobacco, gave copies of incriminating documents to lawyers suing tobacco companies. In addition, a professor at the University of California and zealous antitobacco advocate, Sheldon Glantz, received copies of documents, as did sympathetic congressional representatives. After they appeared on the Internet, a judge ruled that the documents were in the public domain and could be used by plaintiffs in cases against Brown and Williamson and other tobacco companies. Another key to success in the third wave of suits came from Jeffrey S. Wigand, a former top research

Tobacco Industry and Smoking

executive at Brown and Williamson. He asserted in testimony and in public that the company knew of the harm and addictiveness of cigarettes. Many other examples of likely tobacco industry misrepresentation, concealment, and failure to disclose followed. With this evidence the new legal strategy of accusing the companies of fraud had much potential for success.

Most important in terms of government regulation, the attorneys general of all states brought claims against tobacco companies to recover their Medicaid costs for tobacco-related illnesses. These efforts began with a suit brought by the state of Mississippi under Attorney General Mike Moore and represented by successful trial lawyers Richard Scruggs and Ron Motley. Mississippi and three other states negotiated their own settlements with the tobacco industry, while 46 other states and the District of Columbia negotiated a 1998 Master Settlement Agreement. The settlement involved payment of $246 billion by tobacco companies over 25 years. It also included several public health provisions, such as restricting youth access to tobacco products, ending brand name sponsorships and promotion activities, limiting outdoor advertising, and contributing to cessation and prevention programs. The agreement created an important precedent in another way: It was the first time the tobacco industry had agreed to settle a suit.

The settlement has brought dispute over how states should spend the funds, with antismoking advocates accusing government officials of using the money for purposes other than tobacco prevention. New York governor George Pataki, for example, has proposed to use the funds for collateral in obtaining loans to help deal with the state's current fiscal crisis. In addition, the huge legal fees of the plaintiff's attorneys have come under criticism—some calculations show payment at rates of more than $100,000 an hour. Despite these disputes the settlement represents an important victory against the tobacco companies.

Numerous other suits remain to be resolved. For example, R. J. Reynolds currently has more than 1,660 cases pending against it. Although the administration of president George W. Bush appears less committed to federal efforts to control tobacco than the previous Clinton administration, such efforts continue. The Justice Department has carried on a 1999 federal suit against the tobacco companies to recover Medicare costs for treatment of elderly persons with smoking-related illnesses. Suits involving smokeless tobacco, flight attendants harmed by secondhand smoke, health insurance companies wanting to recover costs for smoking-related illness, and a variety of other types of injuries keep the threat to the tobacco industry high. The tobacco industry has won some cases, such as not having to pay for medical checkups of smokers in West Virginia and eliminating its restrictions on advertising in Massachusetts. The industry plans to continue fighting the suits (in some cases it has sued groups that criticize the industry and aggressively pursued documents of those bringing the suits). However, with juries increasingly willing to decide against tobacco companies, huge awards are likely. The suits may do little to reduce smoking, but they require tobacco companies to share their profits with the government and individuals.

The litigation strategy has critics, however. Believing that such efforts unfairly penalize legal businesses, remove responsibility from individuals for their actions, limit the freedom of individuals to make their own choices, and enrich trial lawyers, some oppose the tendency toward making huge and numerous awards against tobacco companies. Economists in particular view the awards as a form of tax on cigarettes and argue that such taxes should come from the legislature rather than the judiciary.[59] Yet the litigation strategy seems to be spreading. The European Commission joined in suing U.S. tobacco companies for smuggling cigarettes into Europe without paying import duties and taxes. The World Health Organization similarly recommends that other nations use the U.S.-style litigation strategy to control tobacco.

SMOKERS' RIGHTS

The vigorous efforts of federal, state, and local governments, the medical profession, nonprofit agencies, and trial lawyers to eliminate or control tobacco have spawned a countermovement devoted to smokers' rights. Critics of antitobacco polices argue that the goal of community health has come to conflict with and override individual liberty and freedom of choice. They argue that adults have the right to choose smoking pleasure over longevity of life, and efforts to prevent this choice can result in government tyranny.[60] Numerous smokers' rights organizations have developed over the years (often with support of the tobacco industry).

These groups have responded to policies that implement high cigarette taxes, restrict advertising, ban smoking in public places, and encourage litigation. First and foremost, smokers' rights advocates oppose special cigarette taxes. Excessively high taxes on cigarettes, they say, unfairly punish smokers and businesses that sell cigarettes. According to some, smokers do not impose special costs on society that would warrant having to pay special taxes. Because smokers tend to die younger than nonsmokers, the short-term cost of treating tobacco-related illness is more than outweighed by other savings. In the long run, nonsmokers cost the government more than smokers in expenses for social security, nursing home care, and health care in old age.

Rather than use the cigarette tobacco revenues for tobacco-related costs, governments typically use them for general expenditures. Yet critics note that these revenues often end up lower than expected, which in turn requires more increases in taxes. The low revenues stem in part from the efforts of smokers to search out cheaper prices in places where taxes are lower. For example, Native Americans can sell tax-free cigarettes at lower prices on their lands, and they advertise their prices on the Internet. Internet purchases and large-scale commercial smuggling across state borders also become common. Critics believe that these problems could be avoided with fairer tax policies.

Second, smokers' rights advocates oppose government programs to restrict the flow of information about tobacco and the choice of individuals to smoke. Limitations in certain forms of advertising represent, according to antitobacco critics, a form of censorship and a threat to freedom. They view smoking as a legal behavior and adults as free to make their choice without government restrictions on the information they can obtain. Government control of information thus represents a step toward prohibition. If government controls access to information about smoking, it may lead to a ban on smoking altogether. They believe that a ban on smoking can then lead to other threats to liberty—bans on the type of food people can eat, the movies they can watch, the alcohol they can drink, the games they can play, and the ideas they can have—and that government should have no such role in controlling the personal choices of individuals.

Smokers' rights advocates reject the claim that they are manipulated by and need protection from tobacco advertising. They believe that people rather than the tobacco companies are responsible for their choices. Indeed, it is difficult to prove scientifically that advertising causes people to smoke. The free market of ideas includes the opportunity to hear about products, even if most people oppose the use of the product.

Third, smokers' rights advocates oppose banning smoking in bars and restaurants. Although smokers recognize their responsibility to consider the wishes of nonsmokers to be free of smoky air, many view efforts to ban smoking totally in private buildings, restaurants, and bars as mistaken. Critics attack the public health literature by suggesting that the evidence of the harm of secondhand smoke is suspect. They say that the amounts of secondhand smoke faced by nonsmokers in daily life are so small as to be difficult to measure and unlikely to harm health. They believe that secondhand smoke does not present sufficient risk to warrant banning smoking in public places.

Even if the evidence were stronger, such bans create problems. They harm small businesses by keeping smokers away and creating problems of enforcement. In New York City, for example, a confrontation about smoking in a club soon after a ban had been imposed in 2003 resulted in the death of an employee. The bans also reveal a lack of understanding about economic choice and property rights. Free-market supporters suggest that business owners have the right to ban or not to ban smoking in their establishments, and patrons have the right to choose to go to smoking or non-smoking establishments. Offering choices to both owners and patrons would create a more satisfying solution than a government-imposed ban. It would provide for those wanting smoke-free places to eat and drink and for those wanting to enjoy cigarettes with their food and beverages. (However, another issue is an employees' right to a smoke-free workplace.)

Finally, smokers' rights advocates oppose litigation against tobacco companies. They believe that such efforts distort economic incentives and hurt rather than help smokers. Perhaps more important, they reflect an unwillingness to hold individual smokers responsible for their own ac tions. Many people believe that smoking is a choice, just as not smoking and quitting are choices (indeed, more than 40 million Americans have quit smoking). Given the widespread knowledge of the harm of smoking, smokers should assume the risks associated with the habit. The increased litigiousness of society has, according to critics, worked to deny this individual responsibility. Even if smokers deserved some compensation for smoking, litigation has failed to provide it. Most of the funds go to the states or trial lawyers rather than to the victims of smoking (who do not survive long enough to see an award). In the end huge awards against tobacco companies do more to punish smokers by raising cigarette prices than help smokers.

Beyond their opposition to specific policies, smokers' rights advocates worry about the increasingly negative view of smoking. Such attitudes can lead to discrimination against smokers in finding jobs, getting insurance, obtaining service in businesses, and participating in everyday activities. Rightly or wrongly smokers often feel as if they are part of a persecuted minority, and many have taken steps to organize themselves in opposition to what they view as a puritanical antismoking crusade.

CONCLUSION

As they have for the last 100 years, controversies over the tobacco industry and smoking will continue. The last century has also seen the growing importance of public health goals for society and increased government control of tobacco. These trends have considerable momentum, but many questions remain to be resolved.

- Should tobacco companies have the right to promote and advertise a product that although legal, undeniably has long-term harm for users?
- Are smokers victims of manipulation by advertising and addictive properties of nicotine or individual consumers who freely choose a product they enjoy?

Tobacco Industry and Smoking

- Does the goal of improving community health through government tobacco control efforts outweigh the value of individual freedom of choice?
- Is the tobacco industry, despite the mandated warnings on cigarette products, responsible for the harm of cigarettes, or should individuals assume the risk?
- Does secondhand smoke from the cigarettes of others represent a serious threat to nonsmokers that requires banning of smoking in all public indoor places, including restaurants and bars?

These questions about tobacco use and smoking policies affect most everyone in their daily lives and will make debates over the tobacco industry and smoking crucial ones for decades to come.

---

[1] Iain Gately. *Tobacco: The Story of How Tobacco Seduced the World.* New York: Grove Press, 2001, p. 3.

[2] *Ibid.*, p. 23.

[3] Arlene B. Hirschfelder. *Encyclopedia of Smoking and Tobacco.* Phoenix, Ariz.: Oryx Press, 1999, pp. 109, 151, 225–226.

[4] Quoted in Robert Sobel. *They Satisfy: The Cigarette in American Life.* Garden City, N.Y.: Anchor Press, 1978, p. 51.

[5] Jack Gottsegen. *Tobacco: A Study of Its Consumption in the United States.* New York: Pittman, 1940, pp. 57, 65.

[6] Sobel. *They Satisfy*, p. 20.

[7] Quoted in Gately. *Tobacco*, p. 234.

[8] Joseph R. Gusfield. *Symbolic Crusade: Status Politics and the American Temperance Movement.* 2d ed. Urbana: University of Illinois Press, 1986, pp. 7–8.

[9] Gottsegen. *Tobacco*, p. 144.

[10] Quoted in Gately. *Tobacco*, p. 234.

[11] John C. Burnham. *Bad Habits: Drinking, Smoking, Taking Drugs, Gambling, Sexual Misbehavior, and Swearing in American History.* New York: New York University Press, 1993, illustration I.22.

[12] Jordan Goodman. *Tobacco in History: The Cultures of Dependence.* London: Routledge, 1993, p. 106.

[13] Gottsegen. *Tobacco*, pp. 149–150.

[14] Richard Tennant. *The American Cigarette Industry.* New Haven, Conn.: Yale University, 1950, pp. 136–142.

[15] Luther L. Terry. "The Surgeon General's First Report on Smoking and Health." In Alan Blum, ed., *The Cigarette Underworld: A Front Line Report on the War Against Your Lungs.* Secaucus, N.J.: Lyle Stuart, 1985, p. 15.

[16] U.S. Department of Health and Human Services. *The Health Consequences of Smoking: Cancer. A Report of the Surgeon General.* Washington, D.C.: U.S. Department of Health and Human Services, 1982, p. xi.

[17] Alan Kluger. *Ashes to Ashes: America's Hundred-Year Cigarette War, the Public Health, and the Unabashed Triumph of Philip Morris.* New York: Alfred A. Knopf, 1996, p. 239.

[18] Gately. *Tobacco*, p. 317.

[19] David Krogh. *Smoking: The Artificial Passion.* New York: W. H. Freeman, 1991, p. 59.

[20] U.S. Department of Health and Human Services. *The Health Consequences of Smoking: Nicotine Addiction. A Report of the Surgeon General.* Washington, D.C.: U.S. Department of Health and Human Services, 1988, p. v.

[21] Paul Slovic. "Cigarette Smokers: Rational Actors or Rational Fools?" In Paul Slovic, ed., *Smoking: Risk, Perception, and Policy.* Thousand Oaks, Calif.: Sage Publications, 2001, pp. 97–124.

[22] Kluger. *Ashes to Ashes*, p. 702.

[23] U.S. Department of Health and Human Services. *Preventing Tobacco Use among Young People. A Report of the Surgeon General.* Washington, D.C.: U.S. Department of Health and Human Services, 1994.

[24] Morton Hunt. *The Story of Psychology.* New York: Anchor Press, 1993, p. 347.

[25] Elizabeth Whelan. *A Smoking Gun: How the Tobacco Industry Gets Away with Murder.* Philadelphia: George F. Stickley, 1984, pp. 105–106.

[26] Whelan. *A Smoking Gun*, p. 110.

[27] Sobel. *They Satisfy*, p. 184.

[28] U.S. Department of Health and Human Services. *Reducing the Health Consequences of Smoking: 25 Years of Progress. A Report of the Surgeon General.* Washington, D.C.: U.S. Department of Health and Human Services, 1989, p. 11.

[29] U.S. Department of Health and Human Services. *Healthy People 2010.* Washington, D.C.: U.S. Department of Health and Human Services, 2000, p. 27-12.

[30] Fred C. Pampel. "Cigarette Diffusion and Sex Differences in Smoking." *Journal of Health and Social Behavior,* vol. 42 (December 2001): 388–404.

[31] "Cigarette Smoking among Adults—United States, 2000." *MMWR Weekly,* vol. 51 (July 26, 2002): 642–645.

[32] "Monitoring the Future." In U.S. Department of Health and Human Services, *Women and Smoking. A Report of the Surgeon General.* Washington, D.C.: U.S. Department of Health and Human Services, 2001, pp. 59–63.

[33] U.S. Department of Health and Human Services. *Women and Smoking,* pp. 453–527.

[34] Quoted in Jacob Sullum. *For Your Own Good: The Anti-Smoking Crusade and the Tyranny of Public Health.* New York: Free Press, 1998, p. 6.

[35] W. Kip Viscusi. *Smoking: Making the Risky Decision.* New York: Oxford University Press, 1992, pp. 7–8.

[36] Kluger. *Ashes to Ashes*, p. 678.

[37] U.S. Department of Health and Human Services. *Women and Smoking,* pp. 68–69.

[38] Paul Rozin. "The Process of Moralization." *Psychological Science,* vol. 10 (May 1999): 218–221.

[39] Sullum. *For Your Own Good,* p. 13.

[40] Richard Klein. *Cigarettes Are Sublime.* Durham, N.C.: Duke University Press, 1993, p. 3.

[41] U.S. Department of Health and Human Services. *Regulating Tobacco Use: A Report of the Surgeon General.* Washington, D.C.: U.S. Department of Health and Human Services, 2000, p. 49.

[42] National Cancer Institute. *Risks Associated with Smoking Cigarettes with Low Machine-Measured Yields of Tar and Nicotine. Smoking and Tobacco Control Monograph 13.* Washington, D.C.: U.S. Department of Health and Human Services, 2001, pp. 1–10, 193–198.

[43] National Cancer Institute. *Risks Associated with Smoking Cigarettes with Low Machine Measured Yields of Tar and Nicotine,* p. 2.

[44] National Cancer Institute. *Risks Associated with Smoking Cigarettes with Low Machine-Measured Yields of Tar and Nicotine,* pp. 1–10.

[45] U.S. Department of Health and Human Services. *Tobacco Use among U.S. Racial/Ethnic Minority Groups: African Americans, American Indians and Alaskan Natives, Asian Americans and Pacific Islanders, and Hispanics. A Report of the Surgeon General.* Washington, D.C.: U.S. Department of Health and Human Services, 1998, pp. 213–224.

[46] Tara Parker-Pope. *Cigarettes: Anatomy of an Industry from Seed to Smoke.* New York: New Press, 2001, p. 27.

[47] World Bank. *Curbing the Epidemic: Governments and the Economics of Tobacco Control.* Washington, D.C.: World Bank, 1999, p. 13.

[48] U.S. Department of Health and Human Services. *Reducing the Health Consequences of Smoking: 25 Years of Progress,* pp. 140–141.

[49] Claire Chollat-Traquet. *Women and Tobacco.* Geneva: World Health Organization, 1992, pp. 31–55.

[50] U.S. Department of Health and Human Services. *Women and Smoking,* pp. 177–376.

[51] Hirschfelder. *Encyclopedia of Smoking and Tobacco,* p. 199.

[52] A. K. Hackshaw, M. R. Law, and N. J. Wald. "The Accumulated Evidence on Lung Cancer and Environmental Tobacco Smoke." *British Medical Journal,* vol. 315 (October 18, 1997): 980–988. Also see U.S. Department of Health and Human Services. *The Health Consequences of Involuntary Smoking: A Report of the Surgeon General.* Washington, D.C.: U.S. Department of Health and Human Services, 1986, pp. 66–96.

[53] U.S. Department of Health and Human Services. *Preventing Tobacco Use among Young People,* p. 135.

[54] E. A. Gilpin, L. Lee, N. Evans, and J. P. Pierce. "Smoking Initiation Rates in Adults and Minors: United States, 1944–1988." *American Journal of Epidemiology,* vol. 140 (September 15, 1994): 535–543.

[55] World Bank. *Curbing the Epidemic,* p. 45.

[56] L. E. Crossett, S. A. Everett, N. D. Brener, J. A. Fishman, and T. F. Pechacek. "Adherence to the CDC Guidelines for School Health Programs to Prevent Tobacco Use and Addiction." *Journal of Health Education* (Supplement), vol. 30 (September/October 1999): S4–S11.

[57] U.S. Department of Health and Human Services. *Regulating Tobacco Use,* pp. 100–128.

[58] U.S. Department of Health and Human Services. *Regulating Tobacco Use,* p. 359.

[59] W. Kip Viscusi. *Smoke-Filled Rooms: A Postmortem on the Tobacco Deal.* Chicago: University of Chicago Press, 2002, p. 8.

[60] Sullum, *For Your Own Good,* p. 13.

CHAPTER 2

THE LAW AND THE TOBACCO INDUSTRY AND SMOKING

FEDERAL LAWS AND REGULATIONS

Given the importance throughout history of tobacco to the American economy, of cigarettes to individual consumers, and of smoking to the health and well-being of the U.S. population, it is surprising that only a few laws and regulations govern the product and activity. The limited legal intervention of the government stems in part from the view of Americans that the purchase of cigarettes and smoking is a personal choice and individual right. It also stems from the power of the tobacco industry to block the actions that the legislative and executive branches might take against the industry. The most important recent actions against the tobacco industry have come from the judiciary; however, this appear to be changing. The public has become more supportive of controls on tobacco advertising to youth and on indoor smoking in public places, and the government has become increasingly active in implementing these controls. This section of the chapter describes the federal laws and regulations that have most affected the tobacco industry and smoking.

FEDERAL CIGARETTE LABELING AND ADVERTISING ACT (1965)

As the first modern federal legislation to address the perils of smoking, the 1965 Federal Cigarette Labeling and Advertising Act signaled an important beginning to the government's battle against the tobacco industry and smoking. Although the law placed only modest requirements on cigarette makers and actually prevented more stringent regulations from going into effect, the entrance of Congress into the realm of tobacco control set a precedent that in years to come would lead to stronger legislation.

After the release of the 1964 Surgeon General's report on health and smoking, the Federal Trade Commission (FTC), which had for some time struggled with the tobacco companies over misleading advertisements about the health benefits of cigarettes, proposed tough new rules. These rules would require warnings about the health risks of smoking on cigarette packages, print advertisements, and broadcast commercials as well as the listing of the tar and nicotine content of cigarettes. With a mandate to restrain unfair and misleading business practices, this agency of the executive branch of the government had the potential to seriously threaten the interests of the tobacco industry.

To forestall such action the tobacco industry proposed to regulate its own advertising. It developed a code to curb ads that appealed directly or indirectly to young people, made unverified claims of health benefits, and implied smoking was essential to sexual attractiveness, social success, virility, and sophistication. Bowman Gray, chairman of the board of R. J. Reynolds Tobacco Company, testified in Congress, "This advertising code represents a sincere effort by the industry to respond to criticisms of the industry's advertising."[1] However, the FTC had little confidence that self-regulation would work.

Believing that it had more clout with Congress than with President Lyndon Johnson and members of the FTC, representatives of the tobacco industry urged various legislators to pass legislation that would override the FTC regulations. The pieces of legislation debated by the House and Senate aimed to provide some sort of warning to consumers but varied in the form the warnings would take. Some legislators favored turning the FTC regulatory proposals into law, while others acting more in concert with the tobacco industry wanted something weaker. At the time antismoking groups had not yet emerged as a strong political force, and groups such as the American Cancer Society and the American Medical Association (AMA), which doubted if warnings would have much effect on smoking, did not lobby for the law. In the end the weaker version of the legislation passed.

The legislation required that cigarette packages include the following (somewhat mild) statement: "Caution: Cigarette Smoking May Be Hazardous to Your Health." The statement did not use more frightening words such as death and lung cancer and qualified its impact with the words *may be hazardous*. The packages would list the warnings on the side in small type rather than on the front in larger type. Unlike the original FTC proposals, the legislation did not include any provisions for warnings on advertisements or commercials and did not require statements of the tar and nicotine content of cigarettes. Two other provisions that seemed less important at the time were included instead. One provision denied all federal and state agencies the power over the next four years to require any additions or revisions to the warning. This provision aimed to produce uniform statements on cigarette packages but also to keep the FTC and other government agencies out of the issue and to assert Congress's power. Another provision required the FTC and the Department of Health, Education, and Welfare through the Office of the Surgeon General to report annually to Congress on cigarette advertising and on smoking and health.

Despite its opposition to the warning, the tobacco industry enjoyed, according to most observers, a victory with the legislation. It preempted more stringent regulations with modest requirements for a warning statement and allowed advertisements to continue as they had in the past. The legislation also allowed the industry to drop its efforts at self-regulation that, if followed, would have done much more to change the nature of cigarette advertising. Although less clearly realized at the time, the warnings on cigarette packages had the advantage of serving in the future to protect the industry from lawsuits. Smokers would not easily be able to claim in a suit that they had lacked knowledge of the health risks of smoking or that the tobacco companies had hidden the danger of their product. Warnings would play an important role in suits to follow.

However, the provision requiring annual reports to Congress by the FTC and the Surgeon General allowed antismoking forces in the government to continue their steady criticism of smoking and cigarette advertisements. Year after year, the Surgeon General published reports listing the harm of cigarette use. These reports would become increasingly critical over the years, eventually concluding that nicotine was an addictive drug and claiming that 400,000 persons a year died prematurely from smoking. The FTC also continued its condemnation of tobacco advertising as misleading and manipulative and recommended in the years to come that the government mandate more strongly worded warnings and exert greater control on advertisements.

FAIRNESS DOCTRINE APPLIED TO TOBACCO (1967)

Extending the fairness doctrine to issues of tobacco by the Federal Communications Commission (FCC) represented an important victory for antismoking forces. The decision gave them free television and radio air time to counter claims made on behalf of cigarettes in paid advertising. By most accounts the antismoking ads effectively persuaded many consumers not to smoke. The benefit of the antismoking ads did not last long, as banning all cigarette television and radio ads in 1971 ended free air time for anticigarette ads. Still the use of the fairness doctrine to battle tobacco companies offered a new and valuable form of smoking regulation.

Tobacco Industry and Smoking

The fairness doctrine had since 1949 required television and radio stations that presented material on important and controversial issues to give air time to both sides of the issues. Since television and radio stations used the public airwaves (unlike magazines and newspapers), and broadcast frequencies in the years before cable were relatively scarce, the government had a responsibility to ensure that stations used their airwaves for the good of the public. One way to do so involved the fair treatment of opposing viewpoints. The doctrine initially applied largely to politicians and interest groups representing competing sides of political issues and prevented stations from bias in favor of one political party or set of interests.

Angered by a cigarette commercial he saw on television in 1966, John Banzhaf III, a young New York City lawyer, requested air time from WCBS-TV in New York City to rebut the cigarette ads the station carried. After being turned down by the station, he filed a complaint with the FCC, which enforced the doctrine. In 1967 the FCC ruled in Banzhaf's favor by requiring that stations provide a significant amount of air time for the other side of the controversial issue of the health hazards of smoking. The commission did not force stations to air an equal number of anti- and prosmoking commercials but threatened to revoke their licenses if they did not give significant time to the antitobacco side. After a court ruled in support of the commission's decision, Banzhaf and others proceeded to set up organizations that monitored the compliance of stations with the ruling.

The rule had a considerable impact. In practice about one antismoking commercial appeared for every three smoking commercials, which translated into donations by broadcasters of $75 million in air time (more than $300 million in 1997 dollars).[2] In one effective commercial, William Talman, a well-known actor from the *Perry Mason* television show, appeared. He was sick and dying from lung cancer after decades of smoking three packs of cigarettes a day. Introducing his wife and children, he stated he was battling for his life and to enjoy more time with his family. He then urged others not to smoke. His death by the time many of the commercials aired lent power to the ads. Reviewing these antismoking ads, a leading tobacco control scholar claimed that they were more effective than any other technique of persuading people to stop smoking.[3]

PUBLIC HEALTH CIGARETTE SMOKING ACT (1969)

Moving beyond warnings on packages, this act banned cigarette advertising from television and radio (all media subject to the authority of the FTC) beginning on January 2, 1971. It also strengthened the wording of the warnings on cigarette packages and led to the inclusion of warning statements on print advertisements. Although not part of the legislation, a later consent decree from the FTC required warnings on advertisements in newspapers, magazines, and outdoor displays.

The 1965 Federal Cigarette Labeling and Advertising Act included no provisions on tobacco advertising, but the FTC continued its criticism of the tobacco industry for misleading practices in promoting its product. In 1967 the FTC noted that despite warnings on packages, cigarette sales had continued to rise, in large part because advertisements depicted images of healthy smokers. Particularly disconcerting, these images appealed to young people and thereby led teens to start smoking before they fully understood the risks. The FTC first called for stronger warnings on packages and new warnings on ads to counter the influence of the ads. In 1969, however, the FTC took another approach: Six of seven commissioners voted to prohibit cigarette advertising from television and radio. Such a ban had been implemented in England in 1965 and seemed an effective way to moderate the influence of the tobacco companies in promoting smoking.

Addressing the issue in 1969, the House of Representatives responded to concerns of both the tobacco industry and the National Association of Broadcasters (which received 10 percent of its advertising revenue from tobacco companies) with a bill. In exchange for acceptance of stronger warnings by the tobacco industry, the bill would prohibit state and federal agencies from taking any action on cigarette advertising. However, stronger opposition to the tobacco industry had emerged in the Senate, and it appeared that a bill to ban advertising would pass in that chamber. Recognizing defeat, the tobacco industry accepted the proposed ban, and the act passed in 1969.

The act specified that cigarette advertising on television and radio would cease on January 2, 1971. The date chosen allowed cigarette companies to flood the airwaves with commercials during the New Year's Day football games. The act also strengthened the warning on cigarette packages to state:

WARNING: The Surgeon General has Determined that Cigarette Smoking is Dangerous to Your Health.

The warning replaced *may be* with *is* and cited the Surgeon General's office as the source of the claim. As in earlier legislation the 1969 act also preempted other government agencies from requiring changes in the warning. A group of broadcasters rather than the cigarette companies challenged the restrictions on their right to free speech with the television and radio ban on tobacco ads, but in *Capital Broadcasting v. Mitchell*, the D.C. district court affirmed the constitutionality of the prohibition.

The law effectively and quickly eliminated ads from television and radio but did little to slow the advertising efforts of tobacco companies. The companies saved more than $200 million on electronic advertising and could use these savings for promotions and space in magazines, in newspapers, and on outdoor billboards. Before the ban tobacco companies spent $205 million on television advertising, $12.5 million on radio advertising, $14 million on newspaper advertising, and $50 million on magazine advertising. By 1979 newspaper advertising had soared to $241 million and magazine advertising to $257 million.[4] Tobacco companies spent other funds on promotional items such as coupons, lighters, key chains, and clothing with brand names, and on sponsorship of sporting and entertainment events. The continued growth in advertising led the American Cancer Society, the American Medical Association, the American Public Health Association, and the American Heart Association to advocate (unsuccessfully) a ban on all advertising.

Not only did the ban not appear to harm tobacco companies with the shift of advertising to different media, but it may have actually helped them in another way. The ban also eliminated free airtime given to antismoking groups. The cigarette counteradvertising appeared effective, as smoking had declined every year since it started in 1967. Tobacco industry executives admitted that they accepted the ban in part to end free antismoking commercials. The fairness doctrine did not apply to magazines and newspapers, and antismoking groups did not have the resources to pay for ads to balance those of the tobacco industry. The act ended the application of the fairness doctrine to tobacco and ultimately appeared to benefit more than it harmed the tobacco industry.

COMPREHENSIVE SMOKING EDUCATION ACT (1984)

The 1984 Comprehensive Smoking Education Act strengthened the wording of the warnings placed on cigarette packages and required that the warnings also be displayed prominently on advertisements. Its importance comes not only from further efforts to limit the ability of tobacco companies to attract new smokers but also from the emerging signs that the tobacco industry had lost much of its traditional influence on the political process in Washington, D.C. The 1980s saw the emergence of new leaders in Congress who had the skill and political power to guide antitobacco legislation through both the Senate and House of Representatives.

As in earlier legislation, the impetus for this act came from the FTC. In monitoring advertisements in magazines, newspapers, posters, and billboards, the FTC once again accused the tobacco industry of misleading business practices. Ads tended to appeal to young people by depicting smokers as youthful, healthy, active, and confident (even though the known harm of cigarettes contradicted these images). A 1981 report concluded that the existing warnings did little to counter these positive images, and regulations needed to limit more forcefully the appeal of cigarettes.[5]

The Law and the Tobacco Industry and Smoking

Taking up the recommendations of the FTC, Representative Henry Waxman of California, a Democrat, held hearings on the business practices of the tobacco industry and developed a bill in the House of Representatives that would more stringently control tobacco advertising. In the Senate, Al Gore, a new Democratic senator from Tennessee, managed to negotiate a milder form of the bill by finding a way to compromise between antismoking and tobacco interests. In much of these negotiations, however, tobacco company executives and lobbyists offended prominent senators with inflexible views and untrustworthy actions. The industry's dealings on the bill actually furthered antismoking attitudes in Congress. In the end a bill emerged that was weaker than the one envisioned by Henry Waxman but still represented a victory for antismoking forces.

The public most noticed the provision of the bill that required the rotating of four new warning statements on both packages and on advertisements. The four warning statements used more direct, specific, and unqualified wording than the early ones:

SURGEON GENERAL'S WARNING: *Smoking Causes Lung Cancer, Heart Disease, Emphysema, and May Complicate Pregnancy.*

SURGEON GENERAL'S WARNING: *Quitting Smoking Now Greatly Reduces Serious Risks to Your Health.*

SURGEON GENERAL'S WARNING: *Smoking by Pregnant Women May Result in Fetal Injury, Premature Birth, and Low Birth Weight.*

SURGEON GENERAL'S WARNING: *Cigarette Smoke Contains Carbon Monoxide.*

The warnings did not spell out the harm of carbon monoxide (a poisonous gas that kills in large doses) and avoided reference to death and addiction, but they did state unequivocally that smoking causes specific diseases (rather than stating smoking is hazardous or dangerous). These warnings would appear not just on cigarette packages but also on ads. Countering pictures of smokers having fun, the noticeable insert in the ad would remind readers of the result of smoking.

Other provisions would prove significant in years to come. The act required tobacco companies to provide the government with lists of the additives put in cigarettes during the manufacturing process; government officials would analyze the information on additives but keep it confidential. In 1994, however, the government reversed course and released the lists. The publicity about the additives, many of which are harmful, embarrassed the tobacco industry. In addition the warnings chosen for the packages and advertisements preempted efforts of state and most federal agencies to develop other warnings but did not prevent the FTC from continuing its own efforts to control tobacco advertising.

In some ways the act did not go as far as antismoking advocates would have liked. The warnings did not mention death and addiction and did not include information on the amounts of tar, nicotine, and carbon monoxide inhaled with a cigarette. Still the act represented a substantial change in the willingness of the government to control the tobacco industry.

COMPREHENSIVE SMOKELESS TOBACCO HEALTH EDUCATION ACT (1986)

Although it was slow in coming, strong evidence had accumulated by the mid-1980s that smokeless tobacco caused oral cancer and nicotine addiction. The evidence worried public health officials because smokeless tobacco use had been rising among young boys, in part because they thought it would not cause cancer and was not addictive. The law banned advertising of smokeless tobacco on electronic media and required three rotated warnings on smokeless tobacco packaging and all advertising except billboards:

WARNING: This product may cause serious mouth cancer.

WARNING: This product may cause gum disease and tooth loss.

WARNING: This product is not a safe alternative to cigarettes.

The FTC implemented the act, later coming to decide that T-shirts, jackets, hats, and lighters represented a form of advertising and should not include brand names or logos.

MASTER SETTLEMENT AGREEMENT (1998)

This agreement between 46 state attorneys general, as well as the District of Columbia, and major U.S. tobacco companies settled pending lawsuits by the states for recovery of Medicaid costs they incurred in treating smoking-related illnesses. Its importance shows in the huge size of the award—$246 billion over 25 years—and in the willingness of the tobacco industry to settle rather than fight the suits. In addition four other states settled suits separately.

The initial events leading to the Master Settlement Agreement (MSA) began with a suit filed by the state of Mississippi against tobacco manufacturers, wholesalers, and trade groups. The Mississippi attorney general, Mike Moore, working with successful trial lawyers Richard Scruggs and Ron Motley, led the effort. In a major shift in strategy the suit did not request damages on behalf of injured smokers. After all, courts and juries had not in the past been willing to absolve smokers of their responsibility for choosing to smoke despite knowing the harm of the product. Rather the state, which itself had never assumed the risks of smoking that individuals did, wanted to recover the costs taxpayers had to pay for tobacco-related illnesses. Officials noticed that of the Mississippians whose medical costs the state covered with Medicaid, half were smokers. In this way the state rather than the smokers themselves had been injured by the tobacco companies. In addition to these costs, the state requested costs for reimbursement of legal expenses. In the meantime a group of private plaintiff law firms rather than the state itself fronted the expenses of bringing the suit. The states of Minnesota, Florida, and West Virginia filed their own suits soon after. The new legal approach appeared promising enough that attorneys general from nearly all the other states and the District of Columbia would seek recovery of their own costs for tobacco-related illnesses.

The states made the case that the companies had violated antitrust and consumer fraud laws by withholding information about the harm of smoking, had manipulated nicotine levels to maximize addiction, and conspired to withhold lower risk products from the market. Given these fraudulent actions, the companies were, according to the suits, responsible for the costs to taxpayers of public Medicaid costs for smoking-related illnesses.

Bennett LeBow, the CEO of the Brooke Group, which owned the smallest of the big tobacco companies, Liggett Tobacco, broke ranks first by negotiating with the states. Although the other manufacturers vowed not to give in to the state demands for payment, LeBow believed that fighting would harm the nontobacco parts of his company and saw little chance of winning. Tobacco industry documents on the Internet provided examples of deception and manipulation and also made settlement seem sensible. In 1996 the company agreed to pay up to $50 million, publicize the ingredients of its cigarettes, and strengthen its warning labels. The settlement, although small, shifted the balance of power against the tobacco companies.

The other tobacco companies, Philip Morris, R. J. Reynolds, Brown and Williamson (part of the British-American Tobacco Company), and Lorillard, soon followed in reaching agreements. On July 2, 1998, they settled with Mississippi by agreeing to pay $3.4 billion over 25 years. Separate agreements were also reached with Minnesota, Florida, and West Virginia. More important, the companies proposed a settlement with 41 other states that would end all pending lawsuits brought by government agencies and all other pending class-action lawsuits. Given the goal of ending certain types of lawsuits, the agreement needed the force of national law to make it work; however, Congress could not agree on the terms for such legislation, and the proposed agreement failed.

Tobacco Industry and Smoking

From this failure both sides accepted the Master Settlement Agreement on November 23, 1998. Dealing directly with the state attorneys general (except for the four states that negotiated agreements separately), 11 tobacco companies made concessions to the states in return for dropping the suits for Medicaid reimbursement. The major concession of the tobacco companies was to pay $246 billion to the states over 25 years; however, the agreement included many other provisions.

- **Youth access:** Tobacco companies would provide no free samples where underage persons are present, would provide no gifts to youth in return for purchases, would provide no gifts through the mail without proof of age, and would offer no cigarettes in packages of fewer than 20 until December 31, 2001.
- **Marketing:** Tobacco company brand names would not sponsor sporting events, concerts, and events with a significant youth audience, paid underage spectators, or underage participants; in addition tobacco companies would ban the display of tobacco names in stadiums and arenas, the use of cartoon characters in ads, payments to promote tobacco products in movies, and distribution of merchandise with tobacco logos.
- **Lobbying:** Tobacco companies would not support diversion of settlement funds for nonhealth uses, lobby against restrictions of advertising on school grounds, or challenge state and local tobacco control laws enacted before June 1, 1998.
- **Outdoor advertising:** Tobacco companies would ban outdoor advertising such as billboards and transit ads and would pay for ads discouraging youth smoking.
- **Cessation and prevention:** Tobacco companies would contribute $25 million annually for 10 years to charitable programs devoted to preventing teen smoking and the diseases associated with teen smoking, and would contribute $1.45 billion over five years to support a national sustained advertising and education program to counter youth tobacco use.

The payment of the funds to the states has created debate about their use. In some cases the funds have gone for government programs unrelated to tobacco control. Ideally states would use them to prevent youth smoking. Given the potential for statewide prevention and education programs to work better in halting cigarette use than local or school-based programs, the settlement funds used for statewide programs would do much to discourage cigarette use. Settlement funds could also pay for the kind of antismoking ads that had so much success in the past. Debate over the use of the funds continues to the present.

82

Critics of the settlement point to the fact that it represents a financial windfall for the states but otherwise does little to improve the health of citizens. The funds gained from the tobacco companies go not to the victims of smoking-related diseases but to lawyer's fees and the state budgets controlled by politicians. In one sense, the ultimate costs of the settlement fall on smokers. Because the settlement raises the costs of cigarettes, it in essence imposes additional taxes on those who smoke. Some recommend that states replace these hidden taxes imposed by judicial agreements with unconcealed taxes passed by democratic legislation.[6]

From the point of view of the tobacco industry the settlement has done little to ease its litigation problems. Without national legislation from Congress to prevent future suits, the agreement with the states does not prevent others from filing similar suits. Health care organizations such as Blue Cross/Blue Shield, the federal government, state agencies, and individuals continue to file suits based on the same legal principles as those that led to the Master Settlement Agreement. Indeed, R. J. Reynolds reports on its webpage that it stands as the defendant in thousands of suits. If the industry hoped to buy some legal peace with the settlement, it did not succeed.

STATE AND LOCAL LAWS AND REGULATIONS

In the absence of major federal legislation concerning tobacco since 1986, much of the initiative has moved to states and localities. States have always had laws restricting access to minors but in more recent years have strengthened these laws. In addition states have expanded their taxes on cigarettes to reduce the demand for the product and to bring in government revenues. Both states and localities have also addressed issues of clean indoor air with laws and regulations banning or limiting smoking inside buildings. Since the 50 states and the District of Columbia differ greatly in their smoking laws and regulations, this section reviews only the broad outlines of the differing approaches in three areas: access of minors, clear indoor air, and taxes.

Access of Minors

All states restrict the sale of tobacco to youth under age 18 (Alabama and Alaska restrict sales to youth under 19) but vary in the procedures they use to enforce the rules. Regulations in most states require retailers to have a license to sell cigarettes over the counter and post a sign indicating the minimum age of purchase. A smaller number of states also regulate the minimum age for salespersons, and a few attempt to educate employees of the seriousness of the problem of youth cigarette sales. Without strong enforcement efforts and severe punishments, however, these regulations lack power. Historically little effort has gone into policing sales to youth, and significant numbers of minors could purchase cigarettes with little trouble. More recent attempts to strengthen enforcement make youth cigarette purchases more difficult, but recent studies found 22 to 33 percent of sales went to minors.[7]

With the commercial availability of cigarettes from retailers declining, youth can attempt to obtain the product from older friends or by other means. This shifts laws and regulations away from sellers to the youth who purchase, possess, or use cigarettes. Although all states prohibit sales by retailers, fewer states have laws and regulations concerning the buyers. Public health advocates tend to blame retailers for sales to minors more than the minors themselves, who by reacting to advertising seem more like victims than criminals.

The federal government has become involved in these efforts. The U.S. Congress in 1992 passed an amendment sponsored by Representative Mike Synar, a Democrat from Oklahoma as part of the Alcohol, Drug Abuse, and Mental Health Administration Reorganization Act. The amendment required states to adopt and enforce a minimum age for tobacco sales, as well as demonstrate reductions in the retail availability of tobacco products to youth. The federal government does not have authority over state laws, but failure of states to follow these strictures would result in the loss of federal block grant funds for substance abuse. States have followed the requirements by increasing random unannounced inspections, measuring retailer violations of the rules, and restricting access of youth to vending machines.

Some new state laws take a more active approach to fighting youth smoking. Effective January 1, 2002, a set of laws in California prohibiting sales of cigarettes to minors add some new requirements: The laws prohibit smoking of tobacco products within a playground or sandbox area, the sale or display of cigarettes without the supervision or assistance of a clerk, and the sale or importation of bidis. To enforce rules about the sales of cigarettes to minors, the laws now make business owners as well as clerks liable for infractions. The state can use sting operations to determine if retailers sell tobacco products illegally and to investigate sales of cigarettes to minors through the Internet, phone, or mail. Some cities in California have gone even further. In San Diego, for example, ordinances prevent advertising displays in places where children may see them, and cigarette displays near candy and nonalcoholic beverages are not allowed.

Clean Indoor Air

By the end of 1999, 45 states and the District of Columbia had laws that to one degree or another restricted indoor smoking in public places (Alabama, Kentucky, New Mexico, North Carolina, and Wyoming are the exceptions). Among these restrictions smoking was limited in government workplaces in 43 states and the District of Columbia, in restaurants in 31 states, and in private worksites in 21 states. To give a few examples, Maryland in 1995 enacted a smoke-free policy for all workplaces except hotels, bars, restaurants, and private clubs; Vermont in 1995 extended its smoking ban to include restaurants, bars, hotels, and motels; and California in 1998 banned smoking in bars unless there is a separately ventilated smoking area. The restrictions represent a major change. In 1964 no state laws protected indoor air from tobacco smoke. By 1999 nearly 100 such ordinances restricted smoking in workplaces and restaurants, and nearly 300 such ordinances restricted indoor smoking in various public places.

Local ordinances have also become important in the absence of state laws. By 1988 nearly 400 local ordinances had been enacted to protect indoor air from cigarette smoke, and 820 ordinances in 1998 restricted or banned smoking in public places. Debate over banning smoking in restaurants and bars, a major source of conflict between smokers' rights groups and antismoking groups, takes place largely within local areas. For workplaces not covered by state or local laws, private firms have increasingly decided to restrict smoking in their facilities. By 1992, 87 percent of worksites with 50 or more employees had a smoking policy of some kind. A large employer itself, the federal government stringently regulates smoking in its buildings.

Taxes

Although used historically to raise revenues, taxes also help to reduce smoking through raising the price of a pack of cigarettes. Two sorts of taxes can apply to cigarettes. Excise taxes specific to tobacco products are added before purchase, and sales taxes on products in general are added at the time of the purchase. The excise taxes are generally higher. Washington State raised its excise tax to $1.425 in 2001, and New Jersey has a per pack excise tax of $2.05. Tobacco-growing states have the lowest excise taxes: 2.5¢ a pack in Virginia, 3¢ a pack in Kentucky, and 5¢ a pack in North Carolina. Sales taxes can, in addition, add significantly to the cost of cigarettes:

California adds 25¢ a pack, and Illinois and Michigan add 20¢ a pack. On the low end, however, three states—Colorado, Delaware, and New Hampshire—have no special sales taxes on cigarettes.

In 1988 California voters approved the Tobacco Tax and Health Protection Act (Proposition 99), which increased the excise tax on cigarettes by 25 percent. In 1994 Michigan voters enacted a financing plan for public schools that included higher taxes on cigarettes. Similar voter-approved measures operate in Massachusetts, Arizona, and Oregon. The measures often devote part of the increased revenue to tobacco education and prevention programs. Raising taxes in single states requires enforcement against smuggling of cigarettes from nearby states with lower taxes. The Federal Trafficking in Contraband Cigarettes Act of 1978 dealt with smuggling by organized crime, but casual smuggling by individuals may also create problems. Smuggling problems may worsen as counties and cities add their own taxes to the state taxes.

COURT CASES

Suits against the tobacco industry began in the 1950s, but few reached a jury, and none until the 1990s resulted in monetary damages awarded to the plaintiffs. In the 1990s the number and variety of suits increased greatly, but given the drawn-out appeals process, few of the more recent suits have yet resulted in a final verdict. The older as well as the new suits still reflect efforts to control tobacco products. This section reviews court cases involving the tobacco industry and smoking that have set legal precedents for the treatment of both victims of smoking and the tobacco industry.

GREEN V. AMERICAN TOBACCO COMPANY (1957)

Background

This suit against a major tobacco company over the effect of smoking on lung cancer was the first of its type to go to jury. Dr. Larry Hastings, a physician and lawyer specializing in product liability, filed suit in December 1957 against the American Tobacco Company on behalf of Edwin M. Green. A navy veteran of World War II, Green had begun smoking in the 1920s at age 16 and continued the habit for 32 years until he was diagnosed with lung cancer. The American Tobacco Company manufactured Lucky Strike, the brand Green had smoked all those years. Although he died at age 49, only two months after the filing, the case continued on behalf of his survivors.

A flurry of lawsuits had followed the early publicity about the harm of smoking for lung cancer. The Surgeon General had not yet published his

1964 report on health and smoking, and warning labels were not yet required on cigarette packages. Yet enough information had emerged about the likely harm of cigarettes for smokers to seek redress for their injuries. Green's and other suits comprised a first wave of litigation over the harm of cigarettes.

Legal Issues

The court case revolved around the issues of implied warranty and negligence of the tobacco companies. The plaintiffs argued that by selling Lucky Strike to the public, the American Tobacco Company implied that the product was safe, and this warranty was breached when it turned out that cigarettes caused cancer. Cigarette manufacturers were thus liable for their negligence in selling a harmful product just like makers of a defective car were liable for the injury caused by the car. The defendants argued that no proof existed that cigarettes caused cancer. The defense acknowledged a statistical association, as smokers tended to die younger than nonsmokers, but argued that association does not prove causality. Many physicians and researchers, although well aware of the association, admitted that they did not understand the causes of cancer and testified for the defense. Also in favor of the defense, the nature of the harm of cigarettes differed from that of other products used in liability cases. The harm of a defective car brake on the driver who as a result crashes and dies is immediate and obvious, but the harm of cigarettes takes decades to emerge, and for many smokers does not emerge at all. To understand the connection between smoking and lung cancer, a jury would have to rely on the testimony of medical experts rather than their own perceptions.

The plaintiffs called as witnesses many of the pioneering researchers on the link between smoking and lung cancer, but the defense countered the testimony with its own experts. At this early date the plaintiffs had no incriminating documents from the tobacco industry to prove the manufacturers knew of the potential harm of smoking. To the contrary, tobacco industry representatives denied the validity of claims about the dangers of smoking.

Decision

Deliberating for 10 hours, the Florida jury concluded on August 2, 1960, that Edwin M. Green did indeed die of lung cancer caused by smoking Lucky Strikes but declined to award damages because they believed the American Tobacco Company did not and could not know of the harm of the cigarette in 1956 when Green learned he had lung cancer. They therefore concluded the company was not liable under laws of implied warranty. Neither the plaintiffs nor the defendants were happy with the decision.

Counsel for the tobacco company worried that the jury had, in concluding cigarettes caused the lung cancer of Green, come close to making a financial award. Hastings felt that it made no sense to hold the company accountable for the lung cancer but not to award damages on the basis of that accountability. The plaintiffs appealed the decision and gained a new trial, but the second jury in 1964 clearly sided with the defendants.

Impact

Along with similar verdicts in similar cases, the tobacco industry victory ended suits based on implied warranty and negligence. Reflecting the nature of the first wave of lawsuits against the tobacco industry, *Green* was about as close to a victory as any others at the time. In other similar trials such as *Lartigue v. Liggett and Myers* in Louisiana and *Ross v. Philip Morris* in Missouri, juries showed even stronger resistance to the claims of smokers. They tended to view smoking as a personal choice that did not implicate the manufacturers in ultimate health problems and death. Suits against the tobacco industry would have to employ other strategies.

CIPOLLONE V. LIGGETT GROUP, PHILIP MORRIS, AND LOEWS (1992)

Background

Marc Z. Edell, a lawyer involved in asbestos litigation, thought that the case law used by victims of asbestos products to sue the manufacturers might also apply to victims of tobacco products. He knew that tobacco companies had yet to pay a cent in damages but believed he could present a new legal strategy—one that differed from those used in the past and would have a better chance of success. With the support of his law firm, he sought a client who suffered from the ill effects of smoking and lived in New Jersey, the state where the case law seemed best for bringing the suit. He found a resident of Little Ferry, New Jersey, named Rose Cipollone who agreed to file suit.[8]

Cipollone was a 57-year-old smoker with lung cancer. Growing up in New York City, she had started smoking at age 16 because it looked cool and glamorous to her, and by 18 was smoking a pack a day. While married to Tony Cipollone, raising three children, and maintaining a household in New Jersey, she continued her habit, moving up to one and a half packs each day. She began with Chesterfield cigarettes, manufactured by Liggett and Myers (later the Liggett Group), but switched to the company's filtered L&M cigarettes in the hope that they would be milder and safer. She later switched to Philip Morris's Virginia Slims because she thought the style looked glamorous. Later still she changed to Lorillard's low-tar brand, True. During all the years of smoking, she worried about the health effects but could not bring herself to quit. In 1981 an X ray showed a lesion in her lung that upon biopsy proved to be a malignant growth. Despite two lung operations the cancer returned to her lungs by 1984 and soon spread to her brain and the rest of her body. At the time she met Marc Edell she was undergoing chemotherapy but was clearly dying. Alive to file the suit in 1983, she died on October 21, 1984.

The suit specified three defendants, the Liggett Group, Philip Morris, and Loews Corporation (owner of Lorillard), each a maker of cigarettes that Cipollone had smoked. The defendants employed top legal talent with much experience in tobacco litigation. Worried that any victory against them would open the floodgates to further suits, the tobacco industry was prepared to spend as much as necessary to win the suit (ultimately between $30–50 million, compared to the $2 million spent by Marc Edell's firm for the plaintiff). The defendants hoped to wear down the plaintiffs not only by outspending them but also by slowing the process with numerous objections and appeals, and by overwhelming them with documents. However, Edell and his staff progressed further than previous plaintiffs in countering this strategy. The case not only made it to trial but through several appeals before ending.

Legal Issues

The case for the plaintiff relied on changes in product liability laws that had occurred during the 1960s and 1970s. In the past, companies were responsible for damages incurred by users of a defective product, and courts required evidence of negligence on the part of the manufacturers to award damages. More recently, however, courts had come to accept claims that inherently dangerous products, even when not defective, could make the manufacturers liable for harm done to users. Under the new reasoning manufacturers who profited from risky products such as tall ladders and sharp tools should share the costs of the use of the risky product. In other words manufacturers should be strictly liable for their products. If extended to cigarettes, the logic of strict liability could result in damages to smokers dying of smoking-related illnesses. The plaintiff avoided the accusations of negligence or making a defective product but thought the tobacco companies might be liable for the inherent risks of cigarettes.

The fact that warnings had been placed on cigarette packages in 1965 might, however, remove the liability. If smokers knew of the risks they then shared fault in starting or continuing to smoke, and this absolved the manufacturers of liability. The plaintiffs would address this issue in their case against tobacco companies. They claimed that when Cipollone began smoking, she and most everyone else did not know of the full extent of the possible harm of cigarettes. By the time the risks became widely known and makers included warnings on the packages, she was too addicted to stop. Worse, if the tobacco companies themselves had known of the harm and addictiveness of their product, yet reassured the public that despite scientific studies their product was safe, they prevented Cipollone and others from making an informed choice about the product. The plaintiff argued that in trusting what the companies said, she had been deceived. Although she had a choice in smoking, she did not have an informed choice.

A key component of the case of the plaintiff involved showing that the tobacco makers knew of the harm of cigarettes and deceived the public by denying such harm. Edell and his staff thus devoted much effort to requesting and reviewing private documents of the tobacco companies. If he could find evidence that the companies had searched for a safe cigarette, it would imply that they knew of the harm of the product. Even worse for the tobacco companies, if they admitted in private that cigarettes were harmful, it would imply that their public claims were dishonest. For example, memoranda from the Philip Morris chief Helmut Wakeham urged the company to develop a "medically acceptable" cigarette and to stop denying the existence of persuasive evidence of the harm of cigarettes.

The tobacco lawyers presented several arguments in response. Only a statistical association existed between smoking and lung cancer, and scientists did not really know the causes of cancer. After all, many smokers never get lung cancer, and some nonsmokers get lung cancer. Moreover the type of lung cancer of Cipollone rarely occurs among smokers and did not fit the statistical association. No proof therefore existed that the manufacturer's products had caused the health problem.

Even if she had proof, the plaintiff knew of the risks, according to defense attorneys. Well before packages started to include warnings Cipollone had repeatedly received advice from family and friends to stop smoking; she had also adopted filtered cigarettes in the hope that they would not present the same health risks as unfiltered cigarettes. Had the warnings on cigarette packages begun earlier, she would have continued her habit, just as she did in the 1960s and 1970s, after the warnings were added. Cigarettes remained a legal product that contributed to the enjoyment of individuals, the finances of the government, and the growth of the economy. Whatever the risks associated with this beneficial product, individuals had the choice to smoke or not smoke, and Cipollone chose to smoke, argued the defense.

Attorneys for the tobacco companies presented one other legal issue that would cause dispute through the course of the trial and later appeals. The defense claimed that the 1965 and 1969 acts of Congress that required warning labels also blocked liability claims against cigarette manufacturers. The legislation prevented federal and state agencies from changing or adding to the warnings specified by Congress. While some claimed that this provision merely ensured the use of standardized warnings across all states, the tobacco industry had another interpretation. It argued that liability awards involved a form of state regulation that negated the warnings placed on packages by Congress and therefore violated congressional intent.

Decision

Before giving the case to the jury for a decision the presiding judge of the New Jersey federal court, H. Lee Sarokin, ruled on the claim of the tobacco lawyers that congressional legislation prohibited liability suits. He rejected the claim, noting that if Congress wanted to do this it would have stated explicitly that the law would prevent later tort claims. However, an appeals court reversed Sarokin's decision and required the judge to allow the defendants to include this argument in their case. This had the effect of preventing the plaintiffs from introducing evidence of the dishonesty of tobacco companies after the 1965 warnings and during the last 18 years of Cipollone's life.

The 1988 decision of the six-person jury, handed down four years after the death of Cipollone, appeared on first look as a loss for the tobacco industry. The jury awarded $400,000 to Cipollone's husband, Tony, making this the first case ever in which the tobacco companies had to pay damages. Immediate news reports highlighted this aspect of the decision, but in all other ways the tobacco companies came out victors.

The jury had in fact made no award to Cipollone through her survivors. It had concluded that Philip Morris and Lorillard had no responsibility for her death because Cipollone did not start smoking their cigarettes until after the 1965 warnings. They held the Liggett Group partly responsible (20 percent) for Cipollone's death because she smoked their cigarettes before 1966, but most of the responsibility fell on the plaintiff herself. Since the law allowed damages only when a manufacturer was more than 50 percent responsible for the harm, no award could be given to the plaintiff. The jury awarded the husband $400,000, but this made little sense when the victim of the lung cancer received nothing.

Both the Liggett Group and Edell on behalf of Cipollone's survivors appealed the decision. The Liggett Group claimed it could not be liable for $400,000 to the husband if it was not liable for the death of his wife. Edell appealed Judge Sarokin's decision to prohibit evidence concerning tobacco industry behavior after 1965. After a complex appeals process the case ultimately ended up with the U.S. Supreme Court. In a 1992 decision of 7-2, the Court held for the tobacco companies in determining that a damage award based on actions after 1965 would frustrate Congress's efforts to establish a single nationwide standard of warning. They did allow for Edell to bring suit on other grounds, but both Edell's law firm and Cipollone's survivors had neither the resources nor the will to try again—the odds of success seemed too low to continue.

Impact

Cipollone v. Liggett Group, Philip Morris, and Loews ultimately gave a victory to the tobacco companies. The strict liability arguments offered by the plaintiff failed, as had earlier implied warranty and negligence arguments, to supply a satisfactory basis for receiving damages. With the Supreme Court's decision, the tobacco companies had maintained their perfect record of never paying out damages. However, the case's relatively close brush with triumph, particularly given the imbalance of the resources in favor of the tobacco companies, would embolden others to continue the efforts to sue the companies. If one lawyer with a few staff members and a 57-year-old working-class woman could nearly defeat three rich and powerful tobacco companies, then some shifts in strategy might do better in years to come. Plaintiffs would need to find some argument to overcome the tendency of juries to hold smokers largely responsible for their behavior, but solutions would come soon. The case represented the end of a second wave of lawsuits based on strict liability and the beginning of a third wave that, with new legal arguments, would prove more successful for plaintiffs.

ENGLE V. R. J. REYNOLDS TOBACCO CO. (1994)

Background

The first certified class-action suit to reach a jury began in 1994 with a case filed by a Miami lawyer, Stanley M. Rosenblatt, on behalf of Howard A. Engle, a retired pediatrician who had smoked for 50 years and had asthma and emphysema. More important, the Dade County circuit court judge in the case, Harold Solomon, allowed the case to proceed as a class-action suit on behalf of all smokers in the nation injured by the tobacco companies. The plaintiffs requested $200 billion in compensatory and punitive damages on the grounds that the tobacco companies had manipulated nicotine levels in cigarettes with the goal of addicting its customers, fraudulently misrepresented the nature of their product to the public, and caused harm from tobacco-related diseases and the consequent emotional distress.

The use of a class-action suit differed from previous individual suits. A class action has the goal of simplifying trials for a large number of suits by allowing one or more plaintiffs to bring legal action on behalf of themselves and other persons having an identical interest in an alleged wrong. Four conditions must hold to certify a suit as a class action. First, the large number of members of the class must make separate trials impractical. Second, the claims of the members of the class must relate to the same legal question. Third, the claims of the members of the class must be similar enough that the decision in a single trial can resolve the claims. Fourth, the representatives and the attorneys for the class must be able to fairly represent the interests of all class members. In the end these conditions required that a class-action suit include only the issues common to all members of the class.

Such requirements presented a difficult standard for smokers and their attorneys to meet. In another class-action suit against tobacco companies, *Castano v. American Tobacco* (1995) which was filed in Louisiana on behalf of smokers nationwide, the appeal's court determined that the interests of smokers across the 50 states were too diverse to define a single class. The coalition of lawyers behind *Castano* then filed separate state-based class-action suits. However, at the time of the *Engle* trial, no class-action suit had yet gained certification.

Legal Issues

Worried that class-action suits represented a greater threat than individual suits because they raised the potential costs to the tobacco industry and the ability to share resources among plaintiffs, lawyers for the tobacco companies opposed certification of the class in the *Engle* case. They immediately appealed Judge Solomon's decision to certify a nationwide class, arguing as in *Castano* that the interests of the class were too diverse to include together. Even if all members had suffered from the use of cigarettes, their conditions would differ enough that the court would find it impossible to award damages to the class as a whole. Would someone with a cough get the same as someone with lung cancer? Would someone made sick by cigarettes get the same as someone killed by cigarettes? From the view of the defendants, then, a class-action suit would prevent the fair awarding of damages and should instead take the form of individual suits for individual injuries.

Beyond issues specific to class-action certification, the suit involved legal issues similar to other third-wave cases. Issues of the harm of cigarettes for health remained central, but the issues of the addictiveness of nicotine in cigarettes and the alleged conspiracy of tobacco companies to mislead the public about its product took on more importance.

Decision

A Florida state judicial panel unanimously ruled in the appeal made of the class certification that the *Engle* suit could go to trial as a class-action suit. However, the court also ruled that diverse state laws made the nationwide class inappropriate, and only the 500,000 smokers in Florida could serve as a class. The decision thus reduced the size of the class but kept it large enough to seriously hurt the tobacco companies if a jury verdict ruled against them. After some confusing appeals court decisions,[10] the Supreme Court of Florida allowed the procedure developed for the trial—namely, to make a lump-sum punitive damage award—to go forward.

The decision from the trial itself came in three parts. In the first phase of the trial the six-person jury concluded in 1999 in favor of the plaintiffs that the tobacco companies were liable. They agreed that cigarettes not only caused disease and death, addicted smokers, and created an unreasonable danger, but also that the tobacco industry conspired to conceal information about health effects and the addictiveness of cigarettes, failed to exercise the care required in manufacturing products, and engaged in extreme and outrageous conduct. Despite testimony from tobacco executives in the case noting that they had changed their behavior with the settlements they made with states to pay for health care costs and to reduce youth smoking, the jury sided with the plaintiffs in holding the companies accountable for the damages their product caused.

In the second phase of the trial the jury considered damages for three representative class illnesses. It assessed compensatory damages of $2.8 million to one class member, $5.8 million to another, and $4.0 million to a third. These amounts would serve as guidelines for determining damages for the full class of Florida smokers.

In the third phase the jury decided that the tobacco companies should pay $144.8 billion (less than the $200 billion initially requested by the plaintiffs, but an amount to be shared by a smaller class). The award would be split among Florida smokers who could prove injury. If all 500,000 class members received money, the award would provide about $290,000 for each.

The plaintiffs demanded immediate payment of the award, but the defendants noted that it would take several years of appeals before the courts could reach a final verdict. Based on a controversial Florida state law passed during the *Engle* trial, the tobacco companies did not have to pay damages while awaiting a decision under appeal. Still, legal wrangling led some of the companies to post a $2 billion bond and pay $709 million regardless of the outcome of the case. In the meantime, appeals continue to work their way through the court system and may well end up in the U.S. Supreme Court.

Impact

Engle v. R. J. Reynolds to date represents a stunning win for smokers against the tobacco companies. Its importance comes not only from the huge size of the award. It also comes from its standing as the first certified class-action suit against tobacco companies and as one of the first suits in which the jury held tobacco companies liable for the damage caused by their product. Using the issue of addiction of nicotine and misrepresentation by the tobacco industry, the plaintiffs won huge damages. The verdict and the amount of the award represent a major threat to the tobacco industry.

Although some antismoking activists hope that the *Engle* decision and others like it put the tobacco companies out of business, the impact of huge awards such as this one will likely have other consequences. The awards will force the tobacco companies to raise prices—in essence taxing the company for the harm it has done—and thereby, arguably, will reduce smoking in the population. For many this appears as the optimal outcome. Outlawing cigarettes would not work because the addictive qualities of the product would leave nearly 50 million smokers to suffer through withdrawal symptoms and would lead smokers to obtain cigarettes illegally. Putting U.S. tobacco companies out of business would simply allow foreign companies or newly formed American companies to fill the demand for cigarettes; these companies would not face the liability that current companies face over the cigarettes they manufactured in the past. In the end using class-action suits to raise the cost of doing business for existing cigarette manufacturers seems, according to tobacco foes, the best approach to take in controlling the industry.

CARTER V. BROWN AND WILLIAMSON (1996)

Background

After *Cipollone*, the second case leading to an award against tobacco companies helped define a third wave of tobacco litigation incorporating new strategies. Grady Carter, a 66-year-old retired air traffic controller living in Florida, had started smoking Lucky Strike cigarettes in 1947, had switched brands in 1972, and continued the habit until his diagnosis of lung cancer in 1991. He had tried hard to quit but felt hooked by the habit. Upon hearing claims made in 1994 by tobacco company executives that cigarettes were not addictive, he decided to sue. In the suit he and his wife named Brown and Williamson, the maker of Lucky Strike cigarettes, as defendants and requested $1.5 million in damages. Represented by Jacksonville, Florida, lawyer Norwood S. Wilner, who would file hundreds of lawsuits against tobacco companies over the years, they claimed the company was liable because it knew of the harm of cigarettes but did not warn consumers until required to do so by the government.

A key difference between this case and previous ones related to the public release of internal documents from Brown and Williamson that the plaintiff's lawyers could use in the trial. In the past the discovery process compelled plaintiff attorneys to go through the time-consuming process of requesting and reviewing tobacco company documents, a process hindered whenever possible by the companies. However, copies of such documents came from Merrill Williams, a paralegal at a Louisville, Kentucky, law firm. He came across Brown and Williamson documents indicating that tobacco company executives had knowledge of the harm of tobacco products. He made copies of the documents and contacted a lawyer in Mississippi, Richard F. Scruggs, who was suing tobacco companies. A professor at the University of California and zealous antitobacco advocate, Sheldon Glantz, also received copies in the mail of 4,000 pages of the documents from an unknown source. The documents eventually made their way to Congress and appeared on the Internet. A judge then ruled that the documents had become part of the public domain and could be used by plaintiffs in cases such as the Carters' against Brown and Williamson.

Legal Issues

Florida law had some advantages for the plaintiff and made the state a useful place to bring suit. It allowed a damage award even when the plaintiff had major responsibility for the injury. Unlike in New Jersey where an award could be made only if the defendant was at least 50 percent responsible, a Florida plaintiff could receive an award if the defendant was less than 50 percent responsible. This moved legal issues away from whether the smoker, Grady Carter, held primary responsibility for his habit—he would admit that he did. Rather it focused on whether the tobacco industry was also partly responsible.

The legal issues concerned the knowledge Brown and Williamson had of the harm of cigarettes, and the fraud and misrepresentation that occurred when the company refused to admit the harm. Unlike previous cases the plaintiffs did not claim that the company was liable because of the nature of its product but because it misled users about that nature. The plaintiffs presented newly released documents that demonstrated knowledge of the addictiveness of nicotine and the risks of smoking for health that dated back to years before cigarette packs added warnings. For example, one document dated July 17, 1963, from the chief legal counsel for Brown and Williamson stated that "we are, then, in the business of selling nicotine, an additive drug effective in the release of stress mechanisms."[9] Yet the companies did not inform the public of this fact or distribute a safer, less addictive cigarette when it would have benefited the public.

Brown and Williamson responded that the responsibility for the decision to smoke fell on the individual, particularly when cigarette packages had included warning labels for some 30 years. The labels absolved the company of liability for the hazards of smoking. Moreover the defendant claimed that the cigarettes manufactured and sold by the company provided just what smokers wanted.

Decision

Siding with the plaintiff, the Jacksonville, Florida, jury awarded $750,000 to the Carters in 1996. Jurors commented that the tobacco company's dishonesty bothered them, and they wanted to send a message that such dishonesty would no longer be tolerated. The decision represented a major defeat for the tobacco company. However, a Florida appeals court overturned the verdict on an issue unrelated to the culpability of the tobacco industry. The higher court ruled that Carter in waiting for some time after the diagnosis of lung cancer to file the lawsuit, exceeded the four-year statute of limitations for such cases.

Impact

The victory against the tobacco industry in *Carter*, even though a statute of limitations violation overturned the verdict, presented a strategy for success that would guide hundreds, even thousands of lawsuits in the years to come. Taking an approach that differed from previous cases, including the *Green* and *Cipollone* cases, the *Carter* case suggested that juries would respond more favorably to arguments about the deception of tobacco companies than they would to arguments about the harm of smoking by itself. The strategy would not invariably bring victory, as it failed in some other cases. For example, in another case brought by Norwood S. Wilner, the jury rejected the claims for damages of Jean Connor against R. J. Reynolds. She had died at age 49 of lung cancer in 1995 after having smoked Winston and Salem cigarettes for most of her adult life. Despite arguments of Connor's attorneys that tobacco companies had deceived and addicted her, the jury sided with the defendants because the plaintiff had given up smoking several years before getting lung cancer. Juries would consider the facts at hand carefully before siding with the plaintiffs against the tobacco companies. Still *Carter v. Brown and Williamson* set a precedent that would have much importance for future cases against the tobacco companies.

BROWN AND WILLIAMSON TOBACCO CORP. V. U.S. FOOD AND DRUG ADMINISTRATION (2000)

Background

In 1994 Dr. David A. Kessler, the head of the Food and Drug Administration (FDA) as appointed by President Bill Clinton, suggested in a letter to the Coalition on Smoking OR Health that the FDA might have jurisdiction over tobacco. The coalition then formally petitioned the FDA to declare all cigarettes a drug under the Federal Food, Drug, and Cosmetic Act. The wording in the act defined a drug as a product that manufacturers intended to affect the structure or function of the body. Congress had not explicitly intended to include tobacco under this definition, and the FDA had previously claimed it had no authority over tobacco. However, Kessler thought he had new reasons to change the agency's approach to regulating cigarette products.

Several key points of evidence demonstrated the druglike pharmacological and physiological effects of smoking. First, the addictiveness of nicotine made smokers use cigarettes primarily as a nicotine delivery system. The need for smokers to replace dwindling levels of nicotine in their body by lighting another cigarette demonstrates that the product affects the functioning of the body. Indeed, the FDA regulated nicotine gum and patches as drug delivery systems, and cigarettes differed from these products (besides presenting greater health dangers) largely in the way the nicotine gets into the body. Second, the manufacturers knew that cigarettes were addictive. They had supported research on the nicotine levels in their cigarettes and manipulated the level of nicotine in their products by developing strains of tobacco with high levels of the chemical and by including additives such as ammonia that boosted the efficiency of the delivery of nicotine. Tobacco company executives had testified in Congress that they did not believe cigarettes were addictive, but new documents from the internal files of tobacco companies contradicted their contention. Third, advertising highlighted the nicotine benefits of cigarettes by using code words such as *satisfaction*, *strength*, and *impact*. Appealing to youth with misleading images of health and activity, cigarette ads would contribute to a lifelong addiction to the product.

On August 10, 1995, the FDA announced the results of its investigation of whether nicotine in cigarettes fit the definition of a drug and needed regulation. Concluding that it did, the FDA proposed to oversee the sale and distribution of cigarettes and smokeless tobacco, particularly in regard to underage buyers. After undergoing some revisions in response to public comment the proposed regulations required tobacco companies to support tobacco prevention education for children, take actions to ensure underage youth would not have access to cigarettes through vending machines or other unsupervised sales, ban gift or promotional items bearing cigarette brand names, eliminate outdoor advertising near schools, and limit advertising in publications with more than 15 percent of the readership under age 18. President Clinton announced the publication of the final FDA rules on August 23, 1996.

The Law and the Tobacco Industry and Smoking

Tobacco companies filed numerous suits against the FDA. In one major suit heard in federal court in Greensboro, North Carolina, the plaintiffs included the major tobacco companies (Brown and Williamson, Liggett Tobacco, Lorillard, Philip Morris, and R. J. Reynolds), a smokeless tobacco company (United States Tobacco), parts of the advertising industry concerned about restrictions on advertising and free speech, and trade groups representing convenience stores that would have to follow new rules in selling cigarettes.

Legal Issues

The legal issues involved whether the Federal Drug and Cosmetic Act passed by Congress applied to cigarettes. The plaintiffs claimed that cigarettes were not drugs or devices, that congressional legislation did not give the FDA authority to regulate tobacco, and that the agency had exceeded its authority in the regulations. They also claimed that the restrictions on advertising violated First Amendment rights to free speech. In defense of the regulations the government asserted that the evidence used by the FDA to declare cigarettes a drug-delivery system met the definition of a drug in the congressional legislation.

Decision

The initial decision in April 1997 from the federal court in Greensboro agreed that the FDA had regulative authority but limited the actions the agency could take. In favor of the FDA the decision supported the claim that tobacco fit the legal definition of a drug or drug-delivery device but did not find the justification for all the regulatory proposals to be convincing. The court put a stay on all regulations except those prohibiting sales to minors and requiring proof of age with a photo ID for purchasing cigarettes. It concluded that in doing more than restricting sales to minors, the agency had exceeded its jurisdiction. The FDA did not have the authority to restrict advertising or promotion of the product.

When appealed by both sides to the United States Court of Appeals for the Fourth Circuit, in Richmond, Virginia, the initial decision was overturned in 1998 in a 2-1 decision. The court ruled that the interpretation of the FDA might fit the specific congressional wording but ignored the history of the legislation, which provided no evidence of the intent of Congress to treat cigarettes as a drug. Having lost this round, the government appealed to the U.S. Supreme Court. On March 21, 2000, the Supreme Court by a 5-4 vote affirmed the decision of the appeal's court. While recognizing the case made concerning the harm of tobacco, the majority in a decision written by Judge Sandra Day O'Connor concluded that Congress never intended its act to apply to tobacco. It had instead set up its own special regulatory scheme for tobacco rather than give authority for regulation to the FDA. As a result the FDA could not enforce its regulations and had to drop even the requirements concerning sales to minors.

Impact

The importance of the court case against the FDA comes not from blocking the proposed regulations. States implemented most of those anyway with the Master Settlement Agreement. Rather, it comes from the inability of the executive branch to take action on its own to control tobacco. The decision meant regulation of tobacco must come from specific legislative action by Congress. With Congress unwilling or unable to agree on such legislation, and executive branch agencies barred from imposing their own regulations, actions to control tobacco would have to come from litigation and the judicial branch. The decision thereby accelerated the trend of using lawsuits to deal with a contentious issue left unresolved by legislation. Individuals, trial lawyers, judges, and jurors rather than elected legislators and government officials have largely taken over the task of regulating the tobacco industry, and the reliance on litigation rather than legislation continues.

FRENCH V. PHILIP MORRIS (2002)

Background

The tobacco companies' first defeat in a suit involving secondhand smoke came in June 2002. Lynn French had served as a flight attendant since 1976 for TWA on both domestic and international flights. Since the U.S. government did not ban smoking on domestic flights less than six hours until 1990, she was exposed to environmental tobacco smoke on her job for 14 years, which resulted in chronic sinus problems, according to her complaint. She sought damages of $980,000 from the major tobacco companies in a case heard in the Florida circuit court.

The suit was brought under an agreement stemming from a 1991 class-action suit brought on behalf of nonsmoking flight attendants by Stanley M. Rosenblatt in *Broin v. Philip Morris*. As with the other 8,000 flight attendants who had chosen to be included in the suit, Norma Broin, a nonsmoker who developed lung cancer after 13 years as a flight attendant, claimed she was the victim of secondhand tobacco smoke. The lawyers in the *Broin* suit negotiated an agreement in which the tobacco companies donated $300 million for research on smoking-related diseases in Norma Broin's name, and Rosenblatt and his wife received $49 million. The flight attendants received no damages but obtained the right to bring suit to recover individual compensatory (not punitive) damages. Under this agreement French (and eventually 2,800 other flight attendants) brought suit.

The Law and the Tobacco Industry and Smoking

Legal Issues

As a nonsmoker, French did not have to face the problem of most smokers in suits against the tobacco companies. Since the plaintiff had never made the decision to smoke, the tobacco companies could not claim she had individual responsibility for her use of cigarettes. Moreover she could not have known of the risks she faced from secondhand smoke since neither the tobacco companies nor the Surgeon General had provided such warnings. In the defendants' favor the evidence of the harm of secondhand smoke was not as strong as for direct smoking, and the class-action issues in the case were complex. Several previous efforts to sue tobacco companies had failed on these grounds.

The judge in the case, Robert P. Kaye, had overseen the earlier settlement agreement and used the settlement to justify a different criterion than usual to determine product liability. Over the objections of tobacco company lawyers he relieved the flight attendant of the burden of proving that cigarettes and secondhand smoke caused her health problems. The defense presented testimony that the sinus problems experienced by French were more commonly caused by bacteria and allergies than by secondhand smoke. However, the jury could presume under the settlement, according to Judge Kaye, that secondhand smoke can cause debilitating illness. The tobacco lawyers argued that in making $300 million available for research on diseases suffered by flight attendants, they never admitted that environmental tobacco smoke could cause health problems.

Decision

The six-person Miami jury awarded French $5.5 million in compensatory damages—more than five times as much as requested in the suit. The jury gave $2 million for injuries suffered in the past and $3.5 million for injuries she would suffer in the future. However, a Miami-Dade circuit judge reduced the award to $500,000 three months later in September 2002. The judge called the original amount "shocking," noting that French appeared composed and in no physical distress and had shown little evidence that her sinus problems significantly restricted her activities as a flight attendant, wife, and mother. Tobacco company lawyers viewed the ruling as justification for further appeals to overturn the decision altogether.

Impact

As the first defeat for the tobacco companies in a secondhand smoke case, *French v. Philip Morris* could have a potentially great impact on future cases. With thousands of other suits by flight attendants pending the precedent of the award to French, even after being reduced by Judge Smith, would open

101

up tobacco companies to liability to nonsmokers as well as smokers. The tobacco companies will fight the decision and perhaps even try to overturn the original Broin agreement in order to avoid such liability.

[1] U.S. Department of Health and Human Services. *Reducing Tobacco Use. A Report of the Surgeon General.* Washington, D.C.: U.S. Department of Health and Human Services, 2000, p. 164.

[2] Jacob Sullum. *For Your Own Good: The Anti-Smoking Crusade and the Tyranny of Public Health*, New York: Free Press, 1998, p. 88.

[3] Kenneth E. Warner. "Clearing the Airwaves: The Cigarette Ad Ban Revisited." *Policy Analysis*, vol. 5 (Fall 1979): 435–450.

[4] Elizabeth Whelan. *A Smoking Gun: How the Tobacco Industry Gets Away with Murder.* Philadelphia: George F. Stickley, 1984, p. 130.

[5] M. L. Myers, C. Iscoe, C. Jennings, W. Lenox, and E. Sacks. *A Staff Report on the Cigarette Advertising Investigation.* Washington, D.C.: Federal Trade Commission, 1981, pp. 229–239.

[6] W. Kip Viscusi. *Smoke-Filled Rooms: A Postmortem on the Tobacco Deal.* Chicago: University of Chicago Press, 2002, pp. 1–10.

[7] U.S. Department of Health and Human Services. *Reducing Tobacco Use*, p. 208.

[8] Alan Kluger. *Ashes to Ashes: America's Hundred-Year Cigarette War, the Public Health, and the Unabashed Triumph of Philip Morris.* New York: Alfred A. Knopf, 1996, pp. 639–677.

[9] Court TV Case Files. *"Carter v. Williamson."* Available online, URL: http://courttv.com/casefiles/verdits/carter.html, posted December 26, 2002.

[10] Brian H. Barr. *"Engle v. R. J. Reynolds:* The Improper Assessment of Punitive Damages for an Entire Class of Injured Smokers." *Florida State University Law Review*, vol. 28 (Spring 2001): 809–810.

CHAPTER 3

CHRONOLOGY

This chapter presents a chronology of important events relating to the tobacco industry and smoking. Tobacco has a long history, but the chronology focuses in particular on events of the last 40 years—those beginning with the report of the Surgeon General on health and smoking, leading to the development of antismoking laws and regulations, and ending with the legal battles against the tobacco industry. Unless otherwise stated the listed events occurred in the United States.

5000–3000 B.C.

■ Tobacco is first cultivated in the Andes Mountains in South America in current-day Peru and Ecuador.

A.D. 1492

■ Sailors on the first expedition of Christopher Columbus are the first Europeans to smoke tobacco, sharing a pipe with local Indians on the modern-day island of Cuba. Columbus returns to Spain with only a few tobacco seeds and leaves, but stories of smoking intrigue many in Europe.

1550s

■ Tobacco is grown in Portuguese and Spanish palace gardens for its beauty and ease of growth but is also studied and nurtured by physicians who suspect that it has medicinal properties.

1560

■ Jean Nicot, the French ambassador to Portugal, experiments with tobacco as a medicine and claims in a letter to the queen of France that it has curative powers.

Tobacco Industry and Smoking

1565

- Nicolás Monardes, a physician in Seville, Spain, authors a pamphlet called *Joyful News of Our Newe Founde Worlde* that lauds the wonderful healing properties of tobacco. He claims that smoking cleanses the brain and cures among other things bad breath, kidney stones, and wounds from poison arrows.
- Naval commander John Hawkins and his crew bring tobacco from the West Indies to England, but few besides sailors use the product.

1586

- Walter Raleigh returns to England from an expedition to Virginia, where he became a habitual smoker. He brings with him American Indians who can cultivate tobacco and prepare it for smoking. Raleigh enthusiastically advocates use of the product, and tobacco use spreads quickly throughout England.

1595

- The first English-language book on tobacco, *Tabacco*, is published.

1600

- Walter Raleigh persuades Queen Elizabeth I to take a puff of tobacco smoke.

1604

- Newly crowned king of Great Britain James I publishes a pamphlet entitled *Counterblaste to Tobacco* that decries the habit as filthy, harmful, and addictive. In part motivated by his dislike of Walter Raleigh, King James nonetheless uses his views on tobacco as justification for taxing imports of the product.

1612

- John Rolfe, an English settler in Jamestown, Virginia (who later married the Wampanoag princess Pocahontas), plants tobacco, which will become the major crop of the new settlement. The following year he sends the first shipment of the product to England.

1632

- Less enthused about tobacco than colonists in Virginia, the Massachusetts Bay colony, established by Puritans, bans tobacco sales and public smoking.

Chronology

1676

- Angered by the heavy taxes placed on tobacco by the Virginia governor as well as a number of other issues, planter Nathaniel Bacon leads a brief rebellion against colonial administrators.

1700

- Tobacco exports from Virginia reach 38 million pounds. During this period tobacco can be used as currency and to pay salaries.

1713

- An Italian physician, Bernardino Ramazzini, notes that tobacco workers suffer from headaches and stomach troubles because of the tobacco dust they breathe.

1727

- Tobacco notes that attest to the quality and quantity of the product stored in warehouses become legal tender in Virginia.

1753

- Swedish botanist Carolus Linnaeus gives the name *Nicotiana tabacum* to the tobacco plant commonly smoked in Europe.

1761

- English physician Dr. John Hill cautions against the immoderate use of snuff, noting for the first time in a published document that tobacco can cause cancer.

1762

- General Israel Putnum introduces imported cigars from Cuba to the United States.

1776

- Benjamin Franklin uses tobacco as collateral when he obtains loans from France to support the American Revolution's war effort.

1789

- The French Revolution makes the tobacco habits of the aristocrats—snuff and pipes—unfashionable. Many Frenchmen attempt to identify with the working class by smoking cigarettes, a cheaper and smaller product used by those with little money.

1794

- U.S. Congress passes the first excise tax on tobacco products.

1798

- Dr. Benjamin Rush, a signer of the Declaration of Independence, writes an essay claiming that tobacco causes disastrous effects on the stomach, nerves, and mouth. He also suggests that tobacco use leads to drunkenness.

1809

- French scientist Louis-Nicolas Vanquelin isolates nicotine from tobacco smoke.

1829

- A pipe smoker, Rachel Jackson dies soon after her husband, Andrew, is elected president.

1839

- The discovery of a new way of curing the bright tobacco leaf with heat from charcoal produces a particularly mild and pleasant flavor when the tobacco is chewed or smoked.

1848

- The founder of the Seventh-Day Adventists, Ellen Gould Harmon White, comes to see abstaining from tobacco (and coffee and tea) as a crucial part of healthful living. Opposition to tobacco later becomes a central tenet of the Adventist religion.

1849

- The American Anti-Tobacco Society is founded.
- American doctor Joel Shew publishes a book, *Tobacco: Its History, Nature, and Effects on the Body and Mind,* in which he notes that cancers and tumors occur more commonly among men than women. Since men smoke more than women, he infers that smoking may be the cause.

1857

- George Trask begins publishing the *Anti-Tobacco Journal* in Fitchburg, Massachusetts.

- The prestigious British medical journal *Lancet* publishes a series of articles that debate the medical risks of tobacco but fails to offer a clear statement of the harm of smoking.

1863

- Cigarette tobacco is used by soldiers fighting for the North and the South, and returning Union soldiers popularize cigarette smoking in northern U.S. cities.

1864

- President Abraham Lincoln signs a bill that places a tax of $1 per thousand on all manufactured cigarettes. With limited production of cigarettes in the United States, the tax applies largely to foreign imports.

1866

- George Webb, an Ohio farmer, develops a new tobacco leaf product called white burley that turns out to have an unusual ability to absorb other flavors and additives. Used initially in chewing tobacco, it becomes a popular type of tobacco for cigarettes.

1868

- F. S. Kinney begins to sell prerolled cigarettes in New York City.

1874

- James Buchanan Duke, soon to dominate the tobacco industry, joins his father and brother in founding a tobacco firm, W. Duke and Sons.

1875

- Lewis Ginter, the first major figure in the business of cigarette production, begins producing cigarettes in Richmond, Virginia. Among the first to add flavors to cigarettes, he would become dominant in the production, marketing, and sale of cigarettes in the decades to come.

1878

- Manufacturers begin including trading cards in their cigarette packages, and in the years to come these cards will include pictures.

Tobacco Industry and Smoking

1880

- Figures show consumption of large cigars to have reached 47.1 per person, while consumption of cigarettes equals only 8.2 per person.

1881

- James Albert Bonsack invents and patents a cigarette-rolling machine that can produce 40 times as many cigarettes as a skilled production worker who rolls by hand.

1883

- To advocate its opposition to the use of tobacco, as well as alcohol, the National Women's Christian Temperance Union establishes the Department for Overthrow of the Tobacco Habit (renamed the Department of Narcotics in 1885).
- After reaching a peak of $5 per thousand, taxes on cigarettes fall to 50¢ per thousand. The change reduces the price and helps increase the popularity of cigarettes.

1884

- James Buchanan Duke installs two Bonsack machines in his cigarette factory, thereby increasing production without raising costs and gaining a substantial advantage over his competitors. He soon arranges a leasing agreement with James Bonsack to use more machines to manufacture his cigarettes.

1885

- An inveterate cigar smoker, former president Ulysses S. Grant dies of throat cancer. Upon discovering the cancer in 1884, doctors encouraged Grant to limit his smoking to three cigars a day.

1890

- Following a price war stimulated by the increasing use of cigarette manufacturing machines to lower production costs, Duke merges several competitors with his business to form the American Tobacco Company and monopolizes cigarette sales and production.

1893

- Attempting to monopolize sales of chewing tobacco as well as cigarettes, Duke buys several chew producers, forms the National Tobacco Works, cuts prices, and invites other producers to joint his company. Most companies agree to join, further increasing Duke's power in the tobacco industry.

1895

- North Dakota becomes the first state to prohibit cigarette smoking by youth and adults. Many other states follow in the next five years with anticigarette legislation.

1896

- The Diamond match company begins freely distributing small matchbooks with paper rather than wood matches. The matchbooks allow for advertising on the outside and prove popular with cigarette smokers, who do not need to hold the flame as long as cigar and pipe smokers.

1899

- Lucy Page Gaston, who will become the nation's leading antismoking advocate, sets up the Chicago Anti-Cigarette League (changed to the National Anti-Cigarette League in 1901 and the Anti-Cigarette League of America in 1911).

1902

- A British cigarette manufacturer, Philip Morris, opens a small office in New York City. It will in the next century become the largest and most powerful U.S. tobacco company.

1904

- A woman is arrested for smoking in a car on Fifth Avenue in New York City.

1909

- Dr. Charles Pease succeeds in getting smoking banned in New York City subways.
- Responding to the failure of laws to stop its citizens from smoking, Indiana becomes the first state to repeal cigarette prohibition. Antismoking advocates aim to use education and persuasion in the absence of legislation and prohibition.

1911

- The U.S. Supreme Court affirms use of the Sherman Anti-Trust Act by the Justice Department to dissolve the American Tobacco Company and

Duke's trust. The breakup results in four smaller firms—Liggett and Myers, Reynolds, Lorillard, and American—that will dominate cigarette production and sales for the following decades.

1912

- Liggett and Myers Tobacco Company introduces Chesterfield cigarettes, which use a mixture of American white burley and foreign leaf. Emphasizing its Turkish blend of tobacco and its English name, the company makes the new brand a top seller.

1913

- Richard J. Reynolds introduces Camel cigarettes. Although as cheap as other American cigarettes, Camels have a premium Turkish flavor based on a blend of American and foreign tobaccos. An extensive and intriguing advertising campaign helps make the cigarette a top-selling brand.

1916

- Duke's successors at American Tobacco introduce Lucky Strike cigarettes, whose tobacco is promoted with the slogan "It's Toasted." The cigarette is an instant success and along with Chesterfields and Camels dominates cigarette sales in the United States.

1917

- Despite the introduction of new cigarette brands, cigars still remain popular enough that production passes a new record. More than cigarettes, cigars are viewed as a stylish, leisurely form of smoke that appeals to affluent men.

1918

- Cigarettes are among the rations of U.S. soldiers fighting in Europe in World War I. Charitable organizations such as the International Red Cross and the Young Men's Christian Association (YMCA) send cigarettes to soldiers as a way to support the war effort. Many soldiers return to the states after the war with an attachment to cigarettes and support efforts to repeal anticigarette laws.
- Murad brand cigarettes build on feelings of patriotism in an advertisement that, under the drawing of a soldier with a cigarette, has the caption "Murad—After the Battle, the Most Refreshing Smoke is Murad."

Chronology

1919

■ To promote its Helmar brand of cigarettes, Lorillard becomes the first company to picture a woman in a cigarette advertisement. In the ad the woman is seen holding but not smoking a cigarette.

1920

■ Lucy Page Gaston announces she will run for the Republican presidential nomination on an antitobacco platform.

1922

■ Michigan State Normal College expels an 18-year-old woman for smoking cigarettes, a decision later upheld by the Michigan supreme court.

1924

■ *Reader's Digest* publishes the article "Does Tobacco Injure the Human Body?"

1926

■ In a Liggett and Myers ad for Chesterfield cigarettes, a young woman provocatively asks her male companion to blow some smoke her way.

1927

■ Aiming to appeal to a female audience, an ad from Philip Morris claims its new Marlboro cigarettes are "as Mild as May."
■ In response to the growing use of cigarettes and steady repeal of state laws prohibiting cigarettes, the Department of Narcotics of the Women's Christian Temperance Union sponsors thousands of antismoking events.
■ An ad from the American Tobacco Company claims that according to a survey of 20,679 physicians, Lucky Strikes are less irritating to the throat than other cigarettes.

1928

■ Lucky Strike, cigarettes are advertised with a picture of a women and the slogan "Reach for a Lucky Instead of a Sweet."

1930

■ The *Journal of the American Medical Association (JAMA)* criticizes health claims made for cigarettes in advertisements.

Tobacco Industry and Smoking

1933

- To save tobacco farmers from ruin the Agricultural Adjustment Act limits tobacco production, offers government loans, and develops price supports.

1936

- Brown and Williamson introduces Viceroy filter-tip cigarettes but has little success with the new product. It will become popular in the 1950s as information on the negative effects of tobacco tar on health begins to emerge.

1938

- Raymond Pearl publishes an article in the prestigious scientific journal *Science* that is one of the first to show an association between cigarette smoking and a shorter life.

1941

- A jury finds the American Tobacco Company, Liggett and Myers, and R. J. Reynolds guilty under the Sherman Anti-Trust Act of conspiring to fix prices and create a monopoly. After the Supreme Court upholds the verdict, the companies pay a fine totaling $250,000.

1942

- Claiming that the green pigment used in its packaging is needed for the war effort, American Tobacco changes its Lucky Strike package to white. The cigarette successfully uses the slogan "Lucky Strike Green Has Gone to War."

1944

- The military's share of cigarette consumption rises to 85 billion, a quarter of all cigarettes produced in the nation. Given the high demand among soldiers for cigarettes, a shortage develops and retailers begin to ration their sales. A production decrease due to tobacco growers who in aiming to obtain higher prices, allow land to lie fallow contributes to the shortage.

1945

- U.S. soldiers in Europe make extra money selling cigarettes to Russian soldiers and German citizens who lack access to the product. The price Europeans pay for cigarettes greatly exceeds the cost to American soldiers.

Chronology

1948

■ An article in the *Atlantic Monthly* describes the use of cigarettes by actors and actresses to show thoughtfulness, irritation, anxiety, and anger. Indeed, smoking in movies has become common and serves to promote cigarettes.

1950

■ Studies by Ernest Wynder and Evarts A. Graham in the United States and by Richard Doll and A. Bradford Hill in England demonstrate links between smoking and lung cancer.

1952

■ An antismoking article, "Cancer by the Carton," is published in the popular magazine *Reader's Digest*. The scare created by this article and several others like it temporarily results in lower purchases of cigarettes. It also leads tobacco companies to push new brands of filtered cigarettes.

1953

■ Dr. Ernest Wynder and Dr. Evarts A. Graham report that they produced skin cancer in 44 percent of the mice they had painted with tobacco tar condensed from cigarette smoke. Defenders of smoking note that the results using animals, tar paint, and skin cancer do not apply to humans who inhale cigarette smoke into their lungs.

1954

■ The American Cancer Society's Tobacco and Cancer Committee adopts a resolution recognizing an association between smoking and lung cancer.
■ Tobacco groups establish the Tobacco Industry Research Committee to respond to negative publicity about the damage of cigarette smoking. The committee authors an ad entitled "A Frank Statement to Cigarette Smokers" that calls for more study of the possible dangers but also reassures smokers of its belief that cigarettes are safe.

1955

■ The Marlboro Man ad campaign first associates the cigarette brand with cowboys, masculinity, and outdoor activity. It will make the underperforming brand one of the nation's most popular in years to come and contribute to the growth of Philip Morris.
■ The Federal Trade Commission bans advertising claims about the health effects of smoking.

1957

- Congress holds hearings on deceptive filter-tip cigarette advertising.
- Surgeon General Leroy F. Burney issues a statement that evidence points to a causative effect of smoking on lung cancer.

1958

- After having earlier expressed some mild concerns about the harm to health of smoking, the Consumer's Union asserts that a definitive link exists between cigarette use and lung cancer. The organization notes that filter-tip cigarettes provide little protection from cancer and urges smokers to quit or cut down.
- The Tobacco Institute is established in Washington, D.C., to oversee lobbying and public relations efforts.

1959

- An editorial in the *Journal of the American Medical Association* holds research on cigarette smoking to the highest standards of scientific validity in claiming that no authoritative evidence exists either for or against the harm of smoking and lung cancer.

1960

- A Florida jury concludes in a suit against the American Tobacco Company that Edwin M. Green did indeed die of lung cancer caused by smoking Lucky Strikes but declines to award damages. A retrial in 1964 rejects claims against the tobacco company altogether.

1961

- President John F. Kennedy requests that the surgeon general form a committee to assess the current knowledge on smoking and health, which Surgeon General Luther L. Terry does the next year.

1962

- The surgeon general for the U.S. Air Force orders an end to the distribution of free cigarettes in air force hospitals and flight lunches.

1964

- The surgeon general releases his report on smoking and health, which marks the beginning of a change in attitudes toward smoking and the use of cigarettes.

- The Federal Trade Commission proposes that tobacco companies include warning labels on cigarette packages and in advertisements, but Congress proposes legislation of its own that will supercede the proposals.
- The American Medical Association's Alliance House of Delegates refuses to endorse the surgeon general's report. Used to clinical demonstrations of medical causality, such as symptoms that appear in an infection or fever, many physicians are not ready to accept statistical association as evidence of causality. It will take some more time for attitudes to shift the emphasis of disease treatment to one of risk management.
- State Mutual Life Assurance Company of America becomes the first life insurance company to offer discount policies for nonsmokers.

1965

- In response to efforts of the Federal Trade Commission to include warnings on cigarette packages and advertisements, the tobacco industry has published a voluntary code for advertising and marketing practices. The code is abandoned with passage of a bill later requiring warnings on cigarette packages.
- Congress passes the Federal Cigarette Labeling and Advertising Act, which requires a mild warning statement on cigarette packages but no warning on advertisements. The act overrides the 1964 Federal Trade Commission rules.

1966

- John F. Banzhaf III requests that the Federal Communications Commission apply the fairness doctrine to cigarette advertising on television and radio. In the following year the commission agrees with the petition and orders stations to provide airtime for antismoking ads. The policy, which lasts until 1971, leads to several influential antismoking ads.

1967

- The Federal Trade Commission begins publishing tables of the tar and nicotine content in manufactured cigarettes.
- Philip Morris launches an ad campaign for a new cigarette product, Virginia Slims, that uses the slogan "You've Come a Long Way Baby" to appeal to younger, more liberated women.

1969

- In a congressional hearing, all four physicians invited to testify on the hazards of cigarettes, including the surgeon general, are themselves smokers. Along with the rise in cigarette consumption after a few years of decline, this incident illustrates the difficulty smokers will have in quitting and public health advocates will have in eliminating the tobacco problem.

■ Following recommendations from the Federal Trade Commission to ban cigarette ads from television and radio, Congress passes the Public Health Cigarette Smoking Act. It specifies the ban to begin on January 2, 1971, and new wording for the warnings on cigarette packages. Cigarette companies accept the ban but shift advertising dollars to print media and other promotions.

1970

■ A press conference sponsored by the American Cancer Society announces the results of a research study it funded. In the study Oscar Auerbach finds that among 86 beagles taught to smoke, 12 developed tumors. Although scientific reviewers have questions about the study, its results receive much public attention.

1971

■ United Airlines becomes the first to divide seating into smoking and non-smoking sections.
■ The Group Against Smokers' Pollution (GASP) is founded to lobby for nonsmokers' rights.
■ In *Capital Broadcasting v. Acting Attorney General and Capital Broadcasting v. Mitchell*, the U.S. Court of Appeals upholds the constitutionality of the ban on cigarette ads on television and radio.

1972

■ The Surgeon General's annual report reviews the effects of environmental tobacco smoke on nonsmokers and leads to new efforts to protect nonsmokers from the smoke of others.
■ The Civic Aeronautics Board requires smoking sections on commercial air flights.

1973

■ Arizona becomes the first state to ban smoking in public places.
■ After fluctuating since 1964 the level of cigarette consumption peaks before beginning downward trend that continues to the present.

1975

■ Minnesota passes the first statewide act to keep indoor air free of smoke by requiring no smoking areas in all buildings open to the public.
■ Cigarettes are removed from military field rations.

Chronology

1976

- A New Jersey court rules that an office worker who is allergic to tobacco smoke has the right to a smoke-free office.

1977

- Berkeley, California, becomes the first city to limit smoking in restaurants and other public places.

1978

- A New Jersey administrative rule restricts smoking in restaurants and public places, the first to do so without legislative backing.
- Joseph Califano, head of the Department of Health, Education, and Welfare under President Jimmy Carter, proposes several actions to fight cigarette smoking: raising taxes on cigarettes and using the proceeds for antismoking campaigns and programs, eliminating smoking on airplanes and in restaurants, and ending government subsidies to tobacco growers. With little support for the proposals from others in the Carter administration, the opposition from tobacco growers, retail establishments, and the tobacco industry is sufficient to block the proposals.

1979

- Smoking is restricted in all federal buildings.

1981

- At a national conference of antismoking groups, delegates develop a "Blueprint for Action" that defines the start of a more aggressive antismoking movement.
- Dr. C. Everett Koop becomes surgeon general. He emerges as a powerful antismoking advocate, authoring reports on environmental tobacco smoke, addiction, and the negative health consequences of smoking for women.

1982

- The American Cancer Society, the American Lung Association, and the American Heart Association combine to form Coalition on Smoking OR Health to lobby in Washington, D.C., against smoking.

1983

- According to documents released some years later, Sylvester Stallone, actor and writer of the Rocky films, agrees to use Brown and Williamson cigarette products in five feature films in return for payment of $500,000. The document illustrates the common practices among producers of including cigarette products—otherwise prohibited from being advertised on television and radio—in their movies and films in return for payment from tobacco firms.

1984

- The Food and Drug Administration approves nicotine gum products to help smokers quit.
- The 1984 Comprehensive Smoking Education Act requires that four strongly worded warnings be rotated on cigarette packages and advertisements and requires that the warnings also be displayed prominently on advertisements.

1985

- The American Medical Association calls for a complete ban on cigarette advertising and promotion.
- Los Angeles bans smoking in most public places and in businesses employing four or more persons if nonsmokers request the ban.
- A rotating series of warnings in more specific and severe language, and in larger print, begins to appear on cigarette packages.

1986

- The Comprehensive Smokeless Tobacco Health Education Act requires three rotated warning labels on smokeless tobacco packages.
- Reports from the National Research Council and the Office of the Surgeon General review evidence that indicates nonsmokers living with smokers have an increased risk of lung cancer, and children living with smoking parents have an increased risk of respiratory problems.

1988

- The Surgeon General's report describes nicotine as a highly addictive drug and cigarettes as an efficient means of delivering the drug.
- Congress bans smoking on domestic air flights of less than two hours.
- R. J. Reynolds introduces Premier cigarettes, a virtually smokeless product that reduces cancer-causing compounds, but smokers reject the product.

- Aiming to counter the success of Marlboro cigarettes, R. J. Reynolds decides to introduce the Joe Camel (or Old Joe) cartoon character in its ads. The new ads will produce a jump in sales for Camel cigarettes and are followed with the distribution of free Joe Camel products, some of which become collector's items years later.
- California voters approve the Tobacco Tax and Health Protection Act (Proposition 99), which increases the excise tax on cigarettes by 25 percent.
- The husband of Rose Cipollone wins a $400,000 judgment against the Liggett Group for the failure of the cigarette manufacturer to warn his wife about the dangers of its product, but the award is later overturned.

1989

- Philip Morris introduces Next, a cigarette that has the nicotine removed from the tobacco (much like caffeine is removed from coffee beans for decaffeinated coffee). The product flops.
- The Surgeon General's report, *Reducing the Health Consequences of Smoking, 25 Years of Progress*, reports that more than 400,000 smokers a year die prematurely.

1990

- The ban on smoking in airplanes is extended to all U.S. domestic commercial air travel lasting six hours or less.
- Tobacco companies announce the sale of American cigarettes to the Soviet Union. Wall Street analysts view the move as highly profitable for the industry.

1991

- The Food and Drug Administration approves nicotine patches as an aid to smoking cessation.
- The Federal Trade Commission reaches an agreement with Pinkerton Tobacco Company, maker of Red Man chewing tobacco, which allows the company to continue sponsoring its tractor pull event on cable television but without the expansive use of its brand name product and logo.
- Health and Human Services secretary Louis W. Sullivan calls for fans to shun sporting events sponsored by tobacco firms and for promoters to reject tobacco sponsorship.

1992

- The Environmental Protection Agency classifies environmental tobacco smoke as belonging to the most dangerous class of carcinogens.

- The Senate rejects a measure by 56 to 38 to reduce the tax deductibility of advertising and promotion expenses for tobacco products.
- The U.S. Congress passes the Synar Amendment as part of the Alcohol, Drug Abuse, and Mental Health Administration Reorganization Act. The amendment requires states to adopt and enforce minimum age requirements for tobacco sales and to demonstrate reductions in the retail availability of tobacco products to minors. The federal government does not have authority over state laws, but failure of states to follow these strictures will result in the loss of federal block grant funds for substance abuse.

1993

- Smoking is banned in the White House.
- Vermont extends its smoking ban in public buildings to include restaurants, bars, hotels, and motels (except those holding a cabaret license).
- Major League Baseball announces that all minor league players, coaches, and umpires will be banned from smoking or chewing tobacco in their ballparks or team buses.

1994

- Hoping to help schools prevent tobacco use among its students, the Centers for Disease Control and Prevention release "Guidelines for School Health Programs to Prevent Tobacco Use and Addiction."
- Philip Morris experiments with Eclipse, a cigarette that reduces secondhand smoke by 85–90 percent. However, possible attempts by the Food and Drug Administration to regulate the product keep it off the market.
- The government releases a list of 599 ingredients added by tobacco companies to manufactured cigarettes.
- *February 28 and March 3:* An ABC television show, *Day One*, alleges that tobacco companies added nicotine to their cigarettes but later retracts the statement in response to a suit by the tobacco companies.
- *April 1:* In testimony under oath seven leading U. S. tobacco company executives state their belief that cigarettes and nicotine are not addictive.

1995

- New evidence discloses that Philip Morris conducted research for 15 years on nicotine and that the research found the chemical to affect the body, brain, and behavior of smokers. Representative Henry Waxman of California tells company president William I. Campbell that the disclosures contradict his sworn testimony the previous year.

- Dr. Jeffrey Wigand, former vice president for research at Brown and Williamson, testifies in a deposition that the company knew cigarettes were harmful and addictive. Other sworn statements from former tobacco company employees assert that Philip Morris manipulated the nicotine levels in its cigarettes.
- *June 28:* The House Appropriations Committee defeats an attempt to end the 50-year-old federal government subsidy to tobacco growers.
- *July 24:* A class-action lawsuit is filed in Wichita, Kansas, against manufacturers of smokeless tobacco on behalf of all users of the product in the state.
- *August 16:* A federal appeals court rules that congressional representatives do not have to turn over internal company documents of Brown and Williamson, which the company claims were stolen from it.

1996

- The Food and Drug Administration approves nicotine patch products for over-the-counter sales.
- Papers released in a suit brought by the state of Minnesota against tobacco companies to recover Medicaid costs of treating tobacco-related illnesses show that a Philip Morris researcher in 1977 suggested a cover-up if results about nicotine's effects prove damaging.
- Merrill Williams, a paralegal who provided antitobacco lawyers with internal documents about the health dangers of cigarettes from Brown and Williamson, admits that lawyers on the antismoking side gave him more than $100,000. Tobacco industry lawyers call the payment a bribe, while antismoking lawyers call it charity.
- *June:* Republican presidential candidate Robert Dole says he believes that tobacco may not be addictive for some people and that the government should not regulate it. Strong criticism of the statement comes from President Bill Clinton, the media, and antismoking groups.
- *August 9:* A Jacksonville, Florida, jury awards $750,000 to Grady Carter and his wife in a suit against Brown and Williamson based on claims that the tobacco company deceived the public in denying the harm and addictiveness of its products.
- *August 23:* President Clinton approves Food and Drug Administration regulations that restrict the sale, distribution, advertising, and promotion of cigarettes, but tobacco companies sue to prevent implementation of the regulations.

1997

- The Liggett Group, the smallest of the tobacco companies, after having become the first to settle with plaintiffs' attorneys, admits that nicotine is addictive and that the industry targeted minors, and turns over incriminating documents.

- A group of 41 state attorneys general and the tobacco companies propose a settlement of $360 billion to recover state Medicaid costs for treating smokers for smoking-related illnesses. However, the agreement needs the support of national legislation to enforce the provisions.
- *May 28:* The Federal Trade Commission files a complaint against R. J. Reynolds over its Joe Camel ads, accusing the company of advertising to children.
- *July 11:* In response to a suit that the company violated California consumer protection laws by targeting minors with its Joe Camel campaign *(Mangini v. R. J. Reynolds)*, R. J. Reynolds agrees to restrict advertising and to fund antismoking ads for teens in California.
- *August 9:* President Bill Clinton signs an executive order establishing a smoke-free environment for federal employees and members of the public visiting federally owned facilities.
- *October 10:* Tobacco companies settle a class-action suit on behalf of flight attendants *(Broin v. Philip Morris)* by paying $300 million for research on the harm of smoking, paying $49 million for the legal representatives of the flight attendants, and allowing individual flight attendants to bring suit for compensatory (not punitive) damages.

1998

- *January 1:* California becomes the first state in the nation to ban smoking in bars.
- *June 17:* A bill introduced in the Senate to codify the provisions of the proposed tobacco settlement fails to pass. The initial agreement is thus dropped, which forces the sides to negotiate further.
- *November 11:* A U.S. appeals court overrules the lower court in finding that the Food and Drug Administration lacks authority to regulate cigarettes and smokeless tobacco.
- *November 23:* The attorneys general from 46 states and the major U.S. tobacco companies negotiate a Master Settlement Agreement that does not require legislative affirmation from Congress. Among other provisions the tobacco companies agree to pay a total of $246 billion over 25 years to the states in order to settle suits to recover Medicaid costs of treating smoking-related illness.

1999

- *March 9:* R. J. Reynolds announces it will sell its international tobacco unit to Japan Tobacco and split its tobacco and food divisions.

- *July 7:* In the first part of the *Engle v. R. J. Reynolds* class-action suit, a Florida jury concludes the tobacco companies are liable for the harm of their product because they conspired to conceal information about the health effects of smoking. The verdict represents the first successful class-action suit against the major tobacco companies, but determination of damages will follow in later parts of the trial.
- *September 15:* Worried that it might be subject to federal prosecution, online auction site eBay decides to prohibit the sale of tobacco.
- *September 22:* The Justice Department files a civil lawsuit accusing the tobacco industry of conspiring since the 1950s to defraud and mislead the public about the health effects of smoking. Much like the suit of state attorneys general aimed to recover their Medicaid costs, this suit aims to recover federal Medicare costs for elderly patients, military veterans, and federal government employees for smoking-related illnesses.
- *November:* Payments to the states from the tobacco industry under the Master Settlement Agreement are set to begin.

2000

- *March 21:* The Supreme Court ultimately determines that the Food and Drug Administration does not have legislative authority to regulate tobacco as a drug.
- *July 14:* In a second verdict in the *Engle v. R. J. Reynolds* case, a Florida jury makes a record-setting award of $144.8 billion in damages.
- *October:* Officials from 150 nations meet at a World Health Organization summit in Geneva, Switzerland, to lay the groundwork for a global tobacco treaty.
- *November 3:* The European Commission files a civil racketeering lawsuit in the United States against Philip Morris and R. J. Reynolds. The suit alleges that the companies are involved in efforts to smuggle cigarettes into Europe, and as a result European nations lose billions in import duties and taxes.
- *December 11:* Philip Morris acquires Nabisco Holdings, creating the world's second largest food maker.
- *December 19:* Cigarette prices rise by about 17¢ a pack due to increases in the prices Philip Morris and R. J. Reynolds charge to wholesalers. The price rise stems in part from the costs of the tobacco settlement.

2001

- *January:* Critics say that Wisconsin governor Tommy Thompson, President-elect George W. Bush's nomination to head the Department of

Health and Human Services, has not vigorously pursued tobacco control initiatives because of ties to Philip Morris. Spokespeople for the nominee note Governor Thompson has a strong record of opposing youth access to tobacco and has had contact with Philip Morris because it is one of Wisconsin's largest employers.

- *March 15:* After obtaining information under the Freedom of Information Act, the U.S. Chamber of Commerce reports that lawyers in class-action suits for 21 states received fees of $11 billion, amounting in some cases to more than $100,000 per hour.
- *June 28:* Acting on a Massachusetts case, the Supreme Court places limits on the ability of state and local governments to regulate tobacco advertising. The decision to give First Amendment protection is viewed as a victory for tobacco companies.
- *June 28:* Efforts of the Bush administration to settle the lawsuit brought against tobacco companies by the Justice Department lead to accusations that it has stepped back from Clinton administration efforts to protect the public's health against cigarette makers.
- *July 31:* Maryland's program to pay farmers to stop growing tobacco proves successful enough to eliminate much of the crop.
- *August 11:* The National Conference of State Legislators reports that states are spending most of the money from the Master Settlement Agreement on programs other than for smoking prevention and cessation.
- *November 15:* A Wheeling, West Virginia, jury rejects a lawsuit forcing tobacco companies to pay for annual medical tests of 250,000 healthy West Virginia smokers.

2002

- *January 20:* Defending itself against a Justice Department suit, tobacco companies request documents and files dating back to the 1940s from 10 universities. Universities such as Harvard, Johns Hopkins University, and the University of Arizona resist the subpoenas.
- *February 19:* Lorillard Tobacco Company sues the American Legacy Foundation for ads that vilify the tobacco companies. The suit claims that direct attacks on tobacco companies violate the 1998 Master Agreement Settlement.
- *March 21:* Given the successful tactics of antismoking advocates in the United States, the World Health Organization encourages other nations to use litigation in their antismoking efforts.
- *April 5:* A federal judge in Greensboro, North Carolina, allows tobacco farmers to have class-action status in their suit against tobacco manufacturers for conspiring to set prices.

- *April 11:* The Centers for Disease Control and Prevention report estimates that smoking costs the nation $150 billion a year in health costs and lost work. That amount equals $3,391 a year for each smoker.
- *June 7:* A California judge rules that the R. J. Reynolds Tobacco Company continues to pursue advertising targeted at youth, which violates the 1998 Master Settlement Agreement. The company is fined $20 million.
- *June 18:* A six-person Miami jury awards Lynn French, a former flight attendant, $5.5 million in damages for health problems resulting from environmental tobacco smoke. This is the first case to make an award to a nonsmoker, but the amount is later reduced to $500,000.
- *October 4:* A Los Angeles superior court jury awards Betty Bullock, a smoker with lung cancer, a staggering $28 billion in punitive damages. Philip Morris must pay the damages for luring her into a lifelong tobacco habit with fraudulent advertising and marketing. A judge later reduces the punitive damages to $28 million.
- *December 11:* New York governor George Pataki proposes a financial plan to balance the state's budget by issuing bonds backed by the tobacco settlement funds. Although not used directly for normal expenses, the tobacco funds allow the state to borrow to cover current expenses.

2003

- *January 27:* The Vector Group announces that its low-nicotine cigarette, Quest, is available in seven states. The cigarette uses a new process to remove nicotine but keep the flavor of conventional cigarettes.
- *March 5:* Weeks before a tough antismoking ban goes into effect, Philip Morris announces that it will move its headquarters from New York City to Richmond, Virginia.
- *April 1:* Legislation signed earlier by New York City mayor Michael Bloomberg to ban smoking in bars, restaurants, prisons, and city-owned buildings goes into effect. The law depends largely on owners and patrons of bars and restaurants to voluntarily enforce the ban, but city inspectors begin issuing fines on May 1.
- *April 9:* Norway's parliament votes to make the country among the first in the world to outlaw smoking in bars and restaurants nationwide but delays the ban until spring 2004 to make the transition for smokers less difficult.
- *April 14:* A bouncer at a New York City nightclub is stabbed to death after confronting a man who was smoking in defiance of the city's antismoking law. Some bar owners worry the law will lead to more such violence.

- *May 21:* A Florida appeals court rejects the record-setting $145 billion award against the tobacco industry on behalf of Florida smokers in *Engle v. R. J. Reynolds.*
- *May 21:* In Geneva, Switzerland, more than 190 countries approved the first international treaty against smoking. The treaty requires countries to restrict tobacco advertising, sponsorship, and promotion within five years; lays down guidelines for health warnings; recommends tax increases on tobacco products; and calls for a crackdown on cigarette smuggling.
- *June 17:* To restrict the ability of smokers to purchase cigarettes over the Internet without paying state and city taxes, the state of New York begins enforcing a new law that prohibits shipping of cigarettes to anyone but a licensed dealer. The state, which has lost billions in taxes through Internet purchases over the past years, now faces the issue of how to enforce the law.
- *June 24:* Responding to the ban on Internet cigarette sales in New York State, Native American cigarette retailers have challenged the law in state court. Native American businesses have been selling cigarettes over the Internet without charging state taxes.
- *July 15:* In a controversial raid that resulted in scuffling and arrests by police, agents of the state of Rhode Island entered the reservation of the Narragansett tribe and confiscated cigarettes from a store that have been selling them without charging taxes. Governor Don Carcieri defended the raid, which had a court-approved search warrant, as necessary given the illegal sales of cigarettes.
- *July 30:* The world's second largest tobacco company, British American Tobacco, reports that its profits fell in the year's second quarter by 83 percent. Analysts say the company remains strong, but efforts to cut jobs and factories in Canada and Britain and move production facilities and sales to emerging markets in developing countries produced short-term losses. R. J. Reynolds Tobacco Holdings also reports declining earnings.

CHAPTER 4

BIOGRAPHICAL LISTING

This chapter offers brief biographical information on people who have played major roles in developments since the 13th century in the tobacco industry and smoking. Historical figures include those who popularized the product in Europe and the United States, who built the modern tobacco industry, and who changed the perceptions of tobacco with research and antismoking advocacy. Current figures include those involved in litigation over tobacco, nonsmokers' rights movements, and legislation and regulation to control tobacco.

Dr. Oscar Auerbach, principal researcher in a 1967 project funded by the American Cancer Society. After teaching 86 beagles to smoke through small holes in their throats, he found that 12 of the dogs developed tumors. This finding received much public attention, despite some scientific questions about the validity of the study.

John F. Banzhaf III, New York City lawyer who petitioned the Federal Communications Commission (FCC) in 1966 to apply the fairness doctrine to cigarette advertising. The commission accepted the position and until the end of television and radio advertising of cigarettes, required that stations provide free airtime for anticigarette advertising. Much to the concern of the tobacco industry, these early antismoking ads proved effective. Banzhaf left New York City to become a law professor at George Washington University and found an antismoking organization, Action on Smoking and Health (ASH).

James Albert Bonsack, Lynchburg, Virginia, mechanic. He won a $75,000 contest in 1881 by inventing and patenting a cigarette-making machine that could roll more than 200 cigarettes a minute. The machine would replace skilled workers who hand rolled cigarettes and make James Buchanan Duke's cigarette business the most successful in the country.

Norma Broin, nonsmoking flight attendant who developed lung cancer after 13 years on the job. Represented by Stanley Rosenblatt, she brought a class-action suit on behalf of 8,000 other flight attendants against tobacco companies. The lawyers in the case negotiated an agreement in 1977 in which the tobacco companies donated $300 million for research on smoking-related diseases in the name of Norma Broin (who had since died). The flight attendants received no damages but could in the future bring suit to recover individual compensatory (not punitive) damages. It was under this agreement that Lynn French (and eventually 2,800 other flight attendants) sued the tobacco companies.

Leo F. Burnett, founder and president of a Chicago-based advertising agency. He and his firm developed the highly successful Marlboro Man and Marlboro Country ad campaigns in the 1950s and 1960s that would for decades push Marlboro to among the nation's most popular cigarettes. The masculine, independent outdoorsman depicted in the ads became a cultural icon, a symbol of both the attraction to cigarettes and the misleading images advanced by the tobacco companies.

Dr. Leroy F. Burney, surgeon general in 1957. His early and mild statement that prolonged cigarette smoking could cause lung cancer received more in the way of harsh attacks from critics than recognition of the problem by the public. Yet the statement represented the start of efforts that would culminate in the 1964 Surgeon General's report on the harm of smoking.

George W. Bush, 43rd president of the United States. Antismoking critics of President Bush, who took office in 2001, claim that he backed away from the antitobacco efforts of the Clinton administration. As evidence to support their criticisms, they point to the nomination of Tommy Thompson, who as governor of Wisconsin had ties to the tobacco industry, to head the Department of Health and Human Services, and to the willingness to settle the Justice Department suit against tobacco companies to recover Medicare costs for smoking-related illnesses.

Joseph Califano, head of the Department of Health, Education, and Welfare under President Jimmy Carter. He proposed several actions in 1978 to fight cigarette smoking: raising taxes on cigarettes, using the government proceeds for antismoking campaigns and programs, eliminating smoking on airplanes and in restaurants, and ending government subsidies to tobacco growers. With little support from others in the Carter administration, opposition from tobacco growers, retail establishments, and the tobacco industry was sufficient to block these proposals.

Grady Carter, retired air traffic controller living in Florida. He was the first to have success in suing tobacco companies under a new strategy of claiming misrepresentation and fraud. Carter started smoking Lucky Strike cigarettes in 1947, switched brands in 1972, and continued the habit until his diagnosis of lung cancer in 1991. He had tried hard to quit but felt hooked by the habit. Upon hearing claims made in 1994 by tobacco company executives that cigarettes were not addictive, he and his wife sued Brown and Williamson, the maker of Lucky Strikes, for $1.5 million in damages. The Jacksonville, Florida, jury awarded $750,000 to the Carters in 1996, but a Florida appeals court ruled that the Carters in waiting for some time after the diagnosis of cancer to file the lawsuit, exceeded the four-year statute of limitations for such cases.

Rose Cipollone, smoker who died of lung cancer shortly after filing suit against several tobacco companies. Her husband became the first person to win damages against tobacco companies (but lost the award on appeal). Growing up in New York City, Cipollone had started smoking at age 16 and eventually smoked a pack and a half each day. In 1981 an X ray showed a lesion in her lung that upon biopsy proved to be a malignant growth. Despite two lung operations, the cancer returned to her lungs by 1984 and soon spread to her brain and the rest of her body. Alive to file the suit in 1983, she died on October 21, 1984.

Earl C. Clements, lobbyist hired by the tobacco industry in the 1960s. He was a former congressional representative and senator from Kentucky who still had close ties to his colleagues in Congress and to the Lyndon Johnson White House. He shrewdly led the discussion about tobacco toward economic issues and away from health issues. The efforts could not stop movements to restrict advertising and require warning messages on cigarettes but did forestall more drastic measures.

William J. Clinton, 42nd president of the United States (1993–2001), the first to take an active stand against smoking and the tobacco industry. In his administration smoking was banned in the White House; regulations to control tobacco sales, advertising, and promotions were implemented (although later disallowed by the Supreme Court); and a Justice Department suit was filed against tobacco companies to recover Medicare costs for smoking-related illnesses.

Christopher Columbus, explorer who, in aiming to sail west to reach the Near East, discovered the New World. Supported in his 1492 expedition by King Ferdinand and Queen Isabella of Spain, he landed on a small island in the Bahamas and later sailed to Cuba. There some of his crew became the first Europeans to smoke tobacco. Columbus returned with some tobacco leaves and seeds, but Europeans paid little attention to the product until nearly 60 years later.

Robert Dole, former Republican senator from Kansas and presidential nominee of the Republican Party in the 1996 election. He stated during the presidential campaign that tobacco is not addictive for some people and that the government should not regulate it. Strong criticism of the statement came from President Bill Clinton, the media, and antismoking groups.

Sir Francis Drake, English explorer who circumnavigated the globe between 1577 and 1580. During his expedition he obtained tobacco from native peoples off the southwestern coast of North America and returned to England with samples.

James Buchanan Duke (Buck Duke), entrepreneur most responsible for the shape of the modern tobacco industry. In 1874 he joined his father and brother to found a tobacco firm in Durham, North Carolina. Eventually taking over, Duke showed his tremendous organizational and managerial skills in creating a successful cigarette business. He mechanized production, spent lavishly on advertising, cut prices significantly, and became the nation's largest cigarette manufacturer. Having pressured his major competitors to join him, he formed the American Tobacco Company in 1890 and became, at age 33, the first president. Although wildly successful and rich from his efforts, the trust he created was dissolved in 1911 for violating antitrust laws. The breakup created most of the companies that would dominate the industry over the 20th century.

Marc Z. Edell, lawyer who applied the case law used in suits by victims of asbestos products to suits by victims of smoking and tobacco. On behalf of his client, Rose Cipollone (and her surviving husband), in her suit against the Liggett Group, Philip Morris, and Loews Corporation (owner of Lorillard), each a maker of cigarettes that Cipollone had smoked, he became the first lawyer to win damages in a smoking case, in 1988. His arguments relied on changes in product liability law that had occurred during the 1960s and 1970s. These changes made companies more responsible for damages incurred by use of a dangerous product. Edell had more success against the tobacco companies than others before him, but he ultimately failed in his efforts when the initial award was overturned on appeal.

Howard A. Engle, retired pediatrician who after smoking for 50 years suffered from asthma and emphysema. With representation by Stanley Rosenblatt he filed a class-action suit on behalf of smokers nationwide against tobacco companies, which was later changed only to include all Florida smokers. The damages of $144.8 billion awarded to the class in 1999 represented a major defeat of the tobacco industry, but the verdict is still under appeal.

Dr. Hans Eysenck, well-known and respected psychologist in England. He suggested that persons with certain personality traits were prone to both smoking and early death. His research, published in 1965, showed that those unable to express anger, fear, and anxiety had a high risk of getting cancer. If those same traits led to smoking, the association between smoking and lung cancer might be spurious.

Biographical Listing

Benjamin Franklin, American patriot and pipe smoker. Using tobacco as collateral, he negotiated loans from France to support the Revolutionary War (1775–83).

Lynn French, flight attendant beginning in 1976 for TWA on both domestic and international flights who brought the first successful second-hand smoking suit. Exposed to environmental tobacco smoke on her job for 14 years, she developed chronic sinus problems. With her attorney, Stanley Rosenblatt, she sought damages of $980,000 from the major tobacco companies in a suit heard in the Florida circuit court. The six-person Miami jury awarded French $5.5 million in compensatory damages—more than five times the amount requested in the suit, but a Miami-Dade circuit judge reduced the award to $500,000 three months later in September 2002.

Lucy Page Gaston, schoolteacher who nearly halted the fast spread of cigarette use around the turn of the 20th century. In 1899 she used the model of antialcohol groups in founding the Chicago Anti-Cigarette League. Two years later she founded the National Anti-Cigarette League and soon became one of the country's most well-known reformers. She held rallies in schools and towns in which she decried the poisons brought into the body by cigarettes and noted cases of known murderers and criminals who smoked. She further recruited converts to her organization, promoted health clinics in cities that smokers could use to quit the habit, and urged legislatures to ban the product. In 1920 she ran for the Republican Party presidential nomination. The movement led to the outlawing of cigarettes in 21 states during the first two decades of the 20th century but ultimately failed to stop the growth of cigarettes.

Lewis Ginter, leading U.S. tobacco producer until the 1880s. First using bright tobacco to produce cigarettes, he found success with his excellent marketing and sales skills. However, his major contribution came from the use of a new tobacco leaf, white burley, in cigarettes. Ginter used the new leaf, which could incorporate more flavoring than others, in several types of cigarettes. The new blends created a distinctively American style of cigarette that differed from Turkish and Russian cigarettes and could be sold at a cheaper price than the foreign imports.

Stanton Glantz, professor at the School of Medicine, University of California, San Francisco. The longtime critic of tobacco received more than 4,000 pages of secret internal industry documents in the mail from an unknown source in 1994. He publicized the damaging information contained in the documents, which increased the ability of plaintiffs to make the case that industry leaders misled them about the risks of smoking. Although he played a role in pushing the tobacco companies toward a settlement with the states over Medicaid cost reimbursement, he ultimately opposed any bargaining and urged states to do all they could to bankrupt tobacco companies.

Ulysses S. Grant, 18th president of the United States (1868–76) and victim of throat cancer. He smoked cigars throughout his life as a farmer, soldier, general in the Civil War, and president of the United States. Upon making a diagnosis that Grant had throat cancer, his doctor recommended cutting down on cigars to three a day, but Grant soon died of the disease.

Al Gore, senator from Tennessee, vice president of the United States (1992–2001), and presidential candidate in 2000. As a senator, he helped to negotiate the 1984 Comprehensive Smoking Education Act and prevent the blockage of the bill by tobacco interests. The act required more stringent warnings on cigarette packages.

Edwin M. Green, plaintiff in a suit filed in December 1957 against the American Tobacco Company. A navy veteran of World War II, Green had begun smoking in the 1920s at the age of 16 and continued the habit for 32 years until diagnosed with lung cancer. The American Tobacco Company manufactured Lucky Strikes, the brand Green had smoked all those years. Although he died only two months after the filing, at age 49, the case continued on behalf of his survivors. In 1960 the jury in the first trial concluded that cigarettes had caused Green's lung cancer, but that the American Tobacco Company was not liable for this result. The jury in a second trial, in 1964, rejected the plaintiff's claims altogether.

Dr. Larry Hastings, physician and lawyer specializing in product liability. His representation of Edwin Green in a 1957 suit against the American Tobacco Company typified the failure to obtain damages on the basis of arguments of negligence and implied warranty.

John Hawkins, admiral in the English navy who with his sailors brought tobacco to England after a voyage to the Caribbean in 1562. The use of chewing tobacco became common among sailors but did not spread yet to the English population.

George Washington Hill, a successor of James Duke as president of the American Tobacco Company. Hill fully exploited the potential of advertising to increase sales of cigarettes. His efforts made Lucky Strike, a brand introduced in 1916 with the slogan "It's Toasted," tops in sales by the end of the 1920s. He also appealed to the new market of women smokers by linking cigarettes to youth and beauty—a strategy cigarette advertisers would continue. His efforts helped make cigarettes widely fashionable.

King James I, king of Great Britain (1603–25) and one of the first to speak out against tobacco. In 1604 he wrote *A Counterblaste to Tobacco,* which described smoking as filthy, stinking, vile, sinful, shameful, dangerous, and loathsome. The pamphlet contested the claims of the most famous English advocate of smoking, Walter Raleigh, and aimed to stop the growth of a habit of rising popularity. Having had little influence with the pamphlet, however, James I took steps to tax the import of the product.

Robert P. Kaye, Florida judge who oversaw the settlement between flight attendants and tobacco companies and who presided over the class-action suit of Lynn French against tobacco companies for damages from secondhand smoke. In the French case, he used the settlement agreement to relieve individual flight attendants of the burden of proving that the companies were either negligent or liable for making a defective product. The decision paved the way for a favorable verdict on behalf of French in 2002.

John F. Kennedy, 35th president of the United States (1961–63). He made a request in 1962 to the surgeon general to convene a group that would evaluate the evidence on smoking and health. The action led two years later to the Surgeon General's report on smoking and health that warned the public of the dangers of cigarettes.

Dr. David Kessler, commissioner of the Food and Drug Administration (FDA) in the Bill Clinton administration. Proposing regulations to treat tobacco as a drug, he argued that cigarettes served as a nicotine-delivery system, that tobacco companies used their knowledge of the addictiveness of nicotine to make their cigarettes more addictive, and that the FDA could control the product based on existing legislation, much as it controlled nicotine gum and patches. The regulations would restrict the sale and distribution of cigarettes and smokeless tobacco products to children and adolescence. They would also require tobacco companies to support tobacco prevention education for children, take actions to ensure underage youth would not have access to cigarettes through vending machines or other unsupervised sales, ban gift or promotional items bearing cigarette brand names, eliminate outdoor advertising near schools, and limit advertising in publications with more than 15 percent of the readership under age 18. President Clinton announced the publication of the final FDA rules on August 23, 1996. However, suits by tobacco companies against the regulations led to a decision by the Supreme Court that existing law did not allow regulation of tobacco as a drug.

F. S. Kinney, first tobacco producer to successfully mix American bright tobacco with foreign tobaccos. After opening a small cigarette shop in Lower Manhattan in 1868, he hired foreign-born cigarette rollers to make his product, sold cigarettes in paper packages, and became the leading manufacturer in the new industry. His brand, Sweet Caporal, which contained a mix of flavors and sweeteners, became the first with a national rather than local following. As the business grew, he relocated the factories to Richmond, Virginia; the town would become a center of the tobacco industry.

Dr. C. Everett Koop, pediatric surgeon and evangelical Christian appointed as surgeon general during the Ronald Reagan administration. Although first known for his antiabortion views, he became a forceful and charismatic antismoking advocate. During the 1980s he authored reports calling cigarette smoking the nation's number one public health problem, identifying environmental tobacco smoke as a cause of cancer, and emphasizing the strongly addictive nature of nicotine. He fiercely and relentlessly attacked smoking and tobacco makers, and his leadership helped promote antismoking efforts.

Bennett LeBow, CEO of the Brooke Group, which owned the Liggett Group and Liggett Tobacco, the smallest of the major tobacco companies. He broke ranks with the larger companies in deciding to negotiate with state attorneys general who sued to recover Medicaid costs for treating smoking-related illnesses. He worried that the suits would bankrupt the company and had little confidence that the legal strategy of the tobacco companies would prove successful. His defection in settling with the state attorneys general in 1997 led to the eventual settlement with all the major tobacco companies. He admitted on behalf of his company that cigarettes are addictive and included such a warning on the cigarettes his company manufactured.

Mike Moore, Mississippi attorney general since 1988. In 1994 he filed the first state Medicaid suit against the tobacco industry and helped convince other state attorneys general to file their own suits. Based on the suggestion of a friend, he proposed the new strategy of using litigation on behalf of taxpayers rather than smokers. Along with Richard Scruggs and Ron Motley, he brought tobacco companies to the negotiating table and to settlements with the state of Mississippi and with 46 states in the Master Settlement Agreement.

Ron Motley, plaintiff's attorney in state Medicaid suits against tobacco companies. He helped develop the legal strategy with Richard Scruggs for the 1994 case in Mississippi and represented nearly every state that brought a similar suit. Known for his brilliant courtroom tactics, he had already made millions suing asbestos companies. As he told interviewers, he jointed the antitobacco suits because he wanted to expose the dishonesty and damage of the tobacco industry and because his mother (and hundreds of thousands of others like her) had died from a smoking-related disease.

Jean Nicot, appointed French ambassador to Portugal in 1559 under Henri II and Catherine de' Medici. After learning to raise tobacco in the

Biographical Listing

French embassy in Lisbon and concluding that it had strong curative powers, he sent plants and seeds to the queen of France, who was attracted to herbs and potions. Taken as snuff, tobacco soon became popular in the French court and spread quickly throughout the country. In recognition of his role in promoting the product, scientists named the tobacco plant—*Nicotiana*—after him.

Dr. Raymond K. Pearl, medical researcher at Johns Hopkins University. In 1938 he published the first study in the United States to scientifically identify a link between smoking and life expectancy. Based on his access to the medical records of a sample of 6,813 men, he found that only 45 percent of smokers lived to age 60, compared to 65 percent of nonsmokers.

Walter Raleigh, English soldier, explorer, and favorite of Queen Elizabeth I who helped popularize tobacco smoking in his country. After returning from an expedition in 1586 to Virginia, Raleigh used smoking as a symbol of adventure. Pipe smoking spread to the court of England and then to the rest of society. However, he ran afoul of King James I, who detested the habit and Raleigh's independence, and was executed in 1618 for disobeying the king's orders.

Richard J. Reynolds, founder of R. J. Reynolds Tobacco Company. He was forced by economic pressure to merge his company with James Buchanan Duke's to form the American Tobacco Company. With the breakup of the trust in 1911, Reynolds gained back his old company but started out as the smallest of the four new tobacco companies. The introduction in 1913 of Camel cigarettes, a brand with an appealing mix of American and foreign tobaccos and an intriguing advertising campaign, made his company one of the nation's most successful.

John Rolfe, early English settler of Jamestown, Virginia, who married the Wampanoag princess Pocahontas. He helped cultivate, cure, and ship to England the first successful tobacco crop. Although Jamestown would not survive, the production of tobacco would become the major crop of Virginia and a source of much profit when sold in England.

Theodore Roosevelt (Teddy Roosevelt), 26th president of the United States (1901–09) who reformed the regulation of business by attacking trusts that reduced competition. Under his administration efforts began to dissolve the cigarette and tobacco trust that James Buchanan Duke had formed with the American Tobacco Company. The efforts ended in 1911, after Roosevelt had left the presidency, with the breakup of the trust into four tobacco companies that would dominate the industry for the next 50 years.

Stanley M. Rosenblatt, a Miami lawyer who brought class-action suits against the major tobacco companies. In the *Broin* case he first represented flight attendants in their efforts to obtain damages for health problems they experienced as a result of breathing secondhand smoke on air flights. The suit did not go to trial, but Rosenblatt received $49 million in fees in the 1997 settlement. In the *Engle* case he successfully argued to have Florida smokers certified as a class and in 1999 won damages of $144.8 billion against tobacco companies—an enormous and expensive defeat for the tobacco companies that continues under appeal. He followed the legal strategy used successfully in other suits by claiming that tobacco companies misrepresented the information they had on the addictiveness and harm of their products.

Benjamin Rush, prominent physician and signer of the Declaration of Independence. He authored the first significant antitobacco document in the United States, "Observations upon the Influence of the Habitual Use of Tobacco upon Health, Morals, and Property," in 1798.

H. Lee Sarokin, a New Jersey federal court judge who presided over the *Cipollone* case. Seen as an opponent of the tobacco industry, he made decisions in the *Cipollone* case in 1988 that higher courts overruled. Still later, tobacco industry defendants accused him of having shown bias against the industry and had him removed from tobacco cases.

Richard Scruggs, Mississippi lawyer who played a crucial role in the Master Settlement Agreement. After making millions suing asbestos companies on behalf of injured workers, he worked with the state of Mississippi in its 1994 litigation to recover state costs for treating Medicaid patients with smoking-related illnesses from tobacco companies. Scruggs brought in famous trial attorney Ron Motley and fronted the costs of the suit in return for contingency fees. During the process Scruggs protected whistle-blowers Merrill Williams and Jeffrey Wigand and convinced Bennett LeBow, the head of Liggett Tobacco, to defect from other companies that wanted to fight the suit. In the end Scruggs negotiated an agreement in Mississippi, worked on the Florida suit to recover its Medicaid costs for smoking-related illnesses, and helped broker the Master Settlement Agreement in 1998.

Harold Solomon, Florida circuit judge. He allowed the *Engle* case to proceed as a class-action suit in 1994 on behalf of all smokers in the nation injured by the tobacco companies. His decision was later revised on appeal to include only Florida smokers but still led to the first certification of a class in a suit against the tobacco companies.

Mike Synar, Democratic representative from Oklahoma who sponsored an antismoking amendment to the Alcohol, Drug Abuse, and Mental Health Administration Reorganization Act. His 1992 amendment required states to adopt and enforce minimum age laws for tobacco sales and to demonstrate reductions in the retail availability of tobacco products. The federal government does not have authority over state laws, but failure of states to follow these strictures would, under the amendment, result in the loss of federal block grant funds for substance abuse prevention and treatment.

Dr. Luther E. Terry, surgeon general during the administrations of John F. Kennedy and Lyndon Johnson. He convened a panel of experts to evaluate the evidence on the health risks of smoking in 1962 and sponsored in 1964 *A Report of the Surgeon General on Health and Smoking.* More than a summary of scientific findings, the report and the recommended actions bluntly told people interested in their health and a long life to give up or avoid smoking. The publicity received by the report created a stir among the public and serious problems for tobacco companies. Moreover future surgeons general would follow with additional reports that became increasingly strong in their criticism of the use of tobacco and helped to galvanize antismoking movements.

Henry Waxman, Democratic representative from California and persistent foe of the tobacco industry. He held hearings in the House of Representatives on the business practices of tobacco companies and developed a bill that would more stringently control tobacco advertising. Although he did not obtain all the provisions he wanted, Waxman with the aid of Senator Al Gore was able to get an antismoking bill passed (the 1984 Comprehensive Smoker Education Act) that required rotating of four new warning statements on both packages and advertisements. Waxman also was largely responsible for bringing chief executives of the major tobacco firms to a congressional hearing and having them state their belief that smoking was not addictive—testimony that was later contradicted by internal industry documents.

Jeffrey Wigand, biochemistry Ph.D. who worked as vice president of research at Brown and Williamson Tobacco. He became the highest-level industry executive to speak to the media about the industry's efforts to strengthen the nicotine chemical in its cigarettes. He testified in 1995 on behalf of the state of Mississippi in its suit against tobacco companies, claiming that Brown and Williamson hid damaging scientific information about addiction. After appearing on the television news show *60 Minutes* in 1996, he was accused by Brown and Williamson of misconduct, but his testimony proved crucial in the successful suits against the tobacco industry since then. His story was depicted in the movie *The Insider,* starring Russell Crowe.

Merrill Williams, a smoker and paralegal at a Louisville law firm who leaked damaging tobacco industry internal documents. Given the task in 1994 of cataloguing documents from Brown and Williamson in preparation for suits against the company, he found information in the documents that revealed company knowledge of the addictiveness of cigarettes as early as in 1963, the use of carcinogens in cigarettes, and efforts to target young people. He made copies and passed them to Richard Scruggs, the lawyer representing the state of Mississippi in its Medicaid suit against the tobacco companies. Although the documents were stolen, they eventually became public information and were used in suits against tobacco companies.

Norwood S. Wilner, Jacksonville, Florida, lawyer who represented Grady Carter in his suit against Brown and Williamson. Using a legal strategy developed in the 1990s, he claimed that tobacco companies were liable because they knew of the harm of cigarettes but did not warn consumers of the harm until required to do so by the government. The damages awarded in 1996 in *Carter* represented a major defeat for the tobacco company, and Wilner would file hundreds of other suits against tobacco companies.

Dr. Ernest Wynder, pioneering researcher on the health consequences of smoking and outspoken critic of tobacco use. As a medical student at Washington University in St. Louis, he demonstrated with his professor, Dr. Evarts A. Graham, that a connection existed between smoking and lung cancer. His influential study, published in 1950, showed that 96.5 percent of the lung cancer patients smoked compared to 73.7 percent of the other patients. Other studies by E. Cuyler Hammond and Daniel Horn and by Richard Doll and A. Bradford Hill in the 1950s further contributed to the early evidence of the harm of smoking, but more than other researchers, Wynder became a strong and forceful critic of cigarette use. Despite much resistance from other medical researchers at the time, Wynder continued research to demonstrate the harm of smoking for health.

CHAPTER 5

GLOSSARY

Some terms, phrases, and organizations used in the previous chapters have specialized meanings relating to the tobacco industry and smoking. This chapter lists and defines these words and names in terms appropriate for general readers.

Action on Smoking and Health (ASH) A national charitable antismoking and nonsmokers' rights organization that primarily brings legal action in support of a smoke-free society.

addiction A compulsive need for a substance that produces withdrawal symptoms when stopped and requires increasingly larger amounts to produce the desired response. The Office of the Surgeon General similarly defines addiction as behavior controlled by a substance that causes changes in mood from its effects on the brain.

additive A product such as flavors and chemicals that does not naturally occur in the tobacco plant but are added to cigarettes and other tobacco products in the manufacturing process.

American Cancer Society (ACS) A nationwide, community-based voluntary health organization dedicated to eliminating cancer as a major health problem. It early on expressed concerns about the potential for smoking to cause cancer and has campaigned against smoking.

American Heart Association (AHA) A national voluntary health agency committed to reducing disability and death from cardiovascular diseases and strokes. Given the connection between smoking and heart disease, the organization has played an active role in antismoking efforts.

American Medical Association (AMA) An organization of physicians that advocates on behalf of the medical profession and has since the 1980s taken a strong position of opposition to smoking and tobacco advertising.

American Public Health Association (APHA) An organization of professionals concerned with a broad set of public health issues, including advocacy of a smoke-free society.

139

ammonia   A chemical compound with a noxious aroma that is often used with water for cleaning. Small amounts have sometimes been added to cigarettes to boost the impact of nicotine on the human body.

antidepressant   A drug such as bupropion, Prozac, or Zoloft that is used to relieve symptoms of psychological depression and may also moderate withdrawal symptoms from stopping smoking.

asthma   A condition often caused by allergies that involves coughing, breathing problems, and feelings of constriction in the chest. Children living with smoking parents are at higher risk of asthma than others.

bidi   A small brown tobacco product used commonly in India and occasionally used by youth in the United States. It consists of tobacco that is hand rolled in a leaf and tied at one end by a string.

Blue Cross/Blue Shield (BC/BS)   A private health care insurance company that through its many chapters provides health insurance to more than 80 million people. It has pursued tobacco companies legally to recover its costs for treating smoking-related illnesses.

Bonsack machine   A 1880 invention that pours tobacco from a feeder onto a small strip of paper, rolls a single continuous tube, and cuts the tube into equal length cigarettes. The machine did much to help increase cigarette production and sales.

bright tobacco   A popular American tobacco grown in Virginia and North Carolina that, when cured with heat, develops an unusually sweet and pleasant taste and can be smoked in greater quantities than other tobaccos.

bronchitis   In its chronic form, the serious inflammation of the bronchial tubes that lead to the lungs.

Civil Aeronautics Board (CAB)   An independent agency of the federal government that regulates airline activities, include smoking on airplanes.

cancer   A disorderly, uncontrolled growth of abnormal body cells that, as they multiply, invade and push aside the organs of the body. Malignant cancerous growths eventually interfere with normal body functions and result in death. Tobacco and smoking cause cancer in the lungs, esophagus, mouth, throat, and a variety of other organs.

carbon monoxide   A colorless, odorless, and highly toxic gas that is contained in small amounts in tobacco smoke.

carcinogen   A substance or agent producing or inciting cancer.

Centers for Disease Control and Prevention (CDC)   A federal agency with the mission to promote health and quality of life by preventing and controlling disease, injury, and disability. It has been active in protecting health and safety through antismoking research.

chewing tobacco (chew)   A form of smokeless tobacco that is placed as a small clump inside the mouth and next to the cheek. Usually flavored it allows nicotine to be absorbed through the tissue of the oral cavity and requires spitting to eliminate tobacco juices from the mouth.

cigar A dried, prepared, and rolled tobacco leaf used for smoking. Unlike cigarettes, cigar smoke is seldom fully inhaled, but nicotine from the smoke can, though less efficiently than in the lungs, be absorbed in the mouth.

cigarette A slender roll of cut tobacco used for smoking. The tobacco for cigarettes makes inhaling pleasurable and absorption of nicotine through the lungs efficient.

class action A legal action undertaken by one or more plaintiffs on behalf of themselves and all other persons who have an interest in the alleged wrong.

class certified To bring a class-action suit, a class must be certified by showing that the class members share the same interests, can be fairly represented as a class, and is too large to allow lawsuits to be tried individually for each member.

chronic obstructive pulmonary disease (COPD) A category of illnesses typified by chronic bronchitis and emphysema that block the flow of air to the lungs. The disease is often caused by smoking.

compensatory damages Damages awarded for injury or loss, including expenses, loss of time, and physical and mental suffering.

curing The drying process used to prepare tobacco for market. The different methods of curing—flue cured by heat from pipes or flues connected to a furnace; air cured from air while suspended in barns for five weeks; fire cured by heat from wood fires underneath; and sun cured while outside in the sunshine for four weeks—help give different flavor and texture to tobacco products.

emphysema A type of chronic obstructive pulmonary disease that involves dilation of air spaces in the lungs and makes absorption of oxygen difficult.

Environmental Protection Agency (EPA) A federal agency that protects human life and the natural environment. It has labeled cigarette smoke as a dangerous carcinogen.

environmental tobacco smoke (ETS) Smoke in the air exhaled by smokers or emitted from the burning tips of cigarettes in between puffs. Most public health experts believe it poses a health risk to nonsmokers who breathe it in. It is also called secondhand smoke.

excise tax A tax added to a product before sale. Used specifically to gain revenue from and increase the price of cigarettes, excise taxes differ from sales taxes, which are placed on products in general and are added after the sale.

fairness doctrine A guiding principle that the Federal Communications Commission (FCC) employed to regulate electronic media before cable television. Based on the view that the airways are a public resource, the doctrine required equal time for presentation of competing views, usually by politicians and political parties. However, the FCC extended the doctrine to require the airing of antismoking ads as a means to balance smoking advertisements.

Federal Communications Commission (FCC)   An independent agency of the federal government that regulates television and radio broadcasting and in so doing ruled under the fairness doctrine that stations presenting cigarette ads must provide airtime for antismoking commercials.

Federal Trade Commission (FTC)   A federal agency that enforces laws against unfair business practices and since the 1950s has battled with tobacco companies over misrepresentation in cigarette advertising.

filters or filter tips   Fibrous material placed within one end of the cigarette tube that removes some of the harmful matter when tobacco smoke passes through it.

First Amendment   The amendment to the U.S. Constitution that specifies Congress will make no law abridging the freedom of speech or of the press. The interpretation of the amendment proved crucial in allowing congressional legislation to ban television and radio cigarette ads.

Food and Drug Administration (FDA)   A federal agency devoted to promoting and protecting the nation's public health by approving and monitoring food ingredients, drugs, and medical products.

globalization   The process of creating greater ties across nations of the globe through exchange of products through trade, information through the media, and people through travel and immigration. As part of this process, cigarettes and cigarette advertising have rapidly spread across the globe in recent years.

Group Against Smokers' Pollution (GASP)   A nonsmoker's rights organization that works to eliminate tobacco smoke from the air, educate the public about secondhand smoke, and promote smoke-free policies.

Havana cigar   A premium type of cigar made from Cuban tobacco and highly prized for its flavor. Since an embargo on Cuban products, this cigar type has been difficult to obtain in the United States.

heart disease   A life-threatening illness that typically involves blockage of the arteries that feed blood to the heart by a fatty substance called plaque. Smoking causes heart disease in part by injuring the heart vessels in ways that promote the buildup of plaque. The carbon monoxide in cigarette smoke also contributes to heart disease by blocking absorption of oxygen into the blood.

involuntary smoking   Inhaling environmental tobacco or secondhand smoke.

Joe Camel   A cartoon character reintroduced in 1988 by R. J. Reynolds Tobacco to promote Camel cigarettes. The ad campaign proved successful but was harshly criticized for attracting children and youth to smoking.

liability Legal responsibility for an act or omission, as for example, when cigarette manufacturers are held responsible for the harm of their product.

Master Settlement Agreement (MSA) Following negotiations between the major tobacco companies and state attorneys general, this agreement required tobacco companies to pay states $246 billion for the costs of treating smoking-related illnesses of Medicaid patients. It also restricted advertising, marketing, and promotional activities targeted at youth.

Medicaid A public program to pay for medical care of those unable to afford it and financed largely by states with aid from the federal government.

Medicare A public program to pay for medical care of the elderly and financed largely by the federal government.

Nicotiana tabacum One of some 60 species of plants within the *Nicotiana* genus that is most commonly used by Europeans and Americans for smoking and chewing products.

nicotine A chemical compound found in tobacco plants and tobacco smoke that can be absorbed through the body's cell membrane walls. Poisonous in large amounts, the chemical in small amounts is both stimulating and relaxing in ways that make it addictive.

nicotine replacement therapy The use of gum, patches, inhalers, and nasal sprays to moderate the withdrawal symptoms caused by smoking cessation. The products used in the therapy provide the body with its need for nicotine while avoiding the harm of cigarette tar and gases. Ideally the therapy allows former smokers to slowly reduce their nicotine consumption until the withdrawal symptoms become minor.

passive smoking Inhaling environmental tobacco or secondhand smoke.

pipe A tube of varying lengths connected to a bowl of various sizes in which specially prepared and often flavored tobacco is packed, lit, and smoked. Unlike cigarettes, pipe smoke is seldom fully inhaled, but nicotine from the smoke can, though less efficiently than in the lungs, be absorbed in the mouth.

plug A popular type of chewing tobacco.

point-of-purchase advertisement An advertisement displayed at retail outlets where products are sold. Despite banning cigarette advertisements from television and radio, companies have until recently been able to advertise to youth through store displays.

public health A science devoted to protection of the health of members of a community and population through preventive medicine and sanitary living conditions. It differs from clinical medicine that is based on the observation, diagnosis, and treatment of individual patients and has much relevance to the health effects in communities and populations of cigarette use.

punitive damages Damages awarded above and beyond compensatory damages to punish a negligent party for wanton, reckless, or malicious acts or omissions.

relative risk ratio A measure of the health effects of smoking that shows the number of smokers who die from a particular disease for each nonsmoker who dies of the disease. For example, a relative risk ratio of 22 indicates that for every male nonsmoker who dies of lung cancer, 22 male smokers die.

roll-your-own (hand-rolled) cigarettes Cigarettes made by pouring a small amount of finely grained tobacco onto a small paper, rolling the paper and tobacco into a tube, and licking the paper to seal the tube.

"safe" cigarette Products that reduce the tar, nicotine, secondhand smoke, and additives of cigarettes, and that aim to make cigarettes safer to smoke. Experts on both sides of the issues agree, however, that all tobacco products are inherently unsafe, even if some products are less unsafe than others.

secondhand smoke Environmental tobacco smoke.

smokeless tobacco Tobacco in the form of snuff or chew that does not require smoking or inhalation but nonetheless delivers nicotine to the body.

smuggling Process of secretly moving large amounts of products across borders, without paying import or export duties and taxes. As taxes on cigarettes increase the problem of smuggling becomes more serious. European nations have accused U.S. tobacco companies of helping to smuggle cigarettes into Europe to avoid taxes and sell them at cheaper prices. Domestically some state officials are concerned about cigarettes bought without taxes on Native American lands and over the Internet.

snuff A form of powdered and (usually) flavored smokeless tobacco that is placed between the lower gum and lip, or (mostly in the past) sniffed into the nose.

stillborn A fetus dead at birth, an outcome that occurs more often among mothers who smoked during pregnancy than those who did not smoke.

Students Helping Others Understand Tobacco (SHOUT) An intensive and long-term program designed to reduce smoking among youth.

tar A general term that encompasses particles contained in the residue or by-product of the burning of tobacco and are inhaled with tobacco smoke. It is a major source of the harmful effects of tobacco use on health but also a major source of tobacco flavor.

tar derby A term used to describe the competition among cigarette manufacturers over sales of low-tar cigarettes that occurred in the 1950s when evidence of the harm of smoking for health began to emerge. The low tar and health claims made on behalf of cigarettes became so confusing that the Federal Trade Commission took over the testing for cigarette tar.

Glossary

Tobacco Industry Research Council (TIRC)   An organization formed by U.S. tobacco companies in 1954 to counter the negative publicity about cigarettes with its own studies, press releases, and information on smoking.

Tobacco Institute (TI)   A trade organization in Washington, D.C., that was funded by tobacco firms and promoted the interests of the tobacco industry

tort   A wrongful act or breach of contract that may warrant payment to the wronged party of monetary damages.

trust   A combination of firms or corporations formed by legal arrangement particularly for the purpose of reducing competition. The American Tobacco Company formed a trust among the major cigarette manufacturers in 1890.

Turkish tobacco   A type of tobacco from Turkey with a mild fragrance that comprised a popular type of imported cigarette in the 19th century. Cigarettes grew in popularity when tobacco companies blended it with American tobacco and sold the new blends at lower prices than the imported cigarettes.

warranty   An assurance or guarantee of legal standing, as for example, in the claims of tobacco companies that their products were safe and not addictive. A warranty may be expressed or implied.

white burley tobacco   A popular American tobacco first developed in Ohio in 1866 that could absorb additives better and had higher nicotine content than other tobacco products.

withdrawal   The syndrome of painful physical and psychological symptoms that comes from the discontinuation of an addictive substance.

Women's Christian Temperance Union (WCTU)   An organization founded in 1874 that advocated total abstinence from alcohol and opposed related behaviors such as smoking.

World Health Organization (WHO)   An agency of the United Nations devoted to helping people throughout the world obtain the highest possible level of health. It has in recent years made special efforts to stop the global spread of cigarette use.

PART II

GUIDE TO FURTHER RESEARCH

CHAPTER 6

HOW TO RESEARCH
THE TOBACCO INDUSTRY
AND SMOKING

Beginning researchers face a number of challenges in studying the tobacco industry and smoking. First, they can become easily overwhelmed by the amount of information available on the topic. Used in Europe for 500 years and in North America for an even longer period, tobacco has spread further in recent decades to become one of the world's most widely used products. The numbers seem astounding: Across the world, 5.5 trillion cigarettes are produced each year. In the United States estimates of the number of yearly deaths from smoking-related causes exceed 400,000 (about one-sixth of all deaths), and heavy smokers can expect to die 12 years earlier than non-smokers. Worldwide the death toll of tobacco currently numbers about 4 million people per year (about one in 10 adult deaths). Given the wide use and serious harm of cigarettes, the embattled multinational tobacco industry has similarly received much attention, being subject to antismoking legislation, litigation, and international treaties.

The global importance of tobacco has made it one of the most researched products in the world. It has relevance to issues of health, medicine, law, chemistry, biochemistry, politics, public policy, social life, psychology, economics, business, advertising, and education. No wonder the amount of available information is so vast. It spans traditional academic fields, specialized areas of research, national borders, and historical periods. Without some guidance, those new to these issues may find it difficult to comprehend the diverse information they uncover.

Second, the literature on the tobacco industry and smoking often reflects strong moral views and opinions. Once debates centered on the possible harm of smoking for health, but those debates have been settled—even the tobacco companies today admit that smoking brings risks. Debates over the addictiveness of nicotine have also largely died down as scientific evidence has shown strong similarities between use of cigarettes and addictive drugs such as cocaine and heroin. Some scholars deny such addictiveness, but they remain a minority. Instead the debates today center on the conflict between the freedom of individuals to choose their own lifestyle—however self-destructive—and the goals of public health to reduce sickness and premature death in the population. On the former side stand smokers and those devoted to political philosophies of liberty and individual choice. On the latter side stand the government and physicians who believe that society should do all it can outside of banning tobacco use to eliminate the activity. More extreme antismoking advocates see smoking as immoral, smokers as victimized, and cigarette makers as villains. In terms of public opinion most people side with the public health advocates and view smoking with distaste, but few would deny smokers the choice to continue their habit. Congress reveals a similar split in views, with antismoking advocates unable to pass legislation over the resistance of those committed to freedom of choice and supportive of business interests. In any case writings on the tobacco industry and smoking do not always make these underlying views explicit, and researchers need to be aware of them.

Third, research on the tobacco industry and smoking often includes technically difficult matter. Some of the writings focus on the chemistry of cigarettes, smoke, and nicotine, and therefore go beyond the understanding of most nonscientists. Only slightly less problematic, the widespread use of statistical methods in tobacco-related research, even research addressing issues of general importance to the public, can be daunting. In understanding the harm of smoking for health, the evidence comes not from clinical observations of physicians and nurses; rather it comes from the statistical comparison of the health and mortality of smokers and nonsmokers. Similarly, in understanding the psychological and social patterns of smoking, the facts come from statistical analysis of group behaviors. Even efforts to understand the effects of public policies—taxes, advertising restrictions, smoking-prevention programs—rely on statistical techniques to separate real influences from false ones. Issues of randomness of samples, validity of measurements, and appropriateness of statistical techniques that come into play relate more to the skills of specialists than of general researchers. Readers of studies thus run across intimidating terms such as *relative risk ratios, statistical significance*, and *confidence intervals.*

How can researchers overcome these challenges? Here are some general suggestions, followed by more specific advice about where to find material.

TIPS FOR RESEARCHING THE TOBACCO INDUSTRY AND SMOKING

The following are a few things to keep in mind as one does researching:

- Define the topic carefully. To avoid being overwhelmed by the vast amount of material on the tobacco industry and smoking, beginning researchers need to decide in specific terms what aspects of the larger topic they want to examine. The annotated bibliography in Chapter 7 divides writings into six categories: 1) history and background, 2) health and medical aspects, 3) social and psychological aspects, 4) the tobacco business and litigation, 5) tobacco control, and 6) self-help. However, even these categories likely need to be narrowed down. If interested in the history of tobacco, researchers should then decide if they want to focus more specifically on the use of tobacco in the Americas before Columbus, the spread of tobacco through Europe, changes in preferences for tobacco types (snuff, pipes, cigars, chew), the growth of the cigarette industry, the spreading popularity of cigarettes in the early 20th century, the early use of advertising, the development of successful tobacco companies, or the emerging scientific consensus on the harm of tobacco use. With so many choices, making the research manageable requires care and precision in the identification of the issue to study.

- Consider the underlying viewpoints. If understanding the various viewpoints and their implications for tobacco control can help researchers make sense of the diverse literature, it helps to consult works representing these various underlying viewpoints. A researcher should take care not to rely on a single article or book, particularly one that represents one side of the debates over the tobacco industry and smoking. Being familiar with the debates and how various studies fit in the spectrum of beliefs can help researchers put information into perspective.

- Rely on studies in the best journals. Because smoking research is common in a variety of disciplines, and each academic discipline has dozens of journals for published research, one can only rarely master all this work. In general, however, the most prestigious journals in a discipline publish the best studies—those with the most important discoveries, the strongest scientific methodologies, and the greatest influence on the scientific field. Three top journals publish particularly important work on the medical and social aspects of smoking: the *New England Journal of Medicine, Journal of the American Medical Association (JAMA)*, and *American Journal of Public Health*. The first two are the nation's most prestigious medical journals, and articles related to smoking make up only a small part of any issue. Still the articles that do get published there receive much attention. The *American Journal of Public Health* publishes more on smoking than perhaps any other journal: The articles cover topics related to the health consequences of smoking, psychological and social factors influencing smoking, efforts of the tobacco industry to promote smoking, and ways to prevent and control smoking. Although important and valuable articles appear elsewhere, researchers can benefit from beginning their search of the scientific literature with these journals.

- Focus on conclusions and limitations. Few will want, even if they are able, to wade through the complex details of the methodology and statistical procedures in research articles. Most published articles will have met a minimum standard for scientific quality—particularly articles in the top journals. Otherwise they would be weeded out in the scientific review process and not published. Readers can therefore most efficiently concentrate on the conclusions. Articles contain a one- or two-sentence summary of the conclusion in the abstract (a one-paragraph overview that precedes the article). The abstract contains crucial information in a compact form and can prove quite useful. In addition most articles include a few paragraphs at the end on the limitations of the study and the qualifications of the conclusions. These paragraphs can be important as well. No study is perfect and knowing the weaknesses can help one in understanding its importance.

- Be cautious of newspaper, magazine, television, and radio reports on research. These media sources may exaggerate the importance of a study in trying to attract the interest of readers. They sometimes report early results based on press conferences rather than on articles published in top journals that have gone through the review process. The *New York Times* remains an exception to this statement: The weekly Science section often includes health stories with considerable detail and commentary from experts. However, shorter pieces on new findings in most newspapers, magazines, television reports, and radio stories need to be examined with care. If less valuable for obtaining information on research, these sources of news provide much useful reporting on events involving litigation, public policies, and trends in tobacco use. Stories typically do well to explain legal issues in clear terms, highlight their general importance, and get information to readers quickly.

- Become familiar with some basic statistical terms. Research articles and their abstracts often refer to "relative risk ratios." These measure the health risks of smoking (or any other drug, behavior, group membership, or medical procedure) by comparing the number of smokers who die from a particular disease for each nonsmoker who dies from the disease.

A relative risk ratio of 11, for example, would mean in this context that for every nonsmoker who dies of lung cancer during a particular time span, 11 smokers die. Studies also often refer to "statistical significance." The term does not mean a statistic is necessarily important but suggests that a relationship or coefficient found in a sample (between, say, smoking and lung cancer) likely exists in the larger population. Statistical significance depends greatly on the size of the sample as well as on the strength of the relationship. Similarly a "confidence interval" refers to a range of values for a coefficient that likely contain the true value of the coefficient in the population. Although such terms appear complex, these basic definitions can ease the process of understanding research on smoking.

GETTING STARTED: HOW TO FIND HELPFUL SOURCES

BOOKS

A few recent books provide good starting points for those doing research on the tobacco industry and smoking. Tara Parker-Pope's *Cigarettes: Anatomy of an Industry from Seed to Smoke* (New York: New Press, 2001) presents a readable overview of several facets of the tobacco industry and cigarette use. Her book includes many insightful facts and helpful references but not the overwhelming detail of some other general volumes. Tamara L. Roleff, Mary Williams, and Charles P. Cozic, the editors of *Tobacco and Smoking: Opposing Viewpoints* (San Diego, Calif.: Greenhaven Press, 1998) use articles in general circulation magazines to present alternative sides of various debates about smoking. With short and nontechnical selections, the volume presents a helpful overview of the controversies in the area.

For more information on the history of smoking and the tobacco industry, Iain Gately's *Tobacco: The Story of How Tobacco Seduced the World* (New York: Grove Press, 2001) offers much detail on the spread of tobacco use and is written in a style that will appeal to general readers and beginning researchers. Robert Sobel also offers a readable history in *They Satisfy: The Cigarette in American Life* (Garden City, N.Y.: Anchor Press, 1978). This book concentrates more on cigarette use in the United States than does Gately's book and says much more about tobacco companies and their brands than most books. It ends, however, with the 1970s—before many tobacco control efforts began. An impressive and thorough history of the battle between tobacco companies and antitobacco forces can be found in Alan Kluger's *Ashes to Ashes: America's Hundred-Year Cigarette War, the Public Health, and the Unabashed Triumph of Philip Morris* (New York: Alfred A.

Knopf, 1996). It does not include the litigation success against the tobacco industry in the 1990s but covers just about everything on the battle up to then. If this book is too overwhelming in its detail, a less comprehensive (and more one-sided) history of the battle involving medical and public health experts against the tobacco companies can be found in Elizabeth Whelan's *A Smoking Gun: How the Tobacco Industry Gets Away with Murder* (Philadelphia: George F. Stickley, 1984). Updates to the work of Kluger and Whelan appear in any number of books listed in the next chapter on recent suits against the tobacco companies and the steps toward the Master Settlement Agreement.

For those most interested in the health and social aspects of smoking, the various reports issued by the Office of the Surgeon General are helpful. The reports are comprehensive, and the text often assumes technical knowledge. However, each volume provides nontechnical summaries and conclusions in each chapter and makes concrete policy recommendations. Readers can gain much from these summaries and then select specific parts of the longer text to examine in more detail. The text also typically includes many useful charts and graphs. Since the first report in 1964 has become outdated, a useful starting volume is the 1989 report, *Reducing the Health Consequences of Smoking: 25 Years of Progress* (Washington, D.C.: U.S. Department of Health and Human Services, 1989). It provides a comprehensive review of the evidence on the harm of smoking and the public beliefs about the harm of smoking. The 2001 report, *Women and Smoking*, gives special attention to women and makes up for more extensive attention to men in the past. Even so, with 500-some pages it covers most topics related to smoking of both sexes and contains up-to-date information. For those interested in tobacco control efforts the 2000 volume, *Regulating Tobacco*, is a comprehensive and recent source of information. Still other reports on involuntary smoking, addiction, youth, and racial groups that are listed in the bibliography represent valuable resources.

Among writings concerned with smokers' rights, Jacob Sullum's *For Your Own Good: The Anti-Smoking Crusade and the Tyranny of Public Health* (New York: Free Press, 1998), calmly presents the case of those opposed to many current tobacco control efforts.

The bibliography in the following chapter provides many suggestions for additional books to consult, and researchers can search for more books in library catalogs, bookstore lists, and databases. Remember, however, that in these searches broad keywords such as *tobacco, smoking,* and *cigarettes* will return an enormous number of hits; more specific and detailed keywords will work better. In any case a large selection of books can be found through electronic bookstores such as Amazon.com (http://www.amazon.com) and Barnes and Noble's web site (http://www.barnesandnoble.com). The listings sometimes helpfully include summaries and reviews of the books, as well as the comments of individual readers. Besides using a public or university library for a catalog search, researchers can find references using the comprehensive listings of the Library of Congress (http://lcweb.loc.gov). This huge database includes subject headings on a variety of topics related to tobacco and smoking (which again requires care in selecting keywords for a search).

ARTICLES

Two types of articles may be useful for those researching the tobacco industry and smoking: articles published in scientific journals that include original research and articles published in magazines and newspapers that target general audiences. With rare exceptions journals or magazines are not devoted only to tobacco issues. It is therefore necessary to search through journals and magazine databases for relevant articles.

First, for access to scientific articles one might begin with a search of the top medical and public health journals: the *New England Journal of Medicine* (http://www.nejm.org), *JAMA* (http://jama.ama-assn.org), and the *American Journal of Public Health* (http://www.ajph.org). The Internet home pages of these journals allow users to search for and identify the most relevant articles. The searches almost always return the abstract with the bibliographic citation. For those wanting to avoid the details of the scientific method, the abstract provides a helpful summary of the key findings. Many of the editorials, letters, and brief reports available online in these journals can also prove useful. To explore the article text more fully, it is possible for subscribers (and sometimes nonsubscribers) to view the full article online; if not available online in its full form an article can be found in the journals at university and medical school libraries.

One other journal deserves special mention. *Morbidity and Mortality Weekly Report (MMWR)*, published by the Centers for Disease Control and Prevention (CDC), provides much descriptive information on smoking and smoking-related health conditions. Moreover the journal articles are available online (http://www.cdc.gov/mmwr). Unlike the other journals *MMWR* does not focus on development of new ideas and tests of hypotheses, but it does report reliable and useful figures in a way most readers can understand. The figures come from the best available data sets on smoking and can be easily used in reports.

Several databases of scientific articles on health, medicine, and social science can, with appropriate care, be used for searches on the tobacco industry and smoking. In general the larger the database, the narrower the search terms should be. Terms such as tobacco, smoking, and cigarettes may work well when searching a single journal but are too broad when searching databases made up of a large number of journals. With this caution in mind several reference sources prove most helpful. PubMed (http://www.ncbi. nlm.nih.gov/PubMed), a free resource available to the public as part of the National Library of Medicine and sponsored by the National Institutes of Health, contains more than 12 million citations dating back to the mid-1960s. It includes an important medical database, MEDLINE, and tends to list many hard science references, such as physiology, biochemistry, and neuroscience. For those interested in such research rather than in research on the use and prevention of tobacco, PubMed may be ideal. Otherwise OCLC First Search gives users access to more than 72 databases, including Social Science Abstracts, which focuses more on social than medical aspects of smoking. However, OCLC First Search is available only through subscribing libraries.

Second, for access to less technical articles targeted to a general audience those doing research on the tobacco industry and smoking can use several databases. The above-mentioned OCLC First Search contains an electronic version of Reader's Guide Abstracts that lists articles in *Time, Newsweek, Business Week*, and a large number of other magazines. Again, however, users generally need access to a subscribing library for this database. InfoTrac also compiles articles for general interest audiences and sometimes includes an abstract with the citation or an abstract and a full text article. It, too, requires library privileges. Ingenta Library Gateway (http://www.ingenta.com) includes 11 million citations from more than 20,000 journals and allows searches within specific subject areas, such as medicine and social science. Searching Ingenta is free but delivery of an article requires a fee.

Newspaper articles can provide useful information on court cases, legislation, business changes, and current events related to tobacco. The *New York Times* and the *Wall Street Journal* are particularly useful. Libraries usually subscribe to databases that include these newspapers. For example, users can have access to abstracts and full articles through First Search (select the LexisNexis Academic or ProQuest database within First Search). The *Washington Post* has also a series of articles on tobacco litigation and antitobacco legislation that can be accessed online (http://www.washingtonpost. com/wpdyn/nation/specials/socialpolicy/tobacco/index.html).

RESEARCH ON THE INTERNET

Although the Internet represents an extraordinary resource in terms of the wealth of information available to researchers, combing through all the web sites listed by searches can consume much time. Moreover the information obtained is not always reliable and unbiased. Researchers can proceed in several ways.

How to Research the Tobacco Industry and Smoking

Popular and general search engines such as Google (http://www.google.com), Yahoo! (http://www.yahoo.com), AltaVista (http://www.altavista.com), Excite (http://www.excite.com), Hotbot (http://www.hotbot.com), Lycos (http://www.lycos.com), and many others can identify web sites that contain information on the tobacco industry and smoking. Effectively using these search engines requires the thoughtful selection of narrow search terms. Nonetheless, taking the time to work through the hundreds of thousands of web sites found by using general terms can sometimes lead to an unexpected and intriguing discovery.

A more efficient way to proceed involves searching directories relevant to the tobacco industry and smoking. In Yahoo! directories, under "Recreation & Sports > Hobbies > Smoking," one can find web sites and information on antismoking organizations, cigars, Joe Camel, secondhand smoke, and teen smoking; under "Health > Diseases and Conditions > All Diseases and Conditions > Smoking addictions," one can find information on smoking cessation and cessation support groups. In Google relevant directories include "Health > Addictions > Substance abuse > Tobacco" and "Health > Support Groups > Smoking cessation." Other directories besides those of Yahoo! and Google are available as well. The directory indexes have some advantages over general searches. They do not attempt to compile every link but evaluate a link for usefulness and quality before including it in the directory. This selectivity can save time and frustration, even if it may miss some sites a researcher would find useful. In addition the directories organize the links by topic and thus avoid the disorganized listing obtained from a general search. Use of the directories does not, however, eliminate the need to use the links carefully and critically.

Several web sites devoted specifically to tobacco provide useful starting points for researchers. Tobacco.org (http://www.tobacco.org) contains the latest tobacco headlines, an archive of news briefs, quotes about smoking, an information page, tobacco documents, book releases, and graphs (subscribers can obtain additional information). Given its extensive information the web site can best be used with the search command. TobaccoWeek.com (URL: http://www.tobaccoweek.com) similarly includes much news and information relating to the tobacco industry and smoking. The Tobacco Reference Guide (http://www.globalink.org/tobacco/trg), compiled by David Moyer, presents a collection of materials from a variety of public sources. The online tobacco encyclopedia *TobaccoPedia* (http://tobaccopedia.org) is supported by the International Union Against Cancer (UICC) and includes entries relating to a wide range of topics.

For information relating to tobacco control and antismoking efforts it helps to consult the web sites of several organizations. Action on Smoking and Health (ASH) advertises its web page as "Everything for People

Concerned about Smoking and Nonsmokers' Rights, Smoking Statistics, Quitting Smoking, Smoking Risks, and Other Smoking Information" (http://ash.org). As it claims, the site contains an assortment of anti-smoking information. The Campaign for Tobacco Free Kids (http://www.tobaccofreekids.org) offers resources for helping to reduce youth smoking. The Office of Smoking and Health (http://www.cdc.gov/tobacco), a unit within the CDC and the U.S. Department of Health and Human Services, leads and coordinates efforts to prevent tobacco use among youth, promote smoking cessation, protect nonsmokers from secondhand smoke, and eliminate tobacco-related health disparities. The office's web site contains resources for reaching these goals.

Fewer sites support tobacco use than oppose it, but Forces International (http://www.forces.org) presents arguments in favor of smokers' rights and includes links to other web sites with like-minded views. Web sites of the tobacco companies (British-American Tobacco, Philip Morris, R. J. Reynolds) defend their decision to continue producing and selling cigarettes but, perhaps surprisingly, devote space to stating their goal of limiting tobacco use by children.

COURT CASES

Litigation against the tobacco industry has mushroomed in the last few years because of the admission by tobacco companies in the Master Settlement Agreement of past wrongdoing, the availability of internal tobacco company documents to demonstrate their past misrepresentation, and some large awards against tobacco companies. Information on the suits, jury decisions, awards, appeals, and final judgments can be found through searches of newspapers, tobacco web sites (Tobacco.org and TobaccoWeek.com), and general web sites (by using Google, Yahoo!, or other search engines). To obtain the written decisions in tobacco-related cases, electronic law libraries such as Westlaw and LexisNexis include court opinions since 1990 but charge a fee. Opinions of the Supreme Court relevant to tobacco issues can be obtained from the Legal Information Institute (http://www.law.cornell.edu). To read an overview of the history of tobacco litigation and a review of the most important cases, see the Surgeon General's 2000 report on regulating tobacco, which includes a long chapter on legal action to control tobacco.

CHAPTER 7

ANNOTATED BIBLIOGRAPHY

The following bibliography contains six major sections:

- history and background,
- health and medical aspects,
- social and psychological aspects,
- tobacco business and litigation,
- tobacco control, and
- self-help.

Within each of these sections the citations are divided into subsections for books, articles, and Web documents. The topics and citation types cover a vast amount of material and although the bibliography cannot be fully comprehensive, it includes a representative mix of materials on the tobacco industry and smoking. The sections to follow thus list technical and nontechnical works, historical and contemporary sources, and research and opinion pieces. (See Chapter 6 for an overview on how to most effectively use the diverse materials.) The sections cover history, science, and research but also include self-help selections on how to quit smoking. They also include sources of information useful to those interested in becoming involved in tobacco control activities as well as in learning more about the topic.

HISTORY AND BACKGROUND

BOOKS

Breen, T. H. *Tobacco Culture: The Mentality of the Great Tidewater Planters on the Eve of the Revolution.* Princeton, N.J.: Princeton University Press, 1985. This history demonstrates the importance of tobacco to the political as well as economic history of the United States. The author argues that tobacco planters developed values of personal autonomy, which led to their resistance against economic control by Britain and contributed to the American Revolution.

Burnham, John C. *Bad Habits: Drinking, Smoking, Taking Drugs, Gambling, Sexual Misbehavior, and Swearing in American History.* New York: New York University Press, 1993. This study places the acceptance of smoking within a framework of broader social changes that led to permissiveness toward a wider variety of "bad habits." Smoking and other misbehaviors overcame strong and organized opposition in the first part of the 20th century to become common in American society.

Campbell, Tracy. *The Politics of Despair: Power and Resistance in the Tobacco Wars.* Lexington: University of Kentucky Press, 1993. The tobacco wars in the title refer to conflict between tobacco producers and farmers in Kentucky and Tennessee in 1904–08. The efforts of farmers to resist the push by the tobacco monopoly to pay lower prices for tobacco leaf reflect the culture, politics, and economy in tobacco areas of the South.

Collins, Philip. *Cigar Bizarre: An Unusual History.* Los Angeles: General Publishing Group, 1997. An irreverent and entertaining history of cigars rather than a scholarly work, this book contains pictures plus many unusual and interesting facts.

Cooper, Patricia A. *Once a Cigar Maker: Men, Women, and Work Culture in American Cigar Factories, 1900–1919.* Urbana: University of Illinois Press, 1987. This social history of the Cigar Makers International union describes the daily lives of men and women who made 5¢ and 10¢ cigars, and the tensions between male and female workers as well as between management and labor.

Courtwright, David T. *Forces of Habit: Drugs and the Making of the Modern World.* Cambridge, Mass.: Harvard University Press, 2001. Focusing largely on the expansion of European commerce in illicit and licit drugs, the author treats tobacco as part of a larger story that involves alcohol, caffeine, cannabis, opium, and cocaine.

Cox, Howard. *The Global Cigarette: Origins and Evolution of British American Tobacco, 1880–1945.* New York: Oxford University Press, 2000. This history examines efforts of the British American Tobacco Company to pursue markets in colonies across the world. These early efforts would set the groundwork for the later success of multinational cigarette manufacturers in promoting their products in developing nations and begin the process toward internationalization by the cigarette industry.

Daniel, Pete. *Breaking the Land: The Transformation of Cotton, Tobacco, and Rice Cultures since 1880.* Urbana: University of Illinois Press, 1985. This acclaimed study examines the changes faced by small farmers and tenants in the South as agriculture modernized and compares the response to the changes by those farming tobacco, cotton, and rice. It emphasizes the social and cultural life of southern farmers as well as their economic problems.

Durden, Robert Franklin. *Lasting Legacy to the Carolinas.* Durham, N.C.: Duke University Press, 1998. A history of the Duke endowment and the model it provided to other foundations for how to distribute charity, the book has less to do with smoking and the tobacco industry than with the use of tobacco profits by magnate James B. Duke.

Fahs, John. *Cigarette Confidential: The Unfiltered Truth about the Ultimate American Addiction.* New York: Berkley Books, 1996. The author, an investigative reporter, examines the pleasures and pains of nicotine addiction, the costs of the addiction, the actions of the tobacco industry, and the scenes behind the cigarette wars.

Forey, Barbara, et al. *International Smoking Statistics: A Collection of Historical Data from 30 Economically Developed Countries.* 2d ed. Oxford, U.K.: Oxford University Press, 2002. This comprehensive reference work is filled with data on trends in smoking and cigarette consumption and will interest researchers and those wanting to know more about differences across nations in the use of tobacco.

Gately, Iain. *Tobacco: The Story of How Tobacco Seduced the World.* New York: Grove Press, 2001. Beginning with the first use of tobacco by native peoples in the Americas and ending with the spread of tobacco throughout the world, this book asks why tobacco has and continues to have such a hold on humankind, why it has been accepted in so many cultures across the world, and why its use has persisted well after it has been revealed as a killer. In answering the questions the author gives particular attention to the habit in premodern societies.

Goldstein, Michael S. *The Health Movement: Promoting Fitness in America.* New York: Twayne Publishers, 1992. Together with movements supporting nutrition and exercise, movements supporting smoking abatement have played an important role in public life. This history describes the movements and the social conditions that contributed to their success.

Goodman, Jordan. *Tobacco in History: The Cultures of Dependence.* London: Routledge, 1993. Written more for scholars than the public, this study posits that acceptance of tobacco must be understood as part of the history of the product. It focuses on the dependence of producers as well as consumers on tobacco and gives special attention to cultivation and production in premodern as well as modern societies.

Gottsegen, Jack. *Tobacco: A Study of Its Consumption in the United States.* New York: Pittman, 1940. Filled with facts and statistics, this book presents a scientific and data-oriented approach to the history of tobacco use in the United States. It gives much attention to changing fashions in the preferences for snuff, chew, pipes, cigars, and cigarettes and offers many historical examples of the changing fashions.

Hilton, Matthew. *Smoking in British Popular Culture, 1800–2000*. Manchester, U.K.: Manchester University Press, 2000. Although focused on Britain rather than the United States, this historical study describes changes in the cultural acceptability of smoking. The author argues that the rise of smoking has related to strengthening beliefs about the importance of individuality and independence and later to new understandings of masculinity and femininity.

Hirschfelder, Arlene B. *Encyclopedia of Smoking and Tobacco*. Phoenix, Ariz.: Oryx Press, 1999. This encyclopedia is comprehensive in its listings and a useful reference source. However, its reliance on the alphabetical ordering of items means it lacks a coherent framework to organize the vast material on smoking and tobacco.

Howard, Red. *Cigars*. New York: MetroBooks, 1997. This history of cigars offers a guide to choosing, preparing, and enjoying cigars and includes photographs, examples of advertisements, and fine art reproductions.

Hughes, Jason. *Learning to Smoke: Tobacco Use in the West*. Chicago: University of Chicago Press, 2003. Most literature on smoking takes a biological or pharmacological approach that views cigarettes as a nicotine-delivery system. To supplement this approach the author argues that across histories and societies, individuals have interpreted the meaning of these physical cues differently, and that social context is crucial to understanding smoking.

Infante, C. Cabrera. *Holy Smoke*. New York: Harper and Row, 1984. Raised in Cuba and exiled from his country in 1966, the author offers a social history of the cigar and cigar smokers. With stories about Fidel Castro, Groucho Marx, Mark Twain, W. C. Fields, and many others, the book aims to entertain as well as educate about this tobacco product.

Klein, Richard. *Cigarettes Are Sublime*. Durham, N.C.: Duke University Press, 1993. Stimulated by the difficulties he faced in quitting, the author presents a literary-based review of what makes cigarettes so satisfying. He also criticizes current antismoking campaigns as excessive and puritanical.

Kluger, Alan. *Ashes to Ashes: America's Hundred-Year Cigarette War, the Public Health, and the Unabashed Triumph of Philip Morris*. New York: Alfred A. Knopf, 1996. An impressively detailed history of the tobacco industry and the attempts to control it in the United States over the last century, this volume is unique in the comprehensiveness of the story it tells. It relies on interviews with hundreds of people, thoroughly covers relevant documents, and gives special attention to the growth of the Philip Morris tobacco company.

Annotated Bibliography

Kulikoff, Allan. *Tobacco and Slaves: The Development of Southern Cultures in the Chesapeake, 1680–1800.* Chapel Hill: University of North Carolina Press, 1986. This history describes the development of the tobacco economy in eastern Maryland and Virginia from the late 1600s to 1880 and the development of slave-based cultures among whites and blacks associated with the tobacco economy.

Lock, S., L. A. Reynolds, and E. M. Tansey, eds. *Ashes to Ashes: The History of Smoking and Health.* Atlanta Ga.: Rodopi, 1998. Articles in the volume address issues concerning the history of tobacco advertising, antitobacco movements, tobacco in art and literature, and the emergence of policies to control tobacco.

Mackenzie, Compton. *Sublime Tobacco.* New York: Macmillan, 1958. A smoker who started at age four, the author offers a prologue about his own smoking life before describing historical events that led to the spread of tobacco. Of special historical interest is the epilogue, which deals with the benefits tobacco has brought to humanity and provides a perspective on the product quite different from the one that dominates today.

McCusker, John J., and Kenneth Morgan, eds. *The Early Modern Atlantic Economy.* Cambridge, U.K.: Cambridge University Press, 2001. This study of the trade in tobacco and other products between Britain and America during the 1700s emphasizes the role of merchants in colonial commerce.

Norris, James D. *Advertising and the Transformation of American Society, 1865–1920.* Westport, Conn.: Greenwood Press, 1990. This history of the emergence of advertising appropriately gives prominent attention to cigarettes—a product whose growth coincided with the widespread use of various forms of advertising.

Prince, Eldred E., and Robert R. Simpson. *Long Green: The Rise and Fall of Tobacco in South Carolina.* Athens: University of Georgia Press, 2000. This study of tobacco in South Carolina examines the farmers, land owners, and manufacturers of the product.

Proctor, Robert N. *The Nazi War on Cancer.* Princeton, N.J.: Princeton University Press, 1999. This history describes antitobacco policies in Nazi Germany and efforts to control tobacco companies with state pressure.

Ragsdale, Bruce A. *A Planters' Republic: The Search for Economic Independence in Revolutionary Virginia.* Madison: University of Wisconsin 1996. The author argues that the desire for economic independence more than the desire for political liberty led to the war for independence. With tobacco the primary product, concern about the British economic regulation led the planter class in Virginia to support revolution.

Reynolds, Patrick, and Tom Shachtman. *Gilded Leaf: Triumph, Tragedy, and Tobacco: Three Generations of the R. J. Reynolds Family and Fortune.* Boston:

Little, Brown, 1989. A descendant of R. J. Reynolds and a writer tell a story of family wealth and misfortune. Despite his famous relatives, Patrick Reynolds has become an antismoking activist.

Rogozinski, Jan. *Smokeless Tobacco in the Western World: 1550–1950.* Westport, Conn.: Greenwood Press, 1990. In contrast to most books on tobacco this one gives attention to smokeless tobacco and to differences across nations of Europe in the use and regulation of smokeless products

Siegel, Frederick F. *The Roots of Southern Distinctiveness: Tobacco and Society in Danville, Virginia, 1780–1865.* Chapel Hill: University of North Carolina Press, 1987. Danville, Virginia, and the surrounding area became a thriving center of tobacco marketing and manufacturing. In describing the entrepreneurs, planters, and slaveholders in the vicinity, this history reveals how the culture mixed traits of southern agriculture and slavery with northern business traits of entrepreneurship.

Sobel, Robert. *They Satisfy: The Cigarette in American Life.* Garden City, N.Y.: Anchor Press, 1978. Focusing on the tobacco industry, cigarette advertising, and smoking fashions in the United States up to the 1970s, this history gives much detail about tobacco brands, prices, companies, sales, and marketing. It also offers brief biographies of leading tobacco executives and their opponents and stories about the use of cigarettes in U.S. history.

Stern, Lesley. *The Smoking Book.* Chicago: University of Chicago Press, 1999. In this unusual book of 54 chapters, largely recollections stimulated by smoking, the author tells about an upbringing on a tobacco farm in Rhodesia (modern-day Zimbabwe) and meditates on the meaning of smoking.

Tate, Cassandra. *Cigarette Wars: The Triumph of the "Little White Slaver."* Oxford, U.K.: Oxford University Press, 1999. A historical study from the end of the 19th century to the Great Depression, this book describes the early anticigarette movement and its relationship in the United States to the Progressive Era—a period of protest against smoking, drinking, and other habits. It gives particular attention to legal and social restrictions on smoking a century ago and to the cultural trends that overcame the restrictions.

Tennant, Richard. *The American Cigarette Industry.* New Haven, Conn.: Yale University, 1950. Focused largely on economics, this technical study provides much information on the business during the early part of the 20th century but has become dated with the new information accruing about smoking and cigarettes.

Tenner, Edward. *Why Things Bite Back: Technology and the Revenge of Unintended Consequences.* New York: Knopf, 1996. In arguing that technological breakthroughs often have serious unexpected results, the author provides many examples and gives attention to how innovations involving the creation of low-tar cigarettes have encouraged smoking.

Annotated Bibliography

Tilly, Nannie May. *The R. J. Reynolds Tobacco Company.* Chapel Hill: University of North Carolina Press, 1985. Covering the history of the company from 1875 to 1963, this book discusses labor relations, advertising, and competition for sales with other tobacco companies.

Wagner, Susan. *Cigarette Country: Tobacco in American History and Politics.* New York: Praeger Publishers, 1971. Beginning with the use of tobacco by native peoples in the present-day Mexican state of Chiapas, this book traces the history of tobacco up to the 1960s.

Whelan, Elizabeth. *A Smoking Gun: How the Tobacco Industry Gets Away with Murder.* Philadelphia: George F. Stickley, 1984. Vigorously antitobacco, this book offers a clear if opinionated history of tobacco use and industry efforts to promote its products. It treats the tobacco industry as a villain in its battle with scientists, public health experts, and policy makers. The book is dated in terms of current public policies but suggested the use of many strategies to control tobacco that later were adopted.

Winter, Joseph C., ed. *Tobacco Use by Native North Americans: Sacred Smoke and Silent Killer.* Norman: University of Oklahoma Press, 2000. Native Americans continue to view tobacco—when used properly—as a sacred product that has played an important role in their history. The chapters in the edited volume cover the history of tobacco use by American Indians, the contribution of smoking to myth and tradition, and current problems of Native Americans stemming from modern use of cigarettes.

ARTICLES

Centers for Disease Control and Prevention. "Morbidity and Mortality Weekly Report: State-Specific Prevalence of Current Cigarette Smoking among Adults and the Proportion of Adults Who Work in a Smoke-Free Environment—United States, 1999." *JAMA*, vol. 284, December 13, 2000, p. 2,865. States vary widely in the level of cigarette use, with 31.5 percent of residents of Nevada smoking and 13.9 percent of residents of Utah smoking. States also vary in exposure of their residents to second-hand smoke at work: 61.3 percent of indoor workers in Mississippi reported a workplace policy on smoking and 82.0 percent in Washington, D.C. reported such policies.

———. "Morbidity and Mortality Weekly Report: Tobacco Use—United States, 1900–1999." *JAMA*, vol. 282, December 15, 1999, p. 2,202. This brief report helpfully summarizes the short-term and long-term trends in smoking.

Mackay, Judith. "The Global Tobacco Epidemic: The Next 25 Years." *Public Health Reports*, vol. 113, January/February 1998, pp. 14–21. Noting that the worldwide tobacco epidemic has worsened over the last 30 years, the author projects that by 2025 the number of smokers and smoking-related deaths will continue to rise without major global tobacco control efforts.

Rozin, Paul. "The Process of Moralization." *Psychological Science*, vol. 10, May 1999, pp. 218–221. The author, a psychologist at the University of Pennsylvania, describes the process that translates antismoking preferences into views of cigarette use as an immoral act. Moralization shows not just in the dislike of cigarette smoking but also in the outrage of non-smokers when confronted by undesired cigarette smoke, in the crusading views of antismoking advocates, and in the association of smoking with weakness.

Saad, Lydia. "A Half-Century of Polling on Tobacco: Most Don't Like Smoking but Tolerate It." *Public Perspective*, vol. 9, August/September 1998, pp. 1–4. Summarizes polling results on government regulation of smoking, the right to smoke, awareness of hazards, tobacco use, and teen smoking over the period 1954–96. The trends over time reveal more negative public opinions on smoking but continued support for the right to smoke.

Wynder, Ernest L. "Tobacco and Health: A Review of the History and Suggestions for Public Policy." *Public Health Reports*, vol. 103, January/February 1988, pp. 8–18. One of the first physicians to scientifically demonstrate a link between smoking and lung cancer reviews the early evidence of the link and the slow steps toward widespread acceptance of the harm of tobacco use on health. He notes that progress in preventing tobacco use has come even more slowly than the understanding of its harm.

WEB DOCUMENTS

Cable News Network. "A Brief History of Tobacco." Available online. URL: http://www.cnn.com/US/9705/tobacco/history. Downloaded in December 2002. This news story provides a readable, although short, history of tobacco and highlights some of the major events in that history.

Encarta Encyclopedia. "Tobacco." Available online. URL: http://encarta. msn.com/encet/refbages/RefArticle.aspx?refid=761562287. Downloaded in February 2003. A brief but helpful introduction to growing and harvesting, curing, and aging of tobacco in manufacturing of products; the tobacco industry; health effects of smoking; and antismoking actions.

Gallup Organization. "Gallup Poll In-Depth Analyses: Tobacco and Smoking." Available online. URL: http://www.gallup.com/poll/analysis/ia020815.asp. Posted on June 20, 2002. Using Gallup polling data, this report summarizes public opinions in 2001 on smoking in public, legal issues, health consequences, teen smoking, and government policies.

Moyer, David. "The Tobacco Reference Guide." UICC Globalink. Available online. URL: http://www.globalink.org/tobacco/trg. Downloaded in February 2003. Updating an earlier Tobacco Almanac, this web site of the International Union Against Cancer includes material on all aspects of tobacco. The author states that all the material is in the public realm and can be used without copyright permission.

Tobacco.org. "Tobacco News and Information." Available online. URL: http://www.tobacco.org. Downloaded in February 2003. For nonsubscribers this service provides recent tobacco headlines, an archive of news briefs, quotes about smoking, an information page, tobacco documents, book releases, and graphs; subscribers can copy stories and obtain new ones via e-mail.

TobaccoWeek.com. "Tobacco Week in Review." Available online. URL: http://www.tobaccoweek.com. Downloaded in February 2003. In aiming to provide fast and easily accessible tobacco information, to aid in tobacco control, and to provide a resource center, this web site includes short news articles over the past week, summaries of selected research articles, and an archive of less current news articles.

UICC Globalink. "*TobaccoPedia:* The Online Tobacco Encyclopedia." Available online. URL: http://tobaccopedia.org. Downloaded in February 2003. The online tobacco encyclopedia supported by the International Union against Cancer (UICC) includes entries relating to health effects of active and passive smoking, chemistry of addiction, smoking cessation, and tobacco control.

Washington Post Online. "National Tobacco Report." Available online. URL: http://www.washingtonpost.com/wp-dyn/nation/specials/socialpolicy/tobacco. Downloaded in February 2003. The web site compiles recent news stories from the *Washington Post* on tobacco, litigation, and legislative antitobacco efforts.

HEALTH AND MEDICAL ASPECTS

BOOKS

Bailey, William Everett. *The Invisible Drug.* Houston, Tex.: Mosaic Publications, 1996. Topics covered include the hazards of active and passive (secondhand) smoking, federal regulations concerning tobacco, the history of the tobacco industry, the techniques used to promote the spread of tobacco, and the effects of cigarette advertising on children and teens. It is aimed at the general reader who wants to stay informed.

Benowitz, Neal L., ed. *Nicotine Safety and Toxicity.* New York: Oxford University Press, 1998. Nicotine in high doses is deadly, but its toxicity in smaller doses, such as that obtained directly from patches and gum in smoking reduction efforts, is less clear. Based on a symposium on the topic and addressed largely to experts, this edited volume reviews the scientific evidence on the safety and harm to the body of nicotine.

Christian, Arden G., and Jennifer A. Klein. *Tobacco and Your Oral Health.* Chicago: Quintessence Publishing, 1997. Although tobacco use leads in the long run to sickness and death, it can also stain teeth, produce bad breath, decrease the sense of smell and taste, and cause facial wrinkling, gum and tooth problems, and chronic sinus problems.

Committee on Passive Smoking, Board on Environmental Studies and Toxicology, National Research Council. *Environmental Tobacco Smoke: Measuring and Assessing Health Effects.* Washington, D.C.: National Academy Press, 1986. An early volume on the health effects of secondhand smoke that includes much scientific and technical information.

Diana, John N., ed. *Tobacco Smoking and Atherosclerosis: Pathogenesis and Cellular Mechanisms.* New York: Plenum Publishing, 1990. Atherosclerosis, or buildup of materials in vessel walls, is the major cause of heart disease in the United States. This volume examines how cigarette smoking can cause atherosclerosis and produce early death from heart disease.

Ecobichon, Donald J., and Joseph M. Wu, eds. *Environmental Tobacco Smoking: Proceedings of the International Symposium at McGill University, 1989.* Lexington, Mass.: Lexington Books, 1990. An international group of scholars contributes chapters on topics such as the chemical makeup, exposure, physical harm, and risks of environmental tobacco smoke. Although the findings are dated, the book concludes that the evidence of harm is not strong enough to justify regulatory action.

Frenk, Hanan, and Reuven Dar. *A Critique of Nicotine Addiction.* Boston: Kluwer Academic Publishers, 2000. Based on a review of articles and books on the subject the authors criticize claims that nicotine is an addictive drug. The book offers a minority view on this issue, one that the surgeon general and most public health experts dispute.

Gold, Mark S. *Drugs of Abuse.* Vol. 4, *Tobacco.* New York: Plenum, 1995. Covering the history of tobacco, the effects of nicotine on the brain and the body, psychiatric aspects of tobacco use, and treatment programs, the author emphasizes medical and physical aspects of addiction.

Gori, Gio Batta. *Virtually Safe Cigarettes: Reviving an Opportunity Once Tragically Rejected.* Amsterdam: IOS Press, 2000. In the face of the failure to end use of cigarettes, despite clear evidence of the harm of the product, this book argues that developing a safe cigarette could save thousands of lives and discusses issues in creating and marketing such a product.

Greenberg, Michael R. *Urbanization and Cancer Mortality: The United States Experience, 1950–1975.* New York: Oxford University Press, 1983. This

statistical study shows how cancer—and the smoking habits that contribute to cancer—spread from concentration in cities during the 1950s
to rural areas by the 1970s.

Haustein, Knut-Olaf. *Tobacco or Health: Physiological and Social Damages Caused by Tobacco Smoking*. Berlin Springer, 2003. This translation of a German work covers in some 464 pages the history of tobacco, tobacco components and additives, the health effects of smoking, smoking and pregnancy, passive smoking, nicotine dependence, preventing smoking, and the tobacco industry and advertising.

Jenkins, R. A., M. R. Guerin, and B. A. Tomkins. *The Chemistry of Environmental Tobacco Smoke: Composition and Measurement*. Boca Raton, Fla.: Lewis Publishers, 2000. Technical in nature and aimed at experts, this book provides scientific evidence on the makeup of secondhand smoke and its concentration in indoor air.

Koven, Edward L. *Smoking: The Story Behind the Haze*. New York: Nova Science Publishers, 1996. The most interesting chapter of this book describes the smoking habits of famous people, such as Lucille Ball, Leonard Bernstein, Gary Cooper, Waylon Jennings, Michael Landon, and Lyndon Johnson, and how the habit led to early death or health problems. Another unique chapter includes cartoons about the harm of tobacco.

Kozlowski, Lynn T., Jack E. Henningfield, and Janet Brigham. *Cigarettes, Nicotine, and Health: A Biobehavioral Approach*. Thousand Oaks, Calif.: Sage Publications, 2001. The biobehavioral approach focuses on the physical effects and addictiveness of nicotine. The chapters cover the history of nicotine use, the effects of nicotine on the body, smoking as nicotine addiction, the relation of smoking to drinking and drug use, and helping smokers quit.

Krogh, David. *Smoking: The Artificial Passion*. New York: W. H. Freeman, 1991. In addressing the question of why people smoke, this well-written summary of the scientific literature discusses the biological and psychological research on nicotine use. The research finds that smoking creates positive feelings of both stimulation and relaxation, which make it difficult to quit the habit. The author notes that it is more than physical dependence that keeps smokers puffing away—smoking becomes associated with positive social feelings as well.

Kuhn, Cynthia, Scott Swartzwelder, and Wilkie Wilson. *Buzzed: The Straight Facts about the Most Used and Abused Drugs, from Alcohol to Ecstasy*. New York: Norton, 1998. With chapters on each of 12 types of drugs, this book includes discussion of nicotine with alcohol, caffeine, opiates, steroids, stimulants, and other drugs. The book also discusses issues of addiction, the workings of the brain, and the legal treatment of drugs.

Napier, Kristine M., et al., eds. *Cigarettes—What the Warning Label Doesn't Tell You: The First Comprehensive Guide to the Health Consequences of Smoking*.

New York: American Council on Science and Health, 1996. Each chapter addresses the health effects of smoking from the viewpoint of a different medical specialty. The harm involves not only lung cancer and heart disease but also diabetes, cataracts, psoriasis, and impotence.

National Cancer Institute, National Institutes of Health. *Cigars: Health Effects and Trends.* Smoking and Tobacco Control Monograph 9. Washington, D.C.: U.S. Department of Health and Human Services, 1998. A comprehensive volume on how cigars, although less likely to cause lung cancer and heart disease than cigarettes, nonetheless have risks for oral and esophageal cancer similar to those for cigarettes. It also describes the upward trend in cigar use.

———. *The FTC Cigarette Test Method for Determining Tar, Nicotine, and Carbon Monoxide Yields of U.S. Cigarettes: Report of the NCI Expert Committee.* Smoking and Tobacco Control Monograph 7. Washington, D.C.: U.S. Department of Health and Human Services, 1996. More than others in the series, this volume focuses on technical issues of chemical composition and measurement.

———. *Health Effects of Exposure to Environmental Tobacco Smoke: The Report of the California Environmental Protection Agency.* Smoking and Tobacco Control Monograph 10. Washington, D.C.: U.S. Department of Health and Human Services, 1999. This volume updates earlier reports on the same topic with additional studies and evidence of the harmful effects of exposure to secondhand smoke.

———. *Respiratory Health Effects of Passive Smoking: Lung Cancer and Other Disorders. The Report of the U.S. Environmental Protection Agency.* Smoking and Tobacco Control Monograph 4. Washington, D.C.: U.S. Department of Health and Human Services, 1993. Like the earlier report of the Surgeon General on involuntary smoking, this report from the Environmental Protection Agency (EPA) describes the evidence of the harm of environmental tobacco smoke on health and the need for clean indoor air policies.

———. *Risks Associated with Smoking Cigarettes with Low Machine-Measured Yields of Tar and Nicotine.* Smoking and Tobacco Control Monograph 13. Washington, D.C.: U.S. Department of Health and Human Services, 2001. This volume describes the design of low-tar and low-nicotine cigarettes, their effects on health and disease, the public understanding of the risks of these productions, and efforts of tobacco companies to market them. It concludes that the risks of these cigarettes for health problems remain high.

Orleans, C. Tracy, and John Slade, eds. *Nicotine Addiction: Principles and Management.* New York: Oxford University Press, 1993. A comprehensive reference source for clinicians, researchers, and policymakers, this

edited volume includes chapters on the causes, management, and prevention of nicotine addiction.

Peto, Richard, et al. *Mortality from Smoking in Developed Countries,
1950–2000: Indirect Estimates from National Vital Statistics.* Oxford, U.K.:
Oxford University Press, 1994. Data for each country include the number and proportion of deaths due to smoking over the last half of the 20th
century. Although filled with numbers and tables and based on some
complex calculations, the book presents a summary of the information in
the first chapters that readers will find helpful.

Piasecki, Mclissa, and Paul A. Newhouse, eds. *Nicotine in Psychiatry: Psy-
chopathology and Emerging Therapeutics.* Washington, D.C.: American Psychiatric Press, 2000. Designed for practicing clinicians rather than
general readers, the book provides scientific information on the neuro-
logical and biological bases of the effects of nicotine, the association between smoking and mental illness, and the effectiveness of clinical
programs to reduce smoking.

Rippe, James M., ed. *Lifestyle Medicine.* Malden, Mass.: Blackwell Science,
1999. In emphasizing the important connections between positive
lifestyle behaviors and clinical medicine, this volume discusses how a
smoke-free lifestyle can contribute to better health.

Rogers, Richard G., Robert A. Hummer, and Charles B. Nam. *Living and
Dying in the USA: Behavioral, Health, and Social Differentials of Adult Mortality.* San Diego, Calif.: Academic Press, 2000. The material in chapter
13 (Table 13.1 and Figure 13.1 in particular) demonstrates the harm of
smoking for survival chances and does so after adjusting for numerous
other factors that also increase mortality.

Shepard, Roy J. *The Risks of Passive Smoking.* New York: Oxford University
Press, 1982. This effort to review the research on environmental tobacco
smoke predates the more influential volume by the Surgeon General on
the topic and the more current research to follow in the late 1980s and
the 1990s.

Sonder, Ben. *Dangerous Legacy: The Babies of Drug-Taking Parents.* New
York: Watts, 1994. Including tobacco along with cocaine, crack, opiates,
alcohol, and marijuana in its purview, the book describes the short-term
and sometimes long-term effects of drug use by parents on the well-being
of their infants and children.

Stratton, Kathleen, et al., eds. *Clearing the Air: Assessing the Science Base for
Tobacco Harm Reduction.* Washington, D.C.: National Academy Press,
2001. The Institute of Medicine evaluates the methods used to claim that
certain products reduce the harmful health effects of smoking and the addiction to cigarette nicotine. The products evaluated include pharmaceuticals, medical devices, and modified tobacco products.

Terry, Luther L. "The Surgeon General's First Report on Smoking and Health." In Alan Blum, ed., *The Cigarette Underworld: A Front Line Report on the War Against Your Lungs*. Secaucus, N.J.: Lyle Stuart, 1985. The same surgeon general responsible for the famous 1964 report on the harm of cigarette smoking gives his recollections about the production of the report and its reception.

Wald, Nicholas, and Peter Froggatt, eds. *Nicotine, Smoking, and the Low Tar Programme*. Oxford, U.K. Oxford University Press, 1989. Papers in the volume cover such topics as the effects of nicotine on the body, smoking habits in Britain, and the composition and effects of low-tar cigarettes.

Watson, Ronald R., and Mark L. Witten, eds. *Environmental Tobacco Smoke*. Boca Raton, Fla.: CRC Press, 2001. For clinicians and researchers wanting an up-to-date overview of research on environmental tobacco smoking, this volume focuses on the harm of cigarette smoke on nonsmoking pregnant women, newborns, youth, adults, and the elderly, and the association of exposure to secondhand smoke with asthma, heart disease, cancer, problems of the immune system, and DNA damage.

U.S. Department of Health and Human Services. *The Health Consequences of Involuntary Smoking. A Report of the Surgeon General*. Washington, D.C.: U.S. Department of Health and Human Services, 1986. Although now based on dated evidence, this comprehensive review of the harm of environmental tobacco smoke on nonsmokers provides the background for more recent studies.

———. *The Health Consequences of Smoking: Nicotine Addiction. A Report of the Surgeon General*. Washington, D.C.: U.S. Department of Health and Human Services, 1988. This volume lays out in detail the evidence that smoking is more addictive than heroin or cocaine. The information on pharmacology makes the material less accessible than other reports of the Surgeon General, but the introduction clearly summarizes the basis for making claims about addictiveness of nicotine.

———. *Women and Smoking. A Report of the Surgeon General*. Washington, D.C.: U.S. Department of Health and Human Services, 2001. This comprehensive volume of more than 500 pages details the special health risks faced by women smokers, the efforts of tobacco companies to attract women smokers with advertising, and the ways to help prevent smoking among women. More generally it provides an up-to-date overview of the knowledge about the causes and consequences of smoking.

ARTICLES

Atrens, Dale M. "Nicotine as an Addictive Substance: A Critical Examination of the Basic Concepts and Empirical Evidence." *Journal of Drug Is-*

sues, vol. 31, Spring 2001, pp. 325–394. Despite a general consensus about the addictiveness of nicotine, some scientists remain skeptical. This article reviews the reasons for the skepticism, argues that addiction has been too broadly defined to be meaningful, and concludes that the empirical evidence for the addictiveness of tobacco remains lacking.

Bailar, John C., and Heather L. Gornick. "Cancer Undefeated." *New England Journal of Medicine*, vol. 336, May 29, 1997, pp. 1,569–74. In reviewing trends in cancer since 1970 the authors find the lack of change discouraging but note one major exception: Some important declines have occurred due to reduced cigarette smoking. Given that the effects of new treatments for cancer on mortality appear largely disappointing, the most promising approach is to prevent the disease from occurring through lifestyle change.

Baker, Frank, et al. "Health Risks Associated with Cigar Smoking." *JAMA*, vol. 284, August 9, 2000, pp. 735–740. Summarizing the results of a 1998 conference of the American Cancer Society, the article finds consensus that smoking cigars instead of cigarettes does not reduce the risks of nicotine addiction, that inhaling of cigar smoke makes the risks of death similar to those for cigarette smoking, that cigars contain higher concentrations of toxic and carcinogenic chemicals than cigarettes, and that cigar smoking causes cancer of the lung.

Barnes, Deborah E., and Lisa A. Bero. "Why Review Articles on the Health Effects of Passive Smoking Reach Different Conclusions." *JAMA*, vol. 279, May 20, 1998, pp. 1,566–70. Of 106 articles that evaluated the evidence on passive smoking, 37 percent concluded that it was not harmful, but 74 percent of these articles were written by authors with tobacco industry affiliation. Given the strong association between affiliation and conclusions of the studies, the authors recommend that articles disclose conflicts of interest.

Brennan, M. B. "The Good Side of Nicotine." *Chemical and Engineering News*, vol. 78, March 27, 2000, pp. 23–26. This article describes a symposium on the possible benefits of nicotine for brain disorders such as Alzheimer's disease, Parkinson's disease, and Tourette's syndrome. The presenters oppose cigarette use as a recreational habit but see value in exploring the potentially more positive effects of nicotine on the brain.

Centers for Disease Control and Prevention. "Morbidity and Mortality Weekly Report: Annual Smoking-Attributable Mortality, Years of Potential Life Lost, and Economic Costs—United States, 1995–1999." *JAMA*, vol. 287, May 8, 2002, pp. 2,355–58. Estimates indicate that during 1995–99 smoking caused approximately 440,000 premature deaths each year in the United States, and that these deaths and the associated sickness that preceded them caused approximately $157 billion in annual health-related economic losses.

———. "Morbidity and Mortality Weekly Report: Costs of Smoking among Active Duty U.S. Air Force Personnel—United States, 1997." *JAMA*, vol. 283, June 28, 2000, pp. 3,190–96. This study compares lost work time (including smoke breaks, days spent in the hospital, and time spent in outpatient clinics) of smokers and of nonsmokers. With 25 percent of male and 27 percent of female personnel being current smokers, the habit costs the air force an estimated $107.2 million a year.

Chasan-Taber, Lisa, and Meir Stampfer. "Oral Contraceptives and Myocardial Infarction—the Search for the Smoking Gun." *New England Journal of Medicine*, vol. 345, December 20, 2001, pp. 1,841–42. This editorial reviews the evidence that smoking combined with the use of oral contraceptives by women greatly increase the risk of heart attacks. These findings emphasize the importance of reducing smoking among young women.

Cowell, Micheal J., and Brian L. Hirst. "Mortality Differences between Smokers and Nonsmokers." *Transactions of Society of Actuaries*, vol. 32, 1980, pp. 185–261. This reviews the historical evidence on the consequences of smoking for mortality and discusses the emergence of the policy of providing cheaper life insurance to nonsmokers adopted by the State Mutual Life Assurance Company.

Cruickshanks, Karen J. "Cigarette Smoking and Hearing Loss: The Epidemiology of Hearing Loss Study." *JAMA*, vol. 279, June 3, 1998, pp. 1,715–19. To illustrate the diverse harm of smoking this article shows that smokers are more likely to experience hearing loss than nonsmokers.

Doll, Richard, et al. "Mortality in Relation to Smoking: 40 Years' Observations on Male British Doctors." *British Medical Journal*, vol. 309, October 8, 1994, pp. 901–911. In assessing the hazards associated with tobacco, an analysis of data over 40 years on British doctors (a study group that eliminates the influence of occupation and education since all doctors have high prestige jobs and high education) demonstrates that smokers have risks of dying that are two to three times higher than nonsmokers.

Eisner, Mark D., et al. "Measurement of Environmental Tobacco Smoke Exposure among Adults with Asthma." *Environmental Health Perspectives*, vol. 109, August 2001, pp. 809–814. Problems of asthma have increased in the U.S. population, and evidence suggests that exposure to secondhand smoke can adversely affect adults with asthma. The study, which provided nicotine badge monitors to measure exposure to environmental tobacco smoke, finds that subjects most exposed to the smoke had high risks of respiratory problems.

Eisner, Mark D., Alexander K. Smith, and Paul D. Blanc. "Bartenders' Respiratory Health after Establishment of Smoke-Free Bars and Taverns." *JAMA*, vol. 280, December 9, 1988, pp. 1,909–14. Interviewing bartenders before and after a smoking ban in San Francisco restaurants and bars, the authors assess respiratory irritation and infection. Their findings indicate that the establishment of smoke-free bars and taverns was associated with a rapid improvement of respiratory health.

Ernst, Armin, and Joseph D. Zibrak. "Carbon Monoxide Poisoning." *New England Journal of Medicine*, vol. 339, November 26, 1998, pp. 1,603–08. Tobacco smoke is an important source of carbon monoxide, a colorless, odorless, and nonirritating toxic gas. This article describes the physiological harm of carbon monoxide but focuses less on tobacco smoke than on poisoning from other sources.

Ernst, Monique, Eric T. Moolchan, and Miqun L. Robinson. "Behavioral and Neural Consequences of Prenatal Exposure to Nicotine." *Journal of the American Academy of Child and Adolescent Psychiatry*, vol. 40, June 2001, pp. 630–641. A review of the evidence on the consequences of smoking for pregnant women finds that prenatal exposure of the fetus of nicotine leads to problems of brain development and to higher risks of psychiatric problems and substance abuse later in life.

Fichtenberg, Caroline M., and Stanton A. Glantz. "Association of the California Tobacco Control Program with Declines in Cigarette Consumption and Mortality from Heart Disease." *New England Journal of Medicine*, vol. 343, December 14, 2000, pp. 1,772–77. A voter-enacted initiative to use additional taxes to fund antitobacco programs in 1989 accelerated the decline in cigarette consumption in California. This study shows that the program also reduced the death rate from heart disease, which is associated with smoking, but this effect was diminished in 1992 when the program funding was cut back.

Hackshaw, A. K., M. R. Law, and N. J. Wald. "The Accumulated Evidence on Lung Cancer and Environmental Tobacco Smoke." *British Medical Journal*, vol. 315, October 18, 1997, pp. 280–288. A review of numerous studies of environmental tobacco smoke leads the authors to estimate that lung cancer rates among nonsmoking women whose husbands smoke are 24 percent higher than for nonsmoking women whose husbands do not smoke.

Howard, George, et al. "Cigarette Smoking and Progression of Atherosclerosis: The Atherosclerosis Risk in Communities (ARIC) Study." *JAMA*, vol 279, January 14, 1998, pp. 119–124. Atherosclerosis, the buildup of fatty-like materials on artery walls, can cause heart disease and stroke. Over a three-year period the researchers found that progression of atherosclerosis was 50 percent higher in smokers than in nonsmokers and 20 percent higher in nonsmokers exposed to environmental tobacco smoke than other nonsmokers.

Hu, Frank B., et al. "Diet, Lifestyle, and the Risk of Type 2 Diabetes Mellitus in Women." *New England Journal of Medicine*, vol. 345, September 13, 2001, pp. 790–797. Along with lack of exercise, poor diet, and abstinence from alcohol, current cigarette smoking appears associated with an increased risk of diabetes.

————. "Trends in the Incidence of Coronary Heart Disease and Changes in Diet and Lifestyle in Women." *New England Journal of Medicine*, vol. 343, August 24, 2000, pp. 530–537. This study finds that reductions in smoking among a sample of 85,941 women ages 34 to 59 produced a 13 percent decline in the incidence of coronary heart disease.

Hughes, John R., et al. "Recent Advances in the Pharmacotherapy of Smoking." *JAMA*, vol. 281, January 6, 1999, pp. 72–76. This article reviews the evidence on the effectiveness of smoking treatments such as nicotine nasal spray, nicotine inhalers, over-the-counter nicotine gum and patches, and the antidepressant bupropion. The article concludes that all such therapies appear similarly effective, doubling the rate of quitting compared to the effects of a placebo. Counseling combined with the pharmacological treatments can further aid cessation.

Hummer, Robert A., Charles B. Nam, and Richard G. Rogers. "Adult Mortality Differentials Associated with Cigarette Smoking in the USA." *Population Research and Policy Review*, vol. 17, June 1998, pp. 285–304. Presents much information based on a national sample that smoking increases mortality.

Istre, Gregory R., et al. "Deaths and Injuries from House Fires." *New England Journal of Medicine*, vol. 344, June 21, 2001, pp. 1,911–16. Fires started by smoking result in a higher injury rate than fires unrelated to smoking. Although most deaths from smoking involve disease, some involve injuries stemming from smoking-related fires.

Johnson, Jeffrey G. "Association between Cigarette Smoking and Anxiety Disorders during Adolescence and Early Adulthood." *JAMA*, vol. 284, November 8, 2000, pp. 2,348–51. Smokers seem to suffer disproportionately from anxiety disorders, but it is less clear if high anxiety causes smoking or if smoking causes anxiety disorders. The study finds that cigarette smoking may increase the risk of certain anxiety disorders during late adolescence and early adulthood.

Lesser, Karen, et al. "Smoking and Mental Illness: A Population-Based Prevalence Study." *JAMA*, vol. 284, November 22/29, 2000, pp. 2,606–10. Although many studies report higher rates of smoking of persons with mental illness than persons in the general population, this article offers one of the few national studies of the relationship. The results indicate that persons with mental illness are twice as likely to smoke as other persons but also make substantial efforts to quit.

Mascola, Maria A., Helen van Vunakis, and Ira B. Tager. "Exposure of Young Infants to Environmental Tobacco Smoke: Breast-Feeding among Smoking Mothers." *American Journal of Public Health*, vol. 88, June 1998, pp. 893–896. Finds that breast-fed infants of mothers who smoke had much higher exposure to nicotine than bottle-fed infants and suggests that breast-feeding more than environmental tobacco smoke affects infants of smoking mothers.

Nam, Charles B., Richard G. Rogers, and Robert A. Hummer. "Impact of Future Cigarette Smoking Scenarios on Mortality of the Adult Population in the United States, 2000–2050." *Social Biology*, vol. 43, nos. 3–4, pp. 155–168. Quantifies the impact rising cigarette use would have on the number of deaths in the first part of the 21st century.

Ness, Roberta B., et al. "Cocaine and Tobacco Use and the Risk of Spontaneous Abortion." *New England Journal of Medicine*, vol. 340, February 4, 1999, pp. 333–339. Based on a sample of low-income and pregnant women the study finds a significant risk of miscarriage due to tobacco use.

Otsuka, Ryo, et al. "Acute Effects of Passive Smoking on the Coronary Circulation in Healthy Young Adults." *JAMA*, vol. 286, July 25, 2001, pp. 436–441. To demonstrate that breathing passive smoke reduces the flow of blood to the heart an experiment compares smoking and non-smoking subjects before and after a 30-minute exposure to environmental tobacco smoke. The findings suggest that even a little secondhand smoke can negatively affect the body.

Payne, Sarah. "'Smoke Like a Man, Die Like a Man'? A Review of the Relationship between Gender, Sex, and Lung Cancer." *Social Science and Medicine*, vol. 53, October 2001, pp. 1,067–80. Differences in biologically based hormones and social smoking behaviors of men and women result in different risks of lung cancer. A review of evidence in this article indicates that women smokers have a higher risk of getting lung cancer than male smokers.

Perera, Frederica A. "Environment and Cancer: Who Are Susceptible?" *Science*, vol. 278, November 7, 1997, pp. 1,068–73. Environmental factors such as smoking may act in concert with individual susceptibility to produce cancer. As demonstrated by molecular and epidemiological studies, individuals with predisposing genetic traits may have heightened risk of cancer from smoking

Petit-Zeman, Sophie. "Smoke Gets in Your Mind." *New Scientist*, April 13, 2002, pp. 30–32. Although it is clear that mental illness leads to smoking, there is also emerging evidence, according to this article, that smoking may cause mental illness.

Peto, J. "Cancer Epidemiology in the Last Century and the Next Decade." *Nature*, vol. 411, May 17, 2001, pp. 390–396. In describing the trends and patterns of cancer across the world the author notes that the most important discovery in the history of cancer epidemiology is the carcinogenic effect of tobacco.

Rogers, Richard G., and Eve Powell-Griner. "Life Expectancies of Cigarette Smokers and Nonsmokers in the United States." *Social Science and Medicine*, vol. 32, no. 10, 1991, pp. 1,151–59. Using death certification data for smokers and nonsmokers in 1986, this study finds that smokers can expect to live at least a 25 percent shorter life than nonsmokers.

Stoddard, Jeffrey J., and Bradley Gray. "Maternal Smoking and Medical Expenditures for Childhood Respiratory Illness." *American Journal of Public Health*, vol. 87, February 1997, pp. 205–209. Based on a sample of 2,624 children of five years of age and under, a statistical analysis demonstrates that maternal smoking is significantly associated with increased child health expenditures, particularly for respiratory problems.

Thun, Michael J., et al. "Alcohol Consumption and Mortality among Middle-Aged and Elderly U.S. Adults." *New England Journal of Medicine*, vol. 337, December 11, 1997, pp. 1,705–14. Although focused largely on alcohol consumption, this study provides interesting facts on tobacco use. It shows that moderate alcohol consumption slightly reduces overall mortality, but the effect is far smaller than that of smoking, which doubles the risk of death.

———. "Excess Mortality among Cigarette Smokers: Changes in a 20-Year Interval." *American Journal of Public Health*, vol. 85, September 1995, pp. 1,223–30. Premature mortality, which is defined as the difference between death rates of smokers and nonsmokers, doubled in women and continued unabated in men from the 1960s to the 1980s. Smoking thus continues to impact health, even after cigarette consumption began to fall in the 1960s.

Voelker, Rebecca. "Smoke Carcinogen Affects Fetus." *JAMA*, vol. 280, September 23/30, 1998, p. 1,041. The article briefly reviews a study out of the University of Minnesota Cancer Center that offers the first direct evidence of the transmittal of a cancer-causing chemical to the fetus when a pregnant women smokes. The study finds that the cancer-causing chemical shows up in the urine of infants of smoking mothers.

Wells, A. Judson. "Lung Cancer from Passive Smoking at Work." *American Journal of Public Health*, vol. 88, July 1998, pp. 1,025–29. A review of previous studies finds that workers exposed to secondhand smoke on the job face increased lung cancer risks. The increased risks are similar to those experienced by nonsmokers living with smokers and breathing secondhand smoke at home.

WEB DOCUMENTS

Centers for Disease Control and Prevention. "Surgeon General's Reports." Available online. "URL: http://www.cdc.gov/tobacco/sgrpage.htm. Downloaded in December 2002. This site lists the titles and publication dates for each of the 27 Surgeon General reports since 1964 on smoking and tobacco and allows several of the reports to be downloaded.

National Cancer Institute. "Cancer.gov." Available online. URL: http://www. nci.nih.gov/help. Downloaded in February 2003. The web site includes general cancer information, descriptions of clinical studies, research findings on cancer, and specific information relating to tobacco use and cancer.

———. "Statistics." Available online. URL: http://www.nci.nih.gov/statistics. Downloaded in February 2003. This page provides statistics, maps, and graphs on cancer prevalence, mortality, and prognosis; a guide to understanding statistics; and a list of data sources of cancer.

National Heart, Lung, and Blood Institute. "The Heart Truth: A National Awareness Campaign for Women about Heart Disease." Available online. URL: http://www.nhlbi.nih.gov/health/hearttruth. Downloaded in February 2003. Emphasizing the risks of heart disease for women, particularly those ages 40–60, this web site describes the issues related to the leading cause of death among women in the United States and recommends avoidance of tobacco smoke.

National Institute on Drug Abuse. "Facts about Nicotine and Tobacco Products." Available online. URL: http://www.drugabuse.gov/NIDA_ Notes/NNVoll3N3/tearoff.html. Posted in July 1998. A brief summary of research on nicotine addiction and the effects of tobacco use.

National Institutes of Health. "United States National Library of Medicine." Available online. URL: http://www.nlm.nih.gov. Downloaded in February 2003. This online medical library contains much information on health-related tobacco issues.

Samet, Jonathan M., et al. "Environmental Tobacco Smoke: Risk Assessment." Environmental Health Perspective (EHP) Online. Available online. URL: http://ehpnetl.niehs.nih.gov/docs/1999/suppl-6/toc.html. Posted in December 1999. Provides a summary of the latest evidence on the harm of environmental tobacco smoke, particularly in the workplace, and includes a special report on the ability of pharmaceutical products to help smokers quit.

SOCIAL AND PSYCHOLOGICAL ASPECTS

BOOKS

Akers, Ronald L. *Social Learning and Social Structure: A General Theory of Crime and Deviance.* Boston: Northeastern Press, 1998. In presenting a theory of crime, delinquency, and deviance based on association with other criminals, delinquencies, and deviants, this text examines adolescent smoking behavior. The author explains this behavior through learning and reinforcement of smoking by peers.

Bachman, Jerald G., et al. *The Decline of Substance Use in Young Adulthood: Changes in Social Activities, Roles, and Beliefs.* Mahwah, N.J.: Lawrence Erlbaum Associates, 2002. Building on their previous book, the authors examine how changes in social activities, religious experiences, and individual attitudes affect substance use as youth grow into adulthood. Although it examines many forms of substance abuse, the book gives major attention to cigarette smoking.

———. *Smoking, Drinking, and Drug Use in Young Adulthood: The Impacts of New Freedoms and New Responsibilities.* Mahwah, N.J.: Lawrence Erlbaum Associates, 1997. In tracking the use of legal and illegal substances from high school to young adulthood among some 33,000 individuals, this study finds that new freedoms of young adulthood lead to increases in substance use, while the responsibilities of adulthood such as marriage, pregnancy, and parenthood reduce substance use. Chapter 4 focuses specifically on cigarette use.

Barth, Ilene. *The Smoking Life.* Columbus, Mich.: Genesis Press, 1997. Filled with interesting historical facts, stories, and pictures, this book resembles a coffee-table book that one would want to sample more than read straight through. Its stories and facts, however, reflect the importance of cigarettes on life in modern America and elsewhere.

Blaxter, Mildred. *Health and Lifestyles.* London: Tavistock/Routledge, 1990. The author, a well-known British health scholar, demonstrates how lifestyle behaviors—including smoking—combine with components of socioeconomic status to influence fitness, illness, and mental health.

Bolliger, C. T., and Karl-Olav Fagerström, eds. *Progress in Respiratory Research.* Vol. 28, *The Tobacco Epidemic.* New York: Karger Publishing, 1997. Experts from across the world examine the spread of smoking both within the United States and across nations, and the ability of policies to moderate the epidemic. Chapters cover such topics as passive smoking, the psychology of the smoker, smokeless tobacco as a replacement for cigarettes, smoking cessation programs, and regulation of cigarettes.

Borgatta, Edgar F., and Robert R. Evans, eds. *Smoking, Health, and Behavior.* Chicago: Aldine Publishing, 1968. This volume reviews early research on social aspects of smoking behavior and thereby supplements the more common research of the time on the medical consequences of smoking.

Chollat-Traquet, Claire. *Women and Tobacco.* Geneva: World Health Organization, 1992. One of the early efforts to publicize the growing harm of tobacco on the health of women, this book presents a global perspective on the problem. It reviews the health consequences, causes, and strategies

Annotated Bibliography

of preventing smoking among women. Short and readable, it supplies useful information on smoking and women throughout the world.

Edwards, Peggy. *Evening the Odds: Adolescent Women, Tobacco, and Physical Activity.* Ottawa, Canada: Canadian Association for the Advancement of Women and Sport and Physical Activity, 1996. A feminist analysis of smoking and lack of physical activity suggests the need to improve the social circumstances of young women that leads to both problems. Exercise can meet women's needs while at the same time offering a healthy and enjoyable alternative to smoking.

Eysenck, Hans J. *Smoking, Health, and Personality.* Piscataway, N.J.: Transaction Publishers, 2000. The author, an accomplished and respected psychologist with unique views about smoking, argues in this reissue of a 1965 book that evidence of the harm of smoking is potentially flawed and that personality factors better predict heart disease and cancer than smoking. Along with an introduction by Stuart Brody that reviews Eysenck's work, the book provides an unusual and intriguing view of smoking.

Ferrence, Roberta G. *Deadly Fashion: The Rise and Fall of Cigarette Smoking in North America.* New York: Garland Publishing, 1989. The author views the spread of cigarettes throughout the U.S. and Canadian populations as similar to the diffusion of innovative ideas, techniques, products, and behaviors. The diffusion perspective helps make sense of the early adoption of cigarettes by some groups such as high-status men and the late adoption of cigarettes by other groups such as low-status women.

Gladwell, Malcolm. *The Tipping Point: How Little Things Can Make a Big Difference.* Boston: Little, Brown, 2000. This book views the spread of ideas, products, and messages as similar to the epidemic spread of diseases and searches for what leads to the critical mass or tipping point needed to generate the epidemic. In arguing that tipping points are reached through minor changes in the environment and the action of a small number of people, the author applies his ideas to teen smoking in one chapter.

Gottfredson, Michael R., and Travis Hirschi. *A General Theory of Crime.* Stanford, Calif.: Stanford University Press, 1990. The authors argue that smoking shares a similarity with criminal behavior: Each involves the sacrifice of long-term benefits (such as avoiding health problems, trouble in school, and prison time) in favor of short-term pleasures and immediate impulses (such as enjoyment of smoking, profit from theft, and the high of excess drugs and alcohol). Smoking does not cause crime but is associated with it.

Greaves, Lorraine. *Smoke Screen: Women's Smoking and Social Control.* Halifax, Canada: Fernwood Publishers, 1996. Based on in-depth interviews, the author suggests that women use smoking to bond with others, create an image, control emotions, and obtain comfort in times of stress. She

181

also suggests that women smoke not just because they are manipulated by outside forces but also because they actively search out ways to deal with their own life circumstances.

Grossman, Michael, and Chee-Ruey Hsieh, eds. *Economic Analysis of Substance Use and Abuse: The Experience of Developed Countries and Lessons for Developing Countries.* Northhampton, Mass.: Elgar, 2001. Chapters on cigarette use focus on questions of current concern to economists such as whether addicted smokers act rationally in their use of tobacco, whether smokers are too optimistic in perceptions of their health, whether the presence of children affects men's use of cigarettes, and whether smoking costs much in lost labor productivity.

Huber, Gary L., and Robert J. Pandina. "The Economics of Tobacco Use." In C. T. Bollinger and K. O. Fagerström, eds, *The Tobacco Epidemic.* Basel, Switzerland: Karger, 1997. This chapter offers a history of cigarette use and cigarette sales from an economic perspective.

Jacobson, Bobbie. *The Ladykillers: Why Smoking Is a Feminist Issue.* New York: Continuum, 1982. An early statement of concern about smoking among women and the harm it can cause to them, the book argues that the tobacco industry's exploitation of women makes smoking a feminist issue. It also offers practical advice for giving up smoking.

Jeanrenaud, Claude, and Nils Soguel, eds. *Valuing the Cost of Smoking: Assessment Methods, Risk Perception, and Policy Options.* Boston: Kluwer, 1999. Using an economic approach to smoking that aims to determine the financial burden faced by smokers and by nonsmokers who pay for the social costs of the habit, the chapters review the various ways to place an economic value on the health costs of smoking and use economic perspectives to understand the decision to smoke.

Lloyd, Barbara, et al. *Smoking in Adolescence: Images and Identities.* London: Routledge, 1998. In interviewing adolescents rather than adults to see their point of view about smoking, these British researchers find that teens see smokers as fun loving and nonconformist and see cigarettes as fashionable and image enhancing. The authors use these insights about the meanings smoking has for teens to make recommendations for policy.

Manning, Willard G. *The Cost of Poor Health Habits.* Cambridge, Mass.: Harvard University Press, 1991. Provides numerical estimates of the costs poor health habits such as smoking impose on others in society.

McKay, Judith, and Michael Eriksen. *The Tobacco Atlas.* Geneva: World Health Organization, 2002. Each section of the atlas uses full-color maps and graphics to describe the prevalence of tobacco use, tobacco growing, and tobacco control efforts across the world. Although filled with statistics, this book is clear and accessible.

Annotated Bibliography

National Cancer Institute, National Institutes of Health. *Changing Adolescent Smoking Prevalence: Where It Is and Why.* Smoking and Tobacco Control Monograph 14. Washington, D.C.: U.S. Department of Health and Human Services, 2001. Updating the 1994 Surgeon General's report on youth smoking, the chapters cover trends in youth smoking and the programs to limit the initiation and continuation of smoking among adolescents.

———. *Smokeless Tobacco or Health: An International Perspective.* Smoking and Tobacco Control Monograph 2. Washington, D.C.: U.S. Department of Health and Human Services, 1993. Many view smokeless tobacco as a safe alternative to cigarettes. This volume disputes this view by emphasizing the harm to health of smokeless tobacco and the need for control of the product. It also examines use of the product across the world as well as in the United States.

Slovic, Paul, ed. *Smoking: Risk, Perception, and Policy.* Thousand Oaks, Calif.: Sage Publications, 2001. This volume uses data from telephone interviews to examine perceptions of the risks of smoking. Its theme, that young smokers do not fully understand the health risks of the habit and underestimate the difficulty of quitting, suggests the need for policies to do more to educate young people about these risks.

Tollison, Robert D., and Richard E. Wagner. *The Economics of Smoking.* Boston: Kluwer Academic Publishing Group, 1992. Unlike nearly all academic literature on the topic, this book treats the relationship between smoking and health with skepticism. It argues that if the harm of smoking is born by the smokers themselves, then no public policy is necessary. Their arguments bring a classic economic perspective to bear on the issue of smoking and public policy.

Tollison, Robert D., ed. *Smoking and Society: Toward a More Balanced Assessment.* Lexington, Mass.: Lexington Books, 1986. The contributors to this volume, largely economists supportive of individual choice, question conventional understandings about smoking. The chapters argue that the evidence of the harm of cigarettes is flawed, that cigarettes should not be overregulated, and that individual freedom should not be sacrificed for public health goals.

U.S. Department of Health and Human Services. *Tobacco Use among U.S. Racial/Ethnic Minority Groups: African Americans, American Indians and Alaskan Natives, Asian Americans and Pacific Islanders, and Hispanics. A Report of the Surgeon General.* Washington, D.C.: U.S. Department of Health and Human Services, 1998. This report provides a single, comprehensive source of data on how each of four racial/ethnic groups use tobacco, suffer the physical effects of tobacco use, have psychosocial and social factors associated with use of tobacco, and can benefit from strategies to reduce their tobacco use. The attention to diversity in this volume

183

complements other volumes that take a more general perspective on tobacco use and control.

Viscusi, W. Kip. *Smoking: Making the Risky Decision.* New York: Oxford University Press, 1992. The book summarizes the results of a survey that asked smokers and nonsmokers to estimate the harm of smoking for the added risk of death, the likelihood of dying from a smoking-related cause, and the years of life lost. The findings demonstrate that both groups overstate the risks identified by the scientific literature and that smokers recognize the serious health risks they face.

Waldron, Ingrid. "Contributions of Changing Gender Differences in Behavior and Social Roles to Changing Gender Differences in Mortality." In Donald Sabo and David Frederick Gordon, eds., *Men's Health and Illness: Gender, Power, and the Body.* Thousands Oaks, Calif.: Sage Publications, 1995. The author argues that smoking rates among women in modern societies—which have come to approach those of men—reflect some traditional concerns, such as staying slim, as well as new freedom to act in ways that men have acted.

Wetterer, Angelika, and Jürgen Von Troschke. *Smoker Motivation: A Review of the Contemporary Literature.* Berlin: Springer-Verlag, 1986. This book critically reviews literature published in English and German on questions about why some people take up smoking while others do not, why some people continue and others quit, and why so many who try to quit fail in the effort.

World Health Organization. *Tobacco or Health: A Global Status Report.* Geneva: World Health Organization, 1997. The first several chapters summarize the worldwide trends in smoking and smoking-related mortality, but the volume is most useful for the detailed country-by-country compilation of smoking statistics and antismoking policies. It also provides a summary of current global tobacco control efforts.

ARTICLES

Ahluwalia, Jasjit, et al. "Sustained-Release Bupropion for Smoking Cessation in African Americans." *JAMA*, vol. 288, July 24/31, 2002, pp. 468–474. Since African Americans suffer disproportional harm to their health from smoking, medical research needs to do more to understand how to reduce their smoking rates. This study finds that an antidepressant, bupropion, promoted smoking cessation among a sample of 600 African-American adults who smoked 10 or more cigarettes a day.

Anda, Robert F. "Adverse Childhood Experiences and Smoking during Adolescence and Adulthood." *JAMA*, vol. 282, November 3, 1999, pp. 1,652–58. Using a sample of 9,215 adult members of a health maintenance organization (HMO) in San Diego, the study measures the extent of adverse experiences during childhood (for examples, physical, emotional, or sexual abuse; a battered mother; parental separation or divorce; and the presence of substance abuse, mental illness, or incarceration of parents). These adverse experiences were strongly associated with smoking.

Becker, Gary M., and K. M. Murphy. "A Theory of Rational Addiction." *Journal of Political Economy*, vol. 96, August 1988, pp. 675–700. Coauthored by a Nobel Prize winner in economics, Gary Becker, this article presents a mathematically based argument that explains many seemingly irrational behaviors such as use of cigarettes. The authors posit that individuals recognize the addictive nature of the choices they make but still make them because the gains from the addictive behaviors exceed the costs.

Becker, Gary M., and Michael Grossman. "An Empirical Analysis of Cigarette Addiction." *American Economic Review*, vol. 84, June 1994, pp. 396–418. This empirical study partly supports Becker's theory of rational addiction by finding that current cigarette consumption is affected by past and future cigarette price changes. The results indicate that cigarette smoking is addictive but still responsive to prices.

Benowitz, Neal L., et al. "Slower Metabolism and Reduced Intake of Nicotine from Cigarette Smoking in Chinese-Americans." *Journal of National Cancer Institute*, vol. 94, January 16, 2002, pp. 108–115. This study finds that Chinese Americans take in less nicotine per cigarette and metabolize it more slowly than do Latinos or whites, which could help explain why Chinese Americans have lower rates of lung cancer than do other groups. The findings may help members of different ethnic groups in developing strategies of quitting.

Bobo, Janet Kay, and Corinne Husten. "Sociocultural Influences on Smoking and Drinking." *Alcohol Research and Health*, vol. 24, no. 4, 2000, pp. 225–32. Consistent with arguments that smoking reflects a more generally deviant lifestyle, this review of the evidence finds a strong relationship between alcohol use and tobacco use.

Cochran, Susan D., Vickie M. Mays, and Deborah Bowen. "Cancer-Related Risk Indicators and Preventive Screening Behaviors among Lesbian and Bisexual Women." *American Journal of Public Health*, vol. 91, April 2001, pp. 591–597. This study uses seven separate surveys of 11,876 lesbian/bisexual women, a difficult group to study with surveys, to identify the prevalence of cancer risk factors. It confirms that lesbian/bisexual women have higher rates of tobacco use than heterosexual women.

Colby John P. Jr., Arnold S. Linsky, and Murray A. Straus. "Social Stress and State-to-State Differences in Smoking and Smoking-Related Mortality in the United States." *Social Science and Medicine*, vol. 38, no. 2, January

1994, pp. 373–381. An analysis of the 50 American states demonstrates that those with high rates of stress—divorces, business failures, natural disasters—also have high rates of cigarette use and lung cancer. The results suggest that populations under stress tend to engage in behavior that ultimately harms their health.

DuRant, Robert H., Ellen S. Rome, and Michael Rich. "Tobacco and Alcohol Use Behaviors Portrayed in Music Videos: A Content Analysis." *American Journal of Public Health*, vol. 87, July 1997, pp. 1,131–35. About one-quarter of MTV videos portray tobacco use, and even modest levels of viewing of videos results in substantial exposure to glamorized depictions of smoking.

Ebrahim, Shahul H. "Trends in Pregnancy-Related Smoking Rates in the United States, 1987–1996." *JAMA*, vol. 283, January 19, 2000, pp. 361–366. Smoking has declined among pregnant women, but this study finds that the decline results largely from an overall drop in smoking among young people, rather than from women smokers giving up the habit upon pregnancy. As well as helping to prevent young women from starting to smoke, physicians need to make special efforts to help pregnant smokers to stop.

Edmondson, Brad. "Where Smoking Kills Women." *American Demographics*, vol. 19, October 1997, pp. 26–27. Based on data from the Centers for Disease Control's Atlas of United States Mortality, the maps in this article depict levels of lung cancer mortality among women for the years 1988–92.

Escobedo, Luis G., and John P. Peddicord. "Smoking Prevalence in U.S. Birth Cohorts: The Influence of Gender and Education." *American Journal of Public Health*, vol. 86, February 1996, pp. 231–236. An analysis of trend data shows that cigarette use has decreased most among highly educated persons and males. Low-educated persons in particular have benefited less from tobacco control policies and increased knowledge about the health consequences of cigarette smoking.

Escobedo, Luis, and Patrick Remington. "Birth Cohort Analysis of Prevalence of Cigarette Smoking among Hispanics in the United States." *JAMA*, vol. 261, January 6, 1989, pp. 66–69. In examining trend data on smoking among an understudied group—Hispanics—the findings reveal declining rates of smoking among Hispanic men but not Hispanic women.

Evert, Sherry A., Rae L. Schnuth, and Joanne L. Tribble. "Tobacco and Alcohol Use in Top-Grossing American Films." *Journal of Community Health*, vol. 23, August 1998, pp. 317–324. In examining the top 10 money-making films for each year from 1985 to 1995, the authors find most films had references that supported tobacco use, and few had references to discourage use.

Annotated Bibliography

Fiore, Michael, et al. "Trends in Cigarette Smoking in the United States: The Changing Influence of Gender and Race." *JAMA*, vol. 261, January 6, 1989, pp. 49–55. This somewhat dated but influential analysis demonstrates that smoking has decreased among all groups. However, it has decreased at a slower rate for women than men and for blacks than whites.

Gilpin, E. A., et al. "Smoking Initiation Rates in Adults and Minors: United States, 1944–1988." *American Journal of Epidemiology*, vol. 140, September 15, 1994, pp. 535–543. In examining trends in youth smoking over a long time period, the authors reach the discouraging conclusion that public health campaigns providing information on the harm of smoking have not had much influence on youth smoking.

Graham, Hilary. "Cigarette Smoking: A Light on Gender and Class Inequality in Britain?" *Journal of Social Policy*, vol. 24, no. 4, pp. 509–527. Based on interviews with low-income mothers in Britain, the author finds that those women with the heaviest caring responsibilities and lowest income were most likely to smoke. The findings suggest that deprived women use cigarette smoking as a way to help cope with their difficult circumstances.

Greenlund, Kurt J., et al. "Impact of Father's Education and Parental Smoking Status on Smoking Behavior in Young Adults: The CARDIA Study." *American Journal of Epidemiology*, vol. 142, no. 10, pp. 1,029–33. In the Coronary Artery Risk Development in Young Adults (CARDIA) study, the authors find that children of parents with low education have a higher risk of smoking and suggest that public health efforts do more to mitigate the influence of parent's characteristics on their children's smoking behavior.

Howard-Pitney, Beth, and Marilyn A. Winkleby. "Chewing Tobacco: Who Uses and Who Quits? Findings from NHANES III, 1988–1994." *American Journal of Public Health*, vol. 92, February 2002, pp. 250–256. The results of a national survey indicate that rural, lower-income black and white men had the highest regular use of chewing tobacco. Rural high-income men had the second highest regular use, and southern men had the lowest quit rate. Unlike cigarettes, which are adopted in adolescence, chewing tobacco commonly starts in adulthood.

Jessor, Richard, Mark S. Turbin, and Frances M. Costa. "Protective Factors in Adolescent Health Behavior." *Journal of Personality and Social Psychology*, vol. 75, no. 3, pp. 788–800. This study of 1,493 high school students shows that a positive orientation toward school, friendship with conventional peers, and church attendance increase health-enhancing behaviors and reduce harmful habits such as smoking.

Jha, Prabhat, et al. "Estimates of Global and Regional Smoking Prevalence in 1995, by Age and Sex." *American Journal of Public Health*, vol. 92, June 2002, pp. 1,002–06. The tables reveal that 1995 smoking percentages are highest in East Asia and eastern Europe and lowest in sub-Saharan Africa.

187

Kenkel, Donald S. "Health Behavior, Health Knowledge, and Schooling." *Journal of Political Economy*, vol. 99, no. 2, 1991, pp. 287–305. Why does education lead persons to smoke less? This study demonstrates that something more than increased knowledge of the harm of cigarette smoking is involved and educational campaigns alone will not be sufficient to reduce smoking.

Kiefe, Catarina I., O. Dale Williams, and Cora E. Lewis. "Ten-Year Changes in Smoking Among Young Adults: Are Racial Differences Explained by Socioeconomic Factors in the CARDIA Study?" *American Journal of Public Health*, vol. 91, February 2001, pp. 213–218. Although smoking has declined less among African Americans than whites, this study finds that most of the difference is due to disparities in socioeconomic status. The concentration of smoking among lower socioeconomic groups and the lower socioeconomic status of African Americans explain the widening race gap in smoking.

King, Gary. "The 'Race' Concept in Smoking: A Review of the Research on African-Americans." *Social Science and Medicine*, vol. 45, October 1997, pp. 1,075–87. In reviewing studies on the differences between blacks and whites in smoking, the author finds the uncritical use of racial categories to be a problem in most such research.

Mendez, David, Kenneth E. Warner, and Paul N. Courant. "Has Smoking Cessation Ceased? Expected Trends in the Prevalence of Smoking in the United States." *American Journal of Epidemiology*, vol. 148, no. 3, pp. 249–258. Since data for the 1990s suggest that youth smoking initiation rates have increased and that the decline in smoking has stalled, many worry that the downward trends of the past will not continue. This study predicts to the contrary that smoking of adults will at minimum decline from its current levels of 25 percent to about 15–16 percent in the next 50 years.

Michell, Lynn, and Amanda Amos. "Girls, Pecking Order and Smoking." *Social Science and Medicine*, vol. 44, no. 12, 1997, pp. 1,861–69. Although many studies suggest that social insecurities increase the likelihood of smoking, this review of the evidence concludes that smokers have higher self-esteem than nonsmokers. Girls in Scotland who have high status in peer groups and who project an image of self-esteem were viewed as most likely to smoke. The sample is specialized, but the findings are intriguing.

Molarius, Anu, et al. "Trends in Cigarette Smoking in 36 Populations from the Early 1980s to the Mid-1990s: Findings from the WHO MONICA Project." *American Journal of Public Health*, vol. 91, pp. 206–212. A comprehensive comparison of smoking across numerous nations finds that smoking among men decreased significantly in 44 percent of the populations, changed little in most others, and increased in Beijing, China. For women, smoking increased more commonly than for men, particularly in nations where female smoking started at low levels.

Morabia, Alfredo, et al. "Ages at Initiation of Cigarette Smoking and Quit Attempts among Women: A Generation Effect." *American Journal of Public Health*, vol. 92, January 2002, pp. 71–74. The article concludes that young female smokers have a higher propensity to quit smoking compared with older women and suggests that efforts to encourage young smokers to quit can successfully supplement efforts to prevent nonsmokers from starting to smoke.

Novotny, Thomas E., et al. "Smoking by Blacks and Whites: Socioeconomic and Demographic Differences." *American Journal of Public Health*, vol. 78, September 1988, pp. 1,187–89. Although blacks smoke more than whites, this difference appears to result from the lower income and status among African Americans. In addition, black smokers are less likely than white smokers to be heavy users of cigarettes but are less likely to quit than whites. Policies to reduce cigarette use must keep these racial differences in mind.

Orlando, Maria, Phyllis L. Ellickson, and Kimberly Jinnett. "The Temporal Relationship between Emotional Distress and Cigarette Smoking During Adolescence and Young Adulthood." *Journal of Consulting and Clinical Psychology*, vol. 69, December 2001, pp. 959–970. This statistical study offers an insightful perspective on stress and smoking. It finds that emotional distress in 10th graders led to smoking in 12th grade, and that smoking in 12th grade led to emotional distress in young adulthood. In short, stress initially leads to cigarette use, but then cigarette use exacerbates the stress.

Pampel, Fred C. "Cigarette Diffusion and Sex Differences in Smoking," *Journal of Health and Social Behavior*, vol. 42, December 2001, pp. 388–404. This study of smoking of men and women in more than a dozen European nations finds little association between equality of men and women in the social realm and similarity in rates of smoking. Rather, women's use of cigarettes seems to follow that of men after several decades regardless of the degree of gender equality.

———. "Cigarette Use and the Narrowing Sex Differential in Mortality." *Population and Development Review*, vol. 28, March 2002, pp. 77–104. Comparisons across nations reveal that the decline in the female advantage in length of life results largely from the increased smoking rates among women relative to men.

Parrott, Andy C. "Does Cigarette Smoking Cause Stress?" *American Psychologist*, vol. 54, October 1999, pp. 817–820. The author disputes the common notion that smoking and nicotine act as an aid for mood control by arguing that they worsen stress. The evidence in favor of this view (for example, adolescent smokers report increasing levels of stress as they develop regular patterns of smoking) suggests that tobacco use does not alleviate stress but produces withdrawal symptoms that instead increase it.

Patton, George C., J. B. Carlin, and C. Coffey. "Depression, Anxiety, and Smoking Initiation: A Prospective Study Over 3 Years." *American Journal of Public Health*, vol. 88, October 1998, pp. 1,518–22. A study of more than 2,000 14- to 15-year-old students indicates that symptoms of depression and anxiety increase the likelihood of starting to smoke. Promoting psychological well-being may help prevent adolescent tobacco use.

Pérez-Stable, Eliseo J. "Cigarette Smoking Behavior among U.S. Latino Men and Women from Different Countries of Origin." *American Journal of Public Health*, vol. 91, September 2001, pp. 1,424–30. For men smoking differs little among Mexican Americans, Central Americans, Puerto Ricans, Cuban Americans, South Americans, and other Latinos, but for women Puerto Ricans have the highest rates and Central Americans the lowest rates. Interestingly, foreign-born Latinos are less likely to smoke than U.S.-born Latinos.

Pierce, John P., et al. "Trends in Cigarette Smoking in the United States: Educational Differences Are Increasing." *JAMA*, vol. 261, January 6, 1989, pp. 56–60. One of the early studies to identify an important trend in cigarette smoking—usage declined five times faster among highly educated persons than less educated persons. As a result cigarette use is increasingly concentrated in lower education groups, and health promotion policies need to focus on groups with less education.

Plunkett, Mark, and Christina M. Mitchell. "Substance Use Rates among American Indian Adolescents: Regional Comparisons with Monitoring the Future High School Seniors." *Journal of Drug Issues*, vol. 30, Summer 2000, pp. 575–591. The findings reveal that Native American youth use cigarettes less than other students.

Rigotti, Nancy A., Lae Eun Lee, and Henry Wechsler. "U.S. College Students' Use of Tobacco Products: Results of a National Survey." *JAMA*, vol. 284, August 9, 2000, pp. 699–705. A survey of 14,138 students enrolled in 119 colleges reveals that nearly half had used a tobacco product in the last year and one-third currently use tobacco. College-age students continue to experiment with a variety of tobacco products, risk lifelong nicotine addiction with such activities, and can benefit from national efforts to monitor and prevent tobacco use.

Ross, Catherine E. "Walking, Exercising, and Smoking: Does Neighborhood Matter?" *Social Science and Medicine*, vol. 51, July 2000, pp. 265–274. Among a sample from the state of Illinois, male residents (but not female residents) of disadvantaged neighborhoods are more likely to smoke than

residents of other neighborhoods. The study affirms the importance of social context as well as individual traits in determining the use of cigarettes.

Siegel, Michael, Paul D. Mowery, and Terry P. Pechacek. "Trends in
Adult Smoking in California Compared with the Rest of the United
States, 1978–1994." *American Journal of Public Health*, vol. 90, March
2000, pp. 372–379. California differs from most other states in its aggressive tobacco control programs. This comparative study finds a significant decline in adult smoking in California, but not the rest of the
United States, and suggests that other states adopt California policies.

Suranovic, Steven M., Robert S. Goldfarb, and Thomas C. Leonard. "An
Economic Theory of Cigarette Addiction." *Journal of Health Economics*,
vol. 18, January 1999, pp. 1–29. Economists assume that behaviors of individuals reflect self-interest but must confront the question of why
smokers act against their long-term health in adopting smoking. This article reviews answers to this question and posits that unpleasant withdrawal symptoms and the late realization of the harm of smoking explain
how individuals become trapped by earlier decisions to smoke.

Tercyak, Kenneth P., Caryn Lerman, and Janet Audrain. "Association of At-
tention-Deficit/Hyperactivity Disorder Symptoms with Levels of Cigarette
Smoking in a Community Sample of Adolescents." *Journal of the American
Academy of Child and Adolescent Psychiatry*, vol. 41, July 2002, pp. 799–805. A
survey of more than 1,000 10th-grade students reveals that those with inat-
tention, hyperactivity, and impulsivity symptoms are more likely to experiment with smoking and to become regular tobacco users. These
psychological traits can help predict which adolescents will begin to smoke.

Unger, Jennifer B., Tess Boley Cruz, and Kurt M. Ribisl. "English Language Use as a Risk Factor for Smoking Initiation among Hispanic and
Asian-American Adolescents: Evidence for Mediation by Tobacco-
Related Beliefs and Social Norms." *Health Psychology*, vol. 19, September
2000, pp. 403–410. Research reveals that acculturation of immigrants to
American culture increases smoking. In this study use of English was associated with smoking, in part because English speakers saw fewer consequences of smoking and had more friends who smoked than those who
used the native language.

Vastag, Brian. "Quitting Smoking Harder for Women." *JAMA*, vol. 285,
June 20, 2001, p. 2,966. Reporting on a study from the National Institute
on Drug Abuse, this brief article notes that nicotine replacement therapy
works less well for women because they are greatly concerned about gaining weight. The study urges that smoking cessation research focus on developing methods particularly suited for women.

Waldron, Ingrid, and Diane Lye. "Relationships between Teenage Smoking
and Attitudes toward Women's Rights, Sex Roles, Marriage, Sex and

Family." *Women and Health*, vol. 16, nos. 3/4, 1990, pp. 23–46. Using data on high school seniors in 1985, this study finds that smoking is not related to attitudes toward equal opportunities for women but is related to more liberal attitudes toward cohabitation of unmarried couples. Rejection of conventional values toward marriage and toward smoking thus seem to be related.

Williams, Geoffrey C., Elizabeth M. Cox, and Viking A. Hedberg. "Extrinsic Life Goals and Health-Risk Behaviors of Adolescents." *Journal of Applied Social Psychology*, vol. 30, August 2000, pp. 1,757–71. Examination of attitudes among adolescents discloses that smokers have stronger aspirations for wealth, fame, and image, while nonsmokers have stronger aspirations for growth, relationships, and community ties.

Winkleby, Marilyn A., et al. "Hispanic versus White Smoking Patterns by Sex and Level of Education." *American Journal of Epidemiology*, vol. 142, no. 4, August 1995, pp. 410–418. For persons with high levels of education, differences in smoking between whites and Hispanics are small, but for persons with low education, whites have substantially higher rates of smoking than Hispanics.

Wolfinger, Nicholas H. "The Effect of Parental Divorce on Adult Tobacco and Alcohol Consumption." *Journal of Health and Social Behavior*, vol. 39, September 1998, pp. 254–269. The study demonstrates that the adult children of divorced parents have an increased likelihood of smoking.

Wray, Linda A., et al. "The Impact of Heart Attack on Smoking Cessation among Middle-Aged Adults." *Journal of Health and Social Behavior*, vol. 39, December 1998, pp. 271–293. This study extends research showing that education reduces smoking in general by examining smoking among those who have experienced a heart attack. Those heart attack victims with high education were more likely to give up smoking than those with low education.

Yang, Gonghuan. "Smoking in China: Findings of the 1996 National Prevalence Survey." *JAMA*, vol. 282, October 6, 1999, pp. 1,247–53. China stands today as the world's largest producer and consumer of cigarettes and appears to be experiencing a tobacco epidemic. The statistics from this study indicate the seriousness of the situation: 63 percent of men in China smoke (compared to about 25 percent in the United States). While only 3.8 percent of women in China smoke, the potential exists for rates to rise among females.

Zucker, Alyssa N., Zaje A. Harrell, and Kathi Miner-Rubino. "Smoking in College Women: The Role of Thinness Pressure, Media Exposure, and Critical Consciousness." *Psychology of Women Quarterly*, vol. 25, September 2002, pp. 233–241. Among a sample of 188 female undergraduates, smokers are more likely to believe that smoking controls weight, to feel pressures from media sources to stay thin, and to lack skepticism about tobacco advertisements. The authors suggest that antismoking programs address concerns of young women about weight control.

WEB DOCUMENTS

Bloch, Michele. "Women and Tobacco." Freshlife. Available online. URL: http://www.freshlife.com/articles/tobacco.htm. Downloaded in February 2003. This page describes the special problems created for women by tobacco use, the lack of knowledge among women of the ways tobacco can harm health, and the tendency of women to see smoking as a problem only for men.

Canadian Women's Health Network. "Catching Our Breath: A Journal about Change for Women Who Smoke." Available online. URL: http://www.cwhn.ca/resources/breath/index.html. Posted on December 5, 2001. This includes a historical discussion of culture and tobacco use, describes current social patterns of tobacco use, and offers suggestions for ex-smokers on how to avoid relapse.

Centers for Disease Control and Prevention. "Cigarette Smoking in 99 Metropolitan Areas—United States, 2000." Available online. URL: http://www.cdc.gov/mmwr/preview/mmwrhtml/mm5049a3.htm. Posted on December 14, 2001. Figures show smoking is highest in the South and Midwest, and lowest in the Northeast and West.

———. "Trends in Cigarette Smoking among High School Students—United States, 1991–2001." Available online. URL: http://www.cdc.gov/mmwr/preview/mmwrhtml/mm5119al.htm. Posted on May 17, 2002. Statistics from yearly surveys indicate that after rising in the mid-1990s, cigarette smoking among high school students declined during the late 1990s.

National Center on Addiction and Substance Abuse at Columbia University. "The Formative Years: Pathways to Substance Abuse among Girls and Young Women Ages 8–22." Available online. URL: http://www.casacolumbia.org/publications1456/publications_show.htm?doc_id=151006. Posted on February 2003. Among other things this report finds that girls and young women get hooked on cigarettes (as well as on alcohol and other drugs) more quickly and for different reasons than boys and young men. They should therefore receive specialized treatment.

Substance Abuse and Mental Health Services Administration, Office of Applied Studies. "Substance Abuse and Mental Health Statistics." Available online. URL: http://drugabusestatistics.samhsa.gov. Downloaded in February 2003. Users of the web site can download much scientifically reliable information on the use and treatment of tobacco (and other drugs) for the nation as a whole and for individual states. The site also includes a list of available publications.

Turlington, Christy. "Facts on Women and Tobacco." Centers for Disease Control and Prevention. Available online. URL: http://www.cdc.gov/tobacco/christy/women.htm. Posted on September 24, 2001. Lists facts about smoking rates of young and adult women, risks of developing smoking-related diseases, and smoking cessation.

University of Michigan News and Information Services. "Cigarette Smoking among American Teens Declines Sharply in 2001." University of Michigan. Available online. URL: http://www.umich.edu/~newsinfo/Releases/2001/Dec01/r121901c.htm. Posted on December 19, 2001. University of Michigan researchers have been surveying high school students since the 1970s about substance use—including tobacco. This press release summarizes the trends over the last several decades and the more recent drop in cigarette use.

TOBACCO BUSINESS AND LITIGATION

BOOKS

Burrough, Bryan, and John Helyar. *Barbarians at the Gate: The Fall of RJR Nabisco.* New York: Harper and Row, 1990. This fascinating story about a $25 billion leveraged buyout of RJR Nabisco in 1988 includes much information on R. J. Reynolds and its efforts to diversify by merging with the food company Nabisco.

Congdon-Martin, Douglas. *Camel Cigarette Collectibles: 1964–1995.* Atglen, Penn.: Schiffer Publishing, 2000. In describing Camel ads, posters, signs, and merchandise, this book provides a pictorial history of a successful advertising campaign. The fact that many enjoy collecting products with Camel logos reflects the social importance of cigarette advertising and promotion.

Davis, D. Layton, and Mark T. Nielsen, eds. *Tobacco: Production, Chemistry, and Technology.* Oxford, U.K.: Blackwell Science, 1999. Contains much scientific information on parts of the tobacco industry that get much less attention than marketing and sales—growing tobacco, the chemical composition of various types of tobacco, and processing, storing, and blending tobacco.

Glantz, Stanton A., et al. *The Cigarette Papers.* Berkeley: University of California Press, 1996. This volume publishes secret internal documents from Brown and Williamson Tobacco in book form and allows readers to see what tobacco manufacturers knew about the harm of their product while they were denying that any such harm occurred.

Hammond, Ross. *Addicted to Profit: Big Tobacco's Expanding Global Reach.* Washington, D.C.: Essential Action, 1998. A critic of U.S. tobacco companies argues that they now make more profit outside than inside the United States, condemns worldwide marketing and advertising efforts that contribute to rising global smoking rates, and opposes government trade programs and export legislation that promote worldwide tobacco sales.

Heyes, Eileen. *Tobacco U.S.A.: The Industry behind the Smokescreen.* Brookfield, Conn.: Milbrook Press, 1999. This journalistic examination of the U.S. tobacco industry contains information on current tobacco farming, government support and regulation of the industry, marketing trends, and the recent problems of Big Tobacco.

Hilts, Philip J. *Smokescreen: The Truth behind the Tobacco Industry Cover-Up.* Reading, Mass.: Addison-Wesley, 1996. An investigative report on the efforts of the tobacco industry to hide the dangers of cigarette smoking, the book argues that cigarette manufacturers had known of the harm for a long time and had targeted teens with advertising and nicotine addiction to make sure each generation takes up the habit.

Kilbourne, Jean. *Deadly Persuasion: Why Women and Girls Must Fight the Addictive Power of Advertising.* New York: Free Press, 1999. Because advertisers make addictive behaviors involving tobacco, alcohol, sex, and food appear not only normal but as solutions to personal problems, the author is greatly concerned about the degree to which advertisers influence the lives of American women and girls.

Males, Mike A. *Smoked: Why Joe Camel Is Still Smiling.* Monroe, Maine: Common Courage Press, 1999. The author argues that tobacco companies maintain their power through political contributions and lobbying and believes that efforts to stop teen smoking are counterproductive and dishonest when many adults continue to smoke.

McGowan, Richard. *Business, Politics, and Cigarettes: Multiple Levels, Multiple Agendas.* Westport, Conn.: Greenwood Press, 1995. In describing the development of the tobacco industry this book gives special attention to its relationship with public policies. It explores the effects advertising regulation, smoking bans, and excise taxes have on cigarette sales but in so doing relies on complex statistical procedures.

Miller, Karen S. *The Voice of Business.* Chapel Hill: University of North Carolina Press, 1999. A study of the role of public relations in business, this book describes the practices used by the tobacco industry to promote cigarette use and protect itself from regulation.

Mokhiber, Russell. *Corporate Crime and Violence: Big Business Power and the Abuse of Public Trust.* San Francisco: Sierra Club Books, 1988. This study of corporate crimes includes the tobacco industry along with companies that produced defective products and caused environmental disasters.

195

Mollenkamp, Carrick, et al. *The People vs. Big Tobacco: How the States Took on the Cigarette Giants.* Princeton, N.J.: Bloomberg Press, 1998. This work chronicles the negotiations between the major tobacco companies and an alliance of antismoking interests that led to the 1997 settlement (ultimately revised in 1998 to create the Master Settlement Agreement). As reporters for Bloomberg News, the authors helped break the story about the negotiations.

Nuttall, Floyd H. *Memoirs in a Country Churchyard: A Tobaccoman's Plea: Clean Up Tobacco Row!* Lawrenceville, Va.: Brunswick Publishers, 1996. A man who worked 40 years in the tobacco industry as an expert on blending and flavoring tobacco describes changes in the industry from the 1930s to the 1970s. These memoirs supply a detailed look at the tobacco industry during times of increasing government attacks and negative publicity and present the author's views on the need for a cigarette that is less harmful to nonsmokers.

Orey, Michael. *Assuming the Risk: The Mavericks, the Lawyers, and the Whistle-Blowers Who Beat Big Tobacco.* Boston: Little, Brown, 1999. Beginning with the true-life drama about the case of Nathan Horton, a black carpenter with emphysema and lung cancer who sued American Tobacco for damages, the book traces the efforts in the state of Mississippi to bring a lawsuit against the entire industry.

Parker-Pope, Tara. *Cigarettes: Anatomy of an Industry from Seed to Smoke.* New York: New Press, 2001. A readable overview of the tobacco industry and smoking that covers much ground in relatively few pages. Filled with stories, interesting statistics, and up-to-date material, it provides a good starting point for those doing research on this topic.

Pringle, Peter. *Cornered: Big Tobacco at the Bar of Justice.* New York: Holt, 1998. As with several other books (by such authors as Mollenkamp, Orey, Zegart), this one tells the story of the initial settlement between tobacco companies and state attorneys general suing to recoup Medicaid costs for treating smoking-related illnesses. Although the settlement that the book describes is later replaced by another, the background to the initial agreement proves useful in understanding the motives and actions of both sides of the negotiations.

Read, Melvyn D. *The Politics of Tobacco: Policy Networks and the Cigarette Industry.* Aldershot, U.K.: Avebury, 1996. An empirical study of changes in the strategies used by tobacco companies to influence government policy in Britain and to defend itself from antismoking and public health groups, this book uses its findings to help understand the general nature of policy influences in modern democracies.

Rosenbaum, David I., ed. *Market Dominance: How Firms Gain, Hold, or Lose It and the Impact on Economic Performance.* Westport, Conn.: Praeger Publishers, 1998. This collection of essays on companies that attained dominance in their market includes a chapter on American Tobacco, which monopolized cigarette production and sales for several decades from the late 1800s to the early 1900s and remained a dominant company during the rest of the 20th century.

Sobel, Robert. *When Giants Stumble: Classic Business Blunders and How to Avoid Them.* Paramus, N.J.: Prentice-Hall, 1999. An analysis of 15 major business catastrophes in post–World War II America, this book includes a chapter on the events and pivotal mistakes of corporate leaders resulting in the problems of the tobacco industry.

Taylor, Peter. *The Smoke Ring: Tobacco, Money, and Multinational Politics.* New York: Pantheon Books, 1984. An early effort to examine the use of power and money by multinational tobacco companies to gain political advantage. The present context differs from that described by Taylor, but the efforts of the tobacco companies continue.

Thibodeau, Michael, and Jana Martin. *Smoke Gets in Your Eyes: A Fine Blend of Cigarette Packaging, Branding and Design.* New York: Abbeville Press, 2000. In presenting pictures of the designs of cigarette packages, this book offers a history of how cigarettes have been promoted over the years, what factors led to a successful brand, and why some symbols became particularly popular. It covers well-known campaigns for Camel and Marlboro cigarettes, but also many less successful campaigns for now unknown cigarette brands.

Thompson, Argus V., ed. *The Tobacco Industry: Wheezing or Breezing.* New York: Nova Science Publishers, 2002. A chapter on the economic performance of the U.S. tobacco companies in domestic and world markets reviews the business side of the industry. Other chapters examine litigation against and regulation of the tobacco industry.

Twitchell, James B. *Twenty Ads That Shook the World: The Century's Most Groundbreaking Advertising and How It Changed Us All.* New York: Crown Publishers, 2000. Among the 20 advertisers and advertising campaigns discussed in this book is the highly successful effort to promote Marlboro cigarettes.

Tye, Larry. *The Father of Spin: Edward L. Bernays and the Birth of Public Relations.* New York: Crown, 1998. Bernays's use of psychological insights to develop successful advertising campaigns for American Tobacco in the early part of the 20th century proved important in the widening acceptance of tobacco. This biography supplies much background on the man and on early public relations strategies.

Warner, Kenneth E. *Selling Smoke: Cigarette Advertising and Public Health.* Washington, D.C.: American Public Health Association, 1986. After discussing the public's understandings of the hazards of smoking, the author considers the magnitude of cigarette advertising and its effects and concludes that a ban on tobacco advertising is warranted.

Weems, Robert E. *Desegregating the Dollar.* New York: New York University Press, 1998. This book examines the development of advertising and marketing strategies directed toward African Americans. Part of the book focuses on the serious negative consequences of marketing of cigarette products for the health problems of this group.

White, Larry C. *Merchants of Death: The American Tobacco Industry.* New York: Beech Tree Books, 1988. As indicated by the title, the author is highly critical of the behavior of cigarette companies and their executives for marketing harmful products and then denying that the products cause any harm. He gives attention to early litigation and efforts of tobacco companies to block suits, as well as to political efforts to forestall regulation.

Whiteside, Thomas. *Selling Death: Cigarette Advertising and Public Health.* New York: Liveright, 1971. An early examination of the tobacco executives behind cigarette advertising and a history of the efforts—inadequate, in the author's view—to limit the influence of advertising.

Wright, John R. "Tobacco Industry PACs and the Nation's Health: A Second Opinion." In Paul S. Herrnson, Ronald G. Shaiko, and Clyde Wilcox, eds. *The Interest Group Connection: Electioneering, Lobbying, and Policymaking in Washington.* Chatham, N.J.: Chatham House Publishing 1998. In an analysis of voting in the Senate, the author disputes claims that tobacco Political Action Committees strongly influence voting outcomes and suggests that even with high campaign contributions, tobacco policies respond largely to ideological values.

Zegart, Dan. *Civil Warrior: The Legal Siege on the Tobacco Industry.* New York: Delacorte Press, 2000. Written in the form of a narrative story, this book follows the civil litigation against the tobacco industry from the perspective of the trial lawyers who brought the suits, particularly Ron Motley.

ARTICLES

Alterman, Eric. "How Cigarettes Helped Victor Navasky Prove a Philosophical Truth: Cosa Nostra Syndicate." *New Yorker,* vol. 73, August 25–September 1, 1997, p. 58. Victor Navasky, editor of *Nation* magazine, purchased one share of R. J. Reynolds stock with friends (using the name Cosa Nostra Syndicate) in 1964. The goal was to show that self-destructive behavior, such as cigarette smoking, generates huge profits. Indeed, the sale of the stock in 1995 left them with a large return on their investment.

Barbeau, Elizabeth M., et al. "Does Cigarette Print Advertising Adhere to the Tobacco Institute's Voluntary Advertising and Promotion Code? An Assessment." *Journal of Public Health Policy,* vol. 19, no. 4, 1998, pp. 473–488. Based on the perceptions of 913 students ages 10–15 in the United States, this study concludes that positive messages about smoking continue to reach young people despite agreements of the tobacco industry to eliminate these messages.

Barron, Kelly. "Smoking Gun." *Forbes*, vol. 166, August 21, 2000, p. 54. The largest distributor of cigarettes in the United States outside the tobacco companies themselves is McLane Co., a subsidiary of Wal-Mart Stores. The article describes the ability of the company to both avoid lawsuits and produce profits from cigarette distribution.

Bicner, Lois, and Michael Siegel. "Tobacco Marketing and Adolescent Smoking: More Support for a Causal Inference." *American Journal of Public Health*, vol. 90, May 2000, pp. 407–411. Scientific studies have trouble proving that advertising by tobacco companies causes smoking rather than merely prodding current smokers to switch brands. This study finds that youth familiar with tobacco brands and products were more likely to adopt smoking than those not familiar. This study proves more effective than others in demonstrating that tobacco advertising leads nonsmoking youth to become smokers.

Capehart, Thomas, Jr. "Cigarette Consumption Continues to Slip." *Agricultural Outlook*, vol. 278, January/February 2001, pp. 8–10. The article views the decline in smoking from the perspective of tobacco growers and producers and gives attention to market prices, taxes, and trade.

Carey, John. "Philip Morris' Latest Smoke Screen: Lobbying the FDA to Rein in Incidence of Teen Smoking." *Business Week*, July 16, 2001, p. 43. This article views efforts by one powerful tobacco company to reduce teen smoking as a gimmick designed to avoid further regulation. It criticizes the claims of Philip Morris that it now is motivated to act in the public interest rather than to maximize profits.

Collins, Glenn. "Two Lawyers Carry on Tobacco Suits." *New York Times*, June 6, 1996, p. D4. Profiles Stanley M. and Susan Rosenblatt, two Miami attorneys who would successfully bring a class action suit against tobacco companies on behalf of Florida smokers.

Dickey, Christopher, and Rod Nordland. "Big Tobacco's Next Legal War." *Newsweek*, vol. 136, July 31, 2000, pp. 36–39. The article reviews battles over the role of cigarette manufacturers in smuggling cigarettes across borders without paying taxes. Critics claim the tobacco companies have intentionally hampered international efforts to regulate tobacco and control its movement across national boundaries.

Enrich, David. "Jeffrey Wigand." *U.S. News and World Report*, vol. 131, August 20–27, 2001, p. 70. As part of a special section on heroes, this article tells the story of Jeffrey Wigand, the former chief research scientist at Brown and Williamson Tobacco who helped government investigators, lawyers, and journalists prove that tobacco companies had set out to addict cigarette users.

Fairclough, Gordon. "As Marlboro Loses Ground, Altria Expands the Brand." *Wall Street Journal*, January 29, 2003, p. B1. Philip Morris, the U.S. tobacco unit of Altria, aims to get tobacco sales and profits up with the introduction of a new variety of Marlboro cigarettes. This article describes the goals of the new product and the strategies of tobacco companies in a strongly antismoking environment.

———. "Cheap Smokes Are Squeezing Big Tobacco." *Wall Street Journal*, November 14, 2002, p. C1. In the 1990s tobacco companies cut the prices of their major brands to complete with discount brands, but such discounting in the 2000s is harder with the need to pay huge damages to the states. Discount brands could cut into the profits of major companies, such as Philip Morris.

———. "Losing Control: Four Biggest Cigarette Makers Can't Raise Prices as They Did—Frugal Smokers Are Jumping to Bargain Brands; Profits Fall at Larger Companies—Buying Marlboro? Forget It." *Wall Street Journal*, October 25, 2002, p. A1. Discount brands have begun to cut into the sales of Marlboro cigarettes and reduce the profits of the major cigarette manufacturers. This does not change overall cigarette sales but affects the marketing and sales strategies of major producers.

Fonda, Daren. "Why Big Tobacco Won't Quit: Profits Up and Setbacks for Lawsuits against Industry." *Time*, vol. 157, July 2, 2001, pp. 38–39. Detailing some reasons why the economic future of the tobacco industry looks positive, this article makes the point that states have become dependent on funds from the tobacco companies and ultimately on the sales of cigarettes. That plus the victories of Republicans in recent elections make the political environment in the 2000s somewhat more supportive of tobacco companies.

France, Mike. "Why 'Little Tobacco' Looms Larger." *Business Week*, no. 3595, September 14, 1998, p. 136. With the tobacco settlement, smaller tobacco companies not burdened by the cost of litigation and payments to the states may make inroads in the market share of Big Tobacco.

Gladwell, Malcolm. "The Spin Myth: Work of E. L. Bernays." *New Yorker*, vol. 74, July 6, 1998, pp. 66–69ff. In the 1920s Edward L. Bernays became one of the first to sell cigarettes by appealing to women's right to smoke. This article tells of his public relations scheme to send 10 women down Fifth Avenue in New York City while smoking cigarettes and demanding freedom and of other campaigns that helped promote acceptance of cigarettes.

Greenblatt, Alan. "Secondhand Spokesman: The Tobacco Industry Remains a Potent Lobbying Force, Partly by Letting Other Groups Advocate on Its Behalf." *Governing*, vol. 15, April 2002, pp. 38–40. According to this article groups acting in ways that benefit the tobacco industry include restaurant associations opposed to banning tobacco in their businesses and taxpayer organizations opposed to higher taxes on consumer products. By focusing on economic issues these organizations distract smoking debates from issues of public health.

Gruber, Jonathan. "Tobacco at the Crossroads: The Past and Future of Smoking Regulation in the United States." *Journal of Economic Perspectives*, vol. 15, Spring 2001, pp. 193–212. An economist reviews the history of the tobacco industry and the effects of regulations on the industry.

Headden, Susan. "The Marlboro Man Lives! Restrained at Home, Tobacco Firms Step Up Their Marketing Overseas." *U.S. News and World Report*, vol. 125, September 21, 1998, pp. 58–59. As described in this article, tobacco companies have made efforts to make up for a stagnant domestic cigarette market with intensified international marketing. Manufacturers argue that U.S. laws cannot dictate their behavior abroad and hope to use open markets in other nations to fuel continued growth in profits.

Howell, Craig, Frank Congelio, and Ralph Yatsko. "Pricing Practices for Tobacco Products, 1980–94." *Monthly Labor Review*, vol. 117, December 1994, pp. 3–16. Evidence demonstrates that prices for tobacco products climbed rapidly throughout the 1980s and into the early 1990s but then fell sharply in 1993. Moreover the rise stemmed largely from prices charged by manufacturers to wholesalers rather than from tax increases.

Lavelle, Marianne. "Big Tobacco Rises from the Ashes: Profits Up at Tobacco Companies Despite Costly Settlement." *U.S. News and Business Report*, vol. 129, November 13, 2000, p. 50. Despite having to make the first installment of the $246 billion payment to the states, tobacco companies have continued, at least initially, to make profits by raising prices.

———. "Tobacco Fighters Find Another Smoking Gun: Documents Describing R. J. Reynolds Attempts to Attract Young Smokers." *U.S. News and World Report*, vol. 124, January 26, 1998, p. 55. This article describes tobacco industry documents made public by Representative Henry Waxman that belie claims of the industry that it did not target youth.

Light, Larry. "Smoke Alarms at RJR." *Business Week*, vol. 3604, November 16, 1998, pp. 75–76. The R. J. Reynolds Tobacco Company has been losing out to industry leader Philip Morris in marketing and international sales. With its Nabisco food division also hurting in the market, RJR profits declined in the late 1990s. Although the tobacco industry remains profitable in general, this company has done less well than others.

Meier, Barry. "Data on Tobacco Show a Strategy Aimed at Blacks." *New York Times*, February 6, 1998, p. A1ff. This article reviews tobacco industry documents on the importance of black smokers to the sales and marketing of tobacco companies.

Mintz, Morton. "Blowing Smoke Rings around the Statehouses. Philip Morris' 'Smoking Gun' Campaign to Prevent Increases in State Cigarette Taxes." *Washington Monthly*, vol. 28, May 1996, pp. 20–22. Since a large share of cigarette taxes comes from legislation at the state level, tobacco companies have made major lobbying efforts in each state. Their success from such efforts has led them to support states' rights in developing tobacco control legislation.

Moore, Stephen, et al. "Epidemiology of Failed Tobacco Control Legislation." *JAMA*, vol. 272, October 19, 1994, pp. 1,171–75. Data on campaign contributions and voting of Congress show that the strongest determinant of opposition to tobacco control legislation was the money a representative received from tobacco industry political action committees. According to the authors campaign money that thwarts antitobacco legislation contributes to the loss of thousands of lives a year.

Noonan, David. "A New Way to Sell Smokes: Star Scientific's Marketing of Advance." *Newsweek*, vol. 136, October 16, 2000, p. 54. Advance, a new cigarette made by a small Virginia tobacco company, contains lower levels of carcinogens and takes a new sales strategy by clearly and bluntly stating the risks of smoking. The warnings go beyond those required by the government and may reduce the risk of lawsuits.

Pascual, Aixa M. "LeBow Turns Over a New Leaf." *Business Week*, no. 3731, May 7, 2001, pp. 71–72. This profile of the CEO of the company that owns the Liggett Group, a relatively small cigarette manufacturer, explains how Bennett LeBow was the first to agree to settle with the states over their suits against the tobacco companies and is now working to have his company develop a safer cigarette with fewer carcinogens and another with no nicotine.

Pierce, John E., et al. "Tobacco Industry Promotion of Cigarettes and Adolescent Smoking." *JAMA*, vol. 279, February 18, 1998, pp. 511–515. This study provides rare evidence that tobacco promotional activities cause youth to start smoking. It finds that adolescents in 1992 who did not smoke were likely to later become susceptible to smoking or start smoking if they had a favorite cigarette advertisement and possessed a cigarette promotional item.

Pollay, Richard W. "The Last Straw? Cigarette Advertising and Realized Market Shares among Youth and Adults, 1979–1993." *Journal of Marketing*, vol. 60, no. 2, 1996, pp. 1–16. Analysis of data over time reveals that competition between cigarette firms works mainly to shift brand market share among the young.

Powledge, T. M. "Tobacco Pharming." *Scientific American*, vol. 285, October 2001, pp. 25–26. One company is attempting to use tobacco that carries the tobacco mosaic virus to create medicines and cure cancer. This article describes a genetic engineering effort that may find a more beneficial use for tobacco than smoking.

Sepe, Edward, and Stanton A. Glantz. "Bar and Club Promotions in the Alternative Press: Targeting Young Adults." *American Journal of Public Health*, vol. 92, January 2002, pp. 75–78. This study of tobacco advertising in alternative newspapers in San Francisco and Philadelphia finds an enormous increase in product advertisements and promotions. It appears that the tobacco industry has increased its use of bars and clubs as promotional venues and its efforts to reach the young adults who frequent these establishments.

Shamasunder, Bhavna, and Lisa Bero. "Financial Ties and Conflicts of Interest between Pharmaceutical and Tobacco Companies." *JAMA*, vol. 288, August 14, 2002, pp. 738–744. Tobacco industry documents reveal that tobacco companies pressured pharmaceutical companies to scale back the smoking cessation educational materials that accompany nicotine gum and to restrict the marketing of nicotine patches. The authors recommend that financial ties between the tobacco companies and pharmaceutical products be made public.

Stone, Peter H. "Blowing Smoke at Its Critics." *National Journal*, vol. 28, April 20, 1996, pp. 884–887. This describes efforts of tobacco companies to boost their lobbying operations in the face of legal and legislative threats and to increase contributions to (largely Republican) candidates.

Yach, Derek, and Stella Aguinaga Bialous. "Junking Science to Promote Tobacco." *American Journal of Public Health*, vol. 91, November 2001, pp. 1,745–48. The authors dispute use of the term *junk science* by tobacco companies to discredit evidence of the harm of secondhand smoke for nonsmokers. They recommend that policymakers recognize the sources and funding of studies in reaching conclusions about appropriate public action.

WEB DOCUMENTS

British American Tobacco. "Welcome to British American Tobacco." Available online. URL: http://www.bat.com. Downloaded in February 2003. This web site contains views on smoking and health, addiction, regulation, litigation, and social responsibility of a major international tobacco maker. The page on smoking and health, for example, states clearly that the pleasures of smoking bring risks of serious disease and that many people find it difficult to quit.

Campaign for Tobacco Free Kids. "Tobacco Advertising Gallery." Available online. URL: http://tobaccofreekids.org/adgallery. Downloaded in December 2002. A group opposed to cigarette advertising and efforts to manipulate users into smoking illustrates the ads used by the tobacco companies. Users of the page can view ads organized by country, brand, company, and type.

Court Library. "Court TV Casefiles: *Carter v. Williamson* (8/96)." Court TV. Available online. URL: http://www.courttv.com/casefiles/verdicts/carter.html. Downloaded in December 2002. The case file summarizes the legal issues and verdict of the case that successfully used grounds of fraud and misrepresentation to obtain damages from tobacco companies in a jury trial. Although overturned on a technicality, the case represented a major victory for antismoking forces.

Frontline. "Inside the Tobacco Deal." PBS Online. Available online. URL: http://www.pbs.org/wgbh/pages/frontline/shows/settlement. Downloaded in December 2002. Based on a PBS documentary on the settlement between the states and Big Tobacco companies, the web site provides biographies and interviews with the main participants, a timeline of major events, and background information on the deal. Because the documentary covers events only up to April 1998, it lacks information on the final outcome of the negotiations.

Khermouch, Gerry, and Jeff Green. "Buzz Marketing." Business Week Online. Available online. URL: http://www.businessweek.com/magazine/content/01_03/b3743001.htm. Posted on July 30, 2001. This article describes efforts by Brown and Williamson to make Lucky Strike cigarettes more popular. The company created the Lucky Strike Task Force, which included attractive couples who would smoke Lucky Strike and talk to smokers about the product in trendy neighborhoods such as Miami's South Beach and New York's Soho.

Lorillard Tobacco Company. "Welcome." Available online. URL: http//www.lorillard.com. Downloaded in February 2003. The fourth largest and oldest cigarette manufacturer in the United States stresses its corporate responsibility and desire to cooperate with rather than confront antismoking forces.

National Center for Chronic Disease Prevention and Health Promotion. "Brown and Williamson Litigation Discovery Website." Available online. URL: http://www.cdc.gov/tobacco/industrydocs/brownandwilliamson.htm. Posted on November 18, 1999. This page contains more than 1 million documents produced by either Brown and Williamson or the American Tobacco Company that were released in Minnesota tobacco litigation and other lawsuits.

———. "Committee on Commerce Tobacco Documents." Available online. URL: http://www.cdc.gov/tobacco/industrydocs/ushouse.htm. Posted on November 8, 1999. These documents come from six companies and organizations involved in the Minnesota tobacco case. Originally withheld as private, they were released to the public in 1998.

————. "Council for Tobacco Research—U.S.A., Inc." Available online. URL: http://www.cdc.gov/tobacco/industrydocs/councilfortobacco.htm. Posted on November 18, 1999. These are documents released by the Council for Tobacco Research, an industry-supported group, in lawsuits of state attorneys general and other civil actions.

————. "Legacy Tobacco Documents Library." Available online. URL: http://www.cdc.gov/tobacco/industrydocs/legacylibrary.htm. Posted on November 18, 1999. This library contains more than 20 million documents relating to scientific research, manufacturing, marketing, advertising, and sales of cigarettes. Sponsored by a foundation created from the Master Settlement Agreement, these documents date back to the 1950s.

————. "Lorillard Tobacco Company Document Site." Available online. URL: http://www.cdc.gov/tobacco/industrydocs/lorillard.htm. Posted on November 18, 1999. These documents were released by Lorillard as part of the Minnesota tobacco litigation.

————. "Philip Morris Incorporated Document Site." Available online. URL: http://www.cdc.gov/tobacco/industrydocs/philipmorris.htm. Posted on November 18, 1999. There are 1.5 million documents released by Philip Morris as part of tobacco litigation.

————. "R. J. Reynolds Tobacco Company On-Line Litigation Document Archive." Available online. URL: http://www.cdc.gov/tobacco/industry docs/rjreynolds.htm. Posted on November 18, 1999. More than 90,000 tobacco litigation documents from R. J. Reynolds Tobacco are available here.

————. "Tobacco Archives. com." Available online. URL: http://www.cdc. gov/tobacco/industrydocs/tobaccoarchives.htm. Posted on November 18, 1999. This site provides links to the document archives of the four major tobacco companies and those of the Council on Tobacco Research and the Tobacco Institute.

————. "Tobacco Industry Documents." Available online. URL: http:// www.cdc.gov/tobacco/industrydocs/docsites.htm. Posted on November 18, 1999. A useful guide to explore the tobacco industry document archives on the web, this site offers background information, a glossary, specific industry documents, and a search engine.

————. "The Tobacco Institute Document Site." Available online. URL: http://www.cdc.gov/tobacco/industrydocs/tobaccoinstitute.htm. Posted on November 18, 1999. This offers documents from the tobacco industry trade association released during Minnesota tobacco litigation.

————. "University of California San Francisco's Brown and Williamson Collection." Available online. URL: http://www.cdc.gov/tobacco/industrydocs/ ucsf.htm. Posted on November 18, 1999. Documents and abstracts have been sorted by topic and were among the first to be released after the

California supreme court turned down an appeal from Brown and Williamson to have the documents kept from the public.

Philip Morris USA. "Philip Morris USA." Available online. URL: http://www.philipmorrisusa.com. Downloaded in February 2003. The largest cigarette manufacturer in the United States and one of the largest companies in the world, Philip Morris is best known for its Marlboro cigarettes.

R. J. Reynolds Tobacco Company. "Home Page." Available online. URL: http://www.rjrt.com. Downloaded in February 2003. The second largest tobacco maker in the United States includes here commentary on the health effects of smoking and information about youth nonsmoking programs, tobacco laws and regulations, litigation, and smokers' rights.

Willemsen, Marc C., and Boudewijn de Blij. "Tobacco Advertising." UICC Tobacco Control Factsheets. Available online. URL: http://factsheets. globalink.org/en/advertising.shtml. Downloaded on February 2, 2003. This reviews the evidence that advertising stimulates tobacco sales and concludes that a ban on advertising is needed for countries to reduce tobacco use.

TOBACCO CONTROL

BOOKS

Abbott, Ann Augustine, ed. *Alcohol, Tobacco, and Other Drugs: Challenging Myths, Assessing Theories, Individualizing Interventions.* Washington, D.C.: NASW Press, 2000. This volume compiles articles by social work educators for social work practitioners on addiction, its consequences, its treatments, and its prevention.

Abrams, David, et al. *The Tobacco Dependence Treatment Handbook: A Guide to Best Practices.* New York: Guilford Press, 2003. The chapters contain up-to-date information for clinicians on the assessment, planning, and evaluation of treatment strategies for tobacco dependence. The recommendations are based on scientific research and experiences of practitioners.

Buckley, Christopher. *Thank You for Smoking.* New York: Random House, 1994. This satirical novel about a public relations specialist working for the tobacco companies pokes fun at the extreme antismoking actions of the 1990s.

Center for Substance Abuse Prevention. *Substance Abuse Resource Guide: Tobacco.* Washington, D.C.: U.S. Department of Health and Human Services, 1999. This offers the latest information and references about for tobacco use prevention for professionals, educators, parents, and the general public.

Annotated Bibliography

Centers for Disease Control and Prevention. *Best Practices for Comprehensive Tobacco Control Programs—August 1999*. Atlanta, Ga.: U.S. Department of Health and Human Services, Centers for Disease Control and Prevention, Office of Smoking and Health, 1999. This book describes the best practices for tobacco control in nine areas: community programs, disease prevention programs, schools, enforcement, statewide, countermarketing, cessation, surveillance, and administration.

Derthick, Martha A. *Up in Smoke: From Legislation to Litigation in Tobacco Politics*. Washington, D.C.: CQ Press, 2002. Arguing that litigation does not work as well as legislation in designing tobacco control policies, this book finds that lawsuits in the 1990s came to replace ordinary politics and legislation and changed public policy for the worse. It also provides a rich description of the various players involved in debates over tobacco use.

Fibkins, William L. *What Schools Should Do to Help Kids Stop Smoking*. Larchmont, N.Y.: Eye on Education, 2000. This book identifies what programs work best to prevent kids from smoking and how teachers and administrators can implement the programs. It presents examples of successful efforts at both the school and state level.

Forst, Marin L., ed. *Planning and Implementing Effective Tobacco Education and Prevention Programs*. Springfield, Ill.: Charles C. Thomas, 1999. The chapters describe experiences with a variety of programs for tobacco education and prevention in Native American, African-American, Hispanic, Asian and Pacific Islander, and gay and lesbian communities. A summary chapter evaluates the effects of the various tobacco control programs.

Friedman, Kenneth Michael. *Public Policy and the Smoking-Health Controversy: A Comparative Study*. Lexington, Mass.: Lexington Books, 1975. A dated book, this nevertheless makes interesting comparisons of policies to control tobacco in the United States, Canada, and Great Britain.

Fritschler, A. Lee, and James M. Hoefler. *Smoking and Politics: Policymaking and the Federal Bureaucracy*. 5th ed. Englewood Cliffs, N.J.: Prentice Hall, 1995. In considering the role of government agencies and bureaucracies in influencing government policies, this text examines, among other things, the government's efforts to discourage cigarette smoking by requiring warning labels on cigarette packages and advertisements.

Glantz, Stanton, and Edith D. Balbach. *Tobacco Wars: Inside the California Battles*. Berkeley: University of California Press, 2000. In tracing the history of tobacco control efforts in California, these antitobacco advocates provide a detailed description of the politics behind tobacco change and the efforts of the tobacco industry to prevent such change. The authors argue that elected officials regularly and repeatedly ignored the wishes of the voters for tobacco control to support instead the interests of the tobacco industry.

207

Jacobsen, Peter D., and Jeffrey Wasserman. *Tobacco Control Laws: Implementation and Enforcement.* Santa Monica, Calif.: Rand Corporation, 1997. In reviewing the results of case studies of tobacco control laws, the authors conclude that such laws can be effectively implemented and enforced locally by the public, businesses, and tobacco sellers, but more efforts and funds need to be devoted to the task.

Jacobson, Peter D., et al. *Combating Teen Smoking: Research and Policy Strategies.* Ann Arbor: University of Michigan Press, 2001. This comprehensive volume reviews the political context of smoking policy, trends in youth smoking, and use of the mass media, tax increases, and regulation as forms of tobacco control. It concludes that antismoking mass media campaigns and regulation of cigarettes would be effective but that a comprehensive set of interventions would do most to reduce teen smoking.

Jha, Prabat, and Frank J. Chaloupka, eds. *Tobacco Control in Developing Countries.* New York: Oxford University Press, 2000. With smoking on the increase in developing countries across the world, public health programs must concentrate on tobacco control in nations outside North America and Europe. This volume, which offers an economic framework for tobacco control, provides much information on the most effective interventions for developing countries and highlights both the importance and potential of such interventions.

Kessler, David. *A Question of Intent: A Great American Battle with a Deadly Industry.* New York: Public Affairs, 2001. The former director of the Food and Drug Administration writes about his efforts and those of the agency to regulate tobacco. The book shows the difficulties and complexities of government policy making in general and of fighting the tobacco industry specifically. In the end the regulatory effort failed.

Koop, C. Everett. *Koop: Memoirs of America's Family Doctor.* New York: Random House, 1991. The second part of this autobiography details the efforts of the former surgeon general to battle smoking and nicotine addiction.

Leichter, Howard M. *Free to Be Foolish: Politics and Health Promotion in the United States and Great Britain.* Princeton, N.J.: Princeton University Press, 1991. The United States and Great Britain take different public health approaches to protecting individuals against their own risky lifestyles and against use of cigarettes in particular. In describing these differences the book offers a case study of comparative public policy.

Lichter, S. Robert, and Stanley Rothman. *Environmental Cancer—A Political Disease?* New Haven, Conn.: Yale University Press, 1999. Surveys of cancer scientists and analysis of the content of media reports suggest that environmental activists, media representatives, and sympathetic politicians overstate the risk of environmental agents, including environmental tobacco smoke, as causes of cancer. The views of the scientists and the scientific studies differ from those presented to the public by nonscientists concerned about the environment.

Lynch, Barbara S., and Richard J. Bonnie, eds. *Growing Up Tobacco Free: Preventing Nicotine Addiction in Children and Youths.* Washington, D.C.: National Academy Press, 1994. Chapters contain arguments to support the need for comprehensive tobacco policies to prevent youth from starting the habit and summarize strategies for addressing the need. Topics covered include the addictiveness of nicotine, advertising, controls and bans on tobacco sales, and use of taxes to prevent smoking.

National Cancer Institute, National Institutes of Health. *Community-Based Interventions for Smokers.* Smoking and Tobacco Control Monograph 6. Washington, D.C.: U.S. Department of Health and Human Services, 1995. An examination of the effectiveness of the Community Intervention Trial for Smoking Cessation (COMMIT) finds a modest decrease in smoking rates and an increased sense of community empowerment due to the intervention.

———. *Population Based Smoking Cessation.* Smoking and Tobacco Control Monograph 12. Washington, D.C.: U.S. Department of Health and Human Services, 2000. The papers from a recent conference evaluate the effectiveness of programs to reduce population levels of cigarette use in the United States.

———. *State and Local Legislative Action to Reduce Tobacco Use.* Smoking and Tobacco Control Monograph 11. Washington, D.C.: U.S. Department of Health and Human Services, 2000. This compiles data for states and cities on smoking restrictions in workplaces and public places, on sales to youth, and on smoking prevalence.

Oakley, Don. *Slow Burn: The Great American Antismoking Scam (And Why It Will Fail).* Roswell, Ga.: Eyrie Press, 1999. Criticizing the nation's (sometimes hysterical, according to the book) three-decade crusade against smoking, the author concludes that much of the evidence of the harm of cigarettes and secondhand smoke is overstated. He views the crusade as a threat to personal freedom and responsibility.

Oaks, Laury. *Smoking and Pregnancy: The Politics of Fetal Protection.* New Brunswick, N.J.: Rutgers University Press, 2001. Using interviews with 46 women and 27 health professionals and antitobacco advocates, and a range of written sources, the author examines how concerns about the effects on fetuses of smoking by pregnant women became a crucial public policy concern and could erode the reproductive rights of women.

Peele, Stanton. *The Diseasing of America.* Lexington, Mass.: Lexington Books, 1989. In taking a view that departs from the dominant opinions about chemical dependency, the author argues that individuals have choice and personal responsibility for participating in misbehaviors such as smoking. The term *diseasing* refers to the tendency to treat personal problems as medical diseases.

Pertschuk, Michael. *Smoke in Their Eyes: Lessons in Movement Leadership from the Tobacco Wars.* Nashville Tenn: Vanderbilt University Press, 2001. A longtime antitobacco advocate offers an inside view of the failed efforts of Congress to pass a tobacco control bill. He points not only to the power of tobacco industry lobbying to block legislation but also to internal conflicts in the antismoking movement as contributing to the lost opportunity of Congress to regulate cigarettes.

Proctor, Robert N. *Cancer Wars: How Politics Shapes What We Know and Don't Know about Cancer.* New York: Basic Books, 1995. The author concludes that the war against cancer has failed because of too much emphasis on research and too little emphasis on prevention and treatment. In recounting the political battles over how to fight cancer, the author gives special attention to the efforts of the tobacco industry to counter claims about the harm of cigarette smoking.

Rabin, Robert L., and Stephen D. Sugarman, eds. *Regulating Tobacco.* Oxford, U.K.: Oxford University Press, 2001. Articles in this volume consider the effectiveness of various means to control tobacco use such as raising taxes on tobacco, using tort litigation, and implementing clean indoor air restrictions. The volume gives special attention to the politics of tobacco control in European nations as well as in the United States,

———. *Smoking Policy: Law, Politics, and Culture.* Oxford, U.K.: Oxford University Press, 1993. A group of social and legal scholars examines the strategies used to control smoking and relates them to public attitudes and political institutions. A chapter on the politics of regulation in Canada, France, and the United States illustrates the different approaches each nation has taken to tobacco control.

Rogers, Pamela, and Steve Baldwin. *Controlled or Reduced Smoking: An Annotated Bibliography.* Westport, Conn.: Greenwood Press, 1999. The bibliography was compiled to help practitioners, field workers, and researchers understand diverse scientific literatures from a variety of disciplines. It focuses specifically on helping smokers who do not want to quit or who cannot quit reduce their risk by controlling tobacco use. Each chapter reviews a different type of study, and the final chapter summarizes the overall findings.

Roleff, Tamara L., Mary Williams, and Charles P. Cozic, eds. *Tobacco and Smoking: Opposing Viewpoints.* San Diego, Calif.: Greenhaven Press, 1998. This volume includes nontechnical articles typically from popular magazines that present both sides of questions about the harm of tobacco, the addictiveness of nicotine, the concern about secondhand smoke, the in-

fluence of advertising on smoking, the need for federal control of cigarettes, the importance of individual choice, and the value of the tobacco
settlement.

Schaler, Jeffrey A. *Addiction Is a Choice.* Chicago: Open Court Publishers,
2000. The author disputes the common notion that smoking is an addiction and that addicts cannot help themselves. While recognizing the difficulty of quitting, the author believes people have the choice to stop and
presents research on addiction to support his points.

Schaler, Jeffrey A., and Magada E. Schaler, eds. *Smoking: Who Has the Right?*
Amherst, N.Y.: Prometheus Books, 1998. Expert contributors present diverse viewpoints on the title's question, considering issues of personal responsibility and public health. The book allows readers to form their own
conclusions about the right to smoke versus the public health goal of a
tobacco-free society.

Seidman, Daniel F., and Lirio S. Covey. *Helping the Hard-Core Smoker: A
Clinician's Guide.* Mahwah, N.J.: Lawrence Erlbaum, 1999. Given that the
decline in smoking rates has slowed and that success rates in quitting are
low, the contributions to this volume, edited by clinical psychologists at
Columbia University, explain why current approaches are often inadequate and how to best help today's highly nicotine-dependent smokers. It
is useful for physicians, psychiatrists, nurses, psychologists, counselors,
and other clinicians.

Shaw, David. *The Pleasure Police: How Bluenose Busybodies and Lily-Livered
Alarmists Are Taking All the Fun Out of Life.* New York: Doubleday, 1996.
The author argues that if used with moderation and common sense, tobacco, alcohol, sex, and food bring much pleasure to life. We would be hap-
pier, according to the author, if we stopped worrying so much about these
things and if public health advocates left people alone to enjoy themselves.

Studlar, Donley T. *Tobacco Control: Comparative Politics in the United States
and Canada.* Orchard Park, N.Y.: Broadview Press, 2002. This study of
comparative politics describes differences in the development of regulation and taxation policies used to control tobacco in the United States and
Canada. It relates general differences in political institutions and policymaking procedures to specific differences in tobacco control policies.

Sullum, Jacob. *For Your Own Good: The Anti-Smoking Crusade and the
Tyranny of Public Health.* New York: Free Press, 1998. While recognizing
the harm of smoking for health, the author argues that antismoking advocates have reached the point where they are now attempting to impose
their preferences against cigarettes on another group that has freely chosen to enjoy the product. This book offers a reasoned defense of the view
that government antismoking efforts wrongly threaten the freedom of individuals and businesses.

Sussman, Steve, et al. *Developing School-Based Tobacco Use Prevention and Cessation Programs*. Thousands Oaks, Calif.: Sage Publications, 1995. In thoroughly evaluating programs for schools, the authors describe the development and implementation of the Project Toward No Tobacco Use. They further discuss the curriculum, evaluation, and future directions of such programs.

Tollison, Robert D., ed. *Clearing the Air: Perspectives on Environmental Tobacco Smoke*. Lexington, Mass.: Lexington Books, 1988. Contributors to the volume present chapters on health and policy issues related to environmental tobacco smoke. Supported in part by the tobacco industry, the volume generally views the evidence as not posing a large enough risk to warrant government intervention in the affairs of private citizens.

U.S. Congress, House Committee on Energy and Commerce, Subcommittee on Health and the Environment. *Environmental Tobacco Smoke: Hearings before the Subcommittee on Health and the Environment of the Committee on Energy and Commerce, House of Representatives, One Hundred Third Congress, First Session*. Washington, D.C.: U.S. Government Printing Office, 1988. The hearings are concerned with an amendment to the Public Health Service Act to protect the public from health hazards caused by exposure to environmental tobacco smoke.

————. *Regulation of Tobacco Products: Hearings before the Subcommittee on Health and the Environment of the Committee on Energy and Commerce, House of Representatives, One Hundred Third Congress, Second Session*. Washington, D.C.: U.S. Government Printing Office, 1995. The hearings evaluate proposals to have cigarette use regulated by the government.

————. *Tobacco Advertising: Hearings before the Subcommittee on Health and the Environment of the Committee on Energy and Commerce, House of Representatives, One Hundredth Congress, First Session*. Washington, D.C.: U.S. Government Printing Office, 1988. The hearings consider bills to limit tobacco advertising and prevent the positive depiction of cigarette smoking from influencing the choices of youth to smoke.

————. *Tobacco Control and Marketing: Hearing before the Subcommittee on Health and the Environment of the Committee on Energy and Commerce, House of Representatives, One Hundred First Congress, Second Session*. Washington, D.C.: U.S. Government Printing Office, 1990. The hearings address the conflict between public health efforts to limit tobacco use and public programs to support the export of tobacco to other nations.

————. *The Tobacco Settlement: Hearings before the Subcommittee on Health and the Environment of the Committee on Energy and Commerce, House of Representatives One Hundred Fifth Congress, First Session*. Washington, D.C.: U.S. Government Printing Office, 1999. The hearings address issues relating to the allocation of tobacco settlement funds, the prevention of teen tobacco use, the views of businesses excluded from the settlement, and the views of the public health community.

U.S. Congress, House Committee on Energy and Commerce, Subcommittee on Transportation and Hazardous Materials. *Tobacco Issues: Hearings before the Subcommittee on Transportation and Hazardous Materials of the Committee on Energy and Commerce, House of Representatives, One Hundred First Congress, First Session.* Washington, D.C.: U.S. Government Printing Office, 1989. The hearings consider alleged violations of the Cigarette Labeling and Advertising Act by the tobacco industry and the use of antismoking advertisements to counter prosmoking advertising.

U.S. Congress, Senate Committee on Labor and Human Resources. *Tobacco Settlement: Public Health or Public Harm? Hearings of the Committee on Labor and Human Resources, United States Senate, One Hundred Fifth Congress, First Session.* Washington, D.C.: U.S. Government Printing Office, 1997. The hearings are concerned with the scope of the settlement, the administration's position on the settlement, and public health aspects of the settlement.

U.S. Congress, Senate Committee on the Judiciary. *Raising Tobacco Prices: New Opportunities for the Black Market? Hearings before the Committee on the Judiciary, United States Senate, One Hundred Fifth Congress, Second Session.* Washington, D.C.: U.S. Government Printing Office, 1999. The hearings examine the likely effect of legislation proposing to increase the price of tobacco products on the tobacco industry and opportunities for black market cigarette sales.

U.S. Department of Health and Human Services. *Healthy People 2010.* Washington, D.C.: U.S. Department of Health and Human Services, 2000. Some consider the government goals for reducing smoking by 2010 to be overly ambitious and unlikely to be realized, but the goals play a major role in current public health efforts.

———. *Preventing Tobacco Use among Young People. A Report of the Surgeon General.* Washington, D.C.: U.S. Department of Health and Human Services, 1994. This volume provides an overview of the research on trends and causes of youth smoking, and the successes and failures of policies designed to reduce youth smoking. It makes the case that preventing youth from starting to smoke, despite advertising and promotions encouraging them to do so, will help deal with the public health problem of cigarette use in the future.

———. *Reducing the Health Consequences of Smoking: 25 Years of Progress. A Report of the Surgeon General.* Washington, D.C.: U.S. Department of Health and Human Services, 1989. This volume provides an overview of the new evidence to emerge about the harm of smoking since the 1964 Surgeon General's report, and the progress made in reducing the use of cigarettes and the health problems they cause.

———. *Regulating Tobacco Use. A Report of the Surgeon General*. Washington, D.C.: U.S. Department of Health and Human Services, 2000. After describing the historical efforts to reduce smoking in the United States, this volume reviews the scientific evidence on the effectiveness of several ways to reduce cigarette smoking: education efforts, programs to help smokers quit, government regulation, litigation strategies, economic approaches, and comprehensive programs. An essential guide to understanding current tobacco control endeavors.

———. *Smoking Cessation: Clinical Practice Guideline*. Washington, D.C.: U.S. Department of Health and Human Services, 1996. This short but technical volume based on a review of the scientific literature contains strategies and recommendations designed to assist clinicians, smoking cessation specialists, and health care administrators in helping smokers stop their habit.

Viscusi, W. Kip. *Smoke-Filled Rooms: A Postmortem on the Tobacco Deal*. Chicago: University of Chicago Press, 2002. A prominent critic of public health policy toward smoking, the author argues that smokers pay more in taxes than nonsmokers but consume fewer government benefits because they die earlier. In this book Viscusi criticizes the Master Settlement Agreement between the states and tobacco companies on economic grounds, arguing that the legislative branch more than the judicial branch can efficiently deal with the problem of tobacco use.

Wolfson, Mark. *The Fight against Big Tobacco: The Movement, the State, and the Public's Health*. New York: Adline De Gruyter, 2001. Focusing on Minnesota's tobacco control activities, the author tells the history of the antismoking movement. He emphasizes the connections between the government and antitobacco movements, and links tobacco control efforts to theories about social movements more generally.

World Bank. *Curbing the Epidemic: Governments and the Economics of Tobacco Control*. Washington, D.C.: World Bank, 1999. In addressing the economic aspects of tobacco control from an international perspective, this short book concludes that raising taxes on tobacco can save millions of lives. From a review of existing evidence it also suggests that comprehensive bans on cigarette advertising and promotions can similarly reduce deaths worldwide. It thus encourages leaders and public health officials in developing nations to take action against tobacco use in their countries.

ARTICLES

Bauer, Ursula E., et al. "Changes in Youth Cigarette Use and Intentions Following Implementation of a Tobacco Control Program: Findings from the Florida Youth Tobacco Survey, 1998–2000." *JAMA*, vol. 284,

August 9, 2000, pp. 723–728. According to results of surveys of high school students at the start and end of the two-year Florida Pilot Program on Tobacco Control, tobacco use decreased in each year of the program. The results suggest that comprehensive statewide programs effectively prevent and reduce youth tobacco use.

Bayer, Ronald, et al. "Tobacco Advertising in the United States: A Proposal for a Constitutionally Acceptable Form of Regulation." *JAMA*, vol. 287, June 12, 2002, pp. 2,990–95. The Supreme Court has struck down public health regulation of advertising as a violation of the First Amendment guaranteeing free speech. To continue regulating tobacco without violating free speech rights, the authors recommend taxing tobacco advertisements and promotion and requiring use of half the space in an advertisement for health warnings.

Bigland, Anthony, and Ted K. Taylor. "Why Have We Been More Successful in Reducing Tobacco Use Than Violent Crime?" *American Journal of Community Psychology*, vol. 28, June 2000, pp. 269–302. The authors hold up tobacco control efforts as a successful model for reducing unwanted behavior. As public health advocates have been able to convey the harm of the tobacco problem, to understand the causes of tobacco use, and to develop tobacco reduction programs, so might they use similar strategies to reduce violent crime.

Calfee, John E. "Why the War on Tobacco Will Fail." *Weekly Standard*, vol. 3, July 20, 1998, pp. 23–26. Taking a critical view of tobacco control efforts, this article argues that higher tobacco taxes make governments dependent on revenues generated by tobacco sales and on continued cigarette smoking among citizens.

David, Sean. "International Tobacco Control: A Focus Group Study of U.S. Anti-Tobacco Activists." *Journal of Public Health Policy*, vol. 22, no. 4, 2002, pp. 415–428. Interviews of 1,500 antismoking activists provide insights on their views about tobacco marketing and regulation and progress toward changing public opinion on tobacco issues.

Derthick, Martha. "Federalism and the Politics of Tobacco." *Publius*, vol. 31, Winter 2001, pp. 47–63. A case history of the Master Settlement Agreement that is informed by theory and research in the field of political science.

Farkas, Arthur, et al. "Association between Household and Workplace Smoking Restrictions and Adolescent Smoking." *JAMA*, vol. 284, August 9, 2000, pp. 717–722. Based on data from national surveys, this study finds that adolescents living in smoke-free homes and working in smoke-free workplaces were less likely to smoke than those living in homes and working in places without smoking restrictions. Policies affecting work and home environments can thus do much to prevent smoking among youth and adults.

Fiori, Michael C., et al. "A Clinical Practice Guideline for Treating Tobacco Use and Dependence: A U.S. Public Health Service Report." *JAMA*, vol. 283, June 28, 2000, pp. 3,244–54. This article summarizes a longer publication released by the Public Health Service on recommendations for clinical interventions to treat tobacco use and dependence. Among other conclusions the report finds that although brief treatment can be effective, longer-term treatment brings better results, and various types of counseling and social support prove especially effective.

Fiori, Michael C., Dorothy K. Hatsukami, and Timothy B. Baker. "Effective Tobacco Dependence Treatment." *JAMA*, vol. 288, October 9, 2002, pp. 140–143. Physician-delivered interventions can effectively and inexpensively help smokers quit. To supplement comprehensive programs at the national, state, and local level to treat tobacco dependence, physicians should, according to the authors, do all they can to counsel every tobacco user about the risks of smoking, the benefits of stopping, and how to quit.

Gilpin, Elizabeth A., Arthur J. Farkas, and Sherry L. Emery. "Clean Indoor Air: Advances in California, 1990–99." *American Journal of Public Health*, vol. 92, May 2002, pp. 785–791. A review of surveys on the experiences of individuals with secondhand smoke in workplaces and homes shows considerable progress toward clean indoor air in California. For example, indoor workers reporting smoke-free workplaces increased from 35.0 percent in 1990 to 93.4 percent in 1999.

Glantz, Stanton A., and Annemarie Charlesworth. "Tourism and Hotel Revenues Before and After Passage of Smoke-Free Restaurant Ordinances." *JAMA*, vol. 281, May 26, 1999, pp. 1,911–18. Examining three states (California, Utah, and Vermont) and six cities (Boulder, Colorado; Flagstaff, Arizona; Los Angeles, California; Mesa, Arizona; New York, New York; and San Francisco, California) that banned smoking in restaurants, the authors find that smoke-free ordinances do not appear to adversely affect the tourist business.

Golway, Terry. "Life in the 90s: Ineffectiveness of Big Tobacco Settlement in Curbing Youth Smoking." *America*, vol. 179, December 12, 1998, p. 6. Tobacco companies can work around limitations on direct advertising to youth. For example, with Hollywood continuing to portray attractive smokers in films, the American movie industry influences youth smoking more than advertising.

Gostin, Lawrence O. "Corporate Speech and the Constitution: The Deregulation of Tobacco Advertising." *American Journal of Public Health*, vol. 92, March 2002, pp. 352–355. Noting that the Supreme Court, by invalidating Massachusetts regulations to reduce underage smoking, has sided with business rights to advertise hazardous products, the author argues that the high value of population health should trump the low value of corporate free speech.

Gravelle, Jane G. "Burning Issues in the Tobacco Settlement Payments: An Economic Perspective." *National Tax Journal*, vol. 51, September 1998, pp. 437–451. The article criticizes the efforts of tobacco companies and the states to reach a settlement because it would impose taxes that most hurt the poor and disrupt markets and employment.

Gross, Cary P., et al. "State Expenditures for Tobacco-Control Programs and the Tobacco Settlement." *New England Journal of Medicine*, vol. 347, October 3, 2002, pp. 1,080–86. This evaluation of the state expenditures of funds received for tobacco control from the Master Settlement Agreement in 1998 finds that only a small proportion of the funds are being used as specified by the agreement. In fact, states with higher smoking tend to spend less of the funds on tobacco control than states with lower smoking.

Grossman, Michael, and Frank J. Chaloupka. "Cigarette Taxes: The Straw to Break the Camel's Back." *Public Health Reports*, vol. 112, July/August 1997, pp. 290–297. Two economists argue that a substantial increase in the cigarette tax would do much to discourage smoking.

Jacobson, Peter D., and Jeffrey Wasserman. "The Implementation and Enforcement of Tobacco Control Laws: Policy Implications for Activists and the Industry." *Journal of Health Politics, Policy, and Law*, vol. 24, June 1999, pp. 567–598. Based on the experiences of seven states and 19 cities, the authors describe and evaluate the effectiveness of clean indoor air laws and laws restricting youth access to tobacco.

Jha, Prabhat. "Death and Taxes: Economics of Tobacco Control." *Finance and Development*, vol. 36, December 1999, pp. 46–49. The author argues that regulating tobacco can bring public health benefits without harming the economies of developing nations.

Kaplan, Robert M., Christopher F. Ake, and Sherry L. Emery. "Simulated Effect of Tobacco Tax Variation on Population Health in California." *American Journal of Public Health*, vol. 91, February 2001, pp. 239–244. Economic simulations reveal that higher taxes on cigarettes reduce smoking, sickness, and mortality. The authors conclude that a tobacco excise tax may be among a few policy options that will enhance a population's health status.

Kessler, David A., and Matthew L. Myers. "Beyond the Tobacco Settlement." *New England Journal of Medicine*, vol. 345, August 16, 2001, pp. 535–537. Noting that the tobacco settlement has failed to restrict advertising targeted toward youth or dilute the power of tobacco companies to attract new cigarette users, this article calls for national and state legislation to regulate tobacco and fund comprehensive smoking prevention programs.

Tobacco Industry and Smoking

King, Charles, III, and Michael Siegel. "The Master Settlement Agreement with the Tobacco Industry and Cigarette Advertising in Magazines." *New England Journal of Medicine*, vol. 345, August 16, 2001, pp. 504–511. An analysis of cigarette advertising in 38 magazines from 1995 to 2000 allows the authors to evaluate the effects of the Master Settlement Agreement in prohibiting advertisements that target young people. The study concludes that little change has occurred in the exposure of young people to cigarette advertisements.

Klonoff, Elizabeth A., Hope Landrine, and Delia Lang. "Adults Buy Cigarettes for Underage Youth." *American Journal of Public Health*, vol. 91, July 2002, pp. 1,138–39. In an interesting real-life experiment, 16 youths ages 15–17 approached 1,285 adult strangers to request that they purchase cigarettes for them. Few of the adults asked about the youth's age, and 32.1 percent bought cigarettes for the youths. Adult strangers may be a significant source of tobacco for minors.

Koop, C. Everett, David C. Kessler, and George Lundberg. "Reinventing American Tobacco Control Policy: Sounding the Medical Community's Voice." *JAMA*, vol. 279, February 18, 1998, p. 550. This distinguished group of authors urges the medical community to make even stronger efforts to have its voice heard in regulating tobacco.

Lavelle, Marianne. "Teen Tobacco Wars: Antismoking Campaigns Funded with Tobacco Settlement Versus Cigarette Marketing." *U.S. News and World Report*, vol. 128, February 7, 2000, pp. 14–16. This describes the plans of the Legacy Foundation, an independent organization created using $1.5 billion of the $246 billion paid by the tobacco companies under the Master Settlement Agreement, to produce hard-hitting ads that discourage teen smoking.

Ling, Pamela M., and Stanton A. Glantz. "Using Tobacco-Industry Marketing Research to Design More Effective Tobacco-Control Campaigns." *JAMA*, vol. 287, June 12, 2002, pp. 2,983–89. This article recommends that antismoking ads, in using the knowledge gained by tobacco companies in marketing their products, should include people of all ages, particularly young adults rather than teens alone, should note the monetary costs of smoking, and should help make smoking socially unacceptable by emphasizing the harm of secondhand smoke.

Meier, Barry. "Lost Horizons: The Billboard Prepares to Give Up Smoking." *New York Times*, April 19, 1999, p. A1ff. As part of the Master Settlement Agreement, all cigarette billboard advertising must end. This article describes how the change will affect the visual landscape of the United States.

Meier, Kenneth, and Michael J. Licari. "The Effect of Cigarette Taxes on Cigarette Consumption, 1955 through 1994." *American Journal of Public*

Health, vol. 87, July 1997, pp. 1,126–30. A statistical analysis of the experiences of all 50 states over a 40-year period demonstrates that federal taxes did more than state taxes to reduce smoking. Further efforts to reduce cigarette consumption will, based on the results, require large increases in taxes.

Merrill, Ray M., June E. Stanford, and Gordon B. Lindsay. "The Relationship of Perceived Age and Sales of Tobacco and Alcohol to Underage Customers." *Journal of Community Health*, vol. 25, October 2000, pp. 401–410. Based on estimates of age by 49 gas station and convenience store clerks, the study finds that requesting identification of anyone perceived to be under age 27 works well in minimizing illegal tobacco sales. The results support the policies required by the Food and Drug Administration since 1997 to check IDs for anyone who appears younger than 27.

Mitka, Mike. "Picture This: Smoking Kills." *JAMA*, vol. 283, February 23, 2000, p. 993. A brief report on efforts in Canada to discourage smoking with graphic images of the effects of tobacco use, such as diseased lungs and damaged hearts. Antismoking advocates believe these images will work better than current warning statements about the harm of cigarettes.

Mnookin, Seth. "The Battle over Butts: M. Bloomberg's War on Smoking." *Newsweek*, vol. 140, August 26, 200, p. 37. This provides an overview of the debate in New York City over the mayor's proposal to prohibit smoking in all the city's bars, restaurants, parks, and beaches. As in other towns and cities in the country, the debate pits public health advocates and nonsmokers against smokers and the restaurant business.

Moolchan, Eric T., Monique Ernst, and Jack Henningfield. "A Review of Tobacco Smoking in Adolescents: Treatment Implications." *Journal of the American Academy of Child and Adolescent Psychiatry*, vol. 39, June 2000, pp. 682–693. This article summarizes and evaluates current knowledge about the nature and determinants of adolescent smoking and how it differs from adult smoking. The authors conclude that smoking cessation treatment for adolescents has been disappointing due to low participation and high attrition.

Myers, Matthew L. "Protecting the Public Health by Strengthening the Food and Drug Administration's Authority over Tobacco Products." *New England Journal of Medicine*, vol. 343, December 14, 2000, pp. 1,806–09. The Supreme Court ruling to block efforts of the Food and Drug Administration to regulate tobacco as a drug placed the onus for action on Congress. The author, associated with the National Center for Tobacco-Free Kids, argues that Congress and the president should give the FDA the authority to do so.

Nathanson, Constance A. "Social Movements as Catalysts for Policy Change: The Case of Smoking and Guns." *Journal of Health Politics, Policy, and Law*, vol. 24, June 1999, pp. 421–488. To identify key components of successful public health action, this article compares the antismoking movement with the gun control movement.

Patrick, Steven, and Robert Marsh. "Current Tobacco Policies in U.S. Adult Male Prisons." *Social Science Journal*, vol. 38, 2000, pp. 27–31. Prohibitions of smoking in prisons have followed trends more generally to ban smoking in public places. This article describes the trends and discusses the problems that have emerged in enforcing the bans.

Pierce, John P., et al. "Has the California Tobacco Control Program Reduced Smoking?" *JAMA*, vol. 280, September 9, 1998, pp. 893–899. Lasting from 1989 to 1996, the California Tobacco Control Program initially reduced smoking, but the effects of the program did not persist over the last years. The possible reasons for the lack of long-term benefit may be reduced program funding and increased tobacco industry efforts through pricing and advertising to counter the effects of the program.

Pierce John P., and Elizabeth A. Gilpin. "Impact of Over-the-Counter Sales on Effectiveness of Pharmaceutical Aids for Smoking Cessation." *JAMA*, vol. 288, September 11, 2002, pp. 1,260–64. Surveys of Californians about smoking, efforts to quit smoking, and use of over-the-counter aids such as nicotine patches find increases from 1992 to 1999 in both efforts to quit and use of pharmaceutical aids. However, since becoming available over the counter, nicotine replacement therapies have become less effective in long-term smoking cessation.

Reeves, Hope. "Blowing Smoke." *New York Times Magazine*, November 5, 2000, p. 26. This describes efforts and problems faced by the World Health Organization in negotiating an international antismoking treaty.

Rigotti, Nancy A. "Treatment of Tobacco Use and Dependence." *New England Journal of Medicine*, vol. 346, February 14, 2002, pp. 506–512. The article provides a review of evidence supporting various strategies for physicians to help smoking patients quit their habit and makes clinical recommendations involving the use of nicotine replacement therapy, an antidepressant (bupropion), and counseling.

Rigotti, Nancy A., et al. "The Effect of Enforcing Tobacco-Sales Laws on Adolescents' Access to Tobacco and Smoking Behavior." *New England Journal of Medicine*, vol. 337, November 1997, pp. 1,044–51. A study of six Massachusetts communities, three of which enforced tobacco-sales laws and three of which did not, shows that enforcement efforts reduced illegal sales to minors. However, they did not reduce the self-reported access of youth to cigarettes.

Ringel, Jeanne S., and William N. Evans. "Cigarette Taxes and Smoking during Pregnancy." *American Journal of Public Health*, vol. 91, November 2001, pp. 1,851–56. The study finds that high cigarette excise taxes reduce smoking rates among pregnant women.

"Rout of the New Evil Empire: Tobacco Industry Is the New Great Enemy in the U.S." *Economist*, vol. 353, November 6, 1999, p. 30. This British magazine, which generally supports free-market economic policies, argues that despite the misdeeds of the tobacco industry, disapproval of smoking in the United States has turned intolerance and persuasion into outright bullying.

Satcher, David. "Why We Need an International Agreement on Tobacco Control." *American Journal of Public Health*, vol. 91, February 2001, pp. 191–193. This editorial by the then surgeon general argues that preventing the epidemic of tobacco use in developing countries—and avoiding the physical and financial harm that such an epidemic would bring—requires an international agreement. Satcher strongly supports current negotiations to develop a tobacco control treaty in Geneva, Switzerland.

"Saved by the Smokers." *Economist*, vol. 361, November 24, 2001, p. 33. Citing examples from several states, the article illustrates how funds from the tobacco settlement have been used for purposes other than the antismoking programs for which they were intended. With only about 5 percent being used for tobacco control, the funds largely go to spending on state schools, health care for the poor, and other nontobacco programs.

Spangler, John G. "Current Efforts and Gaps in U.S. Medical Schools." *JAMA*, vol. 288, September 4, 2002, pp. 1,102–09. Noting that U.S. medical schools have been found to inadequately teach tobacco intervention skills, this article reviews the instructional methods currently being taught. It concludes that innovative methods such as counseling and role playing work better than traditional efforts to tell patients of the harm of tobacco, but gaps remain in how medical education trains future physicians to use these techniques.

"Special Report: Cigarette Taxes." *Regulation*, vol. 25, Winter 2003, pp. 52–72. A series of articles in a magazine critical of many government regulations offers viewpoints for and against raising taxes

Stephenson, Joan. "Snuffing the Urge to Smoke." *JAMA*, vol. 284, August 16, 2000, p. 822. The article reviews the results from a National Institute on Drug Abuse study that show a medication used to treat skin problems can help a smoker light up less frequently. The medication partially blocks the body's ability to metabolize nicotine, allows nicotine to linger longer in the body, and reduces the need to smoke more cigarettes to get the nicotine.

"The Tobacco War Goes Global." *Economist*, vol. 357, October 14, 2000, pp. 97–98. This describes the battles over the efforts of the World Health Organization to regulate tobacco use worldwide. Critics of the effort favor allowing nations to tackle the issue on their own rather than to impose international requirements.

Voorhees, Carolyn C., Robert T. Swank, and Frances A. Stillman. "Cigarette Sales to African-American and White Minors in Low Income Areas of Baltimore." *American Journal of Public Health*, vol. 87, April 1997, pp. 652–654. This study provides evidence that age restrictions on sales are often not followed: Six minors ages 14–16 were sent into 83 stores in a low-income neighborhood and were able to purchase cigarettes in 85.5 percent of the stores.

Warner, Kenneth E. "Tobacco." *Foreign Policy*, vol. 130, May/June 2002, pp. 20–28. The author, a well-known tobacco expert, discusses the difficulty of controlling the global spread of tobacco. He recommends that countries across the world implement effective tobacco control policies such as tax increases, bans on smoking in public places, bans on all tobacco advertising and promotion, and public education initiatives.

Waxman, Henry A. "The Future of the Global Tobacco Treaty Negotiations." *New England Journal of Medicine*, vol. 346, March 21, 2002, pp. 936–939. A major critic of tobacco companies, Representative Waxman argues for a stronger role of the United States in supporting negotiations over international tobacco control.

Willemsen, Marc C., and Wil M. de Zwart. "The Effectiveness of Policy and Health Education Strategies for Reducing Adolescent Smoking: A Review of the Evidence." *Journal of Adolescence*, vol. 22, October 1999, pp. 587–599. According to a review of international research, isolated measures to reduce adolescent smoking such as enforcing an age limit for buying cigarettes have little effect. Most effective is the combination of a complete ban on tobacco advertising, increasing prices, restricting sales to tobacco stores, mass media education, and intense antismoking school programs.

Wilson, C. "My Friend Nicotine." *New Scientist*, vol. 172, November 10, 2001, pp. 28–31. The author calls government efforts to slowly reduce cigarette use through propaganda, higher taxes, and medical intervention ineffective against the strong addictive powers of nicotine. He advocates other approaches to tobacco reduction such as using less harmful forms of tobacco as a recreational drug.

Worth, Robert F. "A Smoking Ban in City's Jails Worries Correction Officers." *New York Times*, January 5, 2003, p. 27. The article describes the importance of cigarettes to prisoners and the possible trouble in maintaining control of the population that banning smoking in New York City prisons may create.

Annotated Bibliography

Zhang, Ping, Corinne Husten, and Gary Giovino. "Effect of the Tobacco Price Support Program on Cigarette Consumption in the United States: An Updated Model." *American Journal of Public Health*, vol. 90, May 2000, pp. 746–750. Based on an economic model, the authors conclude that price supports for tobacco farmers increase cigarette prices only slightly, and therefore elimination of the support would do little to reduce smoking. Elimination would, however, create much political opposition.

WEB DOCUMENTS

Action on Smoking and Health. "Everything for People Concerned about Smoking and Nonsmokers' Rights, Smoking Statistics, Quitting Smoking, Smoking Risks, and Other Smoking Information." Available online. URL: http://ash.org. Downloaded in February 2003. As the title suggests, this web site contains an enormous amount of information on a variety of topics, links to other antismoking organizations, news about tobacco control, and helpful actions to control tobacco use. The information supports antismoking goals of the sponsoring organization.

American Lung Association of San Diego and Imperial Counties. "Tobacco Laws and Regulations—Local." Available online. URL: http://www.lungsandiego.org/tobacco/advocate_local.asp. Downloaded in December 2002. This page describes the extensive regulations in San Diego and Imperial County, California, to limit tobacco advertising and youth access to cigarettes. The regulations may serve as a model for other cities and counties aiming to control teen smoking.

American Nonsmokers' Rights Foundation. "Welcome." URL: http://www.no-smoke.org. Downloaded in February 2003. The web site includes news on tobacco control efforts, summaries of recent research articles, alerts about new antitobacco action, position papers, and lists of smoke-free towns and places. It also provides information on youth smoking prevention programs and on avoiding secondhand smoke.

BluePrint for Health. "Smoking and Tobacco Center." Available online. URL: http://blueprint.bluecrossmn.com/topic/smokingcenter. Downloaded in February 2003. Blue Cross/Blue Shield of Minnesota outlines its efforts to reduce tobacco use and provides research papers, forums, and bulletin boards. The web site also includes special reports on smoking in the movies, herbal cigarettes, the joy of not smoking, and the myth of "safe" cigarettes.

Campaign for Tobacco Free Kids Action Fund. "Big Tobacco: Still Addicting Kids." Available online. URL: http://www.tobaccofreekids.org/reports/addicting. Downloaded in February 2003. This site disputes claims of tobacco companies that they have ended efforts to attract kids to smoke.

"Campaign Contributions by Tobacco Interests Quarterly Report: January 2003." URL: http://www.tobaccofreekids.org/reports/contributions. Downloaded in February 2003. This page shows that the tobacco industry has contributed $8.5 million to federal candidates, political parties, and other political action committees, and provides details of the funds by company and political party.

———. "Show Us the Money: A Report on the States' Allocation of the Tobacco Settlement Dollars." Available online. URL: http://www.tobaccofreekids.org/reports/settlements. Downloaded in February 2003. The data show that most states have failed to adequately fund tobacco prevention and cessation programs with the funds they obtained from the tobacco settlement.

Centers for Disease Control and Prevention. "Investment in Tobacco Control: State Highlights 2001" Available online. URL: http://www.cdc.gov/tobacco/statehi/statehi_2001.htm. Posted on March 23, 2001. The study compares investment in tobacco control across states, finding that 45 states made a total investment of $883.2 million in public health programs to reduce the use of tobacco, especially among teenagers. However, the report also notes that tobacco companies spend much more, $6.7 billion, to advertise their products.

———. "Tips for Kids, for Teens, for Adults, for Everyone." Available online. URL: http://www.cdc.gov/tobacco/tips4youth.htm. Downloaded in February 2003. The page includes tobacco information and links, a publications catalog, research, data and reports, advice on how to quit, and educational materials. It also gives access to Surgeon General reports online.

Congressional Record Online. "1995 thru 2003 Congressional Record (Volumes 141 thru 149)." Available online. URL: http://www.access.gpo.gov/su_docs/aces/aces150.html. Downloaded in February 2003. This resource allows researchers to search through proceedings and debates of the U.S. Congress on topics related to smoking and tobacco (or any other topic of interest).

Essential Action. "Essential Information, Encouraging Activism." Available online. URL: http://www.essentialaction.org. Downloaded in February 2003. This web site, which consumer activist Ralph Nader created to alert others about current campaigns for corporate accountability, includes information on a program called the global partnership for tobacco control. The program supports efforts for international tobacco control legislation and notes that the tobacco settlement for the United States does not prevent tobacco companies from continuing to present misleading information outside the country.

Florida Tobacco Control Clearinghouse. "Uniting against Tobacco." Available online. URL: http://www.ftcc.fsu.edu. Downloaded in February 2003. Funded by the Florida Department of Health, this web site provides a centralized resource center with the latest information and materials on tobacco use and its control. It includes lists of antitobacco videos, CDs, meetings, news stories, and publications.

Forces International. "Website on Public Health Fraud and Politics." Available online. URL: http://www.forces.org. Downloaded in February 2003. This web site supports smokers' rights and is devoted to the idea that consumers should be able to choose their own lifestyles without government interference. It aims to provide information on prosmoking views that the media and the government do not present.

Foundation for a Smokefree America. "TobaccoFree.org." Available online. URL: http://tobaccofree.org. Downloaded in February 2003. The site includes educational videos, motivational talks, tips for quitting, antismoking messages for youth and adults, and resources for finding antitobacco information.

Kellard, Joseph. "The Anti-Smoking Crusade's Asphyxiation of Freedom." *Capitalism Magazine*. Available online. URL: http://www.capmag.com/article.asp?ID=2020. Posted on October 18, 2002. This article argues that individuals are responsible for their exposure to secondhand smoke, and if they desire smoke-free air, they should work at or patronize other businesses rather than force employers to ban smoking.

National Cancer Policy Board. "Taking Action to Reduce Tobacco Use." Available online. URL: http://www.nap.edu/books/0309060389/html/R1.html. Downloaded in February 2003. The National Cancer Policy Board recommends increasing the price of tobacco products as the single most direct and reliable method to reduce consumption but also suggests that the government do more to implement and monitor tobacco control measures.

National Center for Chronic Disease Prevention and Health Promotion, Office on Smoking and Health, Centers for Disease Control and Prevention. "State Tobacco Control Highlights—1999." Available online. URL: http://www.cdc.gov/tobacco/statehi/statehi.htm. Downloaded in February 2003. The site presents maps and tables on tobacco use among adults and youth, restrictions on cigarette vending machines, smoke-free indoor air restrictions, tobacco excise taxes, and tobacco agriculture and manufacturing.

Nemours Foundation. "TeensHealth." Available online. URL: http://www.kidshealth.org/teen. Downloaded in February 2003. This web site provides doctor-approved health information for teens, including advice about tobacco use.

Public Health Institute, Technical Assistance Legal Center. "New California Tobacco Laws Effective January 1, 2002." Available online. URL: http://www.phi.org/talc. Downloaded in December 2002. This page summarizes the extensive new California laws to control tobacco, including those to ban smoking on playgrounds, self-service cigarette sales, sales of bidis, and distribution of free sample tobacco products.

Randall, Vernellia R. "Tobacco, Health, and the Law." University of Dayton. Available online. URL: http://academic.udayton.edu/health/syllabi/tobacco. Downloaded in February 2003. This syllabus for a course at the University of Dayton includes many readings relevant to legal issues involving tobacco use, sales, and advertising.

Smokers with Attitude. "The Smoking Section." Available online. URL: http://www.smokingsection.com. Downloaded in February 2003. This web site for smoker's rights includes a smokers' bookstore with many references as well as pages that dispute evidence on the health risks faced by smokers and tally the steep taxes paid by smokers when purchasing cigarettes.

TC Online. "Tobacco Control." Available online. URL: http://tc.bmjjournals.com. Downloaded in February 2003. This is the online version of an international scientific journal devoted to tobacco control. Nonsubscribers are allowed access to older articles, summaries of recent articles, and links to other tobacco control resources.

Tobacco Control Resource Center. "The Multistate Master Settlement Agreement and the Future of State and Local Tobacco Control: An Analysis of Selected Topics and Provisions of the Multistate Master Settlement Agreement of November 23, 1998." Available online. URL: http://www.tobacco.neu.edu/msa. Downloaded in February 2003. There are 10 chapters written by experts about the history, legal background, and participants in the agreement and about the effects of selected provisions on advertising, youth access, lobbying restrictions, and a national foundation.

———. "Tobacco Products Liability Project." Available online. URL: http://www.tobacco.neu.edu. Downloaded in February 2003. This site summarizes efforts of a project at Northeastern University Law School to encourage and coordinate product liability suits against the tobacco industry and government policies to control the sale and use of tobacco.

University of California San Francisco. "Smoke-Free Movies." Available online. URL: http://smokefreemovies.ucsf.edu. Downloaded in February 2003. Lists current movies and videos that glamorize smoking, examines efforts of the tobacco industry to promote their brands in movies, and describes the contribution of movie studios, producers, directors, and actors to the problem of youth cigarette use. This is a project of antitobacco activist and professor at the University of California, San Francisco, Sheldon Glantz.

University of California at San Francisco Library. "Tobacco Control Archives." Available online. URL: http://www.library.ucsf.edu/tobacco. Downloaded in February 2003. The archives collect, preserve, and provide access to papers, unpublished documents, and electronic resources relevant to tobacco control issues (primarily in California). They include millions of documents from tobacco companies and litigation.

U.S. Department of Agriculture, President's Commission on Improving Economic Opportunity in Communities Dependent on Tobacco Production While Protecting Public Health. "Tobacco Communities at a Crossroad." Available online. URL: http://purl.access.gpo.gov/GPO/LPS17840. Downloaded in February 2003. This commission considers options for assisting tobacco farmers and tobacco-farming communities in the economic problems they face as the government continues efforts to reduce public smoking.

U.S. Department of Health and Human Services. "Body FX—Tobacco." Available online. URL: http://www.girlpower.gov/girlarea/bodyfx/tobacco. htm. Downloaded in February 2003. A government-sponsored web site for girls up to age 13, it describes the harms of nicotine and tobacco to health.

U.S. Department of the Treasury. "The Economic Costs of Smoking in the United States and the Benefits of Comprehensive Tobacco Legislation." Available online. URL: http://www.ustreas.gov/press/releases/reports/ tobacco.pdf. Downloaded in February 2003. This press release presents figures showing that smoking in the United States in 1998 costs the country $130 billion in medical care, lost workdays, early death and retirement, and smoking-related fires but notes that legislation could reduce the amount by $78 billion.

U.S. General Accounting Office. "Tobacco Settlement: States' Use of Master Settlement Agreement Payments: Report to the Honorable John McCain, Ranking Minority Member, Committee on Commerce, Science, and Transportation" Available online. URL: http://www.gao.gov/new. items/d01851.pdf. Posted in June 2001. By 2001, 46 states had received $13.5 billion from tobacco companies as part of the Master Settlement Agreement. This government study examines how the funds have been spent and shows about 41 percent of the funds have gone to health, 7 percent to tobacco control, 6 percent to tobacco growers and tobacco-dependent communities, and 26 percent to other budget priorities. The remaining 20 percent has not been allocated.

World Bank. "Economics of Tobacco Control." Available online. URL: http://www1.worldbank.org/tobacco. Downloaded in February 2003. This web site contains information about curbing tobacco use across the world, country profiles on tobacco use and policy, smoke-free workplaces, and key tobacco facts. The site is for researchers, policymakers, advocates, and others who desire to choose and implement effective tobacco control measures.

Youth Media Network. "Tobacco Facts and Resources." Available online. URL: http://www.ymn.org/tobacco/facts.shtml. Downloaded in February

2003. The site offers facts on the composition of cigarettes, youth tobacco use, nicotine addiction, illegal sales, tobacco as a gateway drug, secondhand smoke, advertising, and cigarettes in movies.

SELF-HELP

BOOKS

Brigham, Janet. *Dying to Quit: Why We Smoke and How We Stop.* Washington, D.C.: National Academy Press, 1998. More than most self-help
books on smoking, this one provides much in the way of numerical information on trends and patterns but also describes why smoking is so
difficult to stop and offers personal stories.

Carr, Allen. *Allen Carr's Easy Way to Stop Smoking.* New York: Barnes and
Noble Books, 1999. Recently out in a new edition, this book helps smokers to eliminate the psychological reasons for using cigarettes and avoid
tempting situations to smoke.

Chenoweth, Bruce. *Changing Your Mind about Smoking.* New Plymouth,
Idaho: A.B. Company, 2000. This how-to guide differs from most in recommending that smokers first develop a self-image as a nonsmoker
through autosuggestion before trying to quit.

Embree, Mary. *A Woman's Way: The Stop-Smoking Book for Women.* Waco,
Tex.: WRS Publishing, 1995. Citing research that a woman's addiction to
cigarettes is stronger and different from a man's addiction, this book addresses special problems women face in quitting, such as worrying about
gaining weight. It recommends relaxation and visualization techniques
and diet and exercise programs.

Fisher, Edwin B. *American Lung Association 7 Steps to a Smoke Free Life.* New
York: John Wiley and Sons, 1998. This helps smokers identify the places,
times, moods, and conditions that trigger the need to smoke and offers
techniques to resist the temptation.

Gebhardt, B. Jack. *The Enlightened Smoker's Guide to Quitting.* New York:
Harper Collins, 1998. Among other things the author recommends
avoiding guilt, scare tactics, and negativity when quitting. He instead offers a more positive and emotionally rewarding way of looking at quitting,
one that encourages smokers to feel good about themselves in general and
even better about themselves once they quit.

———. *Help Your Smoker Quit: A Radically Happy Strategy for Nonsmoking
Parents, Kids, Spouses, and Friends.* Minneapolis, Minn: Fairview Press,
1998. This book discourages use of nagging and criticism to get a loved
one to stop smoking, recommends enjoying a family member who smokes

in order to prove that happiness creates the greatest incentive to quit, and offers ways to support a spouse trying to quit.

Gronberg, Erli, and Katherine Srb. *Smokers and Quitters: What Smoking Means to People and How They Manage to Quit.* Commack, N.Y.: Kroshka Books, 1998. Collects personal stories about smoking and quitting that can help current smokers quit and nonsmokers understand smokers.

Hoffman, Elizabeth Hanson, and Christopher Douglas Hoffman. *Recovery from Smoking: Quitting with the 12 Step Process. Updated and Revised Second Edition.* Center City, Minn.: Hazelden Information Education, 1999. Following the model of popular 12-step programs originally developed to deal with alcoholism, the author recommends that smokers accept their powerlessness over the addiction and the need for emotional as well as physical recovery from addiction.

Holmes, Peter, and Peggy Holmes. *Out of the Ashes: Help for People Who Have Quit Smoking.* Minneapolis, Minn.: Fairview Press, 1992. Less concerned about how to quit smoking than most self-help guides, this book focuses on the continuation of cravings and feelings of emptiness that persist after having quit. It aims to help former smokers deal with these difficulties.

Kleinman, Lowell, et al. *Complete Idiot's Guide to Quitting Smoking.* Indianapolis, Ind.: Macmillan, 2000. Dr. Kleinman, a family practice physician called Dr. Quit, and his coauthors provide a description of the difficulties of smoking cessation and the steps needed to quit. The advice includes setting goals, choosing patches and medication, finding a support network, and dealing with stress and depression.

Klesges, Robert, and Margaret DeBon. *A Smoke-Ending Program Especially for Women.* Alameda, Calif.: Hunter House, 1994. Women appear to have a harder time stopping smoking than men do. The thesis of this book is that techniques that work for men do not work as well for women because the two groups start and continue smoking for different reasons. It offers a smoking-cessation program developed at Memphis State University and designed specifically for women.

Kranz, Rachel. *Straight Talk about Smoking.* New York: Facts On File, 1999. Aimed at young adults (grades six to 12), this book offers clear and up-to-date information on the social and medical aspects of tobacco use and encourages teens to take action against tobacco in their own lives and in their community.

Rustin, Terry A. *Keep Quit: A Motivation Guide to a Life Without Smoking.* Center City, Minn.: Hazelden Information Education, 1996. A daily motivation guide, this book offers exercises to help the new nonsmoker avoid relapse.

Schwebel, Robert. *How to Help Your Kids Choose to Be Tobacco-Free: A Guide for Parents of Children Ages 3 through 19.* New York: Newmarket Press,

1999. The author, a family psychologist, offers advice to parents about helping their children make wise choices about tobacco use and preparing them to meet their physical, social, and emotional needs without tobacco. He argues that antitobacco efforts of parents should begin with preschool children and continue through adolescence.

Taylor, C. Barr, and Joel D. Killen. *The Facts about Smoking*. Yonkers, N.Y.: Consumer Reports Books, 1991. This book discusses the reasons for smoking, the composition of cigarettes, the link between smoking and heart disease and cancer, and ways of quitting.

CHAPTER 8

ORGANIZATIONS AND AGENCIES

The organizations and agencies listed in this chapter fall into six categories:

- federal government agencies,
- business organizations and trade associations,
- research and charitable organizations,
- national advocacy groups,
- international advocacy groups, and
- state and local advocacy groups.

The categories overlap because, for example, research and charitable organizations often take advocacy positions and advocacy organizations often sponsor research. Still, most organizations fit better in one category than the other, and the classification helps organize an otherwise diverse domain. For each organization the listing includes web site and e-mail addresses when available (if no e-mail address is listed, it is sometimes possible to contact the organization through the web site). The listing also includes phone numbers (when available), postal address, and a brief description.

FEDERAL GOVERNMENT AGENCIES

Bureau of Alcohol, Tobacco and Firearms (ATF)
URL: http://www.atf.treas.gov
E-mail: ATFMail@atf.gov

Phone: (202) 927-5000
Office of Alcohol and Tobacco
650 Massachusetts Avenue, NW
Washington, DC 20226
A law enforcement organization within the Department of the Treasury, the ATF is concerned with fair and proper revenue collection of tobacco taxes.

Centers for Disease Control and Prevention (CDC)
URL: http://www.cdc.gov
Phone: (800) 311-3435
1600 Clifton Road
Atlanta, GA 30333
The principal federal agency for protecting the health and safety of Americans both at home and abroad. The CDC carries out extensive research on tobacco use and control as part of its goal of promoting health and quality of life.

Federal Election Commission (FEC)
URL: http://www.fec.gov
Phone: (800) 424-9530
999 E Street, NW
Washington, DC 20463
The FEC enforces federal election campaign laws and provides campaign finance reports and data, including contributions from tobacco companies and related political action committees.

Federal Trade Commission (FTC)
URL: http://www.ftc.gov
Phone: (202) 382-4357
600 Pennsylvania Avenue, NW
Washington, DC 20580
The FTC enforces antitrust and consumer protection laws and has been active in regulating tobacco advertising.

Food and Drug Administration (FDA)
URL: http://www.fda.gov
Phone: (888) 463-6332

5600 Fishers Lane
Rockville, MD 20857
The FDA's mission is to promote public health by reviewing clinical research and regulating food and medical products to ensure they are safe. Its attempt to regulate tobacco was blocked by the Supreme Court.

National Cancer Institute (NCI)
URL: http://www.nci.nih.gov
Phone: (800) 422-6237
6116 Executive Boulevard
MSC 8322
Suite 3036A
Bethesda, MD 20892-8322
As the government's principal agency for cancer research and training, the NCI gives particular attention to tobacco and tobacco-related cancers.

National Center for Health Statistics
URL: http://www.cdc.gov/nchs
Phone: (301) 458-4636
3311 Toledo Road
Hyattsville, MD 20782
Part of the Centers for Disease Control, and Prevention, the nation's principal health statistics agency compiles information to improve the health of Americans, including much information on tobacco use and tobacco-related health problems.

National Heart, Lung, and Blood Institute (NHLBI)
URL: http://www.nhlbi.nih.gov
E-mail:
nhlbiinfo@rover.nhlbi.nih.gov

Phone: (301) 592-8573
Room 5A52
31 Center Drive
MSC 2846
Building 31
Bethesda, MD 20892-2846
Given the influence of smoking on heart, lung, and blood vessel diseases, this institute funds research on the consequences of tobacco use and promotes tobacco control.

National Institute for Occupational Safety and Health (NIOSH)
URL: http://www.cdc.gov/niosh
Phone: (800) 356-4674
Hubert Humphrey Building
Room 715H
200 Independence Avenue, SW
Washington, DC 20201
As the federal agency responsible for conducting research and making recommendations on the prevention of work-related disease and injury, the institute investigates lung disease and other problems related to workplace tobacco smoke.

National Institute of Child Health and Development (NICHD)
URL: http://www.nichd.nih.gov
E-mail: NICHDClearinghouse@ mail.nih.gov
Phone: (800) 370-2943
Room 2A32
31 Center Drive
MSC 2425
Building 31
Bethesda, MD 20892-2425

The institute conducts and supports research on the reproductive, neurobiological, developmental, and behavioral processes that determine the health of adults, families, and children, which includes research about the effect of tobacco use by parents on the health of children.

National Institute of Environmental Health Sciences (NIEHS)
URL: http://www.niehs.nih.gov
Phone: (919) 541-3345
P.O. Box 12233
111 Alexander Drive
Research Triangle Park, NC 27709
This institute focuses on understanding how environmental factors, including cigarette and tobacco smoke, contribute, along with individual susceptibility and age, to human health and disease.

National Institute on Drug Abuse (NIDA)
URL: http://www.drugabuse.gov
E-mail: information@lists.nida. nih.gov
Phone: (301) 443-1124
6001 Executive Boulevard
Room 5213
Bethesda, MD 20892-9561
The institute sponsors research on abuse of and addiction to drugs, including nicotine; the effects of drugs on the brain and behavior; and the treatment and prevention of drug abuse and addiction.

Occupational Safety and Health Administration (OSHA)
URL: http://www.osha.gov
Phone: (800) 321-6742
U.S. Department of Labor
200 Constitution Avenue
Washington, DC 20210
With a mission to save lives, prevent injuries, and protect the health of U.S. workers, this agency is concerned with workplace clean air problems created by tobacco use.

Office of Disease Prevention and Health Promotion (ODPHP)
URL: http://odphp.osophs.dhhs. gov
Phone: (202) 205-8611
200 Independence Avenue, SW
Room 738G
Washington, DC 20201
This office sponsors the National Health Information Center and promotes the Healthy People 2010 goals, which include reducing adult smoking to 15 percent.

Office of Safe and Drug-Free Schools (OSDFS)
URL: http://www.ed.gov/offices/ OSDFS
E-mail: customerservice@inet. ed.gov
Phone: (800) 437-0833
U.S. Department of Education
400 Maryland Avenue, SW
Washington, DC 20202
This office in the Department of Education administers, coordinates, and recommends policy for drug and violence prevention activities.

Office of Smoking and Health
URL: http://www.cdc.gov/ tobacco
E-mail: tobaccoinfo@cdc.gov
Phone: (800) 232-1311
Centers for Disease Control and Prevention Mail Stop K-50
4770 Buford Highway, NE
Atlanta, GA 30341-3717
This office leads and coordinates efforts to prevent tobacco use among youth, promote smoking cessation, protect nonsmokers from secondhand smoke, and eliminate tobacco-related health disparities.

Substance Abuse and Mental Health Services Administration (SAMHSA)
URL: http://www.samhsa.gov
E-mail: info@samhsa.gov
Phone: (301) 443-8956
5600 Fishers Lane
Rockville, MD 20857
In working to improve the quality and availability of prevention, treatment, and rehabilitation for substance abuse and mental illness, SAMHSA makes statistics and data on smoking and tobacco use available to interested users.

U.S. Department of Agriculture (USDA)
URL: http://www.usda.gov
E-mail: agsec@usda.gov
Washington, DC 20250
The USDA includes offices concerned with tobacco statistics, farming, prices, and trade.

U.S. Department of Health and Human Services (HHS)
URL: http://www.hhs.gov
Phone: (202) 619-0257
200 Independence Avenue, SW
Washington, DC 20201
As the major government agency for protecting the health of Americans and providing essential services, particularly for those less able to help themselves, the department aims to reduce the harm of tobacco use in the country.

BUSINESS ORGANIZATIONS AND TRADE ASSOCIATIONS

Alternative Cigarettes
URL: http://www.altcigs.com
E-mail: smoking@altcigs.com
Phone: (800) 225-1838
P.O. Box 678
Buffalo, NY 14207
This business manufactures and sells nicotine-free herbal cigarettes and value-priced cigarettes.

American Bar Association (ABA)
URL: http://abanet.org
E-mail: askaba@abanet.org
Phone: (312) 988-5000
750 North Lake Shore Drive
Chicago, IL 60611
The nation's and the world's largest voluntary professional association, the ABA works to assist lawyers and judges in their work and to improve the legal system for the public. It also offers information on health-related law and litigation associated with tobacco.

British American Tobacco
URL: http://www.bat.com
Phone: (44 207) 845 1000
Globe House
4 Temple Place
London WC2R 2PG
England
This large international tobacco group owns Brown and Williamson Tobacco in the United States.

Brown and Williamson Tobacco Corporation
URL: http://www.brownandwilliamson.com
Phone: (800) 341-5211
P.O. Box 35090
Louisville, KY 40232
The third-largest cigarette manufacturer in the United States, Brown and Williamson makes and sells Kool, Lucky Strike, Pall Mall, and Viceroy cigarettes.

Coalition for Responsible Tobacco Retailing
URL: http://www.wecard.org
Phone: (800) 934-3968
Consisting of wholesale marketers and tobacco companies, this coalition aims to prevent tobacco sales to minors through training and uniform retail policies and supports the "We Card" policy for purchasing tobacco.

Dimon
URL: http://www.dimon.com
Phone: (434) 792-7511
1200 West Marlboro Road
P.O. Box 166
Farmville, NC 27828-0166
As the world's second-largest independent tobacco leaf merchant, Dimon supplies its product to manufacturers around the globe.

General Cigar Holdings
URL: http://www.cigarworld.com
Phone: (212) 448-3800
387 Park Avenue South
New York, NY 10016-8899
This company is the largest U.S. manufacturer of premium brand-name cigars.

Imperial Tobacco Group
URL: http://www.imperial-
  tobacco.com
E-mail: itg@uk.imptob.com
Phone: (0117) 963 6636
P.O. Box 244
Upton Road
Bristol BS99 7UJ
England
This British company has become the fourth-largest international tobacco company in the world.

Liggett Group Inc.
URL: http://www.liggettgroup.
  com
E-mail: consumer.relations@
  liggettgroup.com
100 Maple Lane
Mebane, NC 27302
Having sold its traditional products of L&M, Chesterfield, and Lark,

the Liggett Group now concentrates on discount-priced and generic brands and on low-tar and low-nicotine cigarettes.

Lorillard Tobacco Company
URL: http://www.lorillard.com
Phone: (877) 703-0386
P.O. Box 21688
Greensboro, NC 27420
The fourth-largest and oldest cigarette manufacturer in the United States, it is owned by the Loews Corporation.

**National Association of
  Attorneys General (NAAG)**
URL: http://www.naag.org
E-mail: cdark@naag.org
Phone: (202) 326-6000
750 First Street, NE
Suite 1100
Washington, DC 20002
Since state attorneys general began taking action in suing tobacco companies, this organization has become a major force in the fight for tobacco control.

**National Association of
  Convenience Store Owners
  (NACSO)**
URL: http://www.nacsonline.
  com
E-mail: jgordon@nacsonline.
  com
Phone: (703) 684-3600
1600 Duke Street
Alexandria, VA 22314
This industry trade group addresses policies about cigarette sales and

offers advice on how to comply with state tobacco laws.

Philip Morris USA
URL: http://www.
  philipmorrisusa.com
Phone: (800) 343-0975
120 Park Avenue
New York, NY 10017
The largest cigarette manufacturer in the United States and one of the largest tobacco companies in the world, Philip Morris is best known as the maker of Marlboro cigarettes.

PICS, Inc.
URL: http://www.tobaccoweek.
  com/twl_about.asp?t=PICS
E-mail: info@tobaccoweek.com
Phone: (800) 543-3744
12007 Sunrise Valley Drive
Reston, VA 20191
This company develops products for tobacco addiction and other problems and owns Tobacco Week.com.

**R. J. Reynolds Tobacco
  Company**
URL: http://www.rjrt.com
Phone: (800) 372-9300
P.O. Box 7
Winston-Salem, NC 27102
The second-largest cigarette manufacturer in the United States is the maker of Winston, Salem, Camel, and Doral cigarettes.

**Santa Fe Natural Tobacco
  Company**
URL: http://www.nascigs.com
E-mail: feedback@sfntc.com
Phone: (800) 332-5595
P.O. Box 25140
Santa Fe, NM 87504
The company produces cigarettes advertised as additive free, whole leaf, and unreconstituted.

Swisher International
URL: http://www.swishcr.com
Phone: (203) 656-8000
20 Thorndal Circle
Darien, CT 06820-5421
This company dominates the little cigar market with its Swisher Sweets product, and it also produces smokeless tobacco.

**Tobacco Merchants Association
  (TMA)**
URL: http://www.tma.org
E-mail: tma@tma.org
Phone: (609) 275-4900
P.O. Box 8019
Princeton, NJ 08543
This trade association for tobacco industry companies is a source of information on the worldwide tobacco industry.

**U.S. Smokeless Tobacco
  Company**
URL: http://www.ustinc.com
Phone: (203) 661-1100
100 West Putnam Avenue
Greenwich, CT 06830
This is the world's leading producer and marketer of smokeless tobacco products such as Copenhagen snuff and Skoal fine cut.

RESEARCH AND CHARITABLE ORGANIZATIONS

Adolescent Substance Abuse Prevention (ASAP)
URL: http://asap.bsd.uchicago. edu
E-mail: asap@uchicago.edu
Phone: (773) 702-6368
Department of Psychiatry
University of Chicago Hospitals
5841 South Maryland Avenue
MC3077
Chicago, IL 60637-5416
ASAP sponsors a community service program that combats adolescent substance abuse by having medical students visit schools and intro-duce students to the risks and causes of smoking, drinking, and drug taking.

American Cancer Society
URL: http://www.cancer.org
Phone: (800) 227-2345
1599 Clifton Road
Atlanta, GA 30329
With goals of eliminating cancer as a major health problem and pre-venting cancer through research, education, advocacy, and service, this organization supports a variety of antitobacco policies.

American Council on Science and Health (ACSH)
URL: http://www.acsh.org
E-mail: stier@acsh.org
Phone: (212) 362-7044
1995 Broadway

Second Floor
New York, NY 10023-5860
This consumer education group is concerned with promoting scientif-ically sound public policies related to health and the environment and presenting balanced analyses of current health topics. It is highly critical of tobacco companies and misleading claims made through advertising and other means about tobacco use.

American Heart Association
URL: http://www. americanheart.org
Phone: (800) 242-8721
7272 Greenville Avenue
Dallas, TX 75231
This association has as its goal to reduce disability and death from cardiovascular disease by promot-ing smoke-free lifestyles and lobby-ing for tobacco control.

American Lung Association
URL: http://www.lungusa.org
E-mail: press_contact@lungusa. org
Phone: (212) 315-8700
61 Broadway
Sixth Floor
New York, NY 10006
The oldest voluntary health organi-zation in the United States fights lung disease in all forms and gives special emphasis to tobacco control.

American Medical Association (AMA)
URL: http://www.ama-assn.org
Phone: (312) 464-5000

515 North State Street
Chicago, IL 60610
This organization of physicians is dedicated to improving the health of Americans and in so doing supports a variety of antismoking programs and initiatives.

American Public Health Association (APHA)
URL: http://www.apha.org
E-mail: comments@apha.org
Phone: (202) 777-2742
800 I Street, NW
Washington, DC 20001
This organization of public health professionals deals with a broad set of issues affecting personal and environmental health, including tobacco use and control.

Cancer Research and Prevention Foundation
URL: http://www.preventcancer.org
E-mail: info@preventcancer.org
Phone: (800) 227-2732
1600 Duke Street
Suite 110
Alexandria, VA 22314
The foundation supports prevention and early detection of cancer through scientific research and education, and focuses on cancers that can be prevented by lifestyle change, such as stopping cigarette use.

Center for Substance Abuse and Prevention (CSAP)
URL: http://www.covesoft.com/csap.html

E-mail: dbanks@prevline.health.org
Phone: (301) 459-1591, ext. 244
1010 Wayne Avenue
Suite 850
Silver Spring, MD 20910
CSAP provides technical assistance and training to professionals and volunteers who work to prevent abuse of alcohol, tobacco, and other drugs.

Council on Foundations (COF)
URL: http://www.cof.org
E-mail: new@cof.org
Phone: (202) 466-6512
1828 L Street, NW
Washington, DC 20036
This national association of some 2,000 corporations and foundations aids members in making charitable grants and provides information about community organizations that support tobacco control programs.

The Foundation Center
URL: http://fdncenter.org
E-mail: orders@fdncenter.org
Phone: (800) 424-9836
79 Fifth Avenue
New York, NY 10003-3076
This organization collects, organizes, and publicizes information on U.S. philanthropy and can help grant seekers find foundations supporting tobacco control issues.

National Center for Tobacco-Free Older Persons
URL: http://tcsg.org/tobacco.htm

E-mail: tcsg@tcsg.org
Phone: (734) 665-1126
2307 Shelby Avenue ·
Ann Arbor, MI 48103
Part of the Center for Social Gerontology at the University of Michigan, this group emphasizes the special harm of smoking for older persons and how to reduce that harm.

National Center on Addiction and Substance Abuse at Columbia University
URL: http://www.casacolumbia. org
Phone: (212) 841-5200
633 Third Avenue
19th Floor
New York, NY 10017-6706
This research group offers information about the costs of substance abuse, ways to prevent addiction, and the need to remove the stigma of substance abusers.

National Family Partnership (NFP)
URL: http://www.nfp.org
E-mail: mosendorf@ informedfamilies.org
Phone: (305) 856-4815
2490 Coral Way
Suite 501
Miami, FL 33145
NFP helps families and parents in dealing with drug addiction and prevention issues and supports programs to fight tobacco advertising targeted at minors.

National Latino Council on Alcohol and Tobacco Prevention (NLCATP)
URL: http://www.nlcatp.org
E-mail: lcat@nlcatp.org
Phone: (202) 265-8054
1875 Connecticut Avenue, NW
Suite 732
Washington, DC 20009
This organization uses research, policy analysis, community education, training, and information dissemination to reduce the harm caused by alcohol and tobacco in the Latino community.

Robert Wood Johnson Foundation (RWJF)
URL: http://www.rwjf.org
Phone: (888) 631-9989
P.O. Box 2316
College Road East and Route 1
Princeton, NJ 08543-2316
The foundation is devoted to improving the health and health care of Americans by promoting healthy communities and lifestyles and by reducing the harm due to the abuse of tobacco, alcohol, and illicit drugs.

Society for Research on Nicotine and Tobacco (SRNT)
URL: http://www.srnt.org
E-mail: SRNT@tmahq.com
Phone: (608) 836-3787
7600 Terrace Avenue
Middleton, WI 53562
This organization sponsors scientific meetings and publications and arranges for expert advice to policy-

makers and legislators on issues involving nicotine and tobacco.

NATIONAL ADVOCACY GROUPS

Action on Smoking and Health (ASH)
URL: http://ash.org
Phone: (202) 659-4310
2013 H Street, NW
Washington, DC 20006
The national antismoking and nonsmokers' rights organization promotes legal action on behalf of nonsmokers.

Advocacy Institute
URL: http://www.advocacy.org
E-mail: info@advocacy.org
Phone: (202) 777-7575
1629 K Street, NW
Suite 200
Washington, DC 20006-1629
The institute works to promote effective social justice leadership, achieve a just society, and foster economic equality and public health. Its programs include several devoted to tobacco control.

American Legacy Foundation
URL: http://www.americanlegacy.org
E-mail: info@americanlegacy.org
Phone: (202) 454-5555
1001 G Street, NW
Suite 800
Washington, DC 20001
Established in 1999 as a result of the Master Settlement Agreement and supported by funds from the tobacco companies, this organization is devoted to reducing youth tobacco use, decreasing exposure to secondhand smoke, increasing successful quit rates, and eliminating disparities in access to tobacco prevention and cessation.

Americans for Nonsmokers' Rights
URL: http://www.no-smoke.org
E-mail: anr@no-smoke.org
Phone: (510) 841-3032
2530 San Pablo Avenue
Suite J
Berkeley, CA 94702
A national lobbying organization dedicated to nonsmokers' rights, including protection from secondhand smoke and youth addiction, it has worked in the past for legislation to ban smoking from worksites and public places.

BADvertising Institute
URL: http://www.badvertising.org
E-mail: bv@badvertising.org
Phone: (908) 273-9368
c/o NJ GASP
105 Mountain Drive
Summit, NJ 07901
Supports tobacco counteradvertising with posters and graphics that reveal the truth behind cigarette advertising and the glamorous images usually portrayed in tobacco ads. It is run by the New Jersey

Chapter of the Group Against Smokers' Pollution.

The Bureau for At-Risk Youth
URL: http://www.at-risk.com
E-mail: info@at-risk.com
Phone: (800) 999-6884
135 Dupont Street
P.O. Box 760
Plainview, NY 11803-0760
The company sells guidance and prevention materials for schools, youth service programs, and juvenile justice organizations, including materials for tobacco prevention.

Campaign for Tobacco-Free Kids
URL: http://www.
  tobaccofreekids.org
E-mail: info@tobaccofreekids.org
Phone: (202) 296-5469
1400 I Street
Suite 1200
Washington, DC 20005
A private nonprofit organization committed to protecting children from tobacco addiction and secondhand smoke, it works to inform the public about the harm of tobacco, change public policies, educate young people, and expose tobacco marketing practices that addict kids.

Cato Institute
URL: http://www.cato.org
E-mail: service@cato.org
Phone: (202) 842-0200
1000 Massachusetts Avenue,
  NW
Washington, DC 20001-5403

A policy and research organization that favors individual liberty, limited government, free markets, and peace, it is concerned about excessive regulation of economic activity and personal choice by government in all areas of life, including tobacco use.

Center for Media Education (CME)
URL: http://www.cme.org
E-mail: cme@cme.org
Phone: (202) 331-7833
2120 L Street, NW
Suite 200
Washington, DC 20037
Dedicated to creating a quality electronic media culture for children and youth, their families, and the community, this center works to protect children from exposure to tobacco products on the Internet as well as in other media.

Center for Science in the Public Interest (CSPI)
URL: http://www.cspinet.org
E-mail: cspi@cspinet.org
Phone: (202) 332-9110
1875 Connecticut Avenue, NW
Suite 300
Washington, DC 20009
An advocate for nutrition, health, and food safety, this organization is also involved in antitobacco programs

Children Opposed to Smoking Tobacco (COST)
URL: http://www.costkids.org
E-mail: costkids@costkids.org

Founded by a group of students who want to keep tobacco products away from children, this group offers a list of activities that young people can do to help reach this goal.

CigaretteLitter.org
URL: http://www.cigarettelitter. org
E-mail: info@cigarettelitter.org
P.O. Box 289
Culver City, CA 90232
Devoted to reducing cigarette litter through public awareness and education, this organization includes both smokers and nonsmokers in its efforts to improve the landscape.

Conscientious Consuming
URL: http://www. conscientiousconsuming.com
E-mail: con_suming@hotmail. com
This group calls for a boycott of all products, both tobacco and nontobacco, produced by tobacco companies.

Foundation for a Smokefree America
URL: http://www.tobaccofree. org
E-mail: manager@tobaccofree. org
Phone: (310) 471-4270
P.O. Box 492028
Los Angeles, CA 90049-8028
Toward the goal of motivating youth to stay free of tobacco and to help smokers quit, this organization helps establish local, regional, and

national programs, school educational programs, and peer teaching programs.

Group Against Smokers' Pollution (GASP)
Phone: (301) 459-4791
National Headquarters
P.O. Box 632
College Park, MD 20741-0632
GASP works to eliminate tobacco smoke from the air, educate the public about secondhand smoke, and promote smoke-free policies.

INFACT
URL: http://www.infact.org
E-mail: info@infact.org
Phone: (617) 695-2525
46 Plympton Street
Boston, MA 02118
This corporate watchdog group has been critical of tobacco corporations for undermining public health.

Join Together
URL: http://www.jointogether. org
E-mail: info@jointogether.org
Phone: (617) 437-1500
One Appleton Street
Fourth Floor
Boston, MA 02116-5223
A project of Boston University, it addresses issues of substance abuse and gun violence, including issues involving youth and tobacco.

March of Dimes
URL: http://www.modimes.org
Phone: (800) 996-2724

1275 Mamaroneck Avenue
White Plains, NY 10605
This well-known charitable organization aims to improve the health of babies by preventing birth defects and infant mortality; such efforts include reducing the harm of parental cigarette use to babies.

National Organization for
  Women (NOW) Foundation
URL: http://www.
  nowfoundation.org
Phone: (202) 628-8669
P.O. Box 1848
Merrifield, VA 22116-8048
Affiliated with the nation's largest women's rights organization, the foundation focuses on furthering women's rights through education and litigation and supports a women's health project on tobacco advertising and women.

Project Alert
URL: http://www.projectalert.
  best.org
E-mail: info@projectalert.best.
  org
Phone: (213) 623-0580
725 South Figueroa Street
Suite 970
Los Angeles, CA 90017
The project sponsors a drug prevention program for middle-grade students that focuses on tobacco as well as alcohol, marijuana, and inhalants.

Smoke-Free for Health
URL: http://www.
  smokefreeforhealth.org

E-mail: info@
  smokefreeforhealth.org
Phone: (407) 841-2255
P.O. Box 530106
Orlando, FL 32853-0106
The organization supports anti-smoking initiatives, laws, and constitutional amendments to deal with the health hazards of second-hand smoke.

Smokefree.net
URL: http://www.smokefree.net
E-mail: tac@smokefree.net
  joe@smokefree.net
Phone: (202) 667-6653
2100 R Street, NW
Washington, DC 20008
This network is designed to fight for smoke-free air by facilitating communication and information sharing between smoke-free advocates and decision makers.

Smokers Fighting Discrimination (SFD)
URL: http://www.geocities.com/
  sfd-usa
E-mail: sfdsmoke@hal-pc.org
P.O. Box 5472
Katy, TX 77491
SFD opposes state and federal government actions to intrude on personal lifestyle freedoms with smoking restrictions.

Stop Teenage Addiction to
  Tobacco (STAT)
URL: http://www.smokefreeair.
  org/Org/Orgdet.cfm?ID=2559
Email: STAT@exit3.com
360 Huntington Avenue

Cushing Hall
Room 241
Boston, MA 02115
STAT works with youth in community groups to control tobacco at the local level and make the public aware of unethical and deceitful marketing practices of the tobacco industry.

Student Coalition Against
  Tobacco
URL: http://www.smokefreeair.
  org/Org/Orgdet.cfm?ID=2568
Phone: (888) 234-7228
P.O. Box 584
Parkersburg, WV 26102
This national, student-led organization aims to protect students from the ills of tobacco.

Survivors and Victims of
  Tobacco
URL: http://www.tobacco
  survivors.org
E-mail:
  info@tobaccosurvivors.org
Phone: (704) 826-8186
Route 2
Box 340-A
Wadesboro, NC 28170
In this group survivors of tobacco-related illnesses tell their painful and personal stories about the effects of tobacco to young people and adults.

Tobacco Control Resource
  Center
URL: http://www.tobacco.neu.
  edu
E-mail: tobacco@bigfoot.com

Phone: (617) 373-2026
Northeastern University School
  of Law
400 Huntington Avenue
Boston, MA 02115
The center encourages and coordinates product liability suits against the tobacco industry and policy initiatives to control the sale and use of tobacco.

INTERNATIONAL ADVOCACY GROUPS

European Network for Smoking
  Prevention (ENSP)
URL: http://www.ensp.org
E-mail: sibylle.fleitmann@ensp.
  org
Phone: (32 02) 230 65 15
144 Chaussée d'Ixelles
Brussels 1050
Belgium
In coordinating antitobacco efforts among nations of the European Union, the network makes special efforts to support programs that span national boundaries.

Forces International
URL: http://www.forces.org
E-mail: forcesint@forces.org
Phone: (240) 201-6347
P.O. Box 14347
San Francisco, CA 94114-0347
Devoted to the idea that consumers have a right to choose lifestyles without government interference, this group supports smokers' rights.

International Network of
Women Against Tobacco
(INWAT)
URL: http://www.inwat.org
E-mail: bonnie@inwat.org
Phone: (732) 549-9054
P.O. Box 224
Metuchen, NJ 08840
With the goal of improving
women's health around the world,
the network addresses the problem
of tobacco use among women and
young girls.

International Union Against
Cancer (UICC)
URL: http://www.uicc.org
Phone: (41 22) 809 18 50
3, rue du Conseil General
Geneva 1205
Switzerland
A global organization that has as
members 291 cancer-fighting organizations in 87 countries, this union
promotes awareness and responsibility for the growing global cancer
burden and the need for worldwide
tobacco control.

Tobacco Free Initiative (TFI)
URL: http://tobacco.who.int
E-mail: tfi@who.int
Phone: (41 22) 791 2126
World Health Organization
Avenue Appia 20 1211
Geneva 27
Switzerland
This project of the World Health
Organization works for worldwide
tobacco control with publications,
press releases, web news, and anti-
tobacco information.

World Bank Group
URL: http://www.worldbank.org
Phone: (202) 473-1000
1818 H Street, NW
Washington, DC 20433
Although largely focused on help-
ing nations fight poverty, the World
Bank also works in partnership with
the World Health Organization on
issues of tobacco control.

STATE AND LOCAL ADVOCACY GROUPS

Capital District Tobacco-Free
Coalition
URL: http://www.smokefree
capital.org
E-mail:
info@smokefreecapital.org
Phone: (518) 459-4197, ext. 322
3 Winners Circle
Suite 300
Albany, NY 12205
Composed of local organizations
and individuals in the Albany area,
this coalition works at the local level
to help smokers quit, prevent youth
from starting, protect people from
secondhand smoke, and reduce
group differences in tobacco use.

Georgia Alliance for Tobacco
Prevention
URL: http://www.
chargecoalition.org
E-mail: nancy@
gatobaccoprevention.org
Phone: (770) 437-9950

2452 Spring Road
Smyrna, GA 30080
The alliance encourages individuals to work against tobacco use through contacting state representatives, starting and joining local antismoking organizations, and working with children to prevent their use of tobacco

Massachusetts Tobacco Education Clearinghouse (MTEC)
URL: http://www.jsi.com/health/mtec
E-mail: mtec@jsi.com
Phone: (617) 482-9485
Juha Snow Inc., Research and Training Institute
44 Farnsworth Street
Boston, MA 02212-1211
The clearinghouse offers services to support tobacco education efforts across the state and has a large collection of books, brochures, videos, and other teaching tools for tobacco controls.

Michigan Citizens for Smoke-Free Air (MCSFA)
URL: http://www.smokefreemichigan.org
E-mail: MCSFA@qix.net
The group works for smoke-free environments wherever the public gathers and publishes a book of smoke-free restaurants in Michigan.

NYC Coalition for a Smoke-Free City
URL: http://www.nycsmokefree.org
The coalition aims to make the public and policymakers in New York City aware of smoke-free issues and provide a guide to smoke-free places in New York City.

Partnership for a Tobacco-Free Maine
URL: http://demo.hallsinternet.com
Phone: (207) 287-4627, (800) 207-1230
Bureau of Health
Fourth Floor
11 State House Station
Key Bank Plaza
Augusta, ME 04330-0011
The primary program responsible for tobacco prevention and control in the state of Maine, it is funded by the tobacco settlement and the Centers for Disease Control and Prevention.

Smokefree Indiana
URL: http://www.smokefreeindiana.org
E-mail: inquiry@smokefreeindiana.org
Phone: (317) 241-6398
5610 Crawfordsville Road
Suite 1602
Indianapolis, IN 46224
A group of health-promotion specialists in Indiana work in the community to reduce tobacco use.

Smoke-Free Maryland
URL: http://www.smokefreemd.org
E-mail: kari@smokefreemd.org
Phone: (410) 539-0872, ext. 353

1211 Cathedral Street
Baltimore, MD 21201
A statewide coalition of organizations and individuals working to reduce tobacco-related illness and death by advocating various tobacco control policies.

**Students Teaching Against
  Tobacco in Connecticut
  (STATIC)**
URL: http://www.ctstatic.org
E-mail: michelle@ctstatic.org
Phone: (860) 679-7969
**Health Education Center
  Program**
**University of Connecticut
  School of Medicine**
263 Farmingham Avenue

MC3960
Farmington, CT 06030-3960
This youth-led movement aims to provide information about how the tobacco industry works and to counter the actions of the industry.

**Washington Doctors Ought to
  Care (DOC)**
URL: http://kickbutt.org
E-mail: office@kickbutt.org
Phone: (206) 988-7832
**12401 East Marginal Way South
Tukwila, WA 98168**
The organization aims to prevent tobacco use among youth through educational materials, youth support groups, and technical assistance for policy development.

PART III

APPENDICES

APPENDIX A

FOOD AND DRUG ADMINISTRATION NICOTINE REGULATIONS (1996)

The following is an extract and contains only some of the sections.

EXECUTIVE SUMMARY

This document explains the basis for the Food and Drug Administration's [FDA] assertion of jurisdiction over cigarettes and smokeless tobacco under the Federal Food, Drug, and Cosmetic Act (the Act). FDA regulates a diverse range of products under the Act, including foods, drugs, medical devices, and cosmetics. The distinguishing feature that characterizes these products is their intimate and potentially harmful relationship with the human body. The products that FDA regulates include those that are ingested, inhaled, implanted, or otherwise used in close contact with the human body.

Cigarettes, which deliver a pharmacologically active dose of nicotine to the body through inhalation, and smokeless tobacco, which delivers a pharmacologically active dose of nicotine to the body through buccal absorption, share this distinguishing feature. Like the products that FDA traditionally regulates, cigarettes and smokeless tobacco are inhaled or placed within the human body; like many of these products, they deliver a pharmacologically active substance to the bloodstream; and like these products, they have potentially dangerous effects. Indeed, no products cause more death and disease than cigarettes and smokeless tobacco.

FDA is asserting jurisdiction over cigarettes and smokeless tobacco under the drug and device provisions of the Act. Specifically, FDA has concluded that cigarettes and smokeless tobacco are combination products

251

consisting of nicotine, a drug that causes addiction and other significant pharmacological effects on the human body, and device components that deliver nicotine to the body. FDA last considered whether cigarettes were drugs or devices in the late 1970's. Since that time, substantial new evidence has become available to FDA. This evidence includes the emergence of a scientific consensus that cigarettes and smokeless tobacco cause addiction to nicotine and the disclosure of thousands of pages of internal tobacco company documents detailing that these products are intended by the manufacturers to affect the structure and function of the human body. This new evidence justifies the Agency's determination that cigarettes and smokeless tobacco are delivery systems for the drug nicotine.

Under the Act, a product is a drug or device if it is an article (other than food) "intended to affect the structure or any function of the body." The statutory definition is "intended to define 'drug' far more broadly than does the medical profession." The legal question of whether cigarettes and smokeless tobacco are subject to FDA jurisdiction is one that "FDA has jurisdiction to decide with administrative finality."

After intensive investigation and careful consideration of the public comments, FDA concludes that cigarettes and smokeless tobacco meet the statutory definition of a drug and a device. This conclusion is based on two determinations: (1) nicotine in cigarettes and smokeless tobacco does "affect the structure or any function of the body," and (2) these effects on the structure and function of the body are "intended" by the manufacturers.

The Agency's determination that nicotine in cigarettes and smokeless tobacco does "affect the structure or any function of the body" is based on three central findings:

1. Nicotine in cigarettes and smokeless tobacco causes and sustains addiction.
2. Nicotine in cigarettes and smokeless tobacco causes other psychoactive (mood-altering) effects, including tranquilization and stimulation.
3. Nicotine in cigarettes and smokeless tobacco controls weight.

The Agency's determination that the manufacturers of cigarettes and smokeless tobacco "intend" these effects is based on five central findings:

1. The addictive and other pharmacological effects of nicotine are so widely known and accepted that it is foreseeable to a reasonable manufacturer that cigarettes and smokeless tobacco will cause addiction to nicotine and other significant pharmacological effects and will be used by consumers for pharmacological purposes, including sustaining their addiction to nicotine.

2. Consumers use cigarettes and smokeless tobacco predominantly for pharmacological purposes, including sustaining their addiction to nicotine, mood alteration, and weight loss.
3. Manufacturers of cigarettes and smokeless tobacco know that nicotine in their products causes pharmacological effects in consumers, including addiction to nicotine and mood alteration, and that consumers use their products primarily to obtain the pharmacological effects of nicotine.
4. Manufacturers of cigarettes and smokeless tobacco design their products to provide consumers with a pharmacologically active dose of nicotine.
5. An inevitable consequence of the design of cigarettes and smokeless tobacco to provide consumers with a pharmacologically active dose of nicotine is to keep consumers using cigarettes and smokeless tobacco by sustaining their addiction to nicotine.

This document is divided into six sections. Section I describes the evidence and legal basis supporting the Agency's finding that cigarettes and smokeless tobacco "affect the structure or any function of the body." Section II describes the evidence and legal basis supporting the Agency's finding that the manufacturers "intend" these effects on the structure and function of the body. Section III explains the Agency's conclusion that cigarettes and smokeless tobacco are combination products that contain a "drug" and a "device." Section IV explains why the Agency's decision to assert jurisdiction over cigarettes and smokeless tobacco is justified by the new evidence now available to the Agency. Section V demonstrates that Congress has not precluded or preempted the Agency's assertion of jurisdiction over cigarettes and smokeless tobacco. Section VI addresses procedural issues relating to the Agency's assertion of jurisdiction over cigarettes and smokeless tobacco. These sections are summarized below.

I. CIGARETTES AND SMOKELESS TOBACCO "AFFECT THE STRUCTURE OR ANY FUNCTION OF THE BODY" WITHIN THE MEANING OF THE ACT

The nicotine delivered by cigarettes and smokeless tobacco has significant pharmacological effects on the structure and function of the body.

First, the nicotine in cigarettes and smokeless tobacco causes and sustains addiction. Nicotine exerts psychoactive, or mood-altering, effects on the brain that motivate repeated, compulsive use of the substance. These pharmacological effects create dependence in the user. The pharmacological processes that cause this addiction to nicotine are similar to those that cause addiction to heroin and cocaine.

Second, the nicotine in cigarettes and smokeless tobacco produces other important pharmacological effects on the central nervous system. Under some circumstances and doses, the nicotine has a sedating or tranquilizing effect on mood and brain activity. Under other circumstances and doses, the nicotine has a stimulant or arousal-inducing effect on mood and brain activity.

Third, the nicotine in cigarettes and smokeless tobacco affects body weight.

These effects on the structure and function of the body are significant and quintessentially drug-like. Moreover, these effects are the same as the effects of other drugs that FDA has traditionally regulated, including stimulants, tranquilizers, appetite suppressants, and products, such as methadone, used in the maintenance of addiction. For these reasons, the Agency finds that cigarettes and smokeless tobacco "affect the structure or any function of the body" within the meaning of the Act.

II. CIGARETTES AND SMOKELESS TOBACCO ARE "INTENDED" TO AFFECT THE STRUCTURE AND FUNCTION OF THE BODY WITHIN THE MEANING OF THE ACT

To determine whether effects on the structure or function of the body are "intended" by the manufacturer, the Agency must objectively evaluate all the relevant evidence of intent in the record before it. "The FDA is not bound by the manufacturer's subjective claims of intent," but rather can find actual intent "on the basis of objective evidence." In the case of cigarettes and smokeless tobacco, the Agency finds that three types of objective evidence provide independent bases for finding that the manufacturers intend to affect the structure and function of the body: (1) the evidence of the foreseeable pharmacological effects and uses of cigarettes and smokeless tobacco; (2) the evidence of the actual consumer use of cigarettes and smokeless tobacco for pharmacological purposes; and (3) the evidence of the statements, research, and actions of the manufacturers themselves. Considered independently or cumulatively, this evidence convincingly demonstrates that cigarettes and smokeless tobacco are intended to be used for pharmacological purposes.

A. A Reasonable Manufacturer Would Foresee That Tobacco Products Will Cause Addiction and Other Pharmacological Effects and Will Be Used by Consumers for Pharmacological Purposes

When Congress enacted the current definition of "drug" in 1938, it was well understood that "[t]he law presumes that every man intends the legiti-

mate consequences of his own acts." Consistent with this common understanding, FDA's regulations provide that a product's intended pharmacological use may be established by evidence that the manufacturer "knows, or
has knowledge of facts that would give him notice," that the product is
being widely used for a pharmacological purpose, even if the product is not
being promoted for this purpose. Thus, FDA may find that a manufacturer
intends its product to affect the structure or function of the body when it
would be foreseeable to a reasonable manufacturer that the product will (1)
affect the structure or function of the body and (2) be used by a substantial
proportion of consumers to obtain these effects. For example, when it is
foreseeable to a reasonable manufacturer that a product will produce drug
effects in consumers and be purchased by a substantial proportion of consumers for drug purposes, FDA may consider the product a "drug."

In the case of cigarettes and smokeless tobacco, no reasonable manufacturer could fail to foresee that these products will have significant pharmacological effects on consumers and be widely used by consumers for
pharmacological purposes. All major public health organizations in the
United States and abroad with expertise in tobacco or drug addiction now
recognize that the nicotine delivered by cigarettes and smokeless tobacco is
addictive. The first major organization to do so was the American Psychiatric Association, which in 1980 defined the "tobacco dependence disorder"
and the "tobacco withdrawal syndrome." Since 1980, nicotine in tobacco
products has also been recognized as addictive by the U.S. Surgeon General
(1986 and 1988), the American Psychological Association (1988), the Royal
Society of Canada (1989), the World Health Organization (1992), the
American Medical Association (1993), and the Medical Research Council in
the United Kingdom (1994). Every expert medical organization that sub-
mitted comments to FDA on whether nicotine is addictive concluded that
it is. The tobacco industry's public position that nicotine is not addictive is
simply not credible in light of this overwhelming scientific consensus.

The scientific consensus that cigarettes and smokeless tobacco cause addiction to nicotine makes it foreseeable to a reasonable manufacturer that
these products will affect the structure and function of the body. This scientific consensus also makes it foreseeable that cigarettes and smokeless tobacco will be used by a substantial proportion of consumers for a
pharmacological purpose, namely, to satisfy their addiction.

It is also foreseeable that the nicotine in cigarettes and smokeless tobacco
will cause, and be used for, other significant pharmacological effects. It is well
established that the nicotine in cigarettes and smokeless tobacco has psychoactive or mood-altering effects in the brain. Under some circumstances,
nicotine can have a sedative or tranquilizing effect on the brain; under other
circumstances, nicotine can have a stimulating or arousal-inducing effect. In

this regard, nicotine is similar to other addictive drugs such as opiates, which can have both stimulating and sedating effects. In addition, nicotine plays a role in weight regulation, with substantial evidence demonstrating that cigarette smoking leads to weight loss. Because a reasonable manufacturer would foresee that cigarettes and smokeless tobacco will cause and be used for these well-established pharmacological effects in a substantial proportion of consumers, the Agency finds that these drug effects and drug uses are intended by the manufacturers.

B. Consumers Use Tobacco Products to Obtain the Pharmacoiogical Effects of Nicotine and to Satisfy Their Addiction

A second basis for establishing that a product is intended to affect the structure or function of the body is evidence showing that consumers actually use the product for pharmacological purposes. In fact, courts have recognized that even in the absence of any other evidence of intent to affect the structure or function of the body, such an intent may be established by evidence showing that consumers use the product "predominantly" for pharmacological purposes.

In the case of cigarettes and smokeless tobacco, the evidence establishes that consumers do use these products "predominantly" for pharmacological purposes. Major recent studies have concluded that 77% to 92% of smokers are addicted to nicotine in cigarettes. The U.S. Department of Health and Human Services estimates that 75% of young regular users of smokeless tobacco are addicted to nicotine in these products. The comments from the American Heart Association, the American Lung Association, and the American Cancer Society, whose member physicians provide health care for tobacco users in the United States, confirm that "the vast majority of people who use nicotine containing cigarettes and smokeless tobacco do so to satisfy their craving for the pharmacological effects of nicotine; that is, to satisfy their drug dependence or addiction."

In addition, a large proportion of consumers also use cigarettes and smokeless tobacco for other pharmacological purposes. A recent survey found that over 70% of young people 10 to 22 years old who are daily smokers reported that they use cigarettes for relaxation. The same survey found that over 50% of young people who are daily users of smokeless tobacco reported that they use smokeless tobacco for relaxation. Other surveys show that between one-third and one-half of young smokers report that weight control is a reason for their smoking.

This evidence that consumers actually use cigarettes and smokeless tobacco predominantly to obtain the pharmacological effects of nicotine leads

FDA to find that cigarettes and smokeless tobacco are intended to affect the structure and function of the body.

C. The Statements, Research, and Actions of the Cigarette Manufacturers Show That the Manufacturers Intend to Affect the Structure and Function of the Body

A third basis for establishing that a manufacturer intends to affect the structure or function of the body is evidence from the statements, research, and actions of the manufacturer that reveals that the manufacturer knows that its product will, or designs its product to, affect the structure or function of the body. It is a canon of statutory construction that words used by Congress should ordinarily be interpreted in accordance with their plain meaning. The plain meaning of "intend" includes "to have in mind" or "to design" for a particular use. The *American Heritage Dictionary*, for instance, defines "intend" as: "1. To have in mind; plan. 2.a. To design for a specific purpose, b. To have in mind for a particular use." Consistent with the plain meaning of "intend," FDA may consider whether the statements, research, and actions of the manufacturer show that the manufacturer "has in mind" that its product will, or "designs" its product to, affect the structure or function of the body.

The administrative record contains three decades of documents and other evidence from the major cigarette manufacturers. This evidence, most of which has only recently become available, establishes that the manufacturers do "have in mind" that their products will have and be used for pharmacological effects. First, the evidence shows that the cigarette manufacturers know that nicotine is a pharmacologically active drug. In internal documents, for instance, researchers for Philip Morris Inc. call nicotine "a powerful pharmacological agent with multiple sites of action" and "a physiologically active . . . substance . . . [which] alters the state of the smoker by becoming a neurotransmitter and a stimulant"; a researcher for R. J. Reynolds Tobacco Co. (RJR) calls nicotine "a potent drug with a variety of physiological effects"; and researchers for Brown & Williamson Tobacco Corp. and its parent company, BAT Industries PLC (formerly the British-American Tobacco Co.) (BATCO), call nicotine "pharmacologically active in the brain" and "an extremely biologically active compound capable of eliciting a range of pharmacological, biochemical, and physiological responses."

Second, the evidence establishes that the cigarette manufacturers have conducted extensive research to understand precisely how nicotine affects the structure and function of the body. In one year alone, Philip Morris conducted 16 different studies on the effects of nicotine, including 5 experiments to determine the pharmacological effects of nicotine on the human brain. RJR's similarly extensive research found that the nicotine in cigarettes produces measurable changes in brain wave activity, such as "a significant increase in beta2 magnitude" (an effect associated with anxiety relief) and "a significant decrease in delta magnitude" (an effect associated with improved mental condition). Through the Council for Tobacco Research, an organization formed by the major tobacco companies, the manufacturers funded dozens of sophisticated investigations concerning nicotine, including numerous studies that demonstrate nicotine's ability to alter the function of the human brain.

Third, the evidence shows that the manufacturers know that one of the pharmacological effects of nicotine is to cause and sustain addiction. Researchers and senior officials of Brown & Williamson and BATCO expressly acknowledge this fact in their internal documents, stating that "smoking is a habit of addiction" and that "nicotine is addictive." Philip Morris scientists also know of nicotine's addiction potential. They conducted a series of nicotine "self-administration" experiments using the tests used by the National Institute on Drug Abuse to determine whether a substance has addiction potential. These studies found that rats would self-administer nicotine, which is one of the hallmark characteristics of an addictive drug. Moreover, through the Council for Tobacco Research, the cigarette manufacturers funded research that reported that "smoking is a form of dependence no less binding than that of other addictive drugs."

Fourth, the evidence shows that the manufacturers know that consumers smoke cigarettes primarily to obtain the pharmacological effects of nicotine. This point is repeatedly acknowledged in internal company documents. For example, researchers for Philip Morris have stated that nicotine is "the primary reason why people smoke" and that nicotine is "the physiologically active component of smoke having the greatest consequence to the consumer"; researchers for RJR have stated that "the confirmed user of tobacco is primarily seeking the physiological 'satisfaction' derived from nicotine" and that "[w]ithout any question, the desire to smoke is based upon the effect of nicotine on the body"; and BATCO's director of research has stated that "[t]he tobacco smoking habit is reinforced or dependent upon the psycho-pharmacological effects mainly of nicotine." This knowledge of the central role of nicotine in cigarette smoking was communicated to the highest levels of the companies. In 1969, for instance, Philip Morris' vice president for research and development told the Philip Morris board of directors that "the ultimate explanation for the perpetuated cigarette habit resides in the pharmacological effect of smoke upon the body of the smoker."

Fifth, the evidence shows that in their internal documents, the cigarette manufacturers expressly refer to cigarettes as devices for the delivery of nicotine. For instance, researchers for Philip Morris have described ciga-rettes as a "dispenser for a dose unit of nicotine" and as a "nicotine delivery device"; a senior researcher for RJR has described cigarettes as a "vehicle for delivering nicotine"; and researchers for BATCO have described cigarettes as the "means of providing nicotine dose in a metered fashion" and as a de-vice that provides the smoker "very flexible control over titrating his desired dose of nicotine."

This evidence establishes that cigarettes are intended by the manufactur-ers to affect the structure and function of the body. It demonstrates that the manufacturers know that nicotine is pharmacologically active; that con-sumers smoke primarily to obtain the pharmacological effects of nicotine; and that cigarettes function as devices for the delivery of nicotine. The evi-dence thus shows that when the manufacturers offer cigarettes for sale, they "have in mind" that their products will be used for the particular purpose of affecting the structure and function of the body.

In addition to the evidence showing that cigarette manufacturers "have in mind" the use of cigarettes for pharmacological purposes, the record shows that the manufacturers "design" cigarettes to ensure the delivery of a pharmacologically active dose of nicotine to the smoker. The evidence in the record shows that the manufacturers have conducted extensive product research and development to find ways to maintain adequate nicotine levels in low-tar cigarettes. According to one former senior official at Philip Mor-ris, "a key objective of the cigarette industry over the last 20–30 years" was "maintaining an acceptable and pharmacologically active nicotine level" in low-tar cigarettes. Internal industry documents in the record disclose re-search to determine the dose of nicotine that must be delivered to provide "pharmacological satisfaction" to the smoker, as well as estimates by indus-try scientists of the minimum and optimum doses of nicotine that cigarettes must deliver.

Among the many examples in the record of product research and devel-opment to enhance relative nicotine deliveries, Philip Morris conducted ex-tensive research to identify "the optimal nicotine/tar ratios for cigarette acceptability of relatively low-delivery cigarettes"; RJR developed alternative tobacco products that provide a "more efficient and direct way to provide the desired nicotine dosage than the present system involving combustion of to-bacco"; and Brown & Williamson investigated chemical manipulation to raise smoke pH, thereby increasing "free" nicotine delivery, and used genetic engineering to breed a high-nicotine tobacco plant called Y-1.

The record before the Agency shows that several methods of enhancing nicotine deliveries are used in the manufacture of commercial cigarettes. Tobacco blending to raise the nicotine concentration in low-tar cigarettes is common. As the vice chairman and chief operating officer of Lorillard

Tobacco Co. has stated, "the lowest tar segment is composed of cigarettes utilizing a tobacco blend which is significantly higher in nicotine." Another common technique for enhancing nicotine deliveries in low-tar cigarettes is the use of filter and ventilation systems that by design remove a higher percentage of tar than nicotine. Yet a third type of nicotine manipulation is the addition of ammonia compounds that increase the delivery of "free" nicotine to smokers by raising the alkalinity or pH of tobacco smoke. These ammonia technologies are widely used within the industry.

The record establishes that an important reason why the manufacturers design cigarettes that provide pharmacologically active doses of nicotine is to satisfy the demands of users. The manufacturers concede in their comments that their "intent is to design, manufacture and market . . . cigarettes to meet the preferences of adult smokers." The preferences of most smokers, however, include obtaining sufficient nicotine to sustain their addiction and to experience nicotine's mood-altering effects. What the cigarette manufacturers describe as producing cigarettes that satisfy consumer preferences is, in reality, producing cigarettes that provide the pharmacological effects of nicotine sought by consumers. The effect of maintaining a pharmacologically active dose of nicotine in cigarettes is to keep consumers smoking by sustaining their addiction.

The evidence that the manufacturers "design" cigarettes to provide a pharmacologically active dose of nicotine is further proof that the manufacturers intend cigarettes to affect the structure and function of the body. Taken together, the evidence shows that the cigarette manufacturers: (1) "have in mind" the use of cigarettes for the particular purpose of delivering the pharmacological effects of nicotine, and (2) "design" their products to provide these effects. This evidence convincingly demonstrates that the pharmacological effects of cigarettes are "intended" by the manufacturers.

D. The Statements, Research, and Actions of the Smokeless Tobacco Manufacturers Show That the Manufacturers Intend Their Products to Affect the Structure and Function of the Body

The administrative record also contains evidence of the statements, research, and actions of the smokeless tobacco manufacturers. Like the evidence of the statements, research, and actions of the cigarette manufacturers, this evidence establishes that the smokeless tobacco manufacturers intend to affect the structure and function of the body.

First, the evidence in the record shows that the smokeless tobacco manufacturers know that nicotine is a pharmacologically active drug and that consumers use smokeless tobacco to obtain the pharmacological effects of nicotine. As a senior vice president for United States Tobacco Co. (UST) stated, "virtually all tobacco usage is based upon nicotine, 'the kick,' satisfaction." Researchers affiliated with Brown & Williamson acknowledge that "nicotine . . . absorbed through . . . the lining of the nose or mouth . . . will quickly enter a direct route, in the blood, to the brain."

Second, the evidence shows that the smokeless tobacco manufacturers manipulate the nicotine delivery of their products in a manner that promotes tolerance and addiction to nicotine. This manipulation is accomplished through the use of chemicals that alter the pH of the smokeless tobacco. Moist snuff brands that are marketed as "starter" brands have a low pH and consequently deliver a low level of "free" nicotine to the user, limiting the absorption of nicotine in the mouth. The low nicotine deliveries allow the new user to develop a tolerance to nicotine without experiencing adverse reactions such as nausea and vomiting. In contrast, moist snuff brands that are marketed to experienced users have a high pH and consequently deliver a high level of "free" nicotine to the user, increasing the amount of nicotine available for absorption. The increased nicotine deliveries provide sufficient nicotine to sustain the user's addiction.

Third, the evidence shows that smokeless tobacco use and addiction to nicotine has substantially increased among teenagers since the manufacturers began to manipulate nicotine deliveries. Before the introduction of starter brands with low levels of nicotine delivery, virtually no teenagers and young adults used smokeless tobacco. After the smokeless tobacco manufacturers began to market low-nicotine "starter" brands in the 1970's, however, use of smokeless tobacco by teenagers rose dramatically. Use of smokeless tobacco by adolescent males aged 18 to 19, for instance, increased almost 1,500% between 1971 and 1991. Most of the regular teenage users of smokeless tobacco graduate to higher nicotine brands. An analysis by the Centers for Disease Control and Prevention found that the pattern of smokeless tobacco use by teenagers "support[s] the hypothesis that snuff users in earlier stages of tobacco use and nicotine addiction use brands with low levels of free nicotine and then 'graduate' to brands with high levels."

This evidence of: (1) knowledge of nicotine pharmacology, (2) manipulation of nicotine deliveries, and (3) graduation to higher nicotine brands among young users is a sufficient basis to establish that the smokeless tobacco manufacturers intend to affect the structure and function of the body.

In addition to this industry-wide evidence of intended use, the record contains numerous documents from the nation's largest smokeless tobacco manufacturer, UST. The UST documents in the record show that:

- UST officials in the early 1970's recommended the development of products with "three different . . . strengths of nicotine[:] . . . a. High nicotine, strong tobacco flavor ... b. Medium strength of nicotine ... c. Low nicotine, sweet product." In particular, UST officials recommended the development of a product that provided "mild" nicotine satisfaction targeted at "new users ... age group 15–35."

- Shortly after these recommendations, UST began aggressively to market low-nicotine products, targeted "for you guys just starting out." Marketing techniques included free sampling on college campuses and at sports events. Advertisements included instructions on use for new users.

- Numerous UST documents and statements refer to an explicit "graduation process" in which users of smokeless tobacco are encouraged to start with low-nicotine starter brands and then progress to higher nicotine brands. For instance, a UST vice president has stated that Skoal Bandits, one of UST's low-nicotine brands, "is the introductory product, and we look towards establishing a normal graduation process."

These UST documents confirm that smokeless tobacco manufacturers deliberately produce brands with a range of nicotine deliveries in order to allow users to progress (or "graduate") from low-delivery products to high-delivery products. They thus corroborate the Agency's finding that smokeless tobacco is intended to affect the structure and function of the body.

E. The "Intended Use" of a Product Is Not Determined Only on the Basis of Promotional Claims

The principal legal argument of the tobacco industry is that the intended use of a product must be determined exclusively on the basis of the promotional claims made by the manufacturer. Under the industry's legal theory, the Agency must disregard the voluminous internal tobacco industry documents showing that the manufacturers have in mind, and design their products to provide, the pharmacological effects of nicotine. The tobacco industry also urges the Agency to disregard the evidence of the foreseeable pharmacological effects and uses of cigarettes and smokeless tobacco, as well as the evidence of the actual consumer use of these products for pharmacological purposes.

The Agency rejects the industry's legal argument. First, the industry's position is contrary to the plain language of the Act. The Act does not say that only products "promoted" to affect the structure or function of the body are drugs or devices. Rather, the Act says that products "intended" to affect the structure or function of the body are drugs or devices. The plain meaning of "intend" is significantly broader than the meaning of "promote." As summarized above, the plain meaning of "intend" includes "to have in mind" and "to design" for a particular use. The evidence that is relevant to determining the uses that a manufacturer "has in mind" or "designs" includes not just the promotional claims of the manufacturer, but also the internal statements of the manufacturer, as well as the manufacturer's research and actions. Moreover, the ordinary meaning of "intend" also encompasses the reasonably foreseeable consequences of the manufacturer's actions, thereby making consideration of the foreseeable pharmacological effects and uses of a product relevant to its intended use.

Second, the industry's position is contrary to FDA's regulations. These regulations provide that the term "intended use" refers to the "objective intent" of the manufacturer. Under these regulations, the Agency determines the intent of the manufacturer objectively by evaluating all of the relevant evidence in the record from the perspective of a reasonable fact-finder. FDA's regulations expressly direct the Agency to consider the manufacturer's "knowledge" of the use of the product; the manufacturer's "expressions" and "oral or written statements"; and the "circumstances surrounding the distribution of the article." Thus, the regulations expressly provide that the Agency should consider a broad range of evidence in determining intended use, not merely the manufacturer's promotional claims.

Third, the industry's position is contrary to judicial decisions interpreting the Act. These decisions have applied the Act's definitions of drug and device to two different types of products. The first type of product is one that contains no known drug ingredients and has no known pharmacological effects or uses. In cases involving such products, the courts recognize that a manufacturer's promotional claims have a crucial role in establishing intended use. Even a product like mineral water can be brought within FDA's jurisdiction by advertisements that make pharmacological claims.

The situation is fundamentally different, however, when the product contains a known drug ingredient like nicotine that has known pharmacological effects and uses. When a product is pharmacologically active, the courts have recognized that "a fact finder should be free to pierce . . . a manufacturer's misleading . . . labels to find actual therapeutic intent on the basis of objective evidence." Thus, contrary to the industry's contention, the courts have recognized that in determining intended use, FDA may consider a wide range of evidence beyond the manufacturer's promotional claims, including evidence of the pharmacological effects of the product; the purposes for which consumers actually use the product; the medical use of the product; and how the product was formulated.

Fourth, the industry's position is contrary to FDA's administrative precedent. In a broad range of instances, FDA has asserted jurisdiction over products based on the likely pharmacological effects and uses of the product—not express promotional claims. Indeed, in many of these instances, the manufacturer's promotional claims were designed to disguise the actual intended use of the product.

Fifth, the industry's position is contrary to the public health objectives of the Act. If promotional claims alone determined the intended use of a product, virtually any manufacturer of drugs or devices could avoid the Act's reach by simply refraining from making pharmacological claims for the product. For instance, under the industry's interpretation, a company could market a potent tranquilizer or amphetamine for its "pleasurable" effect and escape FDA regulation. To protect the public from the unregulated distribution of products with pharmacologically active ingredients, the Agency must be able to look beyond a manufacturer's promotional claims when determining whether to regulate such products.

For these reasons, the Agency rejects the tobacco industry's legal theory that intended use is determined exclusively on the basis of promotional claims. The Agency also rejects the premise of the industry's position—namely, that their promotional claims demonstrate that cigarettes and smokeless tobacco are not intended to affect the structure and function of the body. To the contrary, as internal tobacco company documents indicate, promises of "satisfaction" in tobacco advertisements imply that cigarettes and smokeless tobacco will provide consumers with desired pharmacological effects of nicotine. These implied drug claims lend support to the Agency's finding that cigarettes and smokeless tobacco are intended to affect the structure and function of the body.

F. Response to Additional Comments

This section responds to additional comments regarding the evidence of the intended use of cigarettes and smokeless tobacco and the Agency's use of this evidence.

G. Considered Cumulatively, the Evidence Overwhelmingly Demonstrates That Cigarettes and Smokeless Tobacco Are Intended to Affect the Structure and Function of the Body

As summarized above, the evidence in the record provides several independent bases for the Agency's finding that cigarettes and smokeless tobacco are "intended" to affect the structure and function of the body. Independently, each of these distinct categories of evidence is a strong and sufficient basis for the Agency's conclusion that the manufacturers of cigarettes and smokeless tobacco intend the pharmacological effects and uses of their products. Considered together, they are mutually corroborating. Both independently and taken as a whole, therefore, the evidence in the administrative record overwhelmingly establishes that cigarettes and smokeless tobacco are "intended to affect the structure or any function of the body" within the meaning of the Act.

III. CIGARETTES AND SMOKELESS TOBACCO ARE COMBINATION PRODUCTS CONSISTING OF "DRUG" AND "DEVICE" COMPONENTS

The Agency's findings in sections I and II establish that the nicotine in cigarettes and smokeless tobacco is a "drug" under section 201(g)(1)(C) of the Act. These findings show that the nicotine in cigarettes and smokeless tobacco "affect[s] the structure or any function of the body" and that these effects are "intended." These findings thus demonstrate that the nicotine in cigarettes and smokeless tobacco meets the statutory definition of a "drug." Cigarettes and smokeless tobacco are not simply packaged nicotine, however. They also include delivery devices that deliver nicotine to the body. In the case of cigarettes, the device components work together upon combustion outside the body to form a nicotine-containing aerosol, which then delivers nicotine to the body when inhaled by the smoker. In the case of smokeless tobacco, the device components function by presenting nicotine to the consumer in a form that is palatable and absorbable by the buccal mucosa. Unlike the drug nicotine, these device components achieve their primary intended purpose without chemical action in or on the body and without being metabolized. The presence of both drug and device components in cigarettes and smokeless tobacco make these products "combination products" under section 503(g) the Act, 21 U.S.C. 353(g)(1).

IV. FDA'S ASSERTION OF JURISDICTION OVER CIGARETTES AND SMOKELESS TOBACCO AT THIS TIME IS JUSTIFIED

FDA has always exercised jurisdiction over tobacco products when there is sufficient evidence in the record to establish that these products are "intended" to treat or prevent disease or to affect the structure or function of the body. Over thirty years ago, for instance, the Agency asserted jurisdiction over a brand of cigarettes when the evidence established that the brand was intended to reduce body weight. The Agency last considered whether to regulate cigarettes in the late 1970's, when the Agency rejected petitions by Action on Smoking and Health (ASH) urging the Agency to regulate cigarettes as drugs or devices. The Agency agreed with ASH that "objective evidence other than manufacturers' claims can be material to a determination of intended use" and that "evidence of consumer use can be one element of objective evidence to be weighed in determining if the intended purpose of a product subjects it to regulation under the Act." However, the Agency concluded that the evidence presented by ASH in the petition was insufficient to establish that cigarettes and smokeless tobacco were in fact intended to affect the structure and function of the body. The court deferred to the Agency's determination not to regulate cigarettes as drugs but expressly left open the possibility that FDA might, at a later date, revisit its decision and determine that it did indeed have jurisdiction over cigarettes. The evidence regarding the intended use of cigarettes and smokeless tobacco has changed dramatically since ASH. First, a scientific consensus has emerged since 1980 that nicotine is addictive and has other significant pharmacological effects and that cigarettes and smokeless tobacco are used by consumers to obtain pharmacological effects. As summarized above, no major public health organization had determined that nicotine was an addictive drug before 1980. Between 1980 and 1994, however, every leading scientific organization with expertise in addiction concluded that nicotine is addictive. This new evidence thus shows that the pharmacological effects and uses of cigarettes and smokeless tobacco have become foreseeable.

Second, scientific evidence accumulated since 1980 has shown that the vast majority of people who use cigarettes and smokeless tobacco use these products to satisfy addiction or to obtain other pharmacological effects. As summarized above, this new evidence now shows that 77% to 92% of smokers are addicted to nicotine and provides a basis for estimating that 75% of young regular smokeless tobacco users are addicted to nicotine. This new evidence establishes that consumers use cigarettes and smokeless tobacco predominantly for pharmacological purposes.

Third, FDA, congressional, and other investigations have recently uncovered a wealth of documents from a wide range of tobacco companies that show that the manufacturers have long known of the pharmacological effects and uses of nicotine and have designed their products to provide pharmacologically active doses of nicotine to consumers. Virtually none of this information was available to FDA in 1980. Information developed since 1980 also demonstrates that the Agency has a unique public health opportunity to reduce substantially the more than 400,000 deaths from tobacco use each year in the United States. This information shows that for most people tobacco use and nicotine addiction begin in childhood and adolescence, and that an increasing number of American children and adolescents are using cigarettes and smokeless tobacco. The data now suggest that if children and adolescents can be prevented from initiating tobacco use during their teenage years, they are unlikely to begin tobacco use later in life, thereby preventing the onset of tobacco-related disease and premature death.

Appendix A

Before the importance of youth-centered interventions was identified, most of the regulatory approaches available under the Federal Food, Drug, and Cosmetic Act to address tobacco-related disease and death, such as removal of the products from the market, were not believed to be feasible solutions. It is now apparent, however, that FDA's authority to restrict the sale, distribution, and use of cigarettes and smokeless tobacco to people under the age of eighteen is an effective tool to reduce the adverse health consequences of tobacco use. Thus, asserting jurisdiction over cigarettes and smokeless tobacco now presents an opportunity to use the Agency's resources effectively for substantial public health gains.

The court in ASH specifically recognized that FDA was permitted to modify its position and that any new FDA position would be accorded deference by the courts. In light of the substantial new information, FDA has reviewed its earlier determination not to assert jurisdiction over tobacco products. The new evidence persuades the Agency to conclude that its previous position is no longer consistent with the relevant facts and should be changed. The evidence before the Agency is now sufficient to establish that cigarettes and smokeless tobacco are in fact intended to affect the structure and function of the body.

V. CONGRESS HAS NOT PRECLUDED OR PREEMPTED FDA FROM REGULATING CIGARETTES AND SMOKELESS TOBACCO

FDA disagrees with the comments of the tobacco industry that assert that Congress has precluded or preempted FDA from regulating cigarettes and smokeless tobacco. The plain language of the Act does not exclude cigarettes or smokeless tobacco from FDA jurisdiction. Tobacco products are expressly excluded from the jurisdiction of the Consumer Product Safety Commission under the Federal Hazardous Substances Act and from the jurisdiction of the Environmental Protection Agency under the Toxic Substances Control Act. The absence of any similar exclusion in the Federal Food, Drug, and Cosmetic Act demonstrates that Congress has not chosen to exclude cigarettes and smokeless tobacco from FDA jurisdiction.

The legislative history of the Act confirms that the Act should not be interpreted to preclude FDA jurisdiction over tobacco products. Congress has long known that FDA will assert jurisdiction over cigarettes when the evidence establishes that the cigarettes are intended to affect the structure or function of the body. For instance, FDA asserted jurisdiction more than 30 years ago over cigarettes that were intended to reduce weight. This demonstrates that Congress has not "ratified" or "acquiesced in" an interpretation of the Act that would preclude FDA from regulating tobacco products

267

intended to affect the structure or function of the body. Moreover, even if Congress had acquiesced in such an interpretation of the Act, congressional acquiescence in a prior agency interpretation does not prevent an agency from changing its interpretation. In the case of cigarettes and smokeless tobacco, a change in interpretation would be justified by the new evidence in the record—evidence never previously before either the Agency or Congress. The Agency also disagrees that other federal statutes preempt FDA jurisdiction over cigarettes and smokeless tobacco. Both the Federal Cigarette Labeling and Advertising Act and the Comprehensive Smokeless Tobacco Health Education Act have provisions that expressly specify the limited extent to which these laws preempt FDA and other federal agencies from regulating cigarettes or smokeless tobacco. In the Federal Cigarette Labeling and Advertising Act, for instance, federal agencies are preempted only from requiring "statement[s] relating to smoking and health . . . on any cigarette package." The narrow preemption provisions that Congress expressly included in these statutes do not apply to FDA's assertion of jurisdiction over cigarettes and smokeless tobacco. No other federal statutes contain provisions preempting FDA regulation of tobacco products. In the absence of an express preemption provision, one federal statute preempts another federal statute only where there is an irreconcilable conflict between the two laws. There is no irreconcilable conflict between FDA jurisdiction and other federal statutes.

VI. FDA EMPLOYED PROCEDURES THAT PROVIDED AN OPPORTUNITY FOR FULL PUBLIC PARTICIPATION AND EXCEEDED ALL LEGAL REQUIREMENTS

FDA went to great lengths to involve the public in the process by which the Agency made its final jurisdictional determination. The Commissioner made public his intention to investigate the role of nicotine in tobacco products, testified twice before Congress on the Agency's findings, wrote to all the major cigarette and tobacco companies requesting information on the role of nicotine in their products, and held a public advisory committee meeting on the abuse potential of nicotine. Although the Agency is not required to undertake rulemaking to establish jurisdiction over new products, the Agency published in the *Federal Register* its initial jurisdictional findings and comprehensive legal analysis in a 325-page document, supported by over 600 footnotes, and sought public comment on those findings. The Agency placed over 210,000 pages of supporting documents in a public docket. FDA received over 700,000 comments on the Jurisdictional Analysis and the accompanying proposed rule. The Agency has responded to substantive comments in this Annex and in the preamble to the Final Rule.

Appendix A

FDA disagrees with the comments of the tobacco industry that the record supporting the Jurisdictional Analysis or the procedures the Agency followed were inadequate. The procedures the Agency employed in reaching its final determination exceeded the requirements of the Administrative Procedures Act (APA) and the Agency's own procedural requirements.

Source: Federal Register August 28, 1996 (Volume 61, Number 168) Rules and Regulations Pages 44628–44649 (via www.gpoaccess.gov/fr/index.html).

APPENDIX B

FOOD AND DRUG ADMINISTRATION ET AL. PETITIONERS V. BROWN & WILLIAMSON TOBACCO CORPORATION ET AL. (MARCH 21, 2000)

JUSTICE [SANDRA DAY] O'CONNOR delivered the opinion of the Court.

This case involves one of the most troubling public health problems facing our Nation today: the thousands of premature deaths that occur each year because of tobacco use. In 1996, the Food and Drug Administration (FDA), after having expressly disavowed any such authority since its inception, asserted jurisdiction to regulate tobacco products. The FDA concluded that nicotine is a "drug" within the meaning of the Food, Drug, and Cosmetic Act (FDCA or Act), as amended, and that cigarettes and smokeless tobacco are "combination products" that deliver nicotine to the body. Pursuant to this authority, it promulgated regulations intended to reduce tobacco consumption among children and adolescents. The agency believed that, because most tobacco consumers begin their use before reaching the age of 18, curbing tobacco use by minors could substantially reduce the prevalence of addiction in future generations and thus the incidence of tobacco-related death and disease.

Regardless of how serious the problem an administrative agency seeks to address, however, it may not exercise its authority "in a manner that is inconsistent with the administrative structure that Congress enacted into law." And although agencies are generally entitled to deference in the interpretation of statutes that they administer, a reviewing "court, as well as the agency, must give effect to the unambiguously expressed intent of Congress." In this case, we believe that Congress has clearly precluded the FDA from asserting jurisdiction to regulate tobacco products. Such authority is inconsistent with the intent that Congress has expressed in the FDCA's overall regulatory scheme and in the tobacco-specific legislation that it has enacted subsequent to the FDCA. In light of this clear intent, the FDA's assertion of jurisdiction is impermissible.

I

The FDCA grants the FDA, as the designee of the Secretary of Health and Human Services, the authority to regulate, among other items, "drugs" and "devices." The Act defines "drug" to include "articles (other than food) intended to affect the structure or any function of the body." It defines "device," in part, as "an instrument, apparatus, implement, machine, contrivance, . . . or other similar or related article, including any component, part, or accessory, which is . . . intended to affect the structure or any function of the body." The Act also grants the FDA the authority to regulate so-called "combination products," which "constitute a combination of a drug, device, or biologic product." The FDA has construed this provision as giving it the discretion to regulate combination products as drugs, as devices, or as both.

On August 11, 1995, the FDA published a proposed rule concerning the sale of cigarettes and smokeless tobacco to children and adolescents. The rule, which included several restrictions on the sale, distribution, and advertisement of tobacco products, was designed to reduce the availability and attractiveness of tobacco products to young people. A public comment period followed, during which the FDA received over 700,000 submissions, more than "at any other time in its history on any other subject."

On August 28, 1996, the FDA issued a final rule entitled "Regulations Restricting the Sale and Distribution of Cigarettes and Smokeless Tobacco to Protect Children and Adolescents." The FDA determined that nicotine is a "drug" and that cigarettes and smokeless tobacco are "drug delivery devices," and therefore it had jurisdiction under the FDCA to regulate tobacco products as customarily marketed—that is, without manufacturer claims of therapeutic benefit. First, the FDA found that tobacco products "'affect the structure or any function of the body'" because nicotine "has significant pharmacological effects." Specifically, nicotine "exerts psychoactive, or mood-altering, effects on the brain" that cause and sustain addiction, have both tranquilizing and stimulating effects, and control weight. Second, the FDA determined that these effects were "intended" under the FDCA because they "are so widely known and foreseeable that [they] may be deemed to have been intended by the manufacturers"; consumers use tobacco products "predominantly or nearly exclusively" to obtain these effects; and the statements, research, and actions of manufacturers revealed that they "have 'designed' cigarettes to provide pharmacologically active doses of nicotine to consumers." Finally, the agency concluded that cigarettes and smokeless tobacco are "combination products" because, in addition to containing nicotine, they include device components that deliver a controlled amount of nicotine to the body.

Having resolved the jurisdictional question, the FDA next explained the policy justifications for its regulations, detailing the deleterious health effects associated with tobacco use. It found that tobacco consumption was "the single leading cause of preventable death in the United States." According to the FDA, "[m]ore than 400,000 people die each year from tobacco-related illnesses, such as cancer, respiratory illnesses, and heart disease." The agency also determined that the only way to reduce the amount of tobacco-related illness and mortality was to reduce the level of addiction, a goal that could be accomplished only by preventing children and adolescents from starting to use tobacco. The FDA found that 82% of adult smokers had their first cigarette before the age of 18, and more than half had already become regular smokers by that age. It also found that children were beginning to smoke at a younger age, that the prevalence of youth smoking had recently increased, and that similar problems existed with respect to smokeless tobacco. The FDA accordingly concluded that if "the number of children and adolescents who begin tobacco use can be substantially diminished, tobacco-related illness can be correspondingly reduced because data suggest that anyone who does not begin smoking in childhood or adolescence is unlikely ever to begin."

Based on these findings, the FDA promulgated regulations concerning tobacco products' promotion, labeling, and accessibility to children and adolescents. The access regulations prohibit the sale of cigarettes or smokeless tobacco to persons younger than 18; require retailers to verify through photo identification the age of all purchasers younger than 27; prohibit the sale of cigarettes in quantities smaller than 20; prohibit the distribution of free samples; and prohibit sales through self-service displays and vending machines except in adult-only locations. The promotion regulations require that any print advertising appear in a black-and-white, text-only format unless the publication in which it appears is read almost exclusively by adults; prohibit outdoor advertising within 1,000 feet of any public playground or school; prohibit the distribution of any promotional items, such as T-shirts or hats, bearing the manufacturer's brand name; and prohibit a manufacturer from sponsoring any athletic, musical, artistic, or other social or cultural event using its brand name. The labeling regulation requires that the statement, "A Nicotine-Delivery Device for Persons 18 or Older," appear on all tobacco product packages.

The FDA promulgated these regulations pursuant to its authority to regulate "restricted devices." The FDA construed §353(g)(1) as giving it the discretion to regulate "combination products" using the Act's drug authorities, device authorities, or both, depending on "how the public health goals of the act can be best accomplished." Given the greater flexibility in the FDCA for the regulation of devices, the FDA determined that "the device authorities provide the most appropriate basis for regulating cigarettes and smokeless tobacco." Under 21 U.S.C. §360j(e), the agency may "require that a device be restricted to sale, distribution, or use . . . upon such other conditions as [the FDA] may prescribe in such regulation, if, because of its potentiality for harmful effect or the collateral measures necessary to its use, [the FDA] determines that there cannot otherwise be reasonable assurance of its safety and effectiveness." The FDA reasoned that its regulations fell within the authority granted by §360j(e) because they related to the sale or distribution of tobacco products and were necessary for providing a reasonable assurance of safety.

Respondents, a group of tobacco manufacturers, retailers, and advertisers, filed suit in United States District Court for the Middle District of North Carolina challenging the regulations. They moved for summary judgment on the grounds that the FDA lacked jurisdiction to regulate tobacco products as customarily marketed, the regulations exceeded the FDA's authority under 21 U.S.C. §360j(e), and the advertising restrictions violated the First Amendment. The District Court granted respondents' motion in part and denied it in part. The court held that the FDCA authorizes the FDA to regulate tobacco products as customarily marketed and that the FDA's access and labeling regulations are permissible, but it also found that the agency's advertising and promotion restrictions exceed its authority under §360j(e). The court stayed implementation of the regulations it found valid (except the prohibition on the sale of tobacco products to minors) and certified its order for immediate interlocutory appeal.

The Court of Appeals for the Fourth Circuit reversed, holding that Congress has not granted the FDA jurisdiction to regulate tobacco products. Examining the FDCA as a whole, the court concluded that the FDA's regulation of tobacco products would create a number of internal inconsistencies. Various provisions of the Act require the agency to determine that any regulated product is "safe" before it can be sold or allowed to remain on the market, yet the FDA found in its rulemaking proceeding that tobacco products are "dangerous" and "unsafe." Thus, the FDA would apparently have to ban tobacco products, a result the court found clearly contrary to congressional intent. This apparent anomaly, the Court of Appeals concluded, demonstrates that Congress did not intend to give the FDA authority to regulate tobacco. The court also found that evidence external to the FDCA confirms this conclusion. Importantly, the FDA consistently stated before 1995 that it lacked jurisdiction over tobacco, and Congress has enacted several tobacco-specific statutes fully cognizant of the FDA's position. In fact, the court reasoned, Congress has considered and rejected many bills that would have given the agency such authority. This, along with the absence of any intent by the enacting Congress in 1938 to subject tobacco products to regulation under the FDCA, demonstrates that Congress intended to withhold such authority from the FDA. Having resolved the jurisdictional question against the agency, the Court of Appeals did not address whether the regulations exceed the FDA's authority under 21 U.S.C.§360j(e) or violate the First Amendment.

We granted the Government's petition for certioraris to determine whether the FDA has authority under the FDCA to regulate tobacco products as customarily marketed.

II

The FDA's assertion of jurisdiction to regulate tobacco products is founded on its conclusions that nicotine is a "drug" and that cigarettes and smokeless tobacco are "drug delivery devices." Again, the FDA found that tobacco products are "intended" to deliver the pharmacological effects of satisfying addiction, stimulation and tranquilization, and weight control because those effects are foreseeable to any reasonable manufacturer, consumers use tobacco products to obtain those effects, and tobacco manufacturers have designed their products to produce those effects. As an initial matter, respondents take issue with the FDA's reading of "intended," arguing that it is a term of art that refers exclusively to claims made by the manufacturer or vendor about the product. That is, a product is not a drug or device under the FDCA unless the manufacturer or vendor makes some express claim concerning the product's therapeutic benefits. We need not resolve this question, however, because assuming, *arguendo*, that a product can be "intended to affect the structure or any function of the body" absent claims of therapeutic or medical benefit, the FDA's claim to jurisdiction contravenes the clear intent of Congress.

A threshold issue is the appropriate framework for analyzing the FDA's assertion of authority to regulate tobacco products. Because this case involves an administrative agency's construction of a statute that it administers, our analysis is governed by *Chevron U.S.A. Inc. v. Natural Resources Defense Council, Inc.* Under *Chevron,* a reviewing court must first ask "whether Congress has directly spoken to the precise question at issue." If Congress has done so, the court "must give effect to the unambiguously expressed intent of Congress." But if Congress has not specifically addressed the question, a reviewing court must respect the agency's construction of the statute so long as it is permissible. Such deference is justified because "[t]he responsibilities for assessing the wisdom of such policy choices and resolving the struggle between competing views of the public interest are not judicial ones," and because of the agency's greater familiarity with the ever-changing facts and circumstances surrounding the subjects regulated.

In determining whether Congress has specifically addressed the question at issue, a reviewing court should not confine itself to examining a particular statutory provision in isolation. The meaning—or ambiguity—of certain words or phrases may only become evident when placed in context. It is a "fundamental canon of statutory construction that the words of a statute must be read in their context and with a view to their place in the overall statutory scheme." A court must therefore interpret the statute "as a symmetrical and coherent regulatory scheme," and "fit, if possible, all parts into an harmonious whole." Similarly, the meaning of one statute may be affected by other Acts, particularly where Congress has spoken subsequently and more specifically to the topic at hand. In addition, we must be guided to a degree by common sense as to the manner in which Congress is likely to delegate a policy decision of such economic and political magnitude to an administrative agency.

With these principles in mind, we find that Congress has directly spoken to the issue here and precluded the FDA's jurisdiction to regulate tobacco products.

A

Viewing the FDCA as a whole, it is evident that one of the Act's core objectives is to ensure that any product regulated by the FDA is "safe" and "effective" for its intended use. This essential purpose pervades the FDCA. For instance, 21 U.S.C. §393(b)(2) (1994 ed., Supp. III) defines the FDA's "mission" to include "protect[ing] the public health by ensuring that . . . drugs are safe and effective" and that "there is reasonable assurance of the safety and effectiveness of devices intended for human use." The FDCA requires remarket approval of any new drug, with some limited exceptions, and states that the FDA "shall issue an order refusing to approve the application" of a new drug if it is not safe and effective for its intended purpose. If the FDA discovers after approval that a drug is unsafe or ineffective, it "shall, after due notice and opportunity for hearing to the applicant, withdraw approval" of the drug. The Act also requires the FDA to classify all devices into one of three categories. Regardless of which category the FDA chooses, there must be a "reasonable assurance of the safety and effectiveness of the device." Even the "restricted device" provision pursuant to which the FDA promulgated the regulations at issue here authorizes the agency to place conditions on the sale or distribution of a device specifically when "there cannot otherwise be reasonable assurance of its safety and effectiveness." Thus, the Act generally requires the FDA to prevent the marketing of any drug or device where the "potential for inflicting death or physical injury is not offset by the possibility of therapeutic benefit."

In its rulemaking proceeding, the FDA quite exhaustively documented that "tobacco products are unsafe," "dangerous," and "cause great pain and suffering from illness." It found that the consumption of tobacco products "presents extraordinary health risks," and that "tobacco use is the single leading cause of preventable death in the United States." It stated that "[m]ore than 400,000 people die each year from tobacco-related illnesses, such as cancer, respiratory illnesses, and heart disease, often suffering long and painful deaths," and that "[t]obacco alone kills more people each year in the United States than acquired immunodeficiency syndrome (AIDS), car accidents, alcohol, homicides, illegal drugs, suicides, and fires, combined." Indeed, the FDA characterized smoking as "a pediatric disease," because "one out of every three young people who become regular smokers . . . will die prematurely as a result."

These findings logically imply that, if tobacco products were "devices" under the FDCA, the FDA would be required to remove them from the market. Consider, first, the FDCA's provisions concerning the misbranding of drugs or devices. The Act prohibits "[t]he introduction or delivery for introduction into interstate commerce of any food, drug, device, or cosmetic that is adultered or misbranded." In light of the FDA's findings, two distinct FDCA provisions would render cigarettes and smokeless tobacco misbranded devices. First, §352(j) deems a drug or device misbranded "[i]f it is dangerous to health when used in the dosage or manner, or with the frequency or duration prescribed, recommended, or suggested in the labeling thereof." The FDA's findings make clear that tobacco products are "dangerous to health" when used in the manner prescribed. Second, a drug or device is misbranded under the Act "[u]nless its labeling bears . . . adequate directions for use . . . in such manner and form, as are necessary for the protection of users," except where such directions are "not necessary for the protection of the public health." Given the FDA's conclusions concerning the health consequences of tobacco use, there are no directions that could adequately protect consumers. That is, there are no directions that could make tobacco products safe for obtaining their intended effects. Thus, were tobacco products within the FDA's jurisdiction, the Act would deem them misbranded devices that could not be introduced into interstate commerce. Contrary to the dissent's contention, the Act admits no remedial discretion once it is evident that the device is misbranded.

Second, the FDCA requires the FDA to place all devices that it regulates into one of three classifications. The agency relies on a device's classification in determining the degree of control and regulation necessary to ensure that there is "a reasonable assurance of safety and effectiveness." The FDA has yet to classify tobacco products. Instead, the regulations at issue here represent so-called "general controls," which the Act entitles the agency to impose in advance of classification. Although the FDCA prescribes no deadline for device classification, the FDA has stated that it will classify tobacco products "in a future rulemaking" as required by the Act. Given the FDA's findings regarding the health consequences of tobacco use, the agency would have to place cigarettes and smokeless tobacco in Class III because, even after the application of the Act's available controls, they would "presen[t] a potential unreasonable risk of illness or injury." As Class III devices, tobacco products would be subject to the FDCA's premarket approval process. Under these provisions, the FDA would be prohibited from approving an application for premarket approval without "a showing of reasonable assurance that such device is safe under the conditions of use prescribed, recommended, or suggested on the labeling thereof." In view of the FDA's conclusions regarding the health effects of tobacco use, the agency would have no basis for finding any such reasonable assurance of safety. Thus, once the FDA fulfilled its statutory obligation to classify tobacco products, it could not allow them to be marketed.

The FDCA's misbranding and device classification provisions therefore make evident that were the FDA to regulate cigarettes and smokeless tobacco, the Act would require the agency to ban them. In fact, based on these provisions, the FDA itself has previously taken the position that if tobacco products were within its jurisdiction, "they would have to be removed from the market because it would be impossible to prove they were safe for their intended us[e]."

Congress, however, has foreclosed the removal of tobacco products from the market. A provision of the United States Code currently in force states that "[t]he marketing of tobacco constitutes one of the greatest basic industries of the United States with ramifying activities which directly affect interstate and foreign commerce at every point, and stable conditions therein are necessary to the general welfare." More importantly, Congress has directly addressed the problem of tobacco and health through legislation on six occasions since 1965. When Congress enacted these statutes, the adverse health consequences of tobacco use were well known, as were nicotine's pharmacological effects. Nonetheless, Congress stopped well short of ordering a ban. Instead, it has generally regulated the labeling and advertisement of tobacco products, expressly providing that it is the policy of Congress that "commerce and the national economy may be . . . protected to the maximum extent consistent with" consumers "be[ing] adequately informed about any adverse health effects." Congress' decisions to regulate labeling and advertising and to adopt the express policy of protecting "commerce and the national economy . . . to the maximum extent" reveal its intent that tobacco products remain on the market. Indeed, the collective premise of these statutes is that cigarettes and smokeless tobacco will continue to be sold in the United States. A ban of tobacco products by the FDA would therefore plainly contradict congressional policy.

The FDA apparently recognized this dilemma and concluded, somewhat ironically, that tobacco products are actually "safe" within the meaning of the FDCA. In promulgating its regulations, the agency conceded that "tobacco products are unsafe, as that term is conventionally understood." Nonetheless, the FDA reasoned that, in determining whether a device is safe under the Act, it must consider "not only the risks presented by a product but also any of the countervailing effects of use of that product, including the consequences of not permitting the product to be marketed." Applying this standard, the FDA found that, because of the high level of addiction among tobacco users, a ban would likely be "dangerous." In particular, current tobacco users could suffer from extreme withdrawal, the health care system and available pharmaceuticals might not be able to meet the treatment demands of those suffering from withdrawal, and a black market offering cigarettes even more dangerous than those currently sold legally would likely develop. The FDA therefore concluded that, "while taking cigarettes and smokeless tobacco off the market could prevent some people from becoming addicted and reduce death and disease for others, the record does not establish that such a ban is the appropriate public health response under the act."

It may well be, as the FDA asserts, that "these factors must be considered when developing a regulatory scheme that achieves the best public health result for these products." But the FDA's judgment that leaving tobacco products on the market "is more effective in achieving public health goals than a ban," is no substitute for the specific safety determinations required by the FDCA's various operative provisions. Several provisions in the Act require the FDA to determine that the *product itself* is safe as used by consumers. That is, the product's probable therapeutic benefits must outweigh its risk of harm. In contrast, the FDA's conception of safety would allow the agency, with respect to each provision of the FDCA that requires the agency to determine a product's "safety" or "dangerousness," to compare the aggregate health effects of alternative administrative actions. This is a qualitatively different inquiry. Thus, although the FDA has concluded that a ban would be "dangerous," it has *not* concluded that tobacco products are "safe" as that term is used throughout the Act.

Consider 21 U.S.C. §360c(a)(2), which specifies those factors that the FDA may consider in determining the safety and effectiveness of a device for purposes of classification, performance standards, and premarket approval. For all devices regulated by the FDA, there must at least be a "reasonable assurance of the safety and effectiveness of the device." Title 21 U.S.C. §360c(a)(2) provides that

> *"the safety and effectiveness of a device are to be determined —*
>
> *"(A) with respect to the persons for whose use the device is represented or intended,*
>
> *"(B) with respect to the conditions of use prescribed, recommended, or suggested in the labeling of the device, and*
>
> *"(C) weighing any probable benefit to health from the use of the device against any probable risk of injury or illness from such use."*

A straightforward reading of this provision dictates that the FDA must weigh the probable therapeutic benefits of the device to the consumer against the probable risk of injury. Applied to tobacco products, the inquiry is whether their purported benefits—satisfying addiction, stimulation and sedation, and weight control—outweigh the risks to health from their use. To accommodate the FDA's conception of safety, however, one must read "any probable benefit to health" to include the benefit to public health stemming from adult consumers' continued use of tobacco products, even though the *reduction* of tobacco use is the *raison d'être* of the regulations. In other words, the FDA is forced to contend that the very evil it seeks to combat is a "benefit to health." This is implausible.

The FDA's conception of safety is also incompatible with the FDCA's misbranding provision. Again, §352(j) provides that a product is "misbranded" if "it is dangerous to health when used in the dosage or manner, or with the frequency or duration prescribed, recommended, or suggested in the labeling thereof." According to the FDA's understanding, a product would be "dangerous to health," and therefore misbranded under §352(j), when, in comparison to leaving the product on the market, a ban would not produce "adverse health consequences" in aggregate. Quite simply, these are different inquiries. Although banning a particular product might be detrimental to public health in aggregate, the product could still be "dangerous to health" when used as directed. Section 352(j) focuses on dangers to the consumer from use of the product, not those stemming from the agency's remedial measures.

Consequently, the analogy made by the FDA and the dissent to highly toxic drugs used in the treatment of various cancers is unpersuasive. Although "dangerous" in some sense, these drugs are safe within the meaning of the Act because, for certain patients, the therapeutic benefits outweigh the risk of harm. Accordingly, such drugs cannot properly be described as "dangerous to health" under 21 U.S.C. §352(j). The same is not true for tobacco products. As the FDA has documented in great detail, cigarettes and smokeless tobacco are an unsafe means to obtaining *any* pharmacological effect.

The dissent contends that our conclusion means that "the FDCA requires the FDA to ban outright 'dangerous' drugs or devices," and that this is a "perverse" reading of the statute. This misunderstands our holding. The FDA, consistent with the FDCA, may clearly regulate many "dangerous" products without banning them. Indeed, virtually every drug or device poses dangers under certain conditions. What the FDA may not do is conclude that a drug or device cannot be used safely for any therapeutic purpose and yet, at the same time, allow that product to remain on the market. Such regulation is incompatible with the FDCA's core objective of ensuring that every drug or device is safe and effective.

Considering the FDCA as a whole, it is clear that Congress intended to exclude tobacco products from the FDA's jurisdiction. A fundamental precept of the FDCA is that any product regulated by the FDA—but not banned—must be safe for its intended use. Various provisions of the Act make clear that this refers to the safety of using the product to obtain its intended effects, not the public health ramifications of alternative administrative actions by the FDA. That is, the FDA must determine that there is a reasonable assurance that the product's therapeutic benefits outweigh the risk of harm to the consumer. According to this standard, the FDA has concluded that, although tobacco products might be effective in delivering certain pharmacological effects, they are "unsafe" and "dangerous" when used for these purposes. Consequently, if tobacco products were within the FDA's jurisdiction, the Act would require the FDA to remove them from the market entirely. But a ban would contradict Congress' clear intent as expressed in its more recent, tobacco-specific legislation. The inescapable conclusion is that there is no room for tobacco products within the FDCA's regulatory scheme. If they cannot be used safely for any therapeutic purpose, and yet they cannot be banned, they simply do not fit.

B

In determining whether Congress has spoken directly to the FDA's authority to regulate tobacco, we must also consider in greater detail the tobacco-specific legislation that Congress has enacted over the past 35 years. At the time a statute is enacted, it may have a range of plausible meanings. Over time, however, subsequent acts can shape or focus those meanings. The "classic judicial task of reconciling many laws enacted over time, and getting them to 'make sense' in combination, necessarily assumes that the implications of a statute may be altered by the implications of a later statute." This is particularly so where the scope of the earlier statute is broad but the subsequent statutes more specifically address the topic at hand. As we recognized recently in *United States* v. *Estate of Romani*, "a specific policy embodied in a later federal statute should control our construction of the [earlier] statute, even though it ha[s] not been expressly amended."

Congress has enacted six separate pieces of legislation since 1965 addressing the problem of tobacco use and human health. Those statutes, among other things, require that health warnings appear on all packaging and in all print and outdoor advertisements; prohibit the advertisement of tobacco products through "any medium of electronic communication" subject to regulation by the Federal Communications Commission (FCC); require the Secretary of Health and Human Services (HHS) to report every three years to Congress on research findings concerning "the addictive property of tobacco;" and make States' receipt of certain federal block grants contingent on their making it unlawful "for any manufacturer, retailer, or distributor of tobacco products to sell or distribute any such product to any individual under the age of 18."

In adopting each statute, Congress has acted against the backdrop of the FDA's consistent and repeated statements that it lacked authority under the FDCA to regulate tobacco absent claims of therapeutic benefit by the manufacturer. In fact, on several occasions over this period, and after the health consequences of tobacco use and nicotine's pharmacological effects had become well known, Congress considered and rejected bills that would have granted the FDA such jurisdiction. Under these circumstances, it is evident that Congress' tobacco-specific statutes have effectively ratified the FDA's long-held position that it lacks jurisdiction under the FDCA to regulate tobacco products. Congress has created a distinct regulatory scheme to address the problem of tobacco and health, and that scheme, as presently constructed, precludes any role for the FDA.

Tobacco Industry and Smoking

On January 11, 1964, the Surgeon General released the report of the Advisory Committee on Smoking and Health. That report documented the deleterious health effects of smoking in great detail, concluding, in relevant part, "that cigarette smoking contributes substantially to mortality from certain specific diseases and to the overall death rate." It also identified the pharmacological effects of nicotine, including "stimulation," "tranquilization," and "suppression of appetite." Seven days after the report's release, the Federal Trade Commission (FTC) issued a notice of proposed rulemaking, the FTC promulgated a final rule requiring cigarette manufacturers "to disclose, clearly and prominently, in all advertising and on every pack, box, carton or other container . . . that cigarette smoking is dangerous to health and may cause death from cancer and other diseases." The rule was to become effective January 1, 1965, but, on a request from Congress, the FTC postponed enforcement for six months.

In response to the Surgeon General's report and the FTC's proposed rule, Congress convened hearings to consider legislation addressing "the tobacco problem." During those deliberations, FDA representatives testified before Congress that the agency lacked jurisdiction under the FDCA to regulate tobacco products. Surgeon General Terry was asked during hearings in 1964 whether HEW had the "authority to brand or label the packages of cigarettes or to control the advertising there." The Surgeon General stated that "we do not have such authority in existing laws governing the . . . Food and Drug Administration." Similarly, FDA Deputy Commissioner Rankin testified in 1965 that "[t]he Food and Drug Administration has no jurisdiction under the Food, Drug, and Cosmetic Act over tobacco, unless it bears drug claims." In fact, HEW Secretary Celebrezze urged Congress *not* to amend the FDCA to cover "smoking products" because, in light of the findings in the Surgeon General's report, such a "provision might well completely outlaw at least cigarettes. This would be contrary to what, we understand, is intended or what, in the light of our experience with the 18th amendment, would be acceptable to the American people."

The FDA's disavowal of jurisdiction was consistent with the position that it had taken since the agency's inception. As the FDA concedes, it never asserted authority to regulate tobacco products as customarily marketed until it promulgated the regulations at issue here. ("In the 73 years since the enactment of the original Food and Drug Act, and in the 41 years since the promulgation of the modern Food, Drug, and Cosmetic Act, the FDA has repeatedly informed Congress that cigarettes are beyond the scope of the statute absent health claims establishing a therapeutic intent on behalf of the manufacturer or vendor").

The FDA's position was also consistent with Congress' specific intent when it enacted the FDCA. Before the Act's adoption in 1938, the FDA's predeces-

282

Appendix B

sor agency, the Bureau of Chemistry, announced that it lacked authority to regulate tobacco products under the Pure Food and Drug Act of 1906, unless they were marketed with therapeutic claims. In 1929, Congress considered and rejected a bill "[t]o amend the Food and Drugs Act of June 30, 1906, by extending its provisions to tobacco and tobacco products." And, as the FDA admits, there is no evidence in the text of the FDCA or its legislative history that Congress in 1938 even considered the applicability of the Act to tobacco products. Given the economic and political significance of the tobacco industry at the time, it is extremely unlikely that Congress could have intended to place tobacco within the ambit of the FDCA absent any discussion of the matter. Of course, whether the Congress that enacted the FDCA specifically intended the Act to cover tobacco products is not determinative; "it is ultimately the provisions of our laws rather than the principal concerns of our legislators by which we are governed." Nonetheless, this intent is certainly relevant to understanding the basis for the FDA's representations to Congress and the background against which Congress enacted subsequent tobacco-specific legislation.

Moreover, before enacting the FCLAA in 1965, Congress considered and rejected several proposals to give the FDA the authority to regulate tobacco. In April 1963, Representative [Morris] Udall [of Arizona] introduced a bill "[t]o amend the Federal Food, Drug, and Cosmetic Act so as to make that Act applicable to smoking products." Two months later, Senator Moss introduced an identical bill in the Senate. In discussing his proposal on the Senate floor, Senator [Frank E.] Moss [of Utah] explained that "this amendment simply places smoking products under FDA jurisdiction, along with foods, drugs, and cosmetics." In December 1963, Representative Rhodes introduced another bill that would have amended the FDCA "by striking out 'food, drug, device, or cosmetic,' each place where it appears therein and inserting in lieu thereof 'food, drug, device, cosmetic, or smoking product.'" And in January 1965, five months before passage of the FCLAA, Representative Udall again introduced a bill to amend the FDCA "to make that Act applicable to smoking products." None of these proposals became law.

Congress ultimately decided in 1965 to subject tobacco products to the less extensive regulatory scheme of the FCLAA, which created a "comprehensive Federal program to deal with cigarette labeling and advertising with respect to any relationship between smoking and health." The FCLAA rejected any regulation of advertising, but it required the warning, "Caution: Cigarette Smoking May Be Hazardous to Your Health," to appear on all cigarette packages. In the Act's "Declaration of Policy," Congress stated that its objective was to balance the goals of ensuring that "the public may be adequately informed that cigarette smoking may be hazardous to health" and protecting "commerce and the national economy . . . to the maximum extent."

Not only did Congress reject the proposals to grant the FDA jurisdiction, but it explicitly preempted any other regulation of cigarette labeling: "No statement relating to smoking and health, other than the statement required by this Act, shall be required on any cigarette package." The regulation of product labeling, however, is an integral aspect of the FDCA, both as it existed in 1965 and today. The labeling requirements currently imposed by the FDCA, which are essentially identical to those in force in 1965, require the FDA to regulate the labeling of drugs and devices to protect the safety of consumers. As discussed earlier, the Act requires that all products bear "adequate directions for use . . . as are necessary for the protection of users," requires that all products provide "adequate warnings against use in those pathological conditions or by children where its use may be dangerous to health;" and deems a product misbranded "[i]f it is dangerous to health when used in the dosage or manner, or with the frequency or duration prescribed, recommended, or suggested in the labeling thereof." In this sense, the FCLAA was—and remains—incompatible with FDA regulation of tobacco products. This is not to say that the FCLAA's preemption provision by itself necessarily foreclosed FDA jurisdiction. But it is an important factor in assessing whether Congress ratified the agency's position—that is, whether Congress adopted a regulatory approach to the problem of tobacco and health that contemplated no role for the FDA.

Further, the FCLAA evidences Congress' intent to preclude *any* administrative agency from exercising significant policymaking authority on the subject of smoking and health. In addition to prohibiting any additional requirements for cigarette labeling, the FCLAA provided that "[n]o statement relating to smoking and health shall be required in the advertising of any cigarettes the packages of which are labeled in conformity with the provisions of this Act." Thus, in reaction to the FTC's attempt to regulate cigarette labeling and advertising, Congress enacted a statute reserving exclusive control over both subjects to itself.

Subsequent tobacco-specific legislation followed a similar pattern. By the FCLAA's own terms, the prohibition on any additional cigarette labeling or advertising regulations relating to smoking and health was to expire July 1, 1969. In anticipation of the provision's expiration, both the FCC and the FTC proposed rules governing the advertisement of cigarettes. After debating the proper role for administrative agencies in the regulation of tobacco, Congress amended the FCLAA by banning cigarette advertisements "on any medium of electronic communication subject to the jurisdiction of the Federal Communications Commission" and strengthening the warning required to appear on cigarette packages. Importantly, Congress extended indefinitely the prohibition on any other regulation of cigarette labeling with respect to smoking and health (again despite the importance of labeling regulation under the FDCA). Moreover, it expressly forbade the FTC from taking any action on its pending rule until July 1, 1971, and it required the FTC, if it decided to proceed with its rule thereafter, to notify Congress at least six months in advance of the rule's becoming effective. As the chairman of the House committee in which the bill originated stated, "the Congress—the body elected by the people—must make the policy determinations involved in this legislation—and not some agency made up of appointed officials."

Four years later, after Congress had transferred the authority to regulate substances covered by the Hazardous Substances Act (HSA) from the FDA to the Consumer Products Safety Commission (CPSC), the American Public Health Association, joined by Senator Moss, petitioned the CPSC to regulate cigarettes yielding more than 21 milligrams of tar. After the CPSC determined that it lacked authority under the HSA to regulate cigarettes, a District Court held that the Act did, in fact, grant the CPSC such jurisdiction and ordered it to reexamine the petition. Before the CPSC could take any action, however, Congress mooted the issue by adopting legislation that eliminated the agency's authority to regulate "tobacco and tobacco products." Senator Moss acknowledged that the "legislation, in effect, reverse[d]" the District Court's decision, and the FDA later observed that the episode was "particularly" "indicative of the policy of Congress to limit the regulatory authority over cigarettes by Federal Agencies." A separate statement in the Senate Report underscored that the legislation's purpose was to "unmistakably reaffirm the clear mandate of the Congress that the basic regulation of tobacco and tobacco products is governed by the legislation dealing with the subject, . . . and that any further regulation in this sensitive and complex area must be reserved for specific Congressional action."

Meanwhile, the FDA continued to maintain that it lacked jurisdiction under the FDCA to regulate tobacco products as customarily marketed. In 1972, FDA Commissioner Edwards testified before Congress that "cigarettes recommended for smoking pleasure are beyond the Federal Food, Drug, and Cosmetic Act." He further stated that the FDA believed that the Public Health Cigarette Smoking Act "demonstrates that the regulation of cigarettes is to be the domain of Congress," and that "labeling or banning cigarettes is a step that can be take[n] only by the Congress. Any such move by FDA would be inconsistent with the clear congressional intent."

In 1977, ASH filed a citizen petition requesting that the FDA regulate cigarettes, citing many of the same grounds that motivated the FDA's rulemaking here. ASH asserted that nicotine was highly addictive and had strong physiological effects on the body; that those effects were "intended" because consumers use tobacco products precisely to obtain those effects; and that tobacco causes thousands of premature deaths annually. In denying

ASH's petition, FDA Commissioner Kennedy stated that "[t]he interpretation of the Act by FDA consistently has been that cigarettes are not a drug unless health claims are made by the vendors." After the matter proceeded to litigation, the FDA argued in its brief to the Court of Appeals that "cigarettes are not comprehended within the statutory definition of the term 'drug' absent objective evidence that vendors represent or intend that their products be used as a drug." The FDA also contended that Congress had "long been aware that the FDA does not consider cigarettes to be within its regulatory authority in the absence of health claims made on behalf of the manufacturer or vendor," and that, because "Congress has never acted to disturb the agency's interpretation," it had "acquiesced in the FDA's interpretation of the statutory limits on its authority to regulate cigarettes." The Court of Appeals upheld the FDA's position, concluding that "[i]f the statute requires expansion, that is the job of Congress." In 1980, the FDA also denied a request by ASH to commence rulemaking proceedings to establish the agency's jurisdiction to regulate cigarettes as devices. The agency stated that "[i]nsofar as rulemaking would relate to cigarettes or attached filters as customarily marketed, we have concluded that FDA has no jurisdiction under section 201(h) of the Act."

In 1983, Congress again considered legislation on the subject of smoking and health. HHS Assistant Secretary Brandt testified that, in addition to being "a major cause of cancer," smoking is a "major cause of heart disease" and other serious illnesses, and can result in "unfavorable pregnancy outcomes." 1983 House Hearings also stated that it was "well-established that cigarette smoking is a drug dependence, and that smoking is addictive for many people." Nonetheless, Assistant Secretary Brandt maintained that "the issue of regulation of tobacco . . . is something that Congress has reserved to itself, and we do not within the Department have the authority to regulate nor are we seeking such authority." He also testified before the Senate, stating that, despite the evidence of tobacco's health effects and addictiveness, the Department's view was that "Congress has assumed the responsibility of regulating . . . cigarettes."

Against this backdrop, Congress enacted three additional tobacco-specific statutes over the next four years that incrementally expanded its regulatory scheme for tobacco products. In 1983, Congress adopted the Alcohol and Drug Abuse Amendments, which require the Secretary of HHS to report to Congress every three years on the "addictive property of tobacco" and to include recommendations for action that the Secretary may deem appropriate. A year later, Congress enacted the Comprehensive Smoking Education Act, which amended the FCLAA by again modifying the prescribed warning. Notably, during debate on the Senate floor, Senator Hawkins argued that the Act was necessary in part because "[u]nder the

Food, Drug and Cosmetic Act, the Congress exempted tobacco products." And in 1986, Congress enacted the Comprehensive Smokeless Tobacco Health Education Act of 1986 (CSTHEA), which essentially extended the regulatory provisions of the FCLAA to smokeless tobacco products. Like the FCLAA, the CSTHEA provided that "[n]o statement relating to the use of smokeless tobacco products and health, other than the statements required by [the Act], shall be required by any Federal agency to appear on any package . . . of a smokeless tobacco product." Thus, as with cigarettes, Congress reserved for itself an aspect of smokeless tobacco regulation that is particularly important to the FDCA's regulatory scheme.

In 1988, the Surgeon General released a report summarizing the abundant scientific literature demonstrating that "[c]igarettes and other forms of tobacco are addicting," and that "nicotine is psychoactive" and "causes physical dependence characterized by a withdrawal syndrome that usually accompanies nicotine abstinence." The report further concluded that the "pharmacologic and behavioral processes that determine tobacco addiction are similar to those that determine addiction to drugs such as heroin and cocaine." In the same year, FDA Commissioner Young stated before Congress that "it doesn't look like it is possible to regulate [tobacco] under the Food, Drug and Cosmetic Act even though smoking, I think, has been widely recognized as being harmful to human health." At the same hearing, the FDA's General Counsel testified that "what is fairly important in FDA law is whether a product has a therapeutic purpose," and "[c]igarettes themselves are not used for a therapeutic purpose as that concept is ordinarily understood." Between 1987 and 1989, Congress considered three more bills that would have amended the FDCA to grant the FDA jurisdiction to regulate tobacco products. As before, Congress rejected the proposals. In 1992, Congress instead adopted the Alcohol, Drug Abuse, and Mental Health Administration Reorganization Act, which creates incentives for States to regulate the retail sale of tobacco products by making States' receipt of certain block grants contingent on their prohibiting the sale of tobacco products to minors.

Taken together, these actions by Congress over the past 35 years preclude an interpretation of the FDCA that grants the FDA jurisdiction to regulate tobacco products. We do not rely on Congress' failure to act—its consideration and rejection of bills that would have given the FDA this authority—in reaching this conclusion. Indeed, this is not a case of simple inaction by Congress that purportedly represents its acquiescence in an agency's position. To the contrary, Congress has enacted several statutes addressing the particular subject of tobacco and health, creating a distinct regulatory scheme for cigarettes and smokeless tobacco. In doing so, Congress has been aware of tobacco's health hazards and its pharmacological effects.

It has also enacted this legislation against the background of the FDA repeatedly and consistently asserting that it lacks jurisdiction under the FDCA to regulate tobacco products as customarily marketed. Further, Congress has persistently acted to preclude a meaningful role for *any* administrative agency in making policy on the subject of tobacco and health. Moreover, the substance of Congress' regulatory scheme is, in an important respect, incompatible with FDA jurisdiction. Although the supervision of product labeling to protect consumer health is a substantial component of the FDA's regulation of drugs and devices, the FCLAA and the CSTHEA explicitly prohibit any federal agency from imposing any health-related labeling requirements on cigarettes or smokeless tobacco products.

Under these circumstances, it is clear that Congress' tobacco-specific legislation has effectively ratified the FDA's previous position that it lacks jurisdiction to regulate tobacco. As in *Bob Jones Univ.* v. *United States*, (1983), "[i]t is hardly conceivable that Congress—and in this setting, any Member of Congress—was not abundantly aware of what was going on." Congress has affirmatively acted to address the issue of tobacco and health, relying on the representations of the FDA that it had no authority to regulate tobacco. It has created a distinct scheme to regulate the sale of tobacco products, focused on labeling and advertising, and premised on the belief that the FDA lacks such jurisdiction under the FDCA. As a result, Congress' tobacco-specific statutes preclude the FDA from regulating tobacco products as customarily marketed.

Although the dissent takes issue with our discussion of the FDA's change in position, our conclusion does not rely on the fact that the FDA's assertion of jurisdiction represents a sharp break with its prior interpretation of the FDCA. Certainly, an agency's initial interpretation of a statute that it is charged with administering is not "carved in stone." As we recognized in *Motor Vehicle Mfrs. Assn. of United States, Inc. v. State Farm Mut. Automobile Ins. Co.* (1983), agencies "must be given ample latitude to 'adapt their rules and policies to the demands of changing circumstances.'" The consistency of the FDA's prior position is significant in this case for a different reason: it provides important context to Congress' enactment of its tobacco-specific legislation. When the FDA repeatedly informed Congress that the FDCA does not grant it the authority to regulate tobacco products, its statements were consistent with the agency's unwavering position since its inception, and with the position that its predecessor agency had first taken in 1914. Although not crucial, the consistency of the FDA's prior position bolsters the conclusion that when Congress created a distinct regulatory scheme addressing the subject of tobacco and health, it understood that the FDA is without jurisdiction to regulate tobacco products and ratified that position.

The dissent also argues that the proper inference to be drawn from Congress' tobacco-specific legislation is "critically ambivalent." We disagree. In that series of statutes, Congress crafted a specific legislative response to the problem of tobacco and health, and it did so with the understanding, based on repeated assertions by the FDA, that the agency has no authority under the FDCA to regulate tobacco products. Moreover, Congress expressly preempted any other regulation of the labeling of tobacco products concerning their health consequences, even though the oversight of labeling is central to the FDCA's regulatory scheme. And in addressing the subject, Congress consistently evidenced its intent to preclude any federal agency from exercising significant policymaking authority in the area. Under these circumstances, we believe the appropriate inference—that Congress intended to ratify the FDA's prior position that it lacks jurisdiction—is unmistakable.

The dissent alternatively argues that, even if Congress' subsequent tobacco-specific legislation did, in fact, ratify the FDA's position, that position was merely a contingent disavowal of jurisdiction. Specifically, the dissent contends that "the FDA's traditional view was largely premised on a perceived inability to prove the necessary statutory 'intent' requirement." A fair reading of the FDA's representations prior to 1995, however, demonstrates that the agency's position was essentially unconditional. To the extent the agency's position could be characterized as equivocal, it was only with respect to the well-established exception of when the manufacturer makes express claims of therapeutic benefit. Thus, what Congress ratified was the FDA's plain and resolute position that the FDCA gives the agency no authority to regulate tobacco products as customarily marketed.

C

Finally, our inquiry into whether Congress has directly spoken to the precise question at issue is shaped, at least in some measure, by the nature of the question presented. Deference under *Chevron* to an agency's construction of a statute that it administers is premised on the theory that a statute's ambiguity constitutes an implicit delegation from Congress to the agency to fill in the statutory gaps. In extraordinary cases, however, there may be reason to hesitate before concluding that Congress has intended such an implicit delegation.

This is hardly an ordinary case. Contrary to its representations to Congress since 1914, the FDA has now asserted jurisdiction to regulate an industry constituting a significant portion of the American economy. In fact, the FDA contends that, were it to determine that tobacco products provide no "reasonable assurance of safety," it would have the authority to ban cigarettes and smokeless tobacco entirely. Owing to its unique place in American history and society, tobacco has its own unique political history. Congress, for better or for worse, has created a distinct regulatory scheme for tobacco products, squarely rejected proposals to give the FDA jurisdiction over tobacco, and repeatedly acted to preclude any agency from exercising significant policymaking authority in the area. Given this history and the breadth of the authority that the FDA has asserted, we are obliged to defer not to the agency's expansive construction of the statute, but to Congress' consistent judgment to deny the FDA this power.

Our decision in *MCI Telecommunications Corp. v. American Telephone & Telegraph Co.*, (1994), is instructive. That case involved the proper construction of the term "modify" in §203(b) of the Communications Act of 1934. The FCC contended that, because the Act gave it the discretion to "modify any requirement" imposed under the statute, it therefore possessed the authority to render voluntary the otherwise mandatory requirement that long distance carriers file their rates. We rejected the FCC's construction, finding "not the slightest doubt" that Congress had directly spoken to the question. In reasoning even more apt here, we concluded that "[i]t is highly unlikely that Congress would leave the determination of whether an industry will be entirely, or even substantially, rate regulated to agency discretion—and even more unlikely that it would achieve that through such a subtle device as permission to 'modify' rate-filing requirements."

As in *MCI*, we are confident that Congress could not have intended to delegate a decision of such economic and political significance to an agency in so cryptic a fashion. To find that the FDA has the authority to regulate tobacco products, one must not only adopt an extremely strained understanding of "safety" as it is used throughout the Act—a concept central to the FDCA's regulatory scheme—but also ignore the plain implication of Congress' subsequent tobacco-specific legislation. It is therefore clear, based on the FDCA's overall regulatory scheme and the subsequent tobacco legislation, that Congress has directly spoken to the question at issue and precluded the FDA from regulating tobacco products.

* * *

By no means do we question the seriousness of the problem that the FDA has sought to address. The agency has amply demonstrated that tobacco use, particularly among children and adolescents, poses perhaps the single most significant threat to public health in the United States. Nonetheless, no matter how "important, conspicuous, and controversial" the issue, and regardless of how likely the public is to hold the Executive Branch politically accountable, *post*, at 31, an administrative agency's power to regulate in the public interest must always be grounded in a valid grant of authority from Congress. And "'[i]n our anxiety to effectuate the congressional purpose of protecting the public, we must take care not to extend the scope of the statute beyond the point where Congress indicated it would stop.'"

Appendix B

Reading the FDCA as a whole, as well as in conjunction with Congress' subsequent tobacco-specific legislation, it is plain that Congress has not given the FDA the authority that it seeks to exercise here. For these reasons, the judgment of the Court of Appeals for the Fourth Circuit is affirmed.
It is so ordered

APPENDIX C

GRAPHS AND FIGURES RELATING TO THE TOBACCO INDUSTRY AND SMOKING

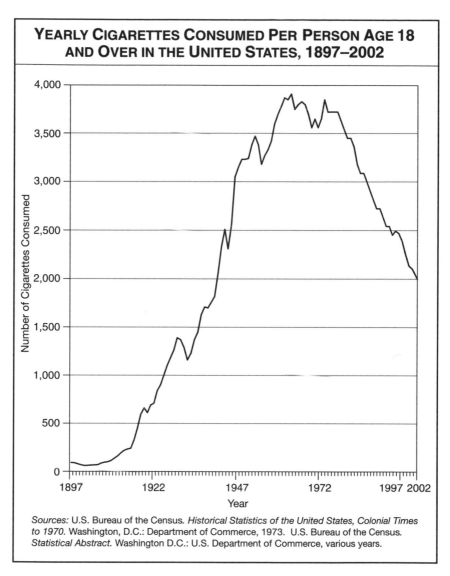

YEARLY CIGARETTES CONSUMED PER PERSON AGE 18 AND OVER IN THE UNITED STATES, 1897–2002

Sources: U.S. Bureau of the Census. *Historical Statistics of the United States, Colonial Times to 1970.* Washington, D.C.: Department of Commerce, 1973. U.S. Bureau of the Census. *Statistical Abstract.* Washington D.C.: U.S. Department of Commerce, various years.

Trends in cigarette consumption show more-or-less steady growth until a peak in 1963. Consumption declined from the late 1960s but reached levels in 1998 that were still higher than in most of the first half of the century.

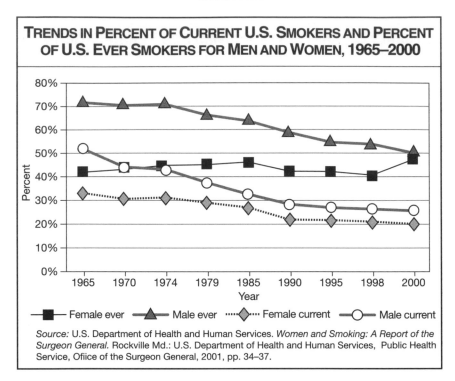

TRENDS IN PERCENT OF CURRENT U.S. SMOKERS AND PERCENT OF U.S. EVER SMOKERS FOR MEN AND WOMEN, 1965–2000

Source: U.S. Department of Health and Human Services. *Women and Smoking: A Report of the Surgeon General*. Rockville Md.: U.S. Department of Health and Human Services, Public Health Service, Ofiice of the Surgeon General, 2001, pp. 34–37.

The percentage of male and female current smokers fell during the last half of the 20th century, and the gap between males and females narrowed considerably. Because of the percent of ever smokers includes former smokers as well as current smokers, it remains at a relatively high level and has even risen a bit for women. Again, however, the gap between men and women narrowed.

Appendix C

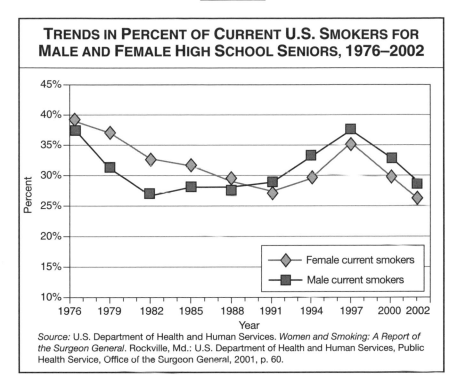

TRENDS IN PERCENT OF CURRENT U.S. SMOKERS FOR MALE AND FEMALE HIGH SCHOOL SENIORS, 1976–2002

Source: U.S. Department of Health and Human Services. *Women and Smoking: A Report of the Surgeon General.* Rockville, Md.: U.S. Department of Health and Human Services, Public Health Service, Office of the Surgeon General, 2001, p. 60.

Smoking among high school seniors dropped steeply during the 1970s, but then declined only slightly during the 1980s and rose during the 1990s. Most recently, the upward trend has begun to reverse.

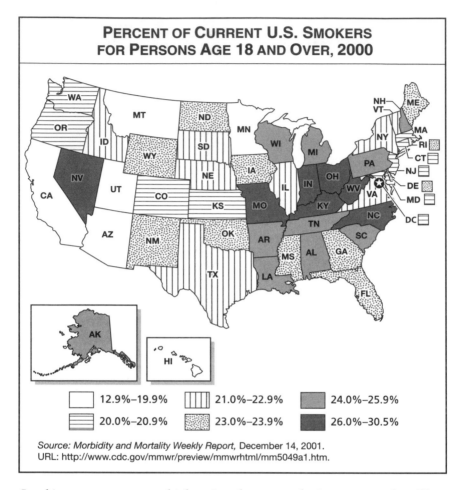

**PERCENT OF CURRENT U.S. SMOKERS
FOR PERSONS AGE 18 AND OVER, 2000**

12.9%–19.9%	21.0%–22.9%	24.0%–25.9%
20.0%–20.9%	23.0%–23.9%	26.0%–30.5%

Source: *Morbidity and Mortality Weekly Report,* December 14, 2001.
URL: http://www.cdc.gov/mmwr/preview/mmwrhtml/mm5049a1.htm.

Smoking percentages are highest in tobacco-producing states such as Kentucky and North Carolina, but also in Missouri, Indiana, and Ohio. The percentages are lower in western states such as Arizona, California, and Utah.

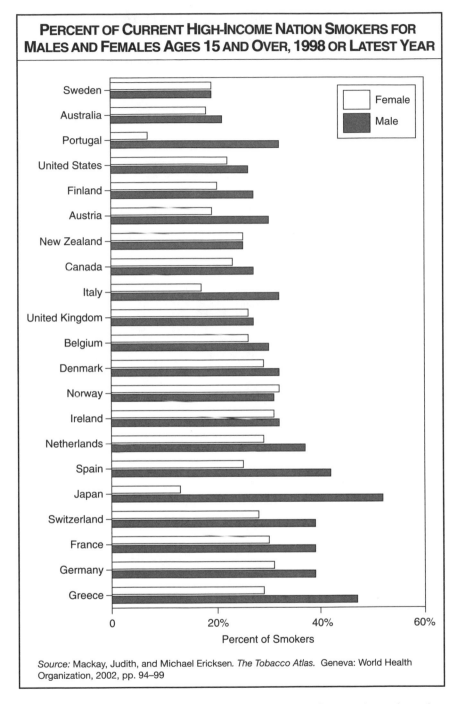

PERCENT OF CURRENT HIGH-INCOME NATION SMOKERS FOR MALES AND FEMALES AGES 15 AND OVER, 1998 OR LATEST YEAR

Female
Male

Sweden
Australia
Portugal
United States
Finland
Austria
New Zealand
Canada
Italy
United Kingdom
Belgium
Denmark
Norway
Ireland
Netherlands
Spain
Japan
Switzerland
France
Germany
Greece

0   20%   40%   60%

Percent of Smokers

Source: Mackay, Judith, and Michael Ericksen. *The Tobacco Atlas.* Geneva: World Health Organization, 2002, pp. 94–99

Compared to other high-income nations, the United States has relatively low levels of smoking. Greece, Germany, France, and Switzerland have among the highest percentage of smokers.

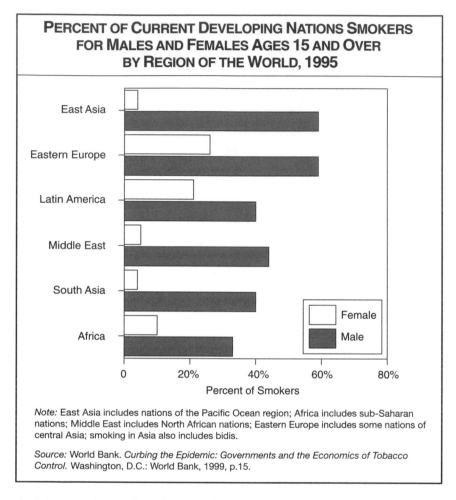

PERCENT OF CURRENT DEVELOPING NATIONS SMOKERS FOR MALES AND FEMALES AGES 15 AND OVER BY REGION OF THE WORLD, 1995

Note: East Asia includes nations of the Pacific Ocean region; Africa includes sub-Saharan nations; Middle East includes North African nations; Eastern Europe includes some nations of central Asia; smoking in Asia also includes bidis.

Source: World Bank. *Curbing the Epidemic: Governments and the Economics of Tobacco Control.* Washington, D.C.: World Bank, 1999, p.15.

A rising numbers of smokers in developing nations has concerned public health experts. At least for men, the percentage of smokers for most regions of the developing world are indeed high.

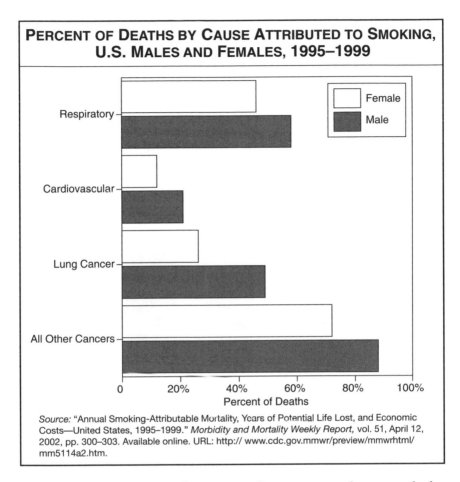

PERCENT OF DEATHS BY CAUSE ATTRIBUTED TO SMOKING, U.S. MALES AND FEMALES, 1995–1999

Source: "Annual Smoking-Attributable Mortality, Years of Potential Life Lost, and Economic Costs—United States, 1995–1999." *Morbidity and Mortality Weekly Report,* vol. 51, April 12, 2002, pp. 300–303. Available online. URL: http:// www.cdc.gov.mmwr/preview/mmwrhtml/ mm5114a2.htm.

Deaths from lung cancer and respiratory diseases are mostly commonly due to smoking, but deaths from other cancers and cardiovascular diseases also often involve smoking.

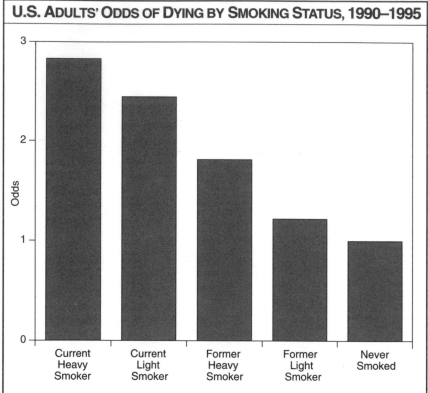

U.S. ADULTS' ODDS OF DYING BY SMOKING STATUS, 1990–1995

Note: Odds for never smokers are set to 1, and odds for other groups are relative to never smokers (for example, current heavy smokers—20+ cigarettes a day—have odds of dying that are nearly three times higher than for never smokers).

Source: Rogers, Richard G., Robert A. Hummer, and Charles B. Nam. *Living and Dying in the USA: Behavioral, Health and Social Differentials of Adult Mortality.* San Diego: Academic Press, 2000, p. 250.

Current heavy smokers are nearly three times as likely to die during a five-year time period as never smokers according to data. Light smokers and former smokers have lower risks of death than heavy smokers, but still higher than never smokers.

INDEX

Locators in **boldface** indicate main topics. Locators followed by *g* indicate glossary entries. Locators followed by *b* indicate biographical entries. Locators followed by *c* indicate chronology entries.

A

ABA (American Bar Association) 235

ACS. *See* American Cancer Society

ACSH (American Council on Science and Health) 238

Action on Smoking and Health (ASH) 127, 139*g*, 157–158, 241, 265–267, 285–286

actors, cigarette use by 113*c*, 118*c*

addictiveness of nicotine **23–26,** 139*g*

Brown and Williamson's knowledge of 121*c*

Brown and Williamson v. FDA 98

Engle v. R.J. Reynolds Tobacco Co. 92, 95

FDA v. Brown and Williamson 271–272

Bennett LeBow 134

Liggett Group's admission of 121*c*–122*c*

and popularity of cigarettes 9

references in 1964 Surgeon General's Report 24

tobacco executives' view of 120*c*

Henry Waxman 137

Merrill Williams 137–138

additives 8, 61, 79, 107*c*, 120*c*, 139*g*. *See also* flavoring

administrative rule 117*c*

adolescents. *See* young people

Adolescent Substance Abuse Prevention (ASAP) 238

advertising **17–19, 27–28.** *See also* antismoking ads; fairness doctrine

AMA's advocacy of ban on 118*c*

John F. Banzhaf III 127

Brown and Williamson v. FDA 98, 99

Leo F. Burnett 128

Camel 110*c*

Capital Broadcasting v. Mitchell 116*c*

cigars 17

Comprehensive Smoking Education Act 118*c*

congressional filter-tip cigarette hearings 114*c*

James Duke cigarette monopoly 11, 12

early cigarette advertising 8

effect on smoking 36–37

Federal Cigarette Labeling and Advertising Act 73–75

global tobacco treaty 126*c*

government regulation of 60–62

and growth in cigarette use 18–19

Helmar 111*c*

George Washington Hill 132

influence of, from 1880s–1930s **17–19**

JAMA criticism of health claims in 18, 111*c*

Lucky Strike 110*c*

Mangini v. R. J. Reynolds 122*c*

Marlboro Man campaign 29, 113*c*

on matchbooks 109*c*

to minorities 47

MSA 82

Murad 110*c*

outdoor 82

physicians in Lucky Strike ads 111*c*

Public Health Cigarette Smoking Act **76–78,** 77, 116*c*

R. J. Reynolds MSA violation 125*c*

radio/television ban 31–32

regulation **60–62**

regulation, limits of 124*c*

"safe" cigarettes 29

Senate rejection of tax deduction reduction 120*c*

and smokers' rights 68

Virginia Slims 34, 115*c*

voluntary code by industry 115*c*

and widespread acceptance of smoking 16–17

women 16, 111*c*

World War I 15

young people **27–28,** 42

advocacy groups 241–248. *See also specific groups*

Advocacy Institute 241

African Americans 39, 47

age and age restrictions 38, 83–84, 120*c*, 136

Agricultural Adjustment Act 112*c*

agricultural subsidies 59–60

Agricultural Adjustment Act 112*c*

during Great Depression 19

House Appropriations Committee 121*c*

Maryland subsidies for not growing tobacco 60, 124*c*

AHA. *See* American Heart Association

air, indoor. *See* clean indoor air regulations; environmental tobacco smoke

Air Force, U.S. 114*c*

airlines 63, 100, 116*c*, 118*c*, 119*c*

Alabama 83, 85

Alaska 83

301

Index

Index